Religion, Politics and Society in Britain, 800–1066

Using a comparative and broad perspective, *Religion, Politics and Society in Britain, 800–1066* draws on archaeology, art history, material culture, texts from charms to chronicles, from royal law-codes to sermons to poems, and other evidence to demonstrate the centrality of Christianity and the Church to Britain, 800–1066. It delineates their contributions to the changes in politics, economy, society and culture that occurred between 800 and 1066, from nation-building to practicalities of government to landscape.

The period 800–1066 saw the beginnings of a fundamental restructuring of politics, society and economy throughout Christian Europe in which religion played a central role. In Britain too the interaction of religion with politics and society was profound and pervasive. There was no part of life which Christianity and the Church did not touch: they affected belief, thought and behaviour at all levels of society.

This book points out interconnections within society and between archaeological, art-historical and literary evidence and similarities between aspects of culture not only within Britain but also in comparison with Armenian Christendom. A.E. Redgate explores the importance of religious ideas, institutions, personnel and practices in the creation and expression of identities and communities, the structure and functioning of society and the life of the individual.

This book will be essential reading for students of early medieval Britain and religious and social history.

A.E. Redgate is a Lecturer in Medieval History at Newcastle University, Newcastle-upon-Tyne, where she has taught Anglo-Saxon history, Armenian history and World history. Her publications include *The Armenians* (1998) and articles drawing on Anglo-Saxon and Welsh history to illuminate Armenian subjects, on Armenian history to illuminate the Anglo-Saxon, and comparing Anglo-Saxon and Armenian kings.

Religion, Politics and Society in Britain
Edited by Keith Robbins

The Conversion of Britain: Religion, Politics and Society in Britain, 600–800
Barbara Yorke

The Age of Reformation: The Tudor and Stewart Realms, 1485–1603
Alec Ryrie

The Post-Reformation: Religion, Politics and Society in Britain, 1603–1714
John Spurr

Eighteenth-Century Britain: Religion and Politics, 1714–1815
Nigel Yates

Providence and Empire: Religion, Politics and Society in the United Kingdom, 1815–1914
Stewart Brown

Religion and Society in Twentieth-Century Britain
Callum G. Brown

Religion, Politics and Society in Britain, 1066–1272
Henry Mayr-Harting

Religion, Politics and Society in Britain, 800–1066

A.E. Redgate

Routledge
Taylor & Francis Group

LONDON AND NEW YORK

First published 2014
by Routledge
2 Park Square, Milton Park, Abingdon, Oxon OX14 4RN

and by Routledge
711 Third Avenue, New York, NY 10017

Routledge is an imprint of the Taylor & Francis Group, an informa business

British Library Cataloguing in Publication Data
A catalogue record for this book is available from the British Library

Library of Congress Cataloging in Publication Data
Redgate, A.E. (Anne Elizabeth)
Religion, politics and society in Britain, 800–1066 / A.E. Redgate.
pages cm – (Religion, politics and society in Britain)
Includes bibliographical references and index.
1. Great Britain–History–Anglo-Saxon period, 449–1066. 2. Christianity and
politics–Great Britain–History–To 1500. 3. Religion and politics–Great
Britain–History–To 1500. 4. Anglo-Saxons–Politics and government.
5. Christianity–Great Britain–History. 6. Anglo-Saxons–Social conditions.
I. Title.
DA152.R37 2014
941.01–dc23
2013034116

ISBN: 978-0-415-73668-8 (hbk)
ISBN: 978-0-582-38250-3 (pbk)
ISBN: 978-1-315-81472-8 (ebk)

Typeset in Baskerville
by Taylor and Francis Books

To Bob,
φιλτάτῳ

Contents

Acknowledgements

I am grateful for the patience of Mari Shullaw at Pearson and Professor Keith Robbins as General Editor of the series whilst I have been writing this book, and for their help and advice in the final stages of its completion. I would like to thank Professor Robbins for his acute comments on the final draft and Professor R.I. Moore for reading and discussing successive versions, enlightening me about Europe and heresy, for his support, encouragement, forbearance and generosity of spirit, both professional and personal. My most recent debt is to Stacey Carter of Routledge for her help and advice. I owe much to the University of Newcastle-upon-Tyne's granting me periods of Research Leave, and to the Inter Library Loan scheme and the efficiency of the Library staff who operate it. The subject of this book was for some years an undergraduate History Special Subject, and teaching the 2006–2007 students Bridget McVennon, Paul Malloy and Amy Telford, one of the best groups I have ever had, contributed significantly to my understanding of it. I am also grateful to Caroline Nielsen and Rachael Redgate for clerical help and for assistance with the index and maps.

Series editor's preface

No understanding of British history is possible without grappling with the relationship between religion, politics and society. How that should be done, however, is another matter. Historians of religion, who have frequently thought of themselves as ecclesiastical historians, have had one set of preoccupations. Political historians have had another. They have acknowledged, however, that both religion and politics can only be understood, in any given period, in a social context. This series makes the interplay between religion, politics and society its preoccupation. Even so, it does not assume that what is entailed by religion and politics remains the same throughout, to be considered as a constant in separate volumes merely because of the passage of time.

In its completed form the series will have probed the nature of these links from c. 600 to the present day and offered a perspective, over such a long period, that has not before been attempted in a systematic fashion. There is, however, no straitjacket that requires individual authors to adhere to a common understanding of what such an undertaking involves. Even if there could be a general agreement about concepts, that is to say about what religion is or how politics can be identified, the social context of such categorisations is not static. The spheres notionally allocated to the one or to the other alter with the circumstances. Sometimes it might appear that they cannot be separated. Sometimes it might appear that they sharply conflict. Each period under review will have its defining characteristics in this regard.

It is the Christian religion, in its manifold institutional manifestations, with which authors are overwhelmingly concerned since it is with conversion that the series begins. It ends, however, with a volume in which Christianity exists alongside other world religions but in a society frequently perceived to be secular. Yet, what de-Christianisation is taken to be depends upon what Christianisation has been taken to be. There is, therefore, a relationship between topics that are tackled in the first volume, and those considered in the last, which might at first seem unlikely. In between, of course, are the 'Christian Centuries' which, despite their label, are no less full of 'boundary disputes', both before and after the Reformation. The perspective of the series, additionally, is broadly pan-insular. The Britain of 600 is plainly not the Britain of the early twenty-first century. However, the current political structures of Britain–Ireland have arguably owed as much to religion as to politics. Christendom has been inherently ambiguous.

It would be surprising if readers, not to mention authors, understood the totality of the picture that is presented in the same way. What is common, how-ever, is a realisation that the narrative of religion, politics and society in Britain is not a simple tale that points in a single direction but rather one of enduring and by no means exhausted complexity.

Keith Robbins

Note on references

The chapter endnotes have been compiled chiefly with the general reader and student in mind, to recommend further reading to them. They also identify the works of scholars that I have particularly drawn on, who are not named in the text itself, and my major and most recent intellectual debts, though many seminal works are absent from both notes and bibliography. Readers who follow up my citations will find identification and discussion of such studies therein. Primary sources (in translation) will be found in the bibliography; references to them (except when quoted) are not given in these notes.

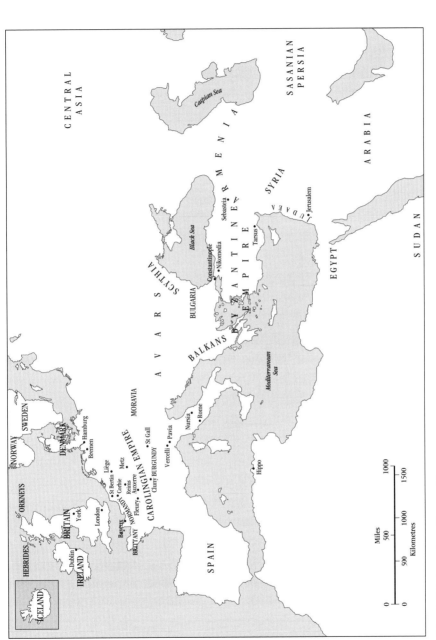

Map 1 Britain and a wider world.

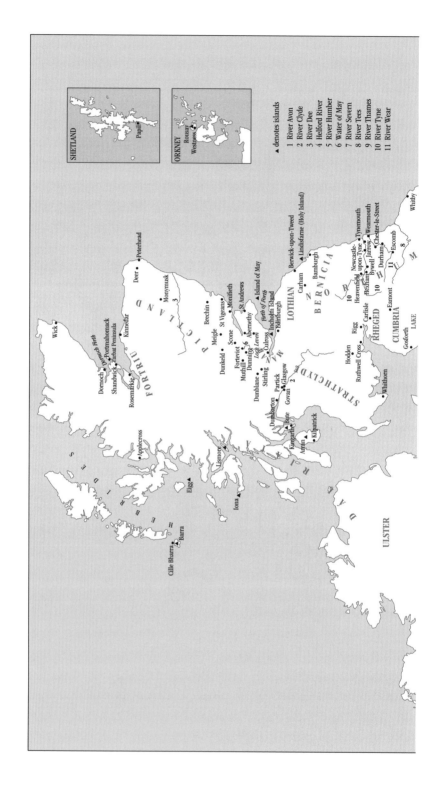

SHETLAND

Papil•

ORKNEY
Rousay▲
Westray▲

▲ denotes islands

1 River Avon
2 River Clyde
3 River Dee
4 Helford River
5 River Humber
6 Water of May
7 River Severn
8 River Tees
9 River Thames
10 River Tyne
11 River Wear

Berwick-upon-Tweed
Lindisfarne (Holy Island)▲

Whitby•

Peterhead
Deer•

Monymusk•

PICTLAND
3
Brechin•

St Vigeans•
Monifieth•
Meigle•   St Andrews•
Scone•   ▲ Island of May
Dunkeld• Abernethy•
Forteviot• Firth of Forth
Muthill• 6 Culross• Inchcolm Island▲
Dunning• Loch Leven Edinburgh•
Dunblane• N W
Stirling•   LOTHIAN
Carham•
Bamburgh•

BERNICIA
Tynemouth•
Newcastle- Wearmouth•
Heavenfield upon-Tyne Jarrow• Chester-le-Street•
•Hexham Bywell• Durham• Escomb•
10
Partick• Glasgow• 2
Dumbarton• Govan•
Kingarth• Bute
Arran•
Kilpatrick•

Wick•

Dornoch Dornoch Firth
Shandwick• Portmahomack•
Tarbat Peninsula
Kinneddar•
Rosemarkie•

FORTRIU

Applecross•

Lismore•

Eigg▲

Iona▲

HEBRIDES

Cille Bharra•▲
Barra

STRATHCLYDE

Hodden•
Rigg•
Ruthwell Cross•
Carlisle•
RHEGED
CUMBRIA
Eamont•
Gosforth• LAKE
Whithorn•

ULSTER

DÁL RIATA

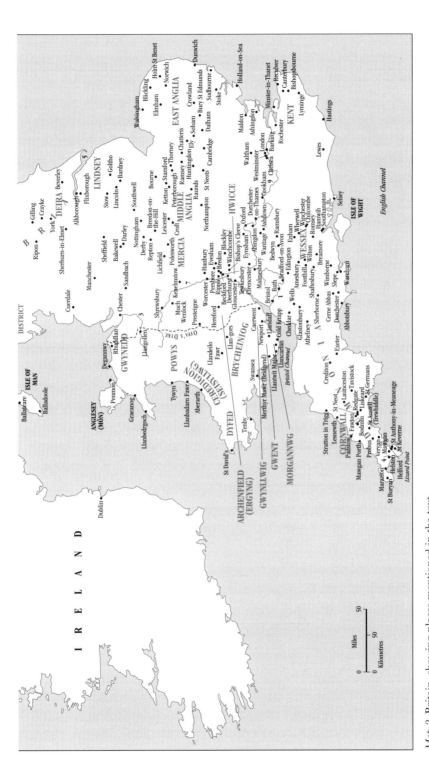

Map 2 Britain, showing places mentioned in the text.

Part I
Britain c. 800–c. 1066

1 Britain in c. 800 and in c. 1066
Changes and continuities

Introduction

People interested in Britain between 800 and 1066 face several challenges. One involves terminology and categorisation. In general, in modern and popular understanding the words England, Scotland and Wales signify three distinct countries and nations; their historical inhabitants were, respectively, English, Scots and Welsh; their experiences included periodic invasion and immigration by foreigners. Furthermore, 'England' and 'English' are often used as if interchangeable with 'Britain' and 'British', despite England's having land borders with Wales and Scotland, running roughly along lines from Bristol in the south to Chester in the north, and from Carlisle in the west to Berwick-upon-Tweed in the east.

The historical reality was very different. Communication depended on travel. In pre-industrial societies, communication without travel is limited to signalling, for example using beacons. In such societies travel by boat, where waters are navigable, is easier and faster than travel by land even where the terrain is easy. Navigable waterways consequently stimulate the cohesion of the lands through which they run rather than their separation, though they may also serve as visual markers of limits of influence. Ranges of mountains or high hills do the reverse. Consequently, the cultural and political units that we might expect to see in early medieval Britain are very different from its modern ones or even subdivisions of them.

Physical geography implies that the 'building blocks' of British history should have been six units. One, straddling the valley of the River Thames and the English Channel would have united present-day south and south-east England with northern France and The Netherlands. Devon, Cornwall and south Wales, united by the Bristol Channel, seems more likely than modern Wales, since travelling overland from Wales' south-east coast to Anglesey off its north coast would have taken eight days.[1] A third natural unit would have combined north-west England, south-west Scotland, the Isle of Man and northern and eastern Ireland, centring around, and united by, the Irish Sea. Likewise, the North Sea links the far north of Scotland with Scandinavia. Fifth, the combinations of south-east Scotland with much of northern and eastern England and sixth, of north Wales with midland England seem geographically plausible.

Sometimes these theoretical units were historical realities. The ninth-century Anglo-Saxon kingdom of Wessex (the West Saxons) was based in the Thames valley but encompassed Kent after c. 825. It was far less significantly involved with northern England than it was with the lands across the Channel, which were ruled by the successors of the Frankish Emperor Charles, now known as Charlemagne (emperor 800–814). In the early tenth century, due to West Saxon success against Viking invaders and to the fragmentation of the Carolingian Empire, Wessex's King Aethelstan (924–939) was the most powerful king in western Christendom. He extended his influence across the Channel, to Brittany. He subjugated, temporarily, what is known nowadays, though not at the time, as the Viking kingdom of York. Originating in Scandinavian conquest and settlement in 876, and lasting until 954, this kingdom stretched, probably, from (modern) Sheffield and Manchester in the south to the River Tees in the north. Its connections with the Viking kingdom of Dublin, in Ireland, were so close that the two sometimes look like halves of the same polity. Another Scandinavian unit dates to the late tenth century. In c. 980 the Norse earldom of Orkney in the north of Scotland was established. Perhaps originally under Danish control, by the mid-eleventh century it had passed to Norway.

The earlier Anglo-Saxon kingdom of Northumbria, of which York had originally been part, had included north-west England and territory north of Carlisle and of Newcastle-upon-Tyne up to the Firth of Forth – that is, the region of Edinburgh. Thus Scottish history and heritage contain English elements. These include Northumbrian rule; involvement in Northumbrian and wider Anglo-Saxon concerns and developments; saints who worked in northern Northumbria, notably the seventh-century King Oswald and monk-bishop Cuthbert; sculpture; and some English poetry, notably *The Dream of the Rood*. A version of this poem is inscribed on the eighth-century north Northumbrian Ruthwell Cross. Conversely, English history includes the history of part of Scotland. In southern Britain, Devon and Cornwall constituted a separate kingdom, Dumnonia, for several centuries. It resembled Welsh rather than Anglo-Saxon kingdoms and had significant contacts with Brittany. Other kingdoms too were, at various times, located on the western side of the island, up to and including the region of Glasgow and across to Edinburgh. They include Rheged in the Carlisle and Lake District area, and Strathclyde and Dumbarton to its north. It is these western kingdoms that are properly called British, distinguishing them from the Anglo-Saxon polities of eastern Britain.

The Anglo-Saxons shared a Germanic language, Old English, the Britons a Celtic one. Since the vicissitudes of political history caused some elements of northern British culture, and people, to move to Wales, Welsh history and heritage includes Scottish elements and vice versa. The poem known as *The Gododdin* has a north British subject, an early-seventh-century raid from Edinburgh into Northumbria, and may be contemporary with it, but it is written in Welsh, and was preserved in Wales. Over the centuries, Scottish as well as Welsh and Cornish enthusiasts have claimed the legendary King Arthur for themselves, locating his headquarters and significant parts of his career in their territory. As portrayed in later texts, Arthur is a figure of fiction, but quests for the historical Arthur start with our earliest known references to an Arthur. The first is a single one in *The Gododdin*; others are in the Latin *History of the Britons* written by a Welsh scholar, who may have been called Ninnius or Nennius, c. 829–830.[2]

Names that are familiar to modern readers are often misleading in themselves though their history can be illuminating. Behind 'Wales' and 'Welsh' lie Germanic words that probably originally signified 'descendants of the former citizens of the Roman Empire' rather than Celts.[3] Old English *wealh* was used in the law code that was attributed by the West Saxon King Alfred (871–899) to his seventh-century forebear King Ine to mean both 'Briton' and 'slave', and in tenth-century texts it meant 'slave'. This development reflects the Welsh–Anglo-Saxon relationship in the ninth, and especially the tenth, centuries when Wessex extended its power into Wales.[4] What the Welsh, then as now, called themselves was very different, *Cymry*, meaning Britons. This name was also applied to Britons elsewhere in Britain, which British writers regarded as their heritage. The fact that 'England' means land of the English may partially explain its frequent current misuse, to refer to Britain. The dominance of England and of the English language and people in today's British government and culture perhaps makes this seem natural and accurate to those who do this. But 'England' is not merely a polity whose size, location and power within Britain changed between 800 and 1066. Its very existence depends on a prior existence of 'the English', that is, a group and regime that thought of itself and was perceptible by outsiders as English, as opposed to, say, West Saxon or East Anglian or Cornish. And there was a time when there was no such thing as the English. In the making of an English people and an England the West Saxon king Alfred and his tenth-century successors played a major role. As for 'Scotland', literally land of the Scots, this actually means the land of the Irish, because *Scotti* was Latin for Irish. For several centuries much of western Scotland was part of the Irish kingdom of Dál Riata, whose base was in eastern Ireland. North-east Scotland on the other hand was contemporaneously the territory of the *Picti* (Picts), a Latin word meaning painted people. The Picts' origin used to be an historical conundrum. Now, however, they are thought to have been the indigenous inhabitants of the lands beyond the frontier of Roman Britain who did not succumb to Romanisation, in contrast to other British groups.[5]

Whether and, if so, when any of these groups had a sense of national identity, distinct from and overriding family, tribal and social identities, is highly debatable. The subject of national identity, its origins and chronology, in world history has generated much scholarly work and disagreement in recent decades. And, though casual use of the word nation still recurs, it has also been debated in relation to medieval case studies, Anglo-Saxon England prominent among them.

Finally, since Britain comprises the island of Britain and the smaller ones around it (Wight, Anglesey, Man, the Hebrides and others), the least confusing term when considering its history between 800 and 1066 may be 'archipelago' (group of islands). 'Britain' after all has a cultural meaning (land of the Britons) and a political one (the Roman diocese Britannia) for this period as well as a geographical one, and these three meanings are far from coincidental on a map. In exploring this archipelago, subdivision into England, Scotland and Wales would be inappropriate. The previous volume in this series divided it into Germanic, British, Irish and Pictish sub-units.[6] To these may be added a further, Scandinavian one, in the later ninth century, when parts of England and Scotland came under Scandinavian domination. This volume will attempt to compare and take account of Scandinavian England, Cornwall, Wales, British Scotland, Dál Riatan Scotland, Pictish Scotland and Scandinavian Scotland as well as Anglo-Saxon England, to which the bulk of our evidence relates. Its focus, however, will be predominantly on England.

The years 800–1066 were very important in the history of the archipelago. Sometimes apparent continuity masks upheaval and crises: in both 800 and 1066 its religion was Christianity but ninth- and tenth-century Scandinavian invasion and settlement had imported and revived paganism, and significantly challenged the established faith and Church. Moreover, by 1066 there had been some long-lasting and significant changes, especially in England. Its boundaries were now roughly the same as its twentieth-century ones and there is a case for considering it the world's first nation-state.[7] Within it, towns flourished. Beyond it, the Picts had disappeared as a political identity, and a kingdom that is recognisable as an early version of modern Scotland had emerged.

Throughout, religion had, and had had, a central importance. In twentieth-century Britain religion came to be widely regarded as an internal and private matter. In this perception, religion comprises faith, spirituality and doctrine, is for individuals, and should neither interfere with society, politics and the state, nor be interfered with by them. For most of the past, however, over most of the planet, as still today over much of it, religion has been a public matter, one of behaviour, and a community concern. This has been true even in cases where religion has also required individual and internal commitment and acceptance of some doctrinal teaching, as Christianity has done, for example about the divine and human nature of Christ and about His Resurrection. Yet Christianity in early medieval Britain, as elsewhere, involved much more than such beliefs. It offered an evolving philosophy of kingship, a body of literature and scholarship. It developed a structure and organisation, of archdioceses, dioceses, parishes and religious communities (minsters, monasteries and nunneries). It acquired widely distributed church buildings and a body of personnel, namely archbishops, bishops, priests and other men in clerical orders (ordained to offices in the Church), abbots, abbesses, monks and nuns (men and women who had taken monastic vows), who provided some degree of pastoral care and played a part in the workings of politics and society. Christian ideas of kingship, Christian texts, writers, bishops and priests played no less a part than did the West Saxon kings in the creation of an English national identity. This involved not only ideas about identities but also practical matters of politics, including kingdoms' unity and unification, administration and internal power structure.

Religion overlapped with economy and culture as well as with politics. By economy, we should understand the population, its distribution and settlement pattern and its livelihood, chiefly based on agriculture, but including some manu-facturing and commerce, revenues in the form of tax or tribute, coinage, trade and towns. Economy supported not only the entirety of society and its life but also its culture more narrowly defined as those areas of its life requiring some individuals and groups to be freed from the work of food production. Culture involves language and literacy, scholarship and learning, attitudes to the past, the future and the afterlife, and awareness of and contacts with a wider 'foreign' world. It includes the composition of scholarly treatises and historical works, poetry, the visual arts (carving, sculpture, manuscript illumination (decoration with painting) and other forms of painting) and architecture and the production of books. Such works were mostly produced at and by ecclesiastical centres. The patronage and finance behind them was usually royal, aristocratic or ecclesias-tical. In many cases works of art, architecture and original writing embodied statements and messages of various kinds on behalf of the patron(s) and these often had a religious element. The attitudes that are thereby revealed may be considered an aspect of social history. There are other social questions too, in which Christian ideas, institutions and personnel were important. They include: socio-economic differentiation, social class and categories, including slavery; the role and status of women, including their legal status and ability to own land; attitudes to sex and marriage; and levels of violence.

Just as religion, politics, society, economy and culture intertwine, so too do such subsidiary questions and the subjects of the chapters of this book. Chris-tianity's manifold contribution to social cohesion, for example, relates both to Part II's consideration of the making of identities and communities and Part III's of the structuring of society. Anglo-Saxon political theory about good kingship and government and their purpose does likewise. Furthermore, the engagement of the Church in government went beyond political philosophy and included practical involvement in the subject of Part IV – the keeping of order and the lives of individuals, in the legal system, taxation, war and diplomacy. The role that was allowed to women is considered in Part III since it relates to the struc-turing of society. It will be approached through the issues of power and property rights, of nuns and abbesses and of female saints, and also those of marriage and of rules and ideas about virginity and celibacy, which overlap with Part IV's of pastoral care and the Christian's life. Before exploring these particular issues, we will consider the extent to which society changed between c. 800 and c. 1066.

Politics, economy, religion, culture and society c. 800

The year 800 did not seem to contemporaries an important date in the history of the archipelago. The *Anglo-Saxon Chronicle* records only that there was an eclipse of the moon on the eve of 16 January.[8] In retrospect, 800's historical importance lies in the fact that on Christmas Day the Pope, in Rome, crowned Charlemagne as Roman emperor.

In a mental review of his Anglo-Saxon neighbours, with whose kingdoms he had already had dealings, Charlemagne would probably have thought first of

midland Mercia and its King Cenwulf. Mercia had recently absorbed a number
of previously independent southern kingdoms, including Kent, which it held
securely from 798, and loosely controlled that of East Anglia. It had an effective,
though now shadowy, administration. It had produced Offa's Dyke, an impressive
earthwork running almost the entire length of the Mercian–Welsh border, and
many high-quality coins, at least two, and possibly as many as ten, million.[9]
Mercian charters (land grants) attest common dues owed by landholders to the
crown. Dominant in the north was Northumbria, under King Eardwulf. Like
Mercia, though less recently, Northumbria had absorbed smaller kingdoms into a
larger one. Unlike Mercia, it had suffered dynastic instability in the later eighth
century. There are different views as to just how deep its political instability ran.[10]
The late-seventh-century Dál Riatan *Law of the Innocents*, which protected non-
combatants from violence in times of internal war or dispute, may have applied in
Northumbria. This is because Northumbria's links with Iona, where it had been
composed, had been very close. It is possible that Northumbria had a hereditary
aristocracy. There may have been a noble council, a hierarchy of royal officials
and some sense of a Northumbrian identity.[11] Northumbrian patriotism is discernible in the poem about the bishops and kings of York written by Alcuin, a
York alumnus,[12] but it may have been restricted to the upper echelons of society.
The fourth Anglo-Saxon kingdom was King Beorhtric's Wessex, long the enemy
of Mercia though suffering its over-lordship. Ine's law code suggests that West
Saxon kings were involved with making law and the administration of justice,
levied revenues and had a range of royal officials.

That there was no sense of a single English national identity is indicated not
only by Alcuin's poem but also by the organisation of war. War has, generally,
been historically important in the creation and maintenance of national identity.
It can generate shared experience and a common outlook against a shared
enemy, and provide occasions for morale-boosting exhortation and for participation in Christian worship (which itself can contribute to a sense of national identity). It becomes an important feature in a shared history. In early Anglo-Saxon
England, war involved the aristocracy intimately but not the peasantry.[13] Kings'
enemies were their dynastic rivals and their immediate neighbours as they
attempted to impose or resist what we can see as the trend towards fewer and
greater kingdoms. Kings needed booty and new lands to reward their followers.
Moreover, the institution of bloodfeud (vendetta) meant that one battle would
generate cause for another. On the other hand there is evidence from Ine's law
code and from the eighth-century Northumbrian historian Bede that using the
English language was perceived as a marker of English as opposed to British
identity.[14] All of the four kingdoms had a history of cultural and political links
with both Francia and the Papacy, and enemies coming from outside the archipelago were beginning to be a concern. Vikings had raided the Northumbrian
monastery of Lindisfarne in 796 but they were not yet an overriding problem.

The Anglo-Saxon economy was developed, varied and prosperous by 800. Its
agriculture produced more food than was needed for mere subsistence, though
estimates of how much more have varied.[15] There was some specialisation in crop

production in the countryside. The high volumes of both Mercian and North-umbrian coinage imply large-scale exchange at low as well as high levels of society, and the trade network of eastern England certainly involved more than just luxury goods. There were glassworks and salt furnaces and production of cloth and wool.[16] For example, at the trading centre of Hamwih, near modern Southampton, in Wessex, sheep were cropped for wool. The beginnings of towns are discernible but trading centres were not necessarily towns.[17] Towns have other attributes besides engaging in trade, such as concentration of settlement, a varied population engaging in different occupations and not growing all its food, and functioning as administrative, political and religious centres. Some types of site other than trading centres had some urban characteristics. Some ecclesiastical settlements were large and populous, and were places where goods were redis-tributed:[18] Bede's monastery at Jarrow seems pre-urban. Thriving York was probably an ecclesiastical centre, not a royal town as sometimes thought.[19] Nei-ther the Anglo-Saxons' royalty and aristocracy nor their settlements, which were not fortified, were urban. When a settlement had a trading centre, a *wīc*, it was not on the same site but close by, as in the case of London and its *wīc* Aldwych.

How many people there were, and exactly how they were settled, is unknown. Most people probably lived within what are often called great estates, or extended, or multiple estates. These were mostly between about 50 and 100 square miles (very much bigger than the typical post-1066 English manor), though there were smaller ones. A great estate would contain different resources, thereby being self-sufficient. At its centre, crafts would be practised, and the estate-owner's officials based. The estate-owner would probably have a home farm. The obligations and the freedom of those who lived on the estate most likely varied depending on how close they lived to the centre: proximity, heavy burdens and lack of freedom going together, and likewise distance, lighter burdens and more freedom. This system covered much though not all of the countryside. People who had holdings on an estate would supply food and other kinds of rent for their landlord. The settlement pattern was predominantly of isolated households and small hamlets.[20] In that respect the landscape differed greatly from that of the present day. In another it did not, since there was not significantly more tree cover then than now.

The Anglo-Saxons' Church was centralised and organised. There were two archbishoprics, subdivided into bishoprics under the archbishops' authority. Of the archbishoprics, Canterbury was senior to York. Including them, there were sixteen sees altogether.[21] In the south, under Canterbury, were Leicester, Winchester, Elmham, Worcester, Hereford, Dunwich, Lindsey, Selsey and London, whose bishops witnessed a 799 charter in this order, plus Rochester, Sherborne and Lichfield. In 800, Lichfield was actually an archbishopric, but it had only recently been elevated to this status and it was short-lived. In 803 it reverted to its former one, as a bishopric. In the north, under York, were Lindisfarne and Hexham. The Church regularly held synods (councils), summoned by the archbishop of Canterbury. The most used meeting place was Clovesho, which may have been within the diocese of London or possibly in Middle Anglia (roughly present-day Leicestershire and Northamptonshire).[22]

Councils considered a variety of business, including disputed inheritances, which often involved legacies to churches. They were attended not only by bishops, heads of religious houses and other ecclesiastics but also by aristocrats and by Mercian kings, who used the occasions to make grants of land. The charter witness lists suggest that the Church north of the River Humber was normally under- or un-represented at the councils.[23] As well as bishoprics there were many religious communities, both male and female, of varying size, standards and ethos, some well known to us from copious evidence, others scarcely and by chance. For example, charter evidence attests some fifty in the diocese of Worcester c. 800[24] and written evidence and sculpture suggest at least sixty-five churches in the counties of Derbyshire, Nottinghamshire, Lincolnshire and Yorkshire before the mid-ninth century.[25] The more important of these were evenly distributed throughout the region. There were some hermits, apparently more in northern Northumbria than elsewhere. Some religious houses enjoyed rights of sanctuary (sheltering fugitives). These rights were, however, not secure, but often violated, certainly in Northumbria.[26]

The Church produced from within itself much criticism, both of its own personnel and of the laity (non-ecclesiastics), but of a kind that shows that Church and faith were in fact securely established. It does not suggest that paganism still lingered. It was directed rather at some surviving practices which had been associated with it, such as the use of amulets and enchantments, at lack of pastoral care and preaching, at backsliding, laxity and immorality. Most famously, in a letter possibly meant for Leicester's bishop (rather than Lindisfarne's as used to be thought), Alcuin regarded the Viking attack on Lindisfarne as divine punishment.[27] This was for the monks' rich dress, lavish food and drink and habit of listening to certain kinds of poetry. Furthermore, there is evidence of piety. Private prayer books were produced, in west Mercia at least, in the eighth and early ninth centuries, for the elite. Penance (a ritual of atonement and purification following confession of sins) was common. The giving of land to the Church could be a penitential act.

A large number of saints were venerated. These included the Virgin Mary and St Peter and other saints known throughout Christendom, and local ones, some of them much more local than others. The emphasis in church dedications was on the universal saints.[28] We have an Old English martyrology (list of saints) which has been reconstructed from five fragments, and was written in the ninth century, perhaps after c. 850. Most of its saints have links with Rome.[29] Some of them appear as English rather than English regional (for example Northumbrian) saints, which was how Bede had presented them in his *Ecclesiastical History of the English People* (written in Latin). Moreover, despite being Mercian, the *Martyrology* contains more saints whose origins and careers were Northumbrian than Mercian.[30] Native saints included some royal women, and some royal men who had died violent deaths and who were venerated in houses that were connected to their families or to others who had an interest in them.[31] Notable examples are the mid-seventh-century King Oswine of Deira (southern Northumbria) killed at the instigation of King Oswy of Bernicia (northern Northumbria) and revered at

Gilling in Northumbria, and Oswy's daughter-in-law Aethelthryth, seventh-century princess of East Anglia and queen of Northumbria. She had retained her virginity through two marriages and was venerated especially in Ely in East Anglia. There were also, probably, many very local saints of seventh- or eighth-century origin whose identities are now lost, and probably had been by the tenth century.

These cults were housed in what became known in English as minsters. According to the so-called 'minster hypothesis',[32] which has generated considerable debate, minsters were mostly royal foundations, established to provide pastoral care for the region in which they were situated, normally quite large. A minster was entitled to dues from its region's people, including some of the services and food-renders that the people owed to the king but which the king had assigned to support the foundation. Minsters were probably originally communities of monks, some of whom may have been in clerical orders, but over time they lost their monastic character, housing itinerant and other clergy. Most became, eventually, entirely clerical, comprising what are termed secular canons, or secular clergy.[33] There may have been a saint for every minster.[34] Saints' relics were venerated and regarded as workers of miracles. Christian magic permeated society, though leaders of the Church disapproved of some of it, for example the use of Christian amulets, such as bones and Gospel quotations on scraps of parchment.[35] By contrast, there were probably neither many church buildings nor priests to serve the people. Worship, preaching and rituals may have taken place at open-air sites. Priests had high social status and were probably not of lowly origin. In 824, there were only fifty for the diocese of Worcester.

Marriage was a religious matter, meant to involve a Mass and a blessing, and to conform to the Church's rules about whom Christians could marry (close kin were forbidden). In 786, legitimacy, that is, one's parents being married at the time of one's birth, was stipulated as a requirement for kingship. Burial by contrast was not something that the Church tried to control.[36] Most lay burials were in rural cemeteries that were not enclosed. Some lay people, probably because they had some close connection with the minster, were interred in a minster cemetery, though not in the same part of it as the deceased religious. In a normal burial the body lay extended, horizontally, head to the east, in a dug grave, and without grave-goods (chattels and personal possessions).[37]

Two late-eighth-century instances testify to the political role of saints. In 798, the body of the seventh-century East Anglian princess Wihtburh (Withburga) was exhumed, to be venerated. This was perhaps in response to Offa of Mercia's beheading of East Anglia's King Aethelbert in 794.[38] At St Alkhmund's church in Derby, in Mercia, is a stone coffin whose exterior decoration suggests that it was meant for display. It may have been the coffin of the Northumbrian king of the same name, Alkhmund. He was killed in Mercia, where he had taken refuge, by his rival Eardwulf in 800. Both the display and the church's dedication were probably meant to signify King Cenwulf of Mercia's alliance with Eardwulf's enemies.[39]

This Alkhmund carving is one of several indications of productivity and vibrancy in the visual arts in turn-of-the-century Mercia. Peterborough and Breedon-on-the-Hill were centres of sculpture, Breedon-on-the-Hill's production beginning perhaps in the 790s.[40] A monument of c. 800 is the standing cross at Sandbach. The glories of Northumbrian – like Kentish – art and scholarship were of earlier date. However, in Northumbria, York's library was impressive, a set of contemporary annals was kept up until the early ninth century, and a monk, Aethelwulf, wrote a Latin poem about the history of his own monastery. It may have been Bywell on the River Tyne or Crayke near York.[41] Anglo-Saxon book production was insignificant by c. 800.[42] There is no evidence for significant lay literacy, but there was a tradition of vernacular (English-language) religious poetry. The date of Cynewulf, who signed four vernacular poems, is debated but may have been early ninth century. His works, like Mercian sculpture, show an awareness of Mediterranean Continental culture. Contacts with the Franks and with Rome, where there was a fortified English School, were strong. In some quarters there was some alienation from parts of the past. Bede had invented a single past for the disparate Anglo-Saxons that they could share. He omitted their pre-Christian experience.

The society in which this Anglo-Saxon culture was embedded was a differentiated one. Under the kings were overseers of areas that had once been independent kingdoms, possibly descendants of their own earlier kings.[43] These are called sub-kings, princes, patricians and dukes (in Old English, *ealdormen*) in surviving texts. Below them were counts (Old English *gesith*s, whose original meaning was companions), who were married property owners. A fourth category was ministers and soldiers (thegns), not aristocrats by birth and inheritance but royal officials dependent on the king for their positions and revenues.[44] These revenues were renders that had previously been paid to the king. The ownership of the lands whence the renders came did not pass to the officials. Laymen had to have been granted lands by royal charter, or to dominate the churches to which such charters had been granted, in order to retain lands. Below these classes, judging by Ine's laws, was that of the *ceorl* (free peasant), whose wergeld (blood-price) was in Wessex one-sixth of a *gesith*'s (though in Kent one-third). A *ceorl* owed military service and food-rent to the king, and normally held one hide of land (enough land to support one household for a year, the acreage of which varied from region to region). Peasant households included slaves, of which there were a large number. The role and status of women within this society is debatable. There are no late-eighth-century examples of powerful and influential abbesses and female monastic houses to parallel those earlier in the eighth century. Furthermore, the last indisputable evidence for any double (with male and female inmates) house ruled by an abbess dates to 796, in a letter written by Alcuin.[45] This might mean that female status and power had declined in general by 800. In Wessex, attitudes to female power were more negative, and its reality less marked, than in Mercia, though why is unclear.

Anglo-Saxon society did not include that of Cornwall, an independent kingdom since the fall of Dumnonia and Wessex's take-over of Devon. Cornwall had dispersed settlement, a bishopric, based at Dinurrin (which lay, probably, a little north of what became Bodmin), and many local churches, whose dedicatees were probably their sixth- and seventh-century founders who had come to be regarded as saintly. Only one cult, however, of Docgwin (Docco), and seven monastic houses are attested by 800.[46] The churches were usually isolated and the names of many of their sites include the Cornish element *lann*, signifying enclosed cemetery or church-town. Carved stones, including decorated sculpted standing crosses, are all that remain of artistic achievement, but the inscriptions on the stones may signify some elite lay literacy.

The elite in the south-west had a tradition of claiming that their identity was Roman as well as Christian, advertising this in how they used Latin in inscriptions.[47] The view that Christianity and Latin were marks of the Britons had obtained too in the British territory west of Offa's Dyke.[48] There, Old Testament personal names were used and claims to biblical and Roman ancestry made for rulers of the major kingdoms. There were, probably, seven kingdoms.[49] Almost no written records survive, yet analysis of those that do suggests that their use may have been significant. Charters associated with Llandaff suggest a tradition of charter-writing[50] and the ninth-century Welsh memorandum and charters written in margins of the Lichfield Gospels may have not have been untypical.[51] There seems to have been some tradition of writing, in Welsh and in Latin, about legal matters. The socio-political structure included notables, or elders, deliberating, and, until c. 800, a social group of 'royal companions'. Kingship was a personal matter. It was heritable property. Kings' financial resources did not include a taxation system but comprised their personal property and what they received in hospitality. On the other hand, there is some evidence for an anointing or inauguration ritual, which would have given kingship an institutional and public character. Kings and nobles used forts as their bases, one example being Degannwy on the north coast, which the Anglo-Saxons destroyed in 822.[52] It is from the kingdom of Gwynedd (in the north-west) in the late 820s that evidence for a sense of national identity comes, in Nennius' work. Here the Britons (not just those of Wales) are one, Christian, people with a shared culture and history, including a lost Golden Age, that of Arthur. Whether Nennius was reflecting sentiment or seeking to shape it is unclear.

As in Anglo-Saxon regions, land was held in great estates. The Welsh economy was less developed than the Anglo-Saxons', though apparently without any problematic poverty. Specialisation in craft was rare though there was some iron-working. There was no free land market, no coinage, no towns and no market economy, perhaps in part because the terrain made communication and movement difficult, though Anglesey was involved in some international trade. The most important exchange mechanism was gift exchange. Hunting was very important, its participants either consuming what it produced or using it to pay dues.[53] The most common way of expressing value was in cows.

The Welsh Church[54] likewise differed from the Anglo-Saxons'. There is only one indication of centralisation: the *Welsh Annals* report that in 768 Easter was changed 'among the Britons'.[55] There were, probably, five bishoprics but no archbishopric. There may have been more than one bishop per kingdom simultaneously, two different grades of bishops, and churches that retained episcopal rank because they had once, though no longer, had a bishop.[56] Very localised church dedications and place-names may indicate that local churches had been founded there quite early. Some such are actually attested, in the Llandaff charters. Gwent had many. There were very few enclosed cemeteries.[57] Infant baptism, private prayer, prayer for protection and, probably, penance, attested in the sixth century, were practised. The Church was dynastic. St David's bishopric and monastery in Dyfed, for example, were dominated by a group of kinsmen. As in Cornwall, there may have been monastic confederations, but there were no religious houses for women. In some cases, the relationship between religious communities and kings may have been close. The burial of eighth-century kings of Brycheiniog at Llan-gors (Llangorse) suggests that it was so there.[58] Llantwit Major's church may have been the cemetery church for the dynasty of Gwent and Glywysing in the eighth and ninth centuries.[59] Most saints who were objects of cults were probably communities' founders. They included David, attested in an inscription of 806, Cadog[60] and Garmon (Germanus).[61] There are different views as to whether the Germanus of the texts was a local saint Garmon, Germanus of Auxerre or a conflation.[62] North Britain's Kentigern was probably venerated by the late eighth century.[63] Non-local saints were venerated too, including the universal saint Michael, and there was a tradition of royal and saintly pilgrimage to Rome and an awareness of both Rome and Jerusalem. One of the latter's sources was Irish pilgrims whose route crossed Wales.[64] As evidenced by Nennius, Wales lacked neither learning nor sophisticated royal courts.[65] Saints' lives were produced.[66] Scholars wrote in Latin. The earliest known vernacular inscription is a ten-line inscription on a stone at Tywyn dated c. 800.[67] Welsh society comprised nobles, peasants and slaves. The aristocracy was violent. Bloodfeud does not seem to have been practised but the kindred had an active social role. Lands were family lands, and women's property rights were inferior to men's.[68]

Our knowledge of Wales is sketchy and that of British Scotland even scantier. The kingdom of Dumbarton may have been partitioned by 800, between Northumbria and the Picts.[69] There was a small kingdom (Manaw) centred on Stirling. There may have been a bishopric, at Glasgow, or at Govan, which first appears in the historical record in 756, and monastic confederations. Penance may have been practised. The Anglo-Saxon saints Cuthbert and Oswald were venerated in the south, the British Uinniau (Ninian) in the south-west, at Whithorn,[70] and the British Kentigern further north, at Glasgow. Two Latin poems about Ninian that were written at Whithorn c. 780 survive.[71] Interest in history is demonstrated by vernacular (Welsh) poems including *The Gododdin*, but there seems not to have been any historical writing. A later source refers to a, now lost, *Life of Kentigern* 'dictated in a Gaelic style'. This has been dated to c. 800, but that is now disputed.[72]

Gaelic-speaking Dál Riatan Scotland comprised Kintyre, where the royal dynasty was based, Arran, parts of Cowal, Lorne and Morvern and various islands.[73] In 800, it was ruled by King Conall. It is possible that kings were anointed. Rulers' bases were hill-forts. Like Northumbria, Dál Riata was threatened by the Vikings, who in 802 attacked the island and monastery of Iona, in whose heritage both kingdoms shared.[74] This heritage included a tradition of penance, scholarship and native poetry. A four-line Gaelic verse about one Oengus, son of Fergus, survives, perhaps composed in 761, following his death.[75] Iona had daughter-monasteries and there may have been one bishopric. Some local saints were venerated: Ionan luminaries, including its sixth-century founder (and evangeliser of the Picts) Columba and late-seventh-century abbot Adomnán; Bláán (Blane) at Kingarth on Bute; Donnán and four others from Eigg;[76] Mo Luag (Molaug), the founder of the monastery there, at Lismore; and Mael Ruba at Applecross.[77] Relics were esteemed but the practice was to acquire secondary relics (items that had been in contact with the saint's body), rather than parts of the body itself, and to leave the interred bodies undisturbed.[78]

In 811, Dál Riata came under the rule of the king of the Picts, Constantín (Constantine) I (789–820), who installed his son there.[79] The Pictish kingdom probably comprised a core region, Fortriu, and others that Fortriu (variably) dominated, possibly extending to Orkney. It may have already been suffering like its neighbours from the Vikings though their first known attack was in 839. Its organisation is very shadowy. Bede implies that its early-eighth-century kings had strong governmental control and a well-ordered state[80] and some twelfth-century evidence has been interpreted as confirmation. There are, however, many uncertainties. Kings' revenues may have come only from Fortriu and their renders from the whole kingdom or just the royal estates; the royal estates might have been merely family estates, not attached to the office of king. Kingship was not partible and only rarely passed from father to son. Land was held in great estates. Secular elite bases were small hill-forts but kings may have spent more time in places that offered more comfort. The most important royal centre was probably Forteviot, then on a promontory almost surrounded by a river, the Water of May. With its residence, church, cemetery and assembly place, Forteviot was an estate centre and a place of ritual activities.[81] Paradoxically, kings' need to raid others' territories to obtain resources to reward the members of their warbands may have stimulated unification. Royal conquest, confiscation of land and subsequent granting of it to supporters would have been concentrated in the areas that were least loyal, rendering them much more so.[82]

There is no evidence for written or oral law. However, the symbol stones, namely stones carved with symbols whose meaning is unknown, may have served as boundary markers. Some of the symbols may have been statements of title to land and of threats to transgressors. Symbol stones were certainly used to mark burial sites which themselves often functioned as boundary markers. Pictish kingship resembled the Anglo-Saxons' not only in its martial and possibly its administrative aspects but also in looking to biblical parallels and role models. The Old Testament King David appears in scenes, including a lion-hunt, in the sculpture on the exterior of the St Andrews sarcophagus (so called because it was found in St Andrews), whose date lies between c. 775 and c. 850.[83] He also features on another sarcophagus at St Andrews.[84] The Dupplin Cross, from the 810s, may have been meant to commemorate the victory with which Constantín I had begun his reign and to imply a parallel with the Roman Emperor Constantine I and the cross that he had set up in the Holy Land. Its decoration includes an equestrian warrior, possibly a portrait of Constantín himself, and a David and the Lion scene.[85]

Pictish representations of kingship in fact drew more than those of the Anglo-Saxons on the art and ideas of the late antique and early medieval eastern world. The St Andrews sarcophagus drew on Sasanian models,[86] that is, from the art of the Persian Empire, ruled by the Sasanian dynasty from the early third to the mid-seventh centuries, whose religion was Zoroastrianism. Furthermore, hunt scenes, customised like other horse-riding scenes for Pictish society, for example in the style of dress, are more prominent in Scotland than anywhere else in western Europe.[87] The importance of this is that further east the hunt had royal and Christian significance. In Iranian culture, it was not merely an elite pastime and preparation for war, but a scene of epiphany, that is, where true character and reality were revealed. It also symbolised the afterlife because of its resonances of good versus evil and ultimate victory. It was an image of fitness to rule. In the Graeco-Roman pagan and Christian worlds the hunt was used in funerary contexts. In Christian Armenia, it had both the funerary and the propagandist senses. How the Picts encountered Sasanian models is mysterious. One possibility is on treasures that Charlemagne is reported to have distributed to 'Scottish' kings after taking them, in 796, as booty from the Avars. The Avars had been allies of the Persians in the early seventh century and dishes and vessels of precious metals are recorded as having been standard Persian diplomatic gifts. The east features in Pictish legend as well as art. In the twelfth-century St Andrews foundation legend, whose origins are perhaps mid-ninth century, eastern monks arrive with saints' relics.

Andrew's cult was introduced in the mid-eighth or early ninth century. If the former, it may have been part of an attempt to emulate the senior–junior, Peter–Andrew commemorative pattern detectable in the Anglo-Saxon Church.[88] If the latter, it came to a society whose dominant cult was that of St Peter.[89] Other cults included that of the Irish Brigit, established since the seventh century at Abernethy,[90] and, as elsewhere, local cults. These included Drostan's and Naiton's (Nechtan),[91] particularly associated with Deer (Old Deer), Serf's at Culross, possibly since c. 700, and less famous ones, for example that of Ethernan (died 669), who was thought to be buried on the island of May.[92] There were no Pictish royal saints though some religious communities had royal contacts. The St Andrews' legend suggests that, and one interpretation of its famous sarcophagus is as the tomb of King Onuist (c. 729–761).[93] Dunkeld, associated with Constantín, and Rosemarkie in Ross were others.

The reach of the Church and the piety of the Picts probably resembled those of the Anglo-Saxons. There was, probably, one bishopric, based at Rosemarkie or possibly at Abernethy in Fife. Something like a structure of parishes is suggested by later arrangements and by the fact that funerary stones are located on later parish boundaries. Monasteries are identifiable by place-names and by material remains. These include cross-marked stones associated with cross-slabs, grave markers and other items of church 'furniture' as at Rosemarkie. Archaeological evidence shows that the monastery of Portmahomack on the Tarbat peninsula flourished up to c. 800.[94] Penance had probably been introduced from Iona and the representation on a panel, from Papil, of pilgrimage may suggest that some Pictish Christians aspired to pilgrimage. There were probably relic-cults: the recesses found in some grave markers have been interpreted as reliquaries.[95] There may have been some lay burial in churches. The known religious communities cluster in the lowland fertile regions, on the east coast and adjacent river valleys. Highland regions may have lacked pastoral care.[96]

The evidence suggests that the Church was active, attempting to provide for the laity. Some sculpture was commemorative. Sculpture that includes exegesis (explanation) may have had a devotional function, and sculpted crosses liturgical and intercessory ones. The subject matter of their decoration may indicate their particular purpose, such as personal prayer or receiving the Eucharist.[97] Such a monument might attract first a cemetery and only later a church, as seems to have been the case at Shandwick.[98] Portable cross-marked stones, which could have been used instead of a building to mark a meeting-place, and a very small portable altar found off the coast of Wick suggest that priests travelled to minister to the people.[99] The material remains certainly show that the Church was wealthy. Religious communities were undying so were not subjected, as it is thought that the laity were, to partition of their resources between heirs (partible inheritance). Instead they could increase their wealth over generations and through long-term planning. For their work, they needed wine, oil and precious vessels, and books, some decorated and all made from parchment (animal skin). These needs stimulated specialised animal husbandry, industry and trade, to supply the requisite materials.[100] At Portmahomack parchment and metalwork were produced in buildings designed for the purpose. But there were no towns or trading places and no use of money.

Although their contacts with the Continent seem to have been indirect, through Anglo-Saxon territory, the Picts were aware of religious developments there. Their sculpture's iconography and content has been described as intellectual, literary and ostentatiously erudite, showing that their scholarship was not inferior to their neighbours'.[101] Examples include use of number symbolism, and of monstrous animals known from texts. Some representations show that books were known. The St Andrews' foundation legend refers to a scribe at the royal court. This may mean that in the ninth century production of written text was normal for elite households.[102] Fragmentary and whole inscriptions, most notably at Portmahomack where Insular Display Capitals and rare Latin invocations are used, and on the Dupplin Cross, attest familiarity with scripts and hence indirectly persons able to produce books.[103] It is very likely that books were indeed produced but no known manuscripts are identifiable as Pictish. Likewise, since links between manuscript illumination and sculpture are discernible in other early Christian cultures it is possible that the Picts produced illuminated manuscripts too.[104]

The entirety of Pictish culture is thus represented in and by its sophisticated stone carving and sculpture.[105] This comprises cross-slab and cross-marked stones, dressed slabs ornamented with plain relief crosses, recumbent and erect slabs, and pillars, with more or less decoration. It does not include free-standing crosses. There were no schools of sculpture with particular styles, but there were centres. In c. 800 there was one at Abernethy, another, very prolific, at Meigle. Pictish sculpture seems idiosyncratic in form and content and so may be interpreted as a manifestation, perhaps deliberate, of a Pictish identity. A unique form was the ornamented recumbent grave marker. Few survive. They had a slot to hold an upright cross, and sometimes a recess for relics. The decorative repertoire included the unique symbols.[106] Hunting scenes were favoured more than elsewhere. Davidic ones were not unique to the Picts but include innovative imagery.[107] Whether any historical works were written is unknown.[108] Some sculpture, including the Dupplin Cross, may have been meant as a record of the recent past. A cross-slab at St Vigeans, inscribed with three names, may be an indication that by c. 800 the recording of names had become a function of public monuments.[109] There was certainly an attachment to the past. The Pictish symbols derive from the culture of the period c. 100 BC to c. AD 100, and in the use of martial and hunt themes in Christian art the ethos of a heroic past was transformed into a Christian present,[110] a process paralleled in Anglo-Saxon poetry. Only one Pictish, Latin poem survives. It celebrates the taking of Alba by which, perhaps, Scottish Dál Riata is meant.[111] We know a little more about buildings. Surviving fragments of the Forteviot Arch, dated to the 810s, suggest use of wall friezes and a tradition of building in stone.[112] Most churches, however, were, probably, wooden. This would explain why church buildings and manuscripts, which would have been kept there, have not survived, since wood decays.

According to Bede, in the 730s the Picts were a distinct people with their own language.[113] Linguistic distinctiveness may have contributed to their becoming a people. Alternatively, it may have been a consequence of their political distinctiveness.[114] Another contributory element may have been the social structure. Where inheritance is partible, aristocratic power blocks do not necessarily endure over more than a generation. Members of royal warbands came from various places. Rewarding them with lands in insecure areas established loyal men there.

The Pictish economy was one of mixed farming (arable and pastoral, crops and animals), most settlements consisting of a single homestead or a cluster of up to four houses. Most households, probably, had slaves. Women would, probably, have moved on marriage, a wife living with her husband's father's family. There are few references to or depictions of women on Pictish stones. This perhaps suggests their limited status and land-owning capacity compared with Anglo-Saxon women. The laws of marriage are unknown though marriage seems to have been important in royal succession.[115] Matrilineal (through the mother's line) succession for kings has been suspected but the evidence for its being a general rule is weak.[116]

Continuity and change: politics, economy, religion, culture and society on the eve of the Norman Conquest, 1066

1066 was more of an historical landmark for the archipelago than 800 had been. Again there was a momentous coronation on Christmas Day, but this one was in England. In Westminster Abbey Duke William of Normandy, who had defeated the English King Harold II at the battle of Hastings in October, was crowned king of England. If William had been well informed, which he was not, his mental picture of the Anglo-Saxons and their neighbours would have differed significantly from that of Charlemagne, in a number of respects.

Pictish political and cultural identity was no more. Scottish Dál Riata and Pictland had amalgamated. The name Alba was used for the whole kingdom, though not by Anglo-Saxons. Alba included the Strathclyde region and the north-west of former Northumbria, which had split into four power blocks in the late ninth century, under Viking pressure. The kingdoms of Strathclyde and Cumbria, which first appear in the sources for the late ninth and early tenth centuries respectively, were not two separate kingdoms but one and the same. The last recorded king of Strathclyde/Cumbria is Owain, who fought for Alba's King Mael Coluim (Malcolm) II against the earl of the Northumbrians, in the battle of Carham in 1018.[117] One of its results was the securing of the River Tweed as the Anglo-Scottish border. Whether elite secular bases tended now to be located on low-lying land, in palace complexes and associated with churches, as in England is a matter of debate.[118] The most important site was now Scone (since c. 900). Certainly ecclesiastical figures were important in secular politics. Crínán, abbot of Dunkeld, was son-in-law of one king and father of another, in whose accession he played a major role. He himself was killed in battle in 1045.[119]

A major question is whether a precocious Scottish 'state' had come into being with strong political institutions and royal control. Until recently there was something approaching consensus that this was indeed the case.[120] This has now been very effectively challenged, partly on the basis of property records added in the twelfth century to a pocket-sized Latin Gospel book, produced in the late ninth or early tenth century and known as the Book of Deer. Much depends on the significance of the *mormaer*s, first recorded in 918 not long after the first usage of *Alba* for the kingdom, who were the highest-ranking category of layman outside the royal family, and the lower-ranking *toisech*s. They have been interpreted as royal agents, entitled by virtue of their office to a share of the dues and services that were owed to the king. But their rights and demands were more probably their own, those of local lords. The Deer records suggest that Deer's lands were not liable for dues and services to the king.[121]

We know something of social organisation from a thirteenth-century law code that lists *cro*s (blood-prices, the equivalent of Anglo-Saxon wergelds) and is thought to be a version of a Gaelic original compiled in the early eleventh century. Below the *mormaer*s were thanes, probably lords of multiple estates, perhaps a minister class or perhaps landowners, or both. Their blood-price, over six times that of the peasants, was similar to that of Anglo-Saxon thegns, who qualified for thegnly status by owning 5 hides of land. From these figures, notional norms of landholdings of between 100 and 600 acres for peasants and of over 500 acres for thanes have been extrapolated. Status was heritable but lost by the fourth generation if not supported by landholding.[122]

The development of a state in Scotland is thus uncertain, but other changes are clear. Some of the Picts' great church-settlements were extinct, including many in areas where Scandinavian immigrants had settled, and others in decline, including Meigle and St Vigeans. The Church's wealth too had declined, as evidenced in its sculpture. For most of the tenth and eleventh centuries little was produced, though some sites, notably Govan (in Strathclyde) and St Andrews, were productive, and what survives is of lesser quality than earlier work.[123] The question of manuscript production in 1066 is nearly as open as in 800. The Book of Deer is the only manuscript thought to be of indigenous origin that survives. Nothing suggests that the tenth- and eleventh-century elite had endowed religious establishments. Yet some parochial organisation may have remained. Lay themes on stones in territory surrounding Meigle, St Vigeans and Govan may suggest this. The later phenomenon of some parishes belonging to a see other than that in which they were located has been interpreted as a remnant of earlier organisation. Finally, the configuration of saints' cults had changed. Either King Constantín or the mid-ninth-century King Cinaed (Kenneth) (842–858) had founded the church of Dunkeld, which had become the centre of the cult of Columba. The fifth-century British Patrick, evangeliser of the Irish, was venerated at Kilpatrick (from c. 900).[124] In addition, there were now some ninth-century royal saints.[125]

As earlier, poetry was part of the culture. Five surviving poems that can be considered part of the Scottish heritage were perhaps composed c. 1066. One is Latin and of uncertain date. Another, dated to c. 1060, and in Gaelic, was probably written by an Irish poet, for an Alban audience. Three, including a long elegy for Earl Thorfinnr of Orkney (died 1064–1065) are in Icelandic Norse, and reconstructed from the later *Orkneyinga saga*.[126] The western and northern isles and the adjacent parts of the mainland were now Scandinavian in language, culture, political allegiance and, possibly, genetics, though Christian. There was a bishopric in Orkney, established in the reign of the first earl's son.[127]

Like that of Alba, the Welsh Church's roster of saints' cults had increased by 1066. The cults of the Welsh Padarn and Illtud[128] are attested, as are those of the Anglo-Saxon Oswald and Cuthbert, and the Irish Brigit from the ninth century. Others include Mary's and Peter's, from the tenth century, and Andrew's in the eleventh.[129] Local saints may have outnumbered universal ones. In Ceredigion there were forty Celtic saints to thirty foreign or biblical ones.[130] Two episcopal sees of c. 800 had lapsed. Their archives had been transferred to Llandaff, which had become the seat of a bishopric by the early eleventh century. The number of religious festivals had increased. Some pastoral care and/or parochial organisation may be implied by a late-eleventh-century reference to preaching every Sunday.[131] Lay involvement with the Church seems to have been primarily through donation, granting land now being the preferred method of penance, though burial in cemeteries and in association with churches had become more common. In contrast to c. 800, there is no evidence c. 1066 for literary activity, and little sign of libraries, except that annals were kept[132] and a Latin inscription was carved in the 1030s, on the Carew standing slab cross. Its decoration does, however, show that as far as sculpture is concerned there had been no significant cultural decline.[133] Oral tradition was preserved by the bards, attested in the twelfth century.

As in Scotland there was some Scandinavian settlement, in north Wales. By the late eleventh century Anglesey was known not as (Welsh) Môn but as (Scandinavian) Ongul's Isle. Land was held predominantly by the laity, and there had been change from greater towards smaller estates. Much in the Welsh–English borderlands was waste, due to ravaging during recent wars.[134] In these regions, hunting, for food, was very important. Some economic development, most noticeable in the south-east, near England had begun. Some surplus was produced, some renders in the east were paid in money rather than in kind, and the concept of wealth as something movable and some ideology of exchange had developed in the tenth and eleventh centuries.[135] There are also hints of the beginnings of towns. There was a trading place near Newport in c. 1050 and in 1086 Rhuddlan, which had been founded as a *burh* by the Anglo-Saxon king Edward the Elder in 921, had a large population and diverse economy.[136] Settlement was dispersed, but there were some villages that clustered round churchyards and secular centres.

Wales had moved towards political unification, but its consolidation was fragile and superficial and England ruled some areas west of Offa's Dyke. In 1066, there were only two Welsh kingdoms, the northern Gwynedd–Powys and southern Seisyllwg–Dyfed. They had been united between 1050 and 1053 under King Gruffudd, who had also expanded eastwards into English territory. Eleventh-century royal titles, however, are thought to embody a sense of national identity.[137]

In 1066, there were aspirations to unite the whole of Britain under one rule. Those who held them may have included the Britons in Wales, for Welsh belief in a future Welsh reoccupation of Britain is reported in the twelfth century. They were certainly embraced by the English establishment. In 1056 the Welsh had recognised as their over-king Edward the Confessor (king of England 1042–1066), descendant of the West Saxon kings who had unified England in the tenth century. In 1063, the English replaced Gruffudd with his two half-brothers as their subordinates. A peace between Mael Coluim III of Alba and Edward in 1059 may have included his recognition of Edward's supremacy.[138] The English combined these aspirations with a strong sense of English national identity. The *Anglo-Saxon Chronicle*, which reported in its obituary of Edward that he ruled Welsh and Scots, survives in five eleventh-century versions. Though compiled at different places, probably Canterbury in Kent, Abingdon in Wessex and Worcester in Mercia or York in Northumbria they have an English rather than local perspective.[139] Texts and textual culture created and recorded a reality and a perception of a shared culture. War too will have contributed to a shared identity. Since the late ninth century the West Saxon kings had made heavy military demands on the whole population. Twenty-five thousand men fought against William at Hastings, a muster not repeated until the twentieth century.[140] Furthermore, the wasting of land in war would be an almost constant reminder of the identities of 'us' and 'them'. Domesday Book, William's land and tax survey which was compiled in 1086, shows that waste land could double its value in twenty years,[141] which implies that wasting could reduce it for something like a generation.

English identity did not, however, involve uniformity. Scandinavians had settled in northern and eastern England in the ninth and tenth centuries. In modern scholarly literature the term 'Danelaw', first recorded in a law code of 1008, signifies the part of England that was in some sense Scandinavian. But it has not been defined consistently. Different criteria have been used, for example forms of land tenure or legal distinctiveness or treaty boundaries. When mapped, these differently defined *Danelaws* do not coincide. Some 'Danelaw' characteristics may have been indigenous regional peculiarities rather than Scandinavian imports.[142] Some may have been merely matters of different terminology. For details we depend a great deal on what Domesday Book records. For example, south-eastern England had linguistic, social and organisational peculiarities. Scandinavian place- and personal names, sokemen (a kind of free peasant), measurement of land in carucates rather than hides were recorded there. Whether these were caused directly by settlement or by other, indirect, Scandinavian influence has been debated. In Northumbria, West Saxon influence was slight. The system of local administration and geld (tax) had only recently been imposed, the first reference to the shire of Yorkshire being in 1065. The tenth-century monastic reformation had not reached Northumbria. The kings had no significant Northumbrian landholdings and did not include the north on their regular itinerations.[143] But the 1065 Northumbrian rebellion sought a new earl, not a revival of independence.

A famous characterisation of the late Anglo-Saxon state is that it was strong everywhere except at the head. The king's control could be weak, but the administrative system was highly organised and efficient. Earls, entrusted with huge provinces and lands to support them, were a factor in both. The major earldoms were Northumbria, Mercia and Wessex. Domesday Book's information has been interpreted as showing that in 1066 the value (in annual income) of the king's lands put him in a weak position in relation to his wife's family, the Godwinesons. Furthermore the king had very little or no land, and hence no direct presence, in Middlesex, Hertfordshire, Essex, Lincolnshire, Rutland, Cheshire, Cornwall (by now incorporated into England), Norfolk, Suffolk or Yorkshire.[144] On the other hand, until the late 1050s the earls had been very insecure, without quasi-regal powers, their earldoms subject to restructuring, they themselves to exile and execution. Their estates may have been intended merely as loans for the duration of their office. In compensation they competed for local as well as royal favour. Further, different scholars' calculations of the values of the lands have produced different results, thereby suggesting a different balance of power.[145] Individuals' and families' lands were scattered rather than concentrated in blocks. The kingdom was bound together by personal, household government. Men from various localities served in the king's household, and the household itinerated through the kingdom though without covering it all.[146] In addition, the royal court effectively spread a shared aesthetic and consumer culture.[147]

The administration was bureaucratic and used writing extensively. Regional and local courts met regularly and were subjected to royal direction from the king. The country was divided into shires (or ridings in Yorkshire) and subdivided into hundreds (or wapentakes in the north). Some of these units had formed, as it were organically, but many were artificial, the result of the extension of Wessex's shire and hundred system to Mercia in the tenth century. There were officials at many levels. Huge sums in coin had been raised regularly in tax in the late tenth and early eleventh centuries, for example £82,500 in 1018. The coinage was royal, of consistently high-quality silver, and since 973 had been recalled and restruck using centrally manufactured coin dies roughly every three years. The fees that were charged in this process amounted to between 10 and 15 per cent of annual royal income. Perhaps twenty million pennies were minted between 978 and 1035. Forty-six mints struck coins for King Harold II in 1066, thirty-nine for Edward in 1065.[148]

By contemporary western European standards the administration was highly sophisticated and crown and country very wealthy. Behind the coinage lay an economy in which trade, including transactions that transferred coin from shire to shire, and towns, which were centres of industry (cloth-making, pottery, wood-work, metalwork, leatherwork, bone-carving) were important. There were more than a hundred towns, twenty-nine with more than 1,000 inhabitants, at least fourteen with more than 2,000. Norwich covered about 200 acres, with perhaps 6,000–7,000 inhabitants.[149] York's population numbered about 10,000 in 1066 but according to a reliable contemporary estimate about 30,000 in c. 1000.[150] London was pre-eminent and a centre for groups of merchants from the Continent. Like Winchester's its population was probably 10,000 or more. In Cornwall, where the total population was no more than 25,000, there was one town, Bodmin, with about 400 people, and beginnings of town life at Launceston, Helston and Stratton.[151] Nearly 10 per cent of the population lived in towns, whereas before 850 only 2 per cent had done so.[152] Apart from areas that had been wasted in recent wars, the rural economy too was thriving in 1066. There were regional differences depending on terrain. In comparison to c. 800 more land, about seven or eight million acres, was cultivated and there was more intensive management and specialised occupations on estates, for example cow-herds and cheese-makers (female).[153] The rearing of sheep was a major part of the economy. There was a surplus and a land market. Domesday Book suggests a total population of between 2.2 and 2.5 million.

Another development since 800 was that of compact villages of between twelve and sixty households, cultivating adjoining open fields. They lay in eastern England, in the midlands running down to the south coast though not into East Anglia and the south-east. Why and how this change, which was still in train, came about is unclear. One possibility is that villagers themselves had decided on it, another that landowners and lords imposed it.[154] Landholdings in 1066 were smaller and much more numerous than in 800. Many grants to new monasteries, for example, had been for only 2 or 3 square miles. Instead of a few hundred estates, there were now several thousand manors. These were more socially diverse and self-sufficient than the earlier estate centres had been, with resident proprietors. Some families' origins were recent, lying in the aftermath of England's conquest by the Danish King Cnut (1016). Cornwall's incorporation into England had not destroyed its native upper class. Its members still owned property there.[155]

There were great variations of wealth. By the mid-eleventh century, there were some 4,000 thegns. Their status theoretically depended on owning 5 hides (perhaps about 200 acres), which would have generated an income of £5.00 per year. But in practice this status depended on the ability to live like a thegn: generating a surplus of grain; having a residence with a chapel, bell-tower and large hall; displaying wealth through this, by purchasing goods manufactured in England and by patronage of the Church; participating in the local law courts (as jurors and judges), in military service and in payment of tax; and performing royal service in the locality.[156] Some thegns owed their status to the profits of trade, some probably to those of military service. Thegns owned urban as well as rural properties. Above them in the social scale were forty-hide-holding thegns, of whom there were in 1065 at least eighty-eight, king's thegns and ealdormen (in tenth-century terminology) or earls (about twenty persons). Below thegns, and working for them, came the *geneat*, the *ceorl* or *gebur* whose normal landholding was about 30 acres, the *cotsetla* (a smallholder and hired worker), freed men and slaves.[157] Slaves made up about 10.5 per cent of the population, the highest percentage being in Cornwall. Slavery, however, was in decline, many slaves having been freed in the tenth and eleventh centuries.[158]

Within English society there were various types of communities. Service, tenancy, blood kinship, guilds in some towns, spiritual bonds including godparent–godchild relationships all bound people together. Every man had to belong to a tithing, a group of ten that was collectively accountable for its individual members. Every man had to have a surety who was accountable if necessary for his attending a law court and paying judicial fines.[159] Villagers engaging in arable farming of common fields had to co-operate, for individual strips in the same field could not be differently cultivated and resources had to be pooled, for example a ploughteam, of eight oxen, would normally have been mustered by several households rather than one.

Other communities were those of the Church. Apart from York and Canterbury there were thirteen bishoprics.[160] Those of Leicester, Dunwich, Lindsey, Lindisfarne and Hexham had gone, but Wells, Exeter, Dorchester and Durham were now sees. In c. 1060 there were forty-nine male and ten female establishments (six in Wessex) that could be termed reformed monastic houses following a version of the sixth-century *Rule* of St Benedict (of Nursia, Italy). There were some forty-seven 'unreformed' houses, colleges of secular canons.[161] Not all the great houses of the past were in the former category. Whitby was in ruins, Ripon and Beverley houses of canons.

Ecclesiastical establishments varied greatly in their wealth. Altogether, in the shires of Wessex and western Mercia they held between a third and a fifth of the land, but less than one-tenth in the east Midlands and the parts of the north that Domesday Book covers.[162] Glastonbury, the wealthiest monastery, had an annual income of over £800.00 per year, but nineteen others (including four nunneries) had less than £100.00 each. The richest bishopric was Canterbury with about £1,750 per year, and the poorest Chester with under £138.[163] There were many local churches, one estimate being at least 4,000 by 1050. In some counties, every village had a church and priest, the best provision being in eastern England where, according to Domesday Book, there were some 750 in Lincolnshire, very slightly fewer in Norfolk, some 630 in Suffolk. The town of Lincoln had thirty-five, and those of Leicester, Derby and Stamford, only six, five and four respectively.[164]

Which saints were most favoured may be inferred from the nine calendars, recording saints' festivals, which survive from the second half of the eleventh century,[165] and eight mid-eleventh-century litanies of saints.[166] In Canterbury it was the Virgin Mary, Augustine, the first archbishop (sent by Pope Gregory I in 597) and the tenth-century Archbishop Dunstan. In Winchester, the kings' proto-capital, it was Grimbald (Frankish adviser of King Alfred), Birinus (seventh-century Frankish bishop of Wessex), the tenth-century Bishop Aethelwold and another, ninth-century, local saint, Swithun. The saints mentioned in the most litanies are, in order: Matthew; the apostles Peter, Paul and Andrew; the apostle James; Benedict (of Nursia); Stephen martyr. Benedict, like Pope Gregory I and Cuthbert, was regarded as a pillar of the English Church. All three appear in twenty-six calendars. Of the three, Benedict was the most favoured, the other two being roughly equal, according to the calendars, but in the litanies and overall in about 1000, he and Gregory are roughly equal, outstripping Cuthbert.[167] The English also now venerated two seventh-century Frankish queens (Balthild and Radegund). The cults of the seventh-century Bishop Wilfrid and King Oswald, and the kings Edmund of East Anglia (martyred by the Vikings in 869) and Edward the Martyr (975–978), brother of Aethelred II (reigned 979–1016) were widespread. Cornwall had two universal saints, Stephen and Michael, one international (Germanus of Auxerre) and between thirty-four and thirty-nine local or inter-Celtic saints.[168] There was a parish system, probably covering most of the country, in which parish priests routinely said Mass, ministered to the sick, conducted baptisms, burials, which were now in churchyards, and exorcisms and probably marriages, and administered confession and penance.

Later-tenth-century England had been both distinguished and distinctive in its culture. There is evidence for learning and scholarship and for international contacts, which probably means that good education was available in at least some places. Vernacular literature was still being produced. Translation of some Old Testament books in the second quarter of the eleventh century supplemented the biblical translations already available. (These were Alfred's of most of the biblical book Psalms and some by Aelfric, who became abbot of Eynsham in 1005.) Mid-eleventh-century book production was vibrant. British Library Cotton

Ms Claudius B.iv was probably produced at St Augustine's monastery at Canterbury early in the second quarter of the century. It contains 394 illustrations for its translation of six books of the Old Testament, other copies of which were produced elsewhere.[169] Of the manuscripts containing the litanies three are of unknown origin, two are from Worcester, two from Winchester, and one from Canterbury; and there are a number of Psalters (copies of Psalms). Probably hundreds of glossed (that is, with marginal or interlinear translation or commentary) Psalters were produced in the tenth and eleventh centuries.[170]

Monasteries kept historical records and some historical works, apart from the *Anglo-Saxon Chronicle*, were undertaken. Books of remembrance contained lists of people to pray for, often including donors and patrons. The *Liber Vitae* (Book of Life) of St Cuthbert's community (at the church of Durham), possibly started in the 680s, has a mid-ninth-century core of some 3,120 names, about 25 per cent of which date from before about 850.[171] In the 1030s, the community was collecting relics of other Northumbrian saints and it commissioned sculpture that suggests interest in its heritage.[172] In the middle to late eleventh century it used its business records to produce the *History of Saint Cuthbert*.[173] Something similar happened after 1066 at Ely. The *Ely Book* incorporates a 'little book' by Aethelwold and details of property grants and leases.[174] Anxiety about title to property, stimulated by the Norman Conquest, lies behind these texts but the keeping of the records pre-dates it.

In their attitude to the past, the Anglo-Saxons were not, however, parochial. They represented themselves as a new Israel. In the Old Testament the Israelites were God's chosen people. There were no Jews in England but Jewish history was part of English understanding of the past–present relationship, offering lessons and good examples. This is clear for example from the sympathetic identification with biblical figures that the liturgy (worship) encouraged[175] and in the pictures of Cotton Claudius B.iv. In another manuscript, characters in four vernacular biblical-historical poems are accompanied by Anglo-Saxon attributes and a covenant between God and the Anglo-Saxons is evoked in various ways.[176] Finally, the English were aware of the wider, contemporary, world. Edward the Confessor had a seal proclaiming him *basileus* of the English.[177] This signifies an awareness of the past. *Basileus* had first, and frequently, been used by King Aethelstan in his charters. Since it was the Greek word used in Byzantium (what remained of the eastern Roman Empire) for its emperor, Edward's usage might also imply his own knowledge of Byzantium and perhaps a self-perception of equivalence. Most of British Library Cotton Tiberius B.v, probably from the second half of the eleventh century and possibly from Canterbury, relates to far-away places.[178] It includes the only surviving Anglo-Saxon map (10 and 5/8th inches by 6 and 11/16th inches) of the world. Its design suggests an Anglo-Saxon perception that the British Isles were as important in world history as Italy and the biblical lands.[179]

Some aspects of Britain in 1066 were very different from how they had been in 800, whilst others were largely unchanged. Scandinavian settlers had integrated into British and English territories, and parts of north Britain were under

Scandinavian rule. There was much less similarity than formerly between the Anglo-Saxons and Britain's other societies. In the former case, different kingdoms and groups had been forged into a single state and national identity that were the forerunners of modern ones, whilst centralisation and effectiveness of government and Church had increased. Urban life had begun and was flourishing, nourishing a sophisticated economy. Coinage and writing were used extensively and a vernacular literature had developed. Except that Alba had been created out of Pictland and Dál Riata, and was encroaching on Strathclyde, such phenomena are not detectible elsewhere, though our knowledge is incomplete. How we know what we know about change and continuity in Britain between 800 and 1066 is the subject of the next chapter.

Notes

1 W. Davies, *Wales*.
2 Higham, *King*.
3 Charles-Edwards, *Wales*: 231.
4 Faull.
5 Fraser, 'From Ancient'.
6 Yorke, *Conversion*.
7 Campbell, 'United'.
8 *EHDI*: 169.
9 Metcalf, 'How', 'Monetary'.
10 Rollason, *Northumbria*.
11 *Ibid.*
12 Bullough, 'Hagiography'.
13 Rollason, *Northumbria*.
14 Charles-Edwards, 'Making'.
15 Blinkhorn.
16 *Ibid.*
17 Dyer, *Making*.
18 Blinkhorn.
19 Rollason, *Northumbria*.
20 Dyer, *Making*.
21 Hill, *Atlas*.
22 Cubitt, *Anglo-Saxon*; Keynes, *Councils*.
23 Keynes, *Councils*.
24 Campbell, 'Questioning'.
25 Hadley, *Northern*.
26 Yorke, *Conversion*.
27 Foot, *Monastic*; Rollason, *Northumbria*.
28 Cubitt, 'Universal'.
29 S. Irvine.
30 Cubitt, 'Universal'.
31 Yorke, *Conversion*.
32 Explained in Blair, *Church*; S. Wood.
33 Blair, *Church*; S. Wood.
34 Blair, 'Saint'.
35 Yorke, *Conversion*.
36 Bullough, 'Burial'.
37 Yorke, *Conversion*.

38 Plunkett.
39 *Ibid.*
40 *Ibid.*
41 Rollason, *Northumbria.*
42 Gneuss, 'King'.
43 Campbell, *Bede's.*
44 Rollason, *Northumbria.*
45 Foot, *Veiled* I.
46 Padel, 'Local'.
47 Hood; Thomas, *Christian.*
48 Charles-Edwards, 'Making'.
49 W. Davies, *Wales.*
50 W. Davies, *Llandaff.*
51 J.R. Davies, 'Saints'.
52 W. Davies, *Early, Wales.*
53 Arnold and J.L. Davies; W. Davies, *Early, Wales.*
54 See W. Davies, 'Myth', *Wales.*
55 Higham, *King.*
56 Charles-Edwards, *Wales.*
57 Petts.
58 Yorke, *Conversion.*
59 Charles-Edwards, *Wales.*
60 J.R. Davies, 'Saints'.
61 M. Miller.
62 For example, Charles-Edwards, *Wales*; Edwards, 'Rethinking'; Higham, *King.*
63 J.R. Davies, 'Bishop'.
64 W. Davies, *Early, Wales.*
65 Higham, *King.*
66 Sims-Williams, 'Uses'.
67 *Ibid.*
68 W. Davies, *Early, Wales.*
69 Woolf, *From.*
70 T.O. Clancy, 'Scottish'.
71 T.O. Clancy, *Triumph.*
72 Macquarrie, *Saints.*
73 Woolf, *From.*
74 T.O. Clancy, *Triumph.*
75 *Ibid.*
76 Yorke, *Conversion.*
77 T.O. Clancy, 'Scottish'.
78 *Ibid.*
79 For what follows, Woolf, *From.* For eighth-century Pictish culture and history see Part III of Fraser, *From Caledonia.*
80 Campbell, 'Archipelagic'.
81 Aitchison.
82 Woolf, *From.*
83 Mac Lean; Thomas, 'Form'.
84 I. Henderson, 'David', *'Primus'.*
85 Aitchison; G. Henderson and I. Henderson; I. Henderson, 'David'.
86 I. Henderson, *'Primus'.*
87 E. James.
88 Fraser, 'Rochester'.
89 Aitchison.
90 Macquarrie, *Saints.*

91 T.O. Clancy, 'Scottish'.
92 Yorke, *Conversion*.
93 I. Henderson, '*Primus*'.
94 Carver, *Portmahomack*.
95 G. Henderson and I. Henderson.
96 Yorke, *Conversion*.
97 G. Henderson and I. Henderson.
98 *Ibid*.
99 *Ibid*.
100 Woolf, *From*.
101 G. Henderson and I. Henderson.
102 Aitchison.
103 Forsyth, 'Literacy'; G. Henderson and I. Henderson.
104 Forsyth, 'Literacy'; G. Henderson and I. Henderson.
105 For what follows, G. Henderson and I. Henderson.
106 *Ibid*.
107 I. Henderson, '*Primus*'.
108 Hughes.
109 G. Henderson and I. Henderson.
110 *Ibid*.
111 T.O. Clancy, *Triumph*; Woolf, *From*.
112 Aitchison.
113 For what follows, Woolf, *From*.
114 Charles-Edwards, 'Making'.
115 Yorke, *Conversion*.
116 Fraser, 'Rochester'; Woolf, *From*.
117 Woolf, *From* and Rollason, *Northumbria*.
118 Aitchison; Woolf, *From*.
119 Macquarrie, *Saints*.
120 Grant.
121 Broun, 'Property'.
122 Woolf, *From*.
123 *Ibid*.
124 Macquarrie, *Saints*.
125 T.O. Clancy, 'Scottish'.
126 T.O. Clancy, *Triumph*.
127 Woolf, *From*.
128 J.R. Davies, 'Saints'.
129 W. Davies, *Early*, *Wales*.
130 Padel, 'Local'.
131 Pryce, 'Pastoral'.
132 J.R. Davies, 'Saints'.
133 Arnold and J.L. Davies.
134 Darby.
135 W. Davies, *Wales*.
136 Redknap, 'Viking'.
137 W. Davies, *Wales*.
138 Higham, *Death*.
139 Stafford, *Unification*.
140 Wormald, 'Did'.
141 Darby.
142 Abrams, 'Edward', 'King'; Hadley, *Northern*, *Vikings*; Holman.
143 Rollason, *Northumbria*.
144 See e.g. Higham, *Death*.

145 Baxter, *Earls*.
146 Stafford, *Unification*.
147 Fleming, 'Rural'.
148 Hill, *Atlas*.
149 Campbell, 'Aspects'; Dyer, *Making*.
150 Fletcher.
151 Balchin; Pearce.
152 Dyer, *Making*.
153 *Ibid*.
154 *Ibid*.
155 Insley, 'Athelstan'; Padel, *Slavery*.
156 Senecal.
157 Dyer, *Making*.
158 Pelteret.
159 Stafford, *Unification*.
160 Hill, *Atlas*.
161 Dyer, *Making*; Hill, *Atlas*.
162 Hadley, *Vikings*.
163 Giandrea.
164 Hadley, *Vikings*.
165 Rushforth.
166 Lapidge, *Anglo-Saxon*.
167 Rushforth.
168 Padel, 'Local'.
169 Withers.
170 Stanton.
171 Gerchow.
172 Rollason, *Northumbria*.
173 Johnson South.
174 Fairweather.
175 Bedingfield, *Dramatic*.
176 Howe, *Writing*; Withers.
177 Ciggaar.
178 Howe, *Writing*.
179 Valtonen.

2 Records and remains

Religion and reconstructions

A holistic approach

The serious study of any historical period or subject requires some understanding of the nature of the available evidence, of how and why it came into being and has been preserved, and, consequently, of what questions it can and cannot be used to answer. In the case of the history of religion, politics and society in Britain between 800 and 1066 there are additional reasons for identifying and examining the evidence with special care. First, a great deal of it illustrates that these three themes were both inextricably interwoven and perceived as such. Second, the fact that much of it was produced and preserved by ecclesiastics means that everything we know, or can know, is influenced both directly and indirectly by ecclesiastical interests and perceptions.

Material and approaches which may not immediately seem historical are often of crucial importance, as, for example, in our appreciation of King Alfred. Even a narrowly conceived political study would need to consider archaeological and literary material as well as historical writing, legal material and theoretical studies of national identity. The contemporary historical writing comprises the *Anglo-Saxon Chronicle*, and a biography of Alfred by Asser, a Welsh monk, from St David's in Dyfed, whom Alfred invited to join his court and who became bishop of Sherborne. Asser wrote it in 893, aiming it in part at a Welsh audience[1] but also at Alfred himself,[2] and indirectly providing us with evidence for Welsh scholarship, for example through his allusions to earlier texts.[3] Its authenticity has been challenged[4] but is generally accepted. The legal material is Alfred's law-code. We have archaeological evidence of town planning, for example in the excavated layout of the streets and property boundaries in the eastern half of Worcester. Alfred's own English translations of his own selection of Latin texts tell us much about his attitude to kingship, that is, his political philosophy. This is because they are very free translations and incorporate interpretations and reflections that are Alfred's own, whether entirely his own or borrowed from earlier commentaries. Some classic studies argue that the sense of national identity is only a modern phenomenon (eighteenth-century onwards in the western world). But the importance which these same studies attach to vernacular texts and state education in its creation[5] illuminates the political significance of Alfred's translations and educational programme.

Alfred's grandson King Aethelstan collected Christian relics with great enthusiasm. This might seem simple-minded and peripheral, even irrelevant, to his politics – to his conquests and his attempts to create a united kingdom, for example. But it was actually central and important, bringing him prestige and attracting loyalty. The cult of relics was also combined with legal innovation and a strongly centralising, intrusive and continuously developing governmental system of great sophistication. So too was bloodfeud, an integral part of the legal system in late-ninth- and tenth-century Anglo-Saxon England. Yet vengeance might seem, to some people, to be both primitive (in a pejorative sense) and incompatible with devout Christianity, given Christ's teaching to turn the other cheek to assailants. Present-day western notions of compatibility are not those of the early medieval world.

The integration of religion with politics and society, and the Church's domination of the evidence are nowhere more apparent than in the period of the so-called tenth-century Reformation. Its high point was in the reign of King Edgar (959–975), who can be regarded as one of the movement's leaders. The others were saints Dunstan, archbishop of Canterbury from 959 to 988, and his younger contemporaries Aethelwold, bishop of Winchester from 963 to 984 and Oswald, bishop of Worcester from 961 to 992 and archbishop of York from 972 to 992. According to the rhetoric of the reformers, Anglo-Saxon monastic life had declined by the mid-tenth-century to a parlous state. Their ideals were, in brief, that life in monastic houses be conducted in accordance with the *Rule* of the sixth-century St Benedict of Nursia; that these houses be independent of lay aristocratic control and influence and be well endowed with lands; and that king and reformed Church should support each other and work together in the leadership of society. The second generation of reformers tried to improve standards of pastoral care for the general population.

The overriding problems for historians are, however, the lack of evidence and its unequal distribution over Britain. Domesday Book does not include everything but does provide pieces of a jigsaw to construct a picture of much of England that King William had conquered in 1066. There is nothing comparable for Scotland or Wales (or indeed any other European country). Broadly speaking and at the risk of over-simplifying, evidence for the different societies of Britain may be characterised as follows. For Anglo-Saxon England and the Anglo-Saxons it is very diverse; generally, though patchily, relatively voluminous; dominated by native-written texts, some in Latin and some in Old English; with a high proportion of legal or governmental documents. For the Scots and the Picts, it is slight; dominated by sculpture; and marked by an almost total lack of texts, though some Anglo-Saxon and Irish historical ones are important sources. For Scandinavian Scotland, Scandinavian England and Cornwall archaeological and linguistic evidence dominate, together in the latter two cases with sculpture and inscribed stones. For Wales and the Welsh the evidence is more varied, but scant compared to Anglo-Saxon England's. Some items cross categories. An inscription on a stone for example provides text with content and meaning, linguistic, and, through its script style, art-historical evidence.

The introduction offered in this chapter is intended not as an exhaustive list but as an indicative sketch. Within it, particular attention will be given to identifying the religious content, provenance, or both, which much of the evidence has.

Material remains

The known material remains include but are not limited to what falls into the domain of archaeologists, whose finds run the gamut of dry, dusty, evocative and splendid. Among them are Winchester's street-plan; faeces from York; tree-ring evidence for sylvan regeneration in Scotland in the first half of the tenth century, testimony to effective land management; the silver-gilt chalice (cup used in the Christian Mass) from an Anglo-Saxon hoard buried at Trewhiddle near St Austell in Cornwall c. 868. It is from archaeology that much of our knowledge about people below the level of royalty, aristocracy and upper ecclesiastical authorities comes, since historical texts tend to concentrate on the elite.

The English subjects for which archaeology is illuminating include towns and settlement patterns.[6] The excavation of Flixborough, in north Lincolnshire, is especially important, partly because there is no contemporary documentation about the site and partly because excavation has produced a huge amount of evidence suggesting that sites' identities were dynamic rather than static. Flixborough was probably a secular rural estate centre in the eighth century, an ecclesiastical or monastic site in the first half of the ninth, then a low-status settlement until the early tenth, after which it became a manorial centre.[7] Some late cemeteries have been excavated. That at Raunds in Northamptonshire is perhaps the most notable. It was established, with the church, probably in about 950, to supplement the manor house and settlement that had been established some 10–20 years earlier. It served for two centuries a live population numbering about forty, which was probably less than the total population of the manor and its associated settlements. Buried there were 363 people from a wide social spectrum, in twenty-three rows.[8] Other significant cemeteries include that at Winchester's Old Dairy Cottage, one of England's twenty-seven known execution cemeteries, where fourteen graves housing sixteen people, seven of them decapitated, have been excavated. In Cornwall the best excavated cemetery and settlement site, comprising at least two farms, whose buildings were of stone, used between c. 850 and c. 1050, is that of Mawgan Porth.[9] Of burial sites that are identifiable as Scandinavian, there are fewer than twenty-five in all from the period 800–1000, fewer than six in York, despite its having been a Viking centre. Most are single burials but there are two exceptions. In the late ninth century Scandinavians used the royal mausoleum of the Mercian kings at the Christian church at Repton. At the same time, at nearby Heath Wood, fifty-nine burial mounds were built. This cemetery may have been newly created and used for, perhaps, only twenty to thirty years.[10]

Burials suggest a rapid cultural assimilation of Scandinavians in England, but there is disagreement about newcomer–native relations, and also the chronology of Scandinavian settlement, in Scotland. Archaeology suggests though that wide-spread Scandinavian settlement began in the second half of the ninth century.[11] There are some 130 Scandinavian burials dating between the mid-ninth and mid-tenth centuries,[12] but only one cemetery, at Westness, on Rousay, has been completely excavated to modern standards.[13] In eastern Scotland, less well served than Scandinavian Scotland, recent work at the Pictish monastery at Portmaho-mack shows that it suffered a catastrophe in about 800, in which its workshops burnt down, but revived.[14] In Wales, the only definitely datable settlement sites are: the eighth- to tenth-century Llanbedrgoch on Anglesey; Llangorse Lake's crannog (an artificial island, the only known Welsh example) built in the late ninth or early tenth century for a high-status settlement; Rhuddlan, founded 921; tenth- and eleventh-century Graeanog; and eighth- to eleventh-century Cold Knapp.[15] Excavations of Welsh churches have been few, and their results limited. Radiocarbon dating may imply an eighth-century change in the pattern of burial, some cemeteries being abandoned. Four burials that may be pagan Scandinavian works have been discovered, but not excavated to modern standards.[16]

Archaeological finds include coins, the study of which is numismatics. Weight, composition, inscriptions and pictorial designs can indicate levels of wealth, the type of economy, the degree to which governments supervised moneyers, aspirations, ideas and cultural contacts. There is no evidence that coins were minted in Wales, though King Hywel Dda (died 950) minted at Chester in England. The coins found in Welsh coin hoards were probably used as bullion, not as coin. Very many very small coins (*stycas*) minted by Anglo-Saxon Northumbrian kings and archbishops survive. They contain progressively less silver and by the 860s were almost entirely copper. This debasement may signify economic and administrative decline or, conversely, extensive use of coin and governmental exploitation. In the ninth-century south, the West Saxon and Mercian kings and the archbishops of Canterbury were the issuing authorities. Their coins (silver pennies) were of the same design, indicating co-operation and desire for a common currency. The Scandinavians who conquered and ruled East Anglia minted their own coins there, copying a previous design and the Viking kings of York silver pennies with original designs, including the hammer of the pagan god Thor with Christian elements.[17] This choice may have been meant as a statement of Scandinavian (as opposed to English) but Christian identity. The nine hoards, which we know were deposited in northern England between 900 and 930, testify to dangerous times. The earliest, from Cuerdale and dating to c. 905, seems from its composition to have been the property of exiles from Scandinavian Dublin.[18]

Most Anglo-Saxon coins bore a cross or other Christian motifs, and, routinely, portraits of kings, which in other media are very rare. Painted images of Aethelstan, Edgar and Cnut (reigned 1016–1035) survive, in manuscripts. The (probably Anglo-Saxon) Bayeux Tapestry's account of the Norman Conquest features Edward the Confessor and Harold II. Edward is also portrayed on the earliest surviving Anglo-Saxon seal, and his mother Emma, queen successively of Aethelred II and Cnut, in two manuscripts. Such pictures are beguiling but should be regarded as sophisticated messages needing decoding rather than naturalistic representations. Modelled on foreign prototypes and using traditional imagery, portraits offer statements of rights and ideals, policies and perceptions. And if we assume some susceptibility to the messages, the coinage offers some insight too into how the people who handled the coins perceived the regime that issued it. The millions of Anglo-Saxon pennies were one of only two methods of mass communication, the other being the Christian liturgy.

The question 'who is saying what to whom?' should always be asked of works of art, though the ease of answering it and the usefulness of the answer will vary. Other forms of surviving metalwork, besides coins, include jewellery and weapons and come from both lower and higher echelons of society. Some pieces are associated with King Alfred and his immediate family.[19] Its Old English inscription 'Alfred had me made' and its find site 4 miles from Athelney in Somerset, where Alfred once took refuge from the Vikings, suggest that the unprecedented Alfred Jewel was the king's commission. It features a figure in cloisonné enamel probably representing Christ as Wisdom, a quality personified in the Old Testament book of Proverbs, whose necessity especially for those in authority is repeatedly emphasised in Alfred's writings. It was perhaps one of the book-markers that Alfred sent to his bishops with his translation of Pope Gregory I's *Pastoral Rule*. Apart from that there is the Minster Lovell Jewel, probably another such book-marker, and decorated gold rings belonging to Alfred's father King Aethelwulf (839–855) and sister Aethelswith, queen of Mercia. A silver sword-hilt found at Abingdon, a major West Saxon centre, has affinities with Aethelwulf's ring and the Alfred Jewel. Its decoration, with plant ornament and the symbols of Matthew, Mark, Luke and John (to whom the four Gospels of the New Testament are ascribed) may be an expression of the perception of his wars as Christians against pagans that Alfred propagated. Very little Welsh metalwork survives.[20] What does, suggests Welsh–Scandinavian contacts: five ninth- or tenth-century Scandinavian type silver armlets and weapons suggestive of a Viking grave in Caerwent. By contrast in recent years a great deal of various kinds has been discovered in England by metal-detectors. Their finds in East Anglia have been particularly useful in the study of Scandinavian settlement there. On the other hand, we will never know how much evidence has been destroyed by unskilled or irresponsible use of this technology, or what it might have told us.

Non-metal objects include some forty small bone or ivory carvings (most of walrus rather than elephant ivory), all dated to after 900, many being fragments or detached pieces of decoration, but some complete. We have one reliquary in the shape of a crucifix and three seal matrices, all dated late tenth-century. There is a large body of Anglo-Scandinavian Christian stone sculpture, perhaps the most famous piece being the high cross in the churchyard at Gosforth in Cumbria, where a Crucifixion is combined with scenes from Norse mythology. The hogback stones (so-called from their shape), probably grave-markers, are characteristic of northern England though there are two, and a fragment, in Cornwall and one (late tenth-century or later) in Wales (at a pre-Norman church at Llanddewi Aberarth, near Aberarth, in Ceredigion).[21] There are some eighty Scandinavian inscriptions in runes, particularly on Man where there are tenth-century memorial crosses.

From south-west Britain, known inscriptions, on stones, ten now lost, number fifty-eight from Cornwall, twenty from Devon and one from Somerset. At least sixteen of them, all in Roman script, date between the ninth and the eleventh centuries. Almost all the texts are Latin (one is in Old English, one perhaps Irish), but some comprise merely one vernacular name. They all seem to have a commemorative function, some being grave-stones. They testify to literacy, though not to its extent, and to the ability to command resources of materials, skills and labour. One of the least mysterious stones is the lower part of a carved cross-shaft at Redgate in Cornwall, also known as the St Cleer, or Doniert, stone. Datable, by type, to between the ninth and eleventh centuries, it is situated in what seems its original location, a field between Redgate and St Cleer. Its five-line inscription is complete, legible and intelligible, meaning 'Doniert requested' (presumably this monument, or prayers) 'for his soul'.[22] Doniert may be the Dungarth, king of Cornwall whom the *Welsh Annals* report was drowned in 875. This monument clearly has both a memorial and intercessionary function and was probably also a boundary marker for the monastery of St Neot, in whose vicinity a number of stones survive.[23]

The south-western stones have some similarities to some of the over 500 early medieval inscribed and sculpted stones of Wales.[24] Mostly from the south-east, just under half of them are dated 800–1100,[25] though there are over forty pieces from Anglesey, almost all from its south and east, dated between the tenth and earlier twelfth centuries.[26] Their production, or survival, seems to have risen, temporarily, in the ninth century. Some bear human figures, possibly a sign of Anglo-Saxon influence. Near Llangollen is the Pillar of Elise (or Eliseg), a shaft probably originally some 13 feet tall and surmounted by a cross-head,[27] with a long inscription, erected in the mid-ninth century by King Concenn (died c. 854) of Powys. This was to honour his great-grandfather Eliseg and probably also to strengthen his hold on its land and kingship by recording his claim to them. Now illegible, but intelligible from seventeenth-century transcriptions,[28] it proclaims Eliseg's and Concenn's conquests and states that their dynasty's founder was the fifth-century Vortigern, married to the daughter of the great King Maximus. It seems that Maximus had come to symbolise the end of Roman rule, so the claim about the marriage was probably a claim that Vortigern's political authority had been legitimate.[29] This representation of Vortigern is very different from that presented a few years earlier in the kingdom of Gwynedd, in Nennius' *History of the Britons*, which he wrote for Gwynedd's King Merfyn. In this, Vortigern is also associated with Powys but less directly, as head of the genealogy of one of its sub-kingdoms,[30] and he appears as a hated sinner, bigamous and incestuous, destroyed by God, by heavenly fire.[31] As in Cornwall and Scotland some Welsh stones indicated land ownership, sometimes symbolically and by their existence and location (monuments clustering around major monasteries and churches), sometimes explicitly by recording the donation of land to a church.[32] Their original locations are evidence for the sites of early cemeteries and churches, almost nothing of which survive, though there are elements of a pre-Norman building at a church at Presteigne in Powys. Many stones were multi-functional. Functions included being markers, of graves, sites for worship where there was no church building, boundaries and routes, and requesting and embodying prayers for the soul(s) of the patron(s) and other nominated individuals. What the sculpted stones illuminate is as diverse as their functions. Anglo-Saxon crosses may have functioned as markers for processions at Rogationtide (the Monday, Tuesday and Wednesday before Ascension Day) and, in the case of those ornamented with vegetal motifs, as weather crosses, to guard against bad weather and attract good.[33]

Some complete and some fragments of ornamented Anglo-Saxon stone crosses survive and likewise some churches. Perhaps most famous are the two at Deerhurst in Gloucestershire, one founded in the eighth century and enlarged in the early ninth; the other, according to its inscription, founded by Earl Odda and consecrated in 1056. Another, at Wing in Buckinghamshire, may have originated in the eighth or ninth century. St Mary's at Breamore in Hampshire, with a vernacular inscription over the arched entrance from the nave to the south chapel, is mostly late Saxon. The style of Edward the Confessor's Westminster Abbey in London, much changed over the centuries, was Norman, a statement of his political as well as architectural leanings.

The importance of Pictish sculpture, with its ornament, mysterious symbols and inscriptions, was indicated in the previous chapter. Most of it is not precisely datable. The Forteviot Arch, originally part of a church, may depict King Onuist (820–834) and be suggestive of ideas about kingship.[34] The Dupplin Cross was probably one of Forteviot's boundary markers, and commemorates and may even depict Constantín I.[35] It too testifies to royal ideology. The fact that it had a Latin inscription may imply the presence of a monastery. Groups of Pictish stones may be evidence for the presence of religious communities, or in another interpretation, by the ninth and tenth centuries, estate centres. The best assemblage of sculpture is Strathclyde's: forty-seven pieces, forty-three of them recumbent and four upright, from the churchyard at Govan, which seems to have become a major ecclesiastical centre by the end of the tenth century.[36] Little was produced in Alba in the tenth and eleventh centuries. Sculpture from Scandinavian Scotland includes a Christian cross-slab with a runic inscription, in honour of a woman, from Cille Bharra (Barra), and some eleventh-century hogback stones from the Northern Isles.[37] No churches survive.

The last important category of material remains is that of manuscripts. They are informative not just through the texts that they contain, but also through their illustrations, scripts (studied by palaeographers), and characters as artefacts. Sixteen ninth-century Anglo-Saxon manuscripts survive, including some half dozen from Alfred's time and circle.[38] Palaeographic study suggests that at least three, including a version of the *Anglo-Saxon Chronicle*, were probably worked on at Winchester. This means that Winchester was a centre of skill and production, and that it began a new style of handwriting. This owed something to previous Anglo-Saxon style and something to Carolingian development, a characterisation that runs like a leitmotif through scholarly assessment of Alfred's reign.

Known possession of manuscripts, whatever their origins, is evidence about the strength of libraries and possibly, though not certainly, since students do not always make use of the resources available to them, of learning. Alfred himself complained, in his preface to his version of Pope Gregory I's *Pastoral Rule*, that learning had declined in England in the first half of the ninth century. The chronology of surviving manuscripts suggests both that Alfred's complaint was justified and that there was significant improvement thereafter. Of the nearly 1,000 complete or fragmentary manuscripts written before 1100 that were pro- duced or possessed by Anglo-Saxon libraries, some seventy-seven ninth-century ones survive. Of these, more than sixty are of Continental origin, and there is no evidence that they were anywhere in England in the ninth century. Nearly 600 survive from the tenth and eleventh centuries.[39] They include some that feature the handwriting of Archbishop Wulfstan II of York (1002–1023, also bishop of London 996–1002 and of Worcester (as Wulfstan I) 1002–1016), a chief adviser of kings Aethelred II and Cnut. Manuscript as well as textual evidence has been used to identify Wulfstan's works. His authorship lies behind the last six (out of ten) law-codes of Aethelred and the law-code of Cnut, and a number of other legal texts, as well as tracts about status and sanctuary and his sermons.[40] Wulfstan was very influential but unfortunately it is impossible to tell how widely his works circulated. Many of them survive in only one copy.

Also illuminated by manuscripts are Cornish scholarship and influence on and in Wessex. There is a phrase in Cornish among the Latin glosses in a ninth- century manuscript of Boethius' *Consolation of Philosophy* and the name Hercules is rendered Ercol in the Old English Orosius. It has been suggested, though dis- puted, that Ercol is a Cornish form, implying that whoever dictated the Old English version was Cornish or Cornish-educated.[41] The fact that a later manu- script contains an excommunication formula that derives from St Germans, and another has part of a service-book that was also, probably, from there, suggests some Cornish liturgical influence on the later Church.[42] Unfortunately the origin of some 30 per cent of post-Alfredian manuscripts is still uncertain, so the relative strengths of particular places are too.[43] In some cases manuscripts are known to have been destroyed. Almost nothing survives from York, because of the destruction wrought there by King William in 1069.

Manuscript illumination testifies at the least to levels of craftsmanship, creativ- ity and openness to foreign artistic style and iconography, and to the ability to afford and obtain expensive and non-local materials. Depending on what is depicted it informs us about other things too, including religious ideas and pre- ferences and political philosophy. In the Book of Cerne, a prayer-book intended for private devotion and meditation, produced for an ecclesiastic, probably in Mercia between about 820 and about 840, text and images work together to provide multiple meanings. There is an emphasis on the efficacy of intercessory prayer, by the dead for the living and vice versa.[44] Another example is the Aethelstan Psalter, given by King Aethelstan to Winchester's Old Minster. Made in the ninth century, probably in the Liège region in Francia, it was augmented later, probably at Winchester, with Anglo-Saxon illustrations. Its scene of Christ enthroned in Heaven surrounded by choirs of martyrs, confessors and virgins is one indication of the veneration of virginity. Its picture is as much one of a pre- sent as of a future state. Centuries earlier, the Church of the Roman Empire had developed a view that virginity was a type of martyrdom. The intercession of deceased virgins at the court of Heaven, to which all martyrs would go without having to wait for the Last Judgement, was thought beneficial for the living. The presence in society of living ones was likewise perceived as useful. This idea lies behind patronage of monasticism and concern for standards within it.

Another important Winchester painting is in the New Minster's refoundation charter, issued by King Edgar in 966. Preceding the text is a picture of Edgar between, and taller than, the Virgin Mary and St Peter. As its patron saints, they represent the church and the prayers of intercession that its monks offered for Edgar. Edgar presents his charter to Christ in Majesty, the frame of whose picture is held up by four angels.[45] The scene proclaims that Edgar was wealthy, pious and powerful; that his kingship was Christ-centred: Christ, as king and judge rather than infant or crucified, was his role model; that Edgar represented his people and mediated between them and God just as Christ had redeemed humanity; that he had the most illustrious and powerful Heavenly allies; and that, consequently he had an overwhelming claim to obedience and respect. These assertions were directed to the monastic as well as the lay community. The picture also attests reverence for St Peter and for the Virgin, whose cult in England was boosted by the reform movement. Even more along these lines is offered in the splendid Benedictional (a collection of blessings that only bishops could pronounce) that was written and illuminated, probably for his use at Edgar's coronation in 973, for Bishop Aethelwold.[46]

Humbler manuscripts may be as interesting as splendid ones though in different ways. Part II of Corpus Christi College Cambridge 422, known as The Red Book of Darley, is perhaps from Winchester or possibly from Sherborne and dated c. 1061. It contains almost everything that a parish priest would have needed, including material for baptisms and burials, ministry to the sick and exorcisms. This implies that it was designed for parish use and hence suggests active parochial pastoral care.[47]

Very few manuscripts survive that are not Anglo-Saxon. One contains the illuminated Psalter and the Martyrology of Rhygyfarch of Llanbadarn Fawr, son of a bishop of St David's, which was illustrated by his brother Ieuan. This was probably around 1079, the date of the Psalter, though possibly as early as 1064.[48] Only one manuscript is identifiable as having been produced in what we call Scotland. This is the small and heavily illuminated Book of Deer, probably made at Deer itself, and perhaps for parish use.[49] It contains the Gospel of St John and extracts from the other three Gospels, and a rite of Communion for the sick and dying that was added before c. 1000. Its scribe-illuminator's strengths and weaknesses suggest that his community was practised in producing books, but was not in close intellectual contact with the Iona confederation.[50]

Linguistic evidence

Linguistic evidence includes personal and place-names which survive in inscriptions and other texts, especially manumissions (records of the freeing of slaves), charters and Domesday Book. Place-name study has often been regarded as offering evidence about who settled where and when, and how well they got on with any previous inhabitants. Points at issue are language, meaning, distribution and chronology of place-names. They may illuminate, for example, Anglo-Saxon expansion into Cornwall. English place-names are concentrated in the north-east and south-east of Cornwall and there are some hybrids in which an English suffix combines with a Cornish element or vice versa. An example is Helston (*hen lys* being Cornish for old court or old hall). Hybrids with *tun* probably signify Anglo-Saxon take-over of existing Cornish estates. West Cornwall's thinly spread *tun* names are probably late tenth or early eleventh century, for *tun* seems to have dropped out of use by 1066.[51]

Place-names have figured very largely in discussion of Scandinavian settlement.[52] Norse place-names replaced indigenous ones in most of Scotland north of the Dornoch Firth and probably in the Western Isles, but when and how is unknown, in part because of the lateness of the documents that record the names. In Galloway and the Isle of Man, Gaelic language seems to have been introduced during the Viking period. This suggests that some Irish accompanied the Scandinavians who came there from Ireland.[53] There are fifty-five Scandinavian place-names in Wales, including Swansea and Anglesey, all in coastal areas and mostly in the south-west. Many of them though may post-date 1066 and have nothing to do with pre-1066 conditions.[54] There are very many Scandinavian place-names in northern and eastern England. Almost all are beyond the frontier that Alfred established, in about 886, with the Viking King Guthrum. Many, the so-called Grimston hybrids, are Anglo-Scandinavian. These are most common in the East Riding of Yorkshire, the area of the so-called Five Boroughs (Lincoln, Nottingham, Derby, Leicester and Stamford) and East Anglia. The implication of large-scale settlement is clear but is nevertheless disputable and disputed. The questions of prior density of population, and of place-names being coined and used by neighbours and by the ruling class rather than by the inhabitants are among the factors that muddy the picture. Whitby and Derby for example are wholly Scandinavian names that replaced known and completely unrelated Old English ones. It may be that behind some other Scandinavian names lie unknown English ones rather than virgin territory.[55]

Linguistic analysis supplements the picture. The work in which the Cornish name Ercol occurs incorporates a travel account that was given to King Alfred at his court by a Norwegian named Ohthere. The language within this shows Norse influence, which suggests that Ohthere spoke in Norse but was nevertheless understood.[56] Contact at lower social levels has been illuminated by the histories of Old English and Old Norse and of the substitution of Old Norse for Old English elements in 220 place-names. The two languages seem to have been very similar in the ninth century. The substitutions suggest that Norse-speakers mostly understood the words that they heard in the place-names spoken by their English-speaking neighbours. It is as if the two groups spoke different dialects rather than languages, not needing bilingualism or interpreters to communicate. Moreover, the communication and contact that occurred was significant. Everyday present-day English betrays a strong Scandinavian influence, the personal pronoun 'they' being one example. The two languages nevertheless retained separate identities. Old Norse was still a living language in Cumbria in 1066.[57] It is possible that Gaelic–Pictish relations could similarly be illuminated by study of the Scottish Gaelic and Pictish British languages, the evidence being thousands of place-names preserved in Scotland's later charters.

Finally, England enjoyed a standard written language, a phenomenon paralleled by 1066 in no other Germanic language. A late form of the West Saxon dialect was used throughout the country. This development had been deliberate and imposed from above: it was not gradual or reflective of popular usage.[58] For example, texts that had been originally written in Anglian and a large part of the corpus of vernacular poetry were transcribed into West Saxon. Behind this standardisation of the language was Bishop Aethelwold's school at Winchester's Old Minster. It was promoted by his pupils, one of whom was (the later abbot) Aelfric, whose homilies, like some other texts written in close connection with Winchester, exemplify the standard language.

Texts – England

The texts through which the Anglo-Saxons may be studied include historical works: their own accounts, their treatments of others' accounts and close associates' accounts. Some of these are in Old English, others in Latin, and some have attracted a great deal of debate, which will not be surveyed here. There are three contemporary accounts of royal figures: Asser's of Alfred; the Continental *Encomium* of Queen Emma, which superficially is more about Cnut than her; and the Continental *Life* of Edward the Confessor which is more about Edward's wife Edith and her family than about him. These are in Latin. The vernacular *Anglo-Saxon Chronicle* provided an account of the Anglo-Saxons in Britain and the history of the West Saxons, including Alfred's reign, therein. It set them in the context of Roman Britain (that is, from Julius Caesar's invasion in 60 BC) and of world history (very briefly dealt with) up to the mid-fifth century. It was probably composed by someone close to Alfred's court and it was continued thereafter in different places. The so-called D Version for example may have been put together for Archbishop Ealdred of York, who died in 1069. A Latin version was composed by the West Saxon ealdorman Aethelweard, a patron of Aelfric. This is notable as evidence for lay literacy and scholarship.

Given their stature and achievements there is a relative lack of historical source material for Aethelstan, who has a claim to be regarded as an English Charlemagne,[59] and for Edgar, the first ruler to be crowned king of all England, for whom the legal and numismatic evidence are crucial. One explanation is that historical works were often designed to buttress a weak position, Alfred's *Anglo-Saxon Chronicle* being the prime example. Its emphases on the rise of Wessex, the ferocity of Viking invaders and the ultimate effectiveness of Alfred are claims for support at a time when rule by Wessex probably seemed at least as unwelcome to others as Viking rule. Tenth-century failure to generate historical propaganda may signify that tenth-century success made it unnecessary.

But tenth-century propaganda, of a kind, is to be found in saints' *Lives*. These include Aelfric's Old English translation of that of the martyred East Anglian King Edmund, written by Abbo of Fleury, a visiting ecclesiastic at Ramsey Abbey in the mid-tenth century. Both Aelfric and Wulfstan of Winchester produced accounts of their teacher Bishop Aethelwold. The *Lives* of Aethelwold's fellow-reformers Dunstan and Oswald were written some time between 995 and 1005, the latter's by Byrhtferth of Ramsey. The community of St Cuthbert was not the only monastery to keep historical records. Ely's *Little Book of Aethelwold* recorded that Edgar and his queen gave Aethelwold an estate in Suffolk in return for his (Old English) translation of the monastic *Rule* of St Benedict. Aethelwold may actually have written this whilst he was a monk at Glastonbury, in the years between c. 940 and the mid-950s, but only distributed it in the early 970s.[60] Neither Wulfstan nor Aelfric mentions it. The anonymous vernacular *King Edgar's Establishment of Monasteries* is regarded as probably what Aethelwold meant for its preface. Some Anglo-Norman historical texts preserve important information. The monk Symeon of Durham's early-twelfth-century work about the church of Durham, and another work to which he contributed, about the kings of England, for example, are useful for the cult of St Cuthbert, its patronage by the West Saxon kings, tenth-century Northumbria and Anglo-Scottish relations.

The historical, business, records of monasteries were their diplomas (charters). Some 2,000 survive, mostly as copies rather than in their original form, over 80 per cent of the fifty-one ascribed to King Edgar for example from after 1066.[61] Their chronological and geographical distribution, with regard both to where they were kept and the lands in nearby areas to which they refer, is patchy. The century best represented is the tenth. Only thirty-six charters survive from Cnut's long reign. Of the 118 royal diplomas that survive in their original form, 42 per cent are datable to 930–970, 40 per cent were preserved at Canterbury and 30 per cent at Worcester, Abingdon, Winchester and the see of Exeter, formerly Crediton.[62] The estates mentioned in charters and other legal documents, namely leases (that is, temporary grants), wills and writs (brief letters announcing a grant, the earliest of which to survive is from 1020), are concentrated in the south and south-east. Almost nothing is recorded for the north-west and only a little more than that for the north-east.[63] An obvious inference is that many charters perished in the destruction caused there by ninth-century Scandinavian activity. The largest ecclesiastical archive is Worcester's, which has some seventy-six leases, normally for a term of three lives, from the years 957 to 996. Seventy-four date to Bishop Oswald's episcopate (961–992).[64] Frustratingly, in half the Worcester cases there is no reference to beneficiaries owing any service in return for their grant, though in the eleventh century such records were kept in writing. It has been suggested that this implies that services were originally agreed orally, but that later this was not felt to be a sufficient guarantee of performance.

Overall over half the surviving charters are grants to the Church. Charters might be expected to reveal, at their most basic, who gave what to whom, plus when, why, where and in whose company (the witnesses). Sometimes they provide information about the history of, and disputes regarding, their estates. Thus as well as preserving names they can illuminate the landscape, land use and ownership, attitudes and policy, friendships and alliances, attendance of great assemblies, royal itineraries, claims of authority and power, and legal process.[65] Boundary clauses are especially important for our understanding of land use. References to cultivated land, hedges and enclosed woodland for example suggest, respectively, concentration on arable, as in Berkshire's Vale of the White Horse, combination of arable with pasture and woodland, as in north Worcestershire, and hunting parks.[66] References to heathen burials, the first being from 903, probably have nothing to do with paganism. They are thought to be allusions to execution cemeteries. The terminology expresses the fact that criminals were outside the Christian community. Domesday Book suggests that hundred boundaries were the preferred sites for such heathen burials.[67] Charters relating to Cornwall[68] include one, issued by a count, probably in the 930s, whose difference from Anglo-Saxon ones suggests that there was a native Cornish tradition of written land grants. Others suggest that tenth-century English kings redistributed Cornish lands on a large scale. In 967, for example, Edgar granted Lesneage, an estate of the church of St Keverne in south-west Cornwall, to one of his ministers. Recent study, however, points to continuity in Cornwall, of institutions, careers and personnel. The Cornish aristocracy adapted to Anglo-Saxon rule, for example by using Anglo-Saxon names simultaneously with their Cornish ones, as Edgar's minister, Wulfnoth Rumuncant, did.[69]

Belief in some sort of Purgatory (a time and state of the purification of souls, after death) and in the efficacy of intercession is indicated by the normally stated motive for grants to churches: desire for the eternal salvation of the soul of the donor and sometimes of others, for example family members, for which the beneficiary would pray. Other ideas are traceable too. The tenth-century reformers attempted to recreate as well as to eulogise the past, as they perceived it, for example by re-endowing the ancient monasteries.[70] Such attitudes may be embedded in the forgeries of earlier charters that are known. A charter was a record of, or aid to remembering, a grant, not the grant itself, which might have lain in a public ceremony. Yet possession of proof of a grant could be very important, so 'forgeries' might have been works of scholarship and housekeeping rather than attempts to deceive. Original charters might have been lost or their detail about boundaries thought inadequate. In the later tenth century some religious houses seem to have felt that they lacked, but needed, title deeds.[71] It is possible that of Edgar's apparent charters, only the New Minster one of 966 is actually authentic.

These are not the only problems that bedevil the use of charters. Some charters, for example thirteen ninth-century royal ones, indicate that payment was made for the land. Purchase rather than gift may lie behind others, as we know by chance in the case of King Edgar's grant to Ely Abbey (refounded by Bishop Aethelwold) in 970 of 10 hides at Stoke, which according to the *Little Book of Aethelwold*, Aethelwold bought from the king. Some charters, very obviously where kings grant lands to themselves, may be recording changes of the status of lands, from folkland to bookland, rather than possession. Behind others may lie not new grants but temporary gifts, grants of rights or exemptions, confirmations of earlier grants, or changes in conditions of tenure. Not all grants were honoured, and some were later annulled, but we depend on evidence other than their charters to recognise these cases. Furthermore, there is some evidence for layers of land-holding that are not recorded in standard charters.[72] Finally, the implications of witness lists about attendance at assemblies may be misleading. It was the scribe of the charter who wrote the names of the witnesses. Witness lists from four groups of charters dated after 956 probably are indeed related to attendance at four assemblies. Other lists, however, may be of all the people who witnessed one transaction that was actually dealt with in several meetings, or be incomplete because of lack of space, the Anglo-Saxon charter being a single sheet with columns for witnesses.[73]

Other legal documents that dispose of property are manumissions and wills. Manumissions, the earliest dating to 925, include fifty Cornish ones that date from the mid-tenth to the late eleventh or early twelfth century, thirty-three of them from between 946 and 1000. These are all recorded, most in Latin, a few in Old English, in the St Petroc, or Bodmin, Gospels (written, probably, in Brittany c. 900).[74] As well as a Cornish property-owning class they reveal some terms for social status whose meaning is mysterious. The fifty-seven wills include those of King Alfred, Aelfric archbishop of Canterbury 1002–1005, eleven women, four married couples and three from one thegnly family between the mid-1040s and mid-1060s. Their distribution, like that of charters, is patchy. There are some twenty-two from East Anglia, all post-dating Aethelred II, but none from Northumbria. Before the tenth century only bequests of land are normally recorded.[75] These texts certainly do not record the entirety of their testators' property and its distribution between their heirs. First, what was eligible for inclusion was limited. Wills could deal only with movable property, such as bedding, and with land that had been acquired by charter, that is, bookland. Other kinds of land were not alienable, but subject to rules of customary inheritance.[76] Second, an apparent bequest of land might actually be confirmation of an earlier grant that had been made by someone else, or a bequest of a lease, rather than of ownership. Insight into landholding can of course be gained from Domesday Book, and pre-Conquest smaller-scale surveys and documents relating to particular estates or to estate-management generally. The eleventh-century *Rights and Ranks of People* does this.

There is scholarly consensus that from the 930s kings' charters were produced by a royal, central chancery rather than by an ecclesiastical one or, as in previous centuries, in monastic scriptoria (writing offices) in the localities. The output has been estimated at about 100 per year, a workload that would have needed only one scribe. More varied formulae in the 950s and new ones in Edgar's reign suggest that more or different scribes were used then, and full-time royal clerks are detectable in Aethelred II's. Cnut and Edward the Confessor allowed bishops to issue charters for them.[77]

Ecclesiastics were also involved in production of a fourth type of legal text, law-codes. We have one detailed code attributed to Alfred, others to his descendants kings Edward the Elder (899–925), Aethelstan, Edmund (940–946), Edgar and Aethelred II, two in the name of Cnut and twenty anonymous ones.[78] The content and style of the royal codes after 1006 betray the authorship of Archbishop Wulfstan II. The prefaces, in Alfred's case exceptionally so, as well as the clauses, of the codes are of interest. They offer information about a range of subjects. Aethelstan's theft legislation is especially important. It made theft a felony, that is a crime not simply against the victim but against one's lord, and hence king and state, whose punishment involved forfeiture of property and execution.[79] Aethelstan regarded theft as something that threatened the peace, hence potentially a breach of the king's peace and thus an act of disloyalty to the king.[80] But also influential was the idea that, because God had prohibited it in the Ten Commandments, He would be likely to punish a regime or society that failed to prevent theft.

Unfortunately the law-codes do not simply and systematically promulgate new laws thereby enabling us to trace policy, problems and change. Early royal legislation was as much a statement of a king's fitness to rule, following the role models presented in the Old Testament and in the Christian Roman Empire, as anything else. Much was done by oral rather than written means: this explains why, for example, a text may represent as customary practices which had ceased to be current and why Alfred apparently deliberately left some of his laws and innovations out of his code.[81] There are questions about typicality and enforcement: whether instances mentioned were common or unusual, whether recurrence indicates draconian repression and success or continuing struggle and failure. Perhaps most crucially, Wulfstan amended earlier legislation when he wrote it up. Thus the original, or official, texts of Aethelred's codes are out of our reach. Wulfstan intended the laws not to be historical records but guidebooks for a Christian society, and for Christianising backsliders.[82]

Ecclesiastics also produced directives, in addition to exhortations, of their own, which might be considered a fifth category of legal sources. Some record of seventeen synods in the first half of the ninth century, survives, but it is only in the case of Chelsea in 816 that the canons (rulings) survive (eleven in this case).[83] The Latin *Regularis Concordia*, written probably by Bishop Aethelwold, in which the rule for the daily life of reformed monasteries was explained in detail, was issued in King Edgar's name, at the Council of Winchester, probably, c. 970.[84] Some decisions made by other tenth-century councils have been preserved in historical texts. Penitential material appears in some tenth- and eleventh-century manuscripts. Pastoral letters from bishops, comprising instructions for local priests, were both directive and exhortatory. Aelfric's surviving works include five of these: four (Old English and Latin versions of two letters) for Archbishop Wulfstan II and one for Wulfsige III, bishop of Sherborne 993–1002. He also wrote exhortative and exegetical texts. His first series of *Catholic Homilies* was written perhaps as early as 990, and no later than 994, his second series no later than 994. Each had forty pieces to provide a year's sermons.[85] His *Lives of Saints*, surviving as five homilies, twenty-six legends, two Old Testament narratives and three tracts, originally probably did likewise.[86] These works offer insight into Aelfric's perceptions and concerns about contemporary conditions because his characterisation is sometimes very different from that of his biblical and historical sources. Wulfstan's works too include homilies. The most famous is the *Sermon of the Wolf to the English* of 1014, which explains their renewed suffering at Danish hands as God's punishment for a catalogue of English transgressions in matters, he says, of both Church and State.

We have some correspondence, within, to and from Anglo-Saxon England, and a few texts to do with the cults of saints. The correspondence includes some Papal letters[87] and a letter from Aethelstan's reign in which the community of St Samson in Dol, in Brittany, claimed to have prayed unwearyingly for Aethelstan's soul and welfare, promised to continue to do so and sent him bones of saints Senator, Paternus and Scabillion. A list, combining an earlier Mercian and later West Saxon lists, of the locations of relics of saints in England survives from c. 1032. It would have been of interest to anyone planning a pilgrimage, either entirely for its own sake or as a supplement to travel that was undertaken for other reasons. For Cornwall we have the tenth-century Vatican list. Written in Cornwall or Brittany and surviving on one of a group of flyleaves, it comprises forty-eight names, between twenty-four and thirty-two of which are names of saints venerated in Cornwall. Its purpose is unknown.[88]

Besides the homiletic material that Aelfric and Wulfstan wrote, there are other homilies, including anonymous ones written in the vernacular. Twenty-three are in a manuscript produced, probably, at St Augustine's monastery in Canterbury, c. 975, and now in Vercelli in northern Italy. Eighteen and a fragment, eight of them unique, are in the slightly later Blickling manuscript, copied by two scribes at an unknown location probably late in the tenth century, though composed between the late ninth and the later tenth century.[89] Both collections contain anti-Jewish rhetoric, as does the Vercelli manuscript's other content, six vernacular poems.[90] Other vernacular poems survive in, or in copies from, other manuscripts.

The poetic corpus is mostly anonymous and not susceptible to precise dating, but it is at least as important, as historical evidence, as sermons are. Like sermons, many of the poems were composed by ecclesiastics, betray ecclesiastical concerns and survive because of ecclesiastical interest. This is true even where they address military and political subjects. Some of them may have been used to edify and entertain meetings of guilds.[91] The corpus includes five tenth-century historical poems, four being entries in the *Anglo-Saxon Chronicle*. Behind the first, celebrating King Aethelstan's victory in the battle of Brunanburh, in 937, may be the figure of Cenwald, bishop of Worcester 929–958.[92] The second celebrates King Edmund's taking of the Five (Danish) Boroughs in 942 in religious terms, as releasing them from bonds of captivity to heathens. The third and fourth, about the coronation of Edgar in 973 and his death in 975 may have been created as pro-church-reform panegyrics, by monks, or a monk.[93] The free-standing *Battle of Maldon* is concerned with an English defeat at Danish hands in Essex in 991, though it is more literary than historical in character. It may have been written as late as the early eleventh century,[94] though scholars disagree as to whether before or after the accession of Cnut in 1016.[95] Its survival may be due to the fact that its hero, Byrhtnoth, was a supporter of church reform, the poem being preserved, in a monastery, to honour his memory.[96] Some Old Norse saga poetry apparently contains information about Scandinavian Northumbria, the eleventh-century conquest of England, and King Cnut. These sagas, however, were written down centuries later and the scholarly consensus now is that they are literary fictions, not, as once thought, reliable historical sources, though the matter is still debated.[97]

The import of the longest of the surviving Old English poems, *Beowulf*, a heroic adventure story featuring monsters and set in historic Scandinavia, which survives in one manuscript written c. 1000, depends on what date is preferred for its composition. This, like the poem's meaning(s), has been much debated. If it is pre-800, then its later copying suggests simply, though importantly, that a post-800 audience found it interesting. If it is post-800, it is more specifically informative about post-800 concerns, or at least those of its anonymous patron and author. The poet's concept of ideal kingship included some traditional, pre-Christian Germanic values, combined with others that were resolutely Christian qualities of rulers that had been advocated by Pope Gregory I. This combination dovetails neatly with how King Alfred is represented in texts. He was an enthusiastic hunter interested in Saxon (presumably Old English) poems, which he learnt by heart, according to Asser, and in his translation of Gregory's *Pastoral Rule*, he applied its teachings about bishops to his own role as king. Such coincidence has been held to imply an Alfredian context for *Beowulf*'s composition. Study of Beowulf's dragon-fight may be held to support this, or a date in Aethelstan's reign, as some motifs in it may have come to Anglo-Saxon England in the context of contacts with Bretons. Such royal contacts were particularly strong in the late ninth and early tenth century.[98] *Beowulf* could be read as justifying Alfred's style of kingship and offering a role model to subordinates and future kings. Another, very different, suggestion is that it reflects anxieties about the great strength of royal power around c. 1000, when lay literacy was more extensive.[99] In this reading, the name of the hall of the king whom Beowulf visits is particularly important. Heorot, meaning hart, and hence deer-hall, is where the king distributes the products of his military conquests and whose occupants the monster Grendel attacks. Heorot, in this interpretation, symbolises hierarchical society and private property whereas in an earlier, egalitarian, society everybody had had rights to the hunt and its products. Grendel and his mother, who tries to avenge his killing by Beowulf, represent resistance to this development. Yet another view is that the poet was concerned with Cnut's reign and court.[100]

The bulk of the Old English poetry by contrast addresses explicitly Christian subjects. In the possibly tenth-century *Judith*, based on the Old Testament Book of Judith, the virginal heroine kills the Assyrian king Holofernes, who had lusted after her, and the Hebrew city of Bethulia is liberated. A Latin *Life* of Juliana, a female virgin martyred in the late-third-century Roman Empire, in Nikomedia (some 70 miles east of modern Istanbul) for refusing to marry a pagan, is the basis of Cynewulf's *Juliana*. These two poems, like Cynewulf's *Elene*, about the discovery by the Roman Empress Helena of the remains of the True Cross in Jerusalem in the fourth century, present heroines who are strong, determined and effective, two of them with powers of leadership, in terms reminiscent of poetic male warrior heroes. This might indicate that Anglo-Saxon society was at ease, and hence familiar, with the phenomenon of female power, but this interpretation has been questioned, since these heroines' specific context, in time and space, is alien. There are also doubts about Cynewulf's dating. The early ninth century, the Alfredian period and the later tenth century have all been suggested. Other poems signed with Cynewulf's name in runes are the *Fates of the Apostles* and *Christ (II)* concerned with Christ's Ascension into Heaven.

Poetry records aspects of Anglo-Saxon Christianity, for example the cults of the Virgin Mary and the Cross, ideas about Heaven, and different attitudes to war and violence and their compatibility with sanctity. Some poems may hide an inner meaning in allegory: thus *Exodus*, about the biblical Israelites' flight from Egypt in search of the Promised Land, may also be about the soul marching towards Heaven, under God's hand but pursued by the powers of darkness.[101] Some have links, like a number of manuscript illuminations, with the liturgy. They may have been intended for a professional religious audience who would appreciate these links and the poems' theological dimensions.[102] There is for example baptismal imagery, involving water, in *Andreas* (date unknown), which is about the adventures of St Andrew, involving sea travel, pagan cannibals and a flood of their city.[103] Similar imagery in *Beowulf*,[104] which may have been intended for a lay audience, when the hero descends into the lake in which Grendel and his mother lived, is one of a number of affinities between the two. Knowledge of *Beowulf* in fact heightens *Andreas*' impact, so it seems likely that the *Andreas* poet both knew and assumed that his audience knew *Beowulf*.[105]

Besides historical, legal, homiletic and poetic material, the (Latin) liturgy itself constitutes a fifth important source of evidence, although of a kind unfamiliar to most readers.[106] It betrays how Anglo-Saxon ecclesiastical authorities thought about their society and encouraged their congregations to think about it, as well as what was owed to Continental churches and what was idiosyncratic. Unfortunately little is known about the liturgy before the tenth-century reformation but the late Anglo-Saxon liturgy has recently been well studied, using the *Regularis Concordia* and the sixteen surviving Pontificals, that is, liturgical books containing instructions for those rites that only bishops could perform.[107] These date from the later tenth century onwards. The Red Book of Darley offers evidence for parish liturgy.[108] The non-Anglo-Saxon churches of Britain by contrast have left almost no trace of their liturgy.[109]

A sixth corpus of textual evidence is that of Anglo-Saxon scholarly works. Permeated by Christianity and Christian concerns, they were written by Christian authors, almost all of whose religion was, in every sense, their profession. The (Latin) books that Alfred termed 'the most necessary for all men to know',[110] and wanted translated, were concerned with God, His relationship with individuals and groups, and in history. Alfred himself is traditionally regarded as the translator of some Psalms, the *Soliloquies* of St Augustine (bishop of Hippo in Africa 395–430), and the *Consolation of Philosophy* (written in Pavia in Italy in the 520s by the Roman aristocrat Boethius). The most recent editors of the Alfredian Boethius have mounted a strong challenge to this attribution, and by implication to that of the Soliloquies since it is by the same author. They suggest an early-tenth-century date, or a translator of Alfredian date but not in his circle.[111] They have not, however, convinced all scholars. Alfred also translated Pope Gregory's *Pastoral Rule*. Translations of Gregory's *Dialogues* and of Bede's *Ecclesiastical History* and Orosius' *History* were done within his circle. A century later, Aethelwold was accomplished in Latin.[112] Of the next generation, Aelfric and Archbishop Wulf-stan II have been compared favourably with leading Continental theologians,[113] and Wulfstan of Winchester deemed a highly accomplished scholar.[114] The monk Byrhtferth of Ramsey produced an important scientific work, a mathematical and astronomical treatise on the reckoning of time, to help parish priests with their regular duties. These are the peaks of Anglo-Saxon intellectual achievement between 800 and 1066. Lower levels are also interesting. Bald's *Leechbook*, a col-lection of medical texts compiled, it seems, during Alfred's reign, is the earliest Anglo-Saxon medical text to survive, though not to have been composed. Such texts were used by practising physicians (some ecclesiastical, some lay). Its medi-cine was rational, including magical elements that were used in a rational way.[115] One instance is the requirement to chant particular prayers a particular number of times while mixing ingredients. In a society without clocks and watches this would have been an excellent method of timing.

A very great deal of the evidence for England was generated by the Church but this does not detract from what the evidence shows – that Christianity was an inspiration in society and that the Church was its power-house: of education, finance, health care, political advice and policy-making, philosophy, art and literature. It is difficult to identify anything significant that the Christian religion did not touch.

Texts – Scotland and Wales

The texts that are informative about Scotland are not only far fewer than those relating to England.[116] They include a much higher proportion of foreign and later documents. Anglo-Saxon and Irish ones are the most important for political history, though the *Anglo-Saxon Chronicle* incorporates what nowadays is called spin, about Anglo-Scottish relations. The core of the Durham *Liber Vitae* was composed perhaps at Wearmouth or Lindisfarne, and attests by inclusion of their names its community's links with the Pictish kings Constantín and his nephew Wen who died in 839.[117] The very brief mid-tenth-century *Welsh Annals* take some notice of the north. Contemporary Irish annals and later Scottish chronicles are also important, though not detailed, sources. The Ulster annal for 900 contains the earliest usage of the name Alba, hitherto applied to the totality of the island of Britain, to signify only its northern part. The first contemporary reference to the earls of Orkney is likewise Irish, for the year 1014.[118] The Continental *Life* of

St Cathróe abbot of Metz (in north-east France), written about 980, records his early life in Scotland, his birthplace.[119] A version of the St Andrews foundation legend may have been written, as one version states, during the reign of Wrad (Ferat or Ferath) (839–842).

Even later, but with a core composed possibly in the second half of the ninth century, is a liturgical text, the Dunkeld Litany or *Litany* of Giric,[120] who reigned 878–889 but is a shadowy figure, beset by conflicting evidence.[121] Its prayer for the king, his army and the expulsion of enemies of Christianity, and the list of saints that it invokes offer insight into a sense, and making, of a political community in which Church and Christianity were binding elements. So too do its attestation of cults of three royal saints (Ainbchellach who died in 719 and two named Constantin, possibly the ones who died in 820 and 876), and of some martyrs killed during Scandinavian attacks and its concentration on Scottish saints, omitting Northumbrian ones.[122] Also important for the unification of Alba is a very short (eighty-one lines of printed text) historical work, which has been detected through its late-twelfth or early-thirteenth-century version. It designates Cinaed mac Alpín as 'first of the Scots' and destroyer of the Picts, though some scholars now believe that Cinaed was Pictish himself.[123] Now called by some scholars the *Chronicle of the Kings of Alba*,[124] this text was written, or finished, in the second half of the tenth century, possibly begun at Dunkeld and finished at St Andrews. It comprises a list of twelve kings, from the mid-ninth century to c. 990, with other information added to it.[125]

There is almost no poetic evidence, none in Pictish. The possibly ninth- or tenth-century historical poem the *Fall of Rheged* is in Welsh. The Middle Gaelic (Irish) *Duan Albanach* (Song of the Albans) is a verse king-list about the settlement of Alba and its rule, composed during the reign of Mael Coluim, 1058–1093, perhaps revealing more about perceptions then than an earlier reality.[126] The final section (364 lines) of the Middle Gaelic *The Prophecy of Berchán* is concerned with kings from the ninth century to the 1090s and was probably almost entirely composed by an author from Alba shortly before 1070.[127] Some scholars regard it as largely accurate, others as a work of fiction. Surviving poetry of a more literary character is very scanty: the five mid-eleventh-century poems mentioned in the previous chapter; six Gaelic works, of which three including an elegy to King Cinaed (died 858) are only a few lines long; one prayer, praising Iona's founder, by Iona's Abbot Mugron, who died in 980; and two others probably by him. In later Norse texts some earlier, short poems have been detected: four tenth century, two early eleventh and one eleventh or twelfth century.[128]

Nor is there any body of legal material that compares with the Anglo-Saxons'. The thirteenth-century tract that lists payments for offences may reflect earlier conditions. The fourteen land grants that were copied, in Middle Gaelic, between c. 1130 and c. 1150, into the Book of Deer probably began in the early eleventh century, since the seventh in the series is a grant by the Mael Coluim who reigned 1005–1034. However, a man named in the second, which summarises property transactions over more than a century, may have been the son of King Giric. These records are very brief, none taking up more than three lines of modern printed text.[129] Finally, there are neither works of scholarship nor allusions in the sources to eminent learned individuals or groups, who might have been analogous to the Anglo-Saxons'. Our perception of this society's learning depends on its sculpture.

The written sources for Wales are significantly less scanty.[130] Nennius' *History*, which set British and Irish origins in a context of world history and focused on fifth-century history, is the only known extended Welsh historical work. Asser's *Life* of Alfred provides some information about Wales besides demonstrating Welsh learning. Scholarship and teaching are indicated too by ninth- and tenth-century Welsh glosses to some Latin texts, including Boethius' *Consolation of Philosophy*, and by a set of conversations that provide students with practice in Latin, which survives from the tenth century.

Interest in history seems to have peaked in Wales in the mid-tenth century. There is a mid-tenth-century collection of thirty genealogies pertaining to the royal families of the time. Some are very short, others, including that of Owain king of Dyfed 950–c. 970, which goes back to Helena, finder of the Cross and to Anna, cousin of the Virgin Mary, very long.[131] They reveal claims of, rather than actual, descent. The first section of the Latin *Welsh Annals* (which in its entirety goes up to the thirteenth century) covers 447 to 954 and was put together in Dyfed. It contains the earliest attempt to date (at 516) Arthur's victory over the Anglo-Saxons at Mount Badon, first mentioned by Nennius, and to detail his death (dated 537 in the battle of Camlann). It presents Arthur as a Christ-type figure.[132] The annals are very brief, with entries for only seventy-six years before 800 and seventy-five afterwards. Most comprise just one line of printed text. The Arthurian entries take three and two lines and the longest, for 814, six. It may also have been in Dyfed, at St David's, or possibly in Gwynedd, perhaps in the 930s or very early 940s, that the long (199 lines) vernacular poem *Armes Prydein* (The Prophecy of Britain) was composed. This promised complete victory over the Anglo-Saxons by an alliance of all the Britons (in Wales, England, Scotland and Brittany) plus the Irish and Scandinavian Dublin, in wars in which St David was to be a leader. It should be understood as a comment on recent events and recommendation of a policy for the future, supporting the Scandinavians against the Anglo-Saxons, which differed from that of the contemporary king of Dyfed.[133] The survival of heroic poetry relating to the sixth and seventh centuries, some of which was composed between c. 800 and c. 1100 is also suggestive of Welsh historical-political interests. Finally, there are nearly 100, mostly three-line, stanzas about the graves of noble warriors of the past, a poem praising the fort of Tenby and its lord and two other ninth- or tenth-century poems.[134]

To these contemporary Welsh sources may be added the *Anglo-Saxon Chronicle*, the 1086 Domesday Book, works of the twelfth-century Gerald of Wales and a few Breton saints' Lives. The two earliest Welsh saints' *Lives*, of the sixth-century Cadog, and David, were written in the late eleventh century and illuminate their authors' rather than the saints' concerns. There are some Latin poems written between 1085 and 1091 and some vernacular works that are almost certainly post-Norman, though possibly preserving some oral story-telling.[135]

The Welsh law tracts are all later than the eleventh century. Many though refer to Hywel Dda's having collected the laws (in the mid-tenth century), and much of their material is thought to be very old. It is nevertheless unclear to what degree his code, in whose historicity some scholars believe, is recoverable.[136] Original texts of charters, relating almost entirely to the south-east, can by contrast be reconstructed, from the twelfth-century *Book of Llandaff*'s 149 corrupt and undated ones. They run from the late sixth to the late eleventh century. Some thirty are from the second half of the ninth century.[137] Four ninth-century charters, relating to the area of Llandeilo Fawr, and some manumissions were written into the margins of the Lichfield Gospels, while this manuscript was at Llandeilo. There are a few fragmentary charters from elsewhere. There are no ecclesiastical legal, admonitory or liturgical texts from this period.[138]

Approaches and methodologies

The wide range and small quantity of evidence require historians to engage with several disciplines. The relevance of archaeology, art history, epigraphy (study of inscriptions), linguistic, literary and liturgical studies, and numismatics is immediately obvious. Less obvious is the utility of sociology, modern literary criticism and anthropology, but they are equally important, as a few examples make plain. Socio-linguistic theories, approaches and methods of intelligibility testing were explained and used to great effect by Matthew Townend in his demonstration, published in 2002, of the mutual intelligibility of Old Norse and Old English.[139] In 2003 came Katharine Scarfe Beckett's study of Anglo-Saxon perceptions of the Islamic world.[140] This was undertaken as a response to what she termed a provocative annexation of the Middle Ages as a repository of, and source for, later centuries' orientalist or imperial attitudes, of the type that the literary scholar Edward W. Said's hugely influential and still debated *Orientalism*, published in 1978, had deprecated. She showed that Said was over general in his summary of medieval views and literary representation of the Orient and mistaken in the ideas and sentiments that he attributed to them. Anglo-Saxon perception of the Islamic world actually combined current political and military awareness with information and ideas that came from non-Anglo-Saxon Latin texts, some of them pre-dating Islam, and did not include the religion of Islam. Nor did they especially associate Arabs, or Muslims with evil. In patristic (Church Fathers') writings, which were hugely influential upon the West, the seat of evil was located in the north. This representation must have resonated with those Anglo-Saxons who had to deal with Viking invasion and Viking paganism. In his *Grammar* Aelfric gave 'Arab' a simple geographical sense – someone from Arabia.

The value of studies of nationalism and national identity, some of which include historical examples and case studies as well as theory, was alluded to earlier in this chapter. Some scholars of national identity practise, or have backgrounds in, anthropology (the study of human societies with regard to such things as kinship relations and culture in the broad sense). The most famous example of anthropology's usefulness in understanding early medieval society is its illumination of bloodfeud as an ordered system, with known rules and built-in peace-parties (neighbours, mutual kin, religious figures) that can engender stability.[141] This makes its combination both with sophisticated government and with Christianity – its practice in Christian societies, the perception of God as a practitioner, the involvement of clerics in negotiations – far less problematic than might seem at first sight.

Other issues for which an anthropological perspective is helpful include orality and gift-giving. A society can have sophisticated and efficient systems without recording their principles and workings in writing. Acknowledging this affects interpretation, for example, of the lack of law-codes from Alba despite the apparent strength of Alba's kings. Gift-giving either discharges an obligation that the giver has previously incurred or creates an obligation on the part of the recipient. Failure to reciprocate immediately, with a gift of equivalent or greater value constitutes acceptance of inferior status and obligation. This explains the emphasis in poetry on gift-giving and the implications of giving land, treasure or relatives (to be nuns or monks) to the Church. We are looking not at simple-mindedness, greed, credulity and superstition but at political alliances, treaties and agreements, loyalty, service and their rewards. Barbara Rosenwein's 1989 study of the property of the monastery of Cluny, in Burgundy, between 909 and 1049, revealed the social and symbolic significance of donation there. It bound monks, laity and the saints together. Challenges by donors' kin and heirs to ecclesiastical possession, confirmations of it and compromises about it may have been attempts more to reaffirm the original relationships, and incorporate different individuals than to redistribute resources.[142] The same is likely to have been true in England. For example, the see of Rochester appears to have had a dispute with the family that was its greatest benefactor, understandable on this basis as a means of renewing the relationship between the church and its patron.

The anthropological studies that have influenced historians have usually concerned societies very different from their own, in time, place and character – for example the Nuer in the Sudan, in Africa. Their undertaking in the earlier half of the twentieth century and their use later by historians might be regarded as reflective of a process of globalisation. It is a cliché that historians' approaches, questions and perhaps conclusions are influenced by the circumstances and concerns of their own societies. It is useful for those concerned with early British studies to remember it. It is easy enough to relate the interests of the Victorian bishop and historian William Stubbs, in Anglo-Saxon constitutional history and documents, most famously charters, to his society's enthusiasm for the growth of Parliamentary democracy. Sir Frank Stenton's *Anglo-Saxon England*, a foundation for modern Anglo-Saxon studies, published in 1943, has been criticised for insularity. Lack of interest in European parallels and in the possibility that English history was part of a Europe-wide phenomenon does not seem unnatural in the light of British experience in the first half of the twentieth century.

A number of changes of scholarly emphases and opinions about particular subjects may be related to scholars' own backgrounds. One such subject is the role and status of women. Feminism and feminist historiography of the 1960s, influential since about 1970, are a backdrop to the questioning of the view that in Christian Anglo-Saxon England the lot of women was a good one, especially in comparison with the Roman Empire and Norman England. One problem is a relative lack of female monastic houses in the reform period. Yet some references to, or suggestive of, religious women, for example particular garments which might have been marks of a nun or abbess, occur in some women's wills. One solution is to postulate regular nunneries behind such references, whose failure to be otherwise recorded and known is explicable in terms of male authors, then and now, being uninterested in or disapproving of female achievement. A different one is that expounded in a study published in the post-feminist year 2000, by Sarah Foot.[143] A woman could take vows and a nun's attire but live on her own estate with her household. Since this option did not necessitate alienating land, it was probably popular with families and it left neither traces in the charter record nor long-lasting nunneries behind it.

A case study in comparative history: vernacular liturgy

Using insights derived from anthropology essentially implies comparison. One advantage of comparative history is that it facilitates identification of what is really idiosyncratic, creative or problematic about a particular place in a particular time, as opposed to particular manifestations of recurring historical patterns. It may also help in interpretation of sketchy sources. Furthermore, a comparative perspective may suggest new answers to familiar questions. For example, Alex Woolf suggested in his 2007 study of Scotland that the twentieth-century Balkan phenomenon of a patchwork of communities speaking different languages, rather than waves of wholesale language replacement, may have been what tenth-century north-west England and south-west Scotland experienced.[144] Comparative history may also, perhaps more importantly, suggest new questions that would not otherwise be asked. What comparison suggests as possible answers may be tested against the sources. It might produce new interpretations, or newly nuance or strengthen existing ones.

This can be seen very clearly in the case of the Anglo-Saxons' failure to translate the liturgy from Latin into their vernacular, Old English.[145] This is despite the fact that vernacular literature blossomed in the Alfredian period and again in the later tenth century, and despite the Church's concern that the laity be engaged and understand what they were doing in church. Considered in the context of western Christian Europe, this failure is not an issue, because it was normal. Scholars have not pursued it. But a broader comparative perspective makes it more problematic. The later ninth century saw the development of a Slavonic vernacular liturgy, first in Moravia (roughly the present-day Czech Republic) and subsequently in Bulgaria. It was used there instead of the previously available Latin (of the western Church) and Greek (the language of the early Church and of that of Byzantium). In Armenia, at the eastern end of Christendom, Christians had enjoyed vernacular (Armenian) scriptures and liturgy since the fifth century, at the beginning of which the Armenian alphabet had been invented, precisely to facilitate biblical translation (the Old Testament from Hebrew, the New from Greek). And apart from this question of vernacular liturgy, Armenians and Anglo-Saxons were very similar, in the tenth century, in two respects. Each had a well-developed vernacular literature. This included historical writings that offered a vision of a shared past, and a sense of national identity, in which Christianity was a major element.

These two phenomena, of literature and identity, are, historically, connected, and they differentiated both Armenians and Anglo-Saxons from contemporary western Europeans. Liturgy too, and especially vernacular liturgy, can be important in the forging of a community identity. It is a communal activity that generates a sense of belonging to a wider community. Every congregation is aware that others in other places are worshipping at the same time in the same way. Commemoration of regional or national saints or occasions promotes a sense of a shared past. Additionally, praying for other people, both living and dead, promotes a sense of community with them, even a sense of responsibility for their welfare. Armenian liturgy repeatedly conjures up an 'us' who are Armenians. England's monastic *Regularis Concordia* is based on Continental texts, but is original in its emphasis on repeated prayer for the king and queen. We do not know how uniform the liturgy was in England. We do, however, know that in and after the reform period uniformity was an aim and monastic practices were disseminated beyond the monastic context. In the letter composed by Aelfric for the parochial clergy of the bishop of Sherborne, he stipulates that Mass priests are to pray for the king.

It cannot be the case that Anglo-Saxon kings and clerics were discouraged from translating the liturgy by a concern that there was no precedent for it. They were almost certainly aware of the use in Christian worship of languages other than Latin and Greek. This is explicit in Alfred's *Pastoral Rule*, finished perhaps about 890. His preface states that the Law – meaning the scriptures – originally in Hebrew, has been translated successively by the Greeks and the Romans and 'similarly all the other Christian peoples turned some part of them into their own language'.[146] He surely knew of the Slavonic developments, which had begun in the 860s in Moravia. In the 880s they had become a cause célèbre for the Franks and Papacy, and Alfred had significant contacts with both. Furthermore, the Old English Orosius, dated to the late 880s, provides direct evidence of knowledge, before 890, of Moravia and some of its history. In its updating of European geography, Moravia is named, and treated as a 'pivotal' area. The translator also shows awareness of ravaging that had occurred very recently, in 883 and 884. That Alfred also knew of an Armenian vernacular tradition is less certain, though likely. His source could have been Jerusalem, which had a well-established Armenian community and with which he had contact well before 890. Asser refers to letters and gifts sent by Elias, patriarch of Jerusalem (c. 879–907) to Alfred. Some remedies in the *Leechbook* fit symptoms that Asser says Alfred had and are stated there to have been sent by Elias. Another possible source was Constantinople, capital of the Byzantine Empire, through which Alfred's emissaries' route may have lain, and where there were both Armenians and Byzantine dignitaries of Armenian origin.

The case for English awareness of an Armenian vernacular tradition is stronger for the late tenth century, when it probably came through Byzantine contacts. The *Ely Book* records a 'Greek' bishop at Edgar's court, Sigewold. He may have been the Bishop Nikephorus of Herakleia who in 956 incurred the displeasure of the Byzantine emperor, for Sigewold is the Old English equivalent of Nicephorus.[147] There is a very interesting mistake in the northern recension of the *Anglo-Saxon Chronicle*. Its preface asserts that the Britons came from Armenia. The oft-repeated explanation, a misreading of Bede's Armorica, meaning Brittany, must be correct. But it is not impossible that this error was analogous to present-day English typists' miscopying Armenia as America, subconsciously substituting the familiar for the unfamiliar. It might imply a perception of Armenia as in some sense relevant, more so than Armorica.

The Anglo-Saxons did not lack the ability to translate the Latin liturgy, or the self-confidence to be, in a western context, innovative in so doing. Their creativity and self-confidence are perceptible in a number of ecclesiastical fields. They may, however, have felt that Latin was more prestigious and hence more suitable for worship, because it had been made sacred by usage, particularly by its use, according to the Bible, in an inscription on Christ's Cross at the Crucifixion. Latin may also have symbolised community with earlier western Christians and with the Papacy.

Perhaps the most convincing explanation, however, lies in Aelfric's fears of heresy, and that translation might lead to it. He thought there was 'much error in many English books', probably meaning sermons such as the anonymous Vercelli and Blickling ones. He expressed unease that biblical translation might cause misunderstanding, though he nevertheless produced versions of six Old Testament books, half of Genesis and half of Numbers, and, in his homilies, of various biblical passages. At first he preferred literal translation, because imposing interpretation involved a risk of error. But he thought that a lack of commentary could also be dangerous. His later translations were more interpretative than his earlier ones, the reverse of what happened in Armenian biblical translation. Such worries might explain, in part, why the Old English Gospels, the only extant complete translation in a west Germanic language in the early Middle Ages, a late tenth or early eleventh-century West Saxon work, seems not to have been widely known.

England's authorities could afford not to use vernacular liturgy to foster national sentiment, because they had another, different, means of doing it, namely their intrusive, demanding, sophisticated and efficient administration. This was compatible with the self-identification of the English as the, or a, new Israel, because the Old Testament presents Israel as a nation-state ruled ideally by a strong king. From at least the time of Alfred West Saxon royal government was impressive. Eleventh-century Anglo-Saxon England has often been described as having the most advanced and sophisticated administration in western Christendom. The government's reach was deep, its grip tight, its ambition elevated. This, and the shared experience that it gave to the population, was probably a crucial factor in the making of English identity as well as of the English state, well before 1066. The Anglo-Saxon reality was very different from the myth of a golden age of freedom and independence, terminated by the Norman Conquest, that was constructed in sixteenth- and seventeenth-century England, made in the context of Parliamentary opposition to the crown, and, partly, to justify it.

We have almost no evidence for dissent of any kind in late Anglo-Saxon England apart from laxity in obedience and in religious observance and royal succession disputes. By contrast, the contemporary Armenian Tondrakian heresy has sometimes been seen as social and economic protest. Aelfric's remarks about heresy feature heretical stories, for example about the death of the Virgin Mary, rather than substantial points of doctrine or practice such as the nature of Christ and the sacraments, from which the Tondrakians dissented. He does, certainly, refer four times to the arch-heretic Arius. Also, two eleventh-century manuscripts (from Winchester and Canterbury) include Arius in an illustration. Arius had been condemned in 325 for his teaching about the Trinity (God the Father, Son and Holy Spirit).[148] But these references do not necessarily imply significant problems of belief and teaching about the Trinity. They may simply signify awareness of the Church's patristic tradition and of the general potential for misunderstanding complicated doctrine. Furthermore, in Francia at this time, the accusation of Arianism often implied an attack on ecclesiastical authority or property by the 'heretic'.[149] The English Church likewise experienced and was concerned about losses of property, so this too might explain the references to Arius. We do not know what lies behind the apparent lack of English dissent. But consideration of the absence of a vernacular liturgy underlines the strength of successive West Saxon governments and their deliberate policy of creating an English nation-state whose hallmarks included control as well as Christianity.

All in all, the evidence is rich in its variety though patchy in its distribution. Most of it has a religious dimension, and most of it reveals more, or less or different things from what it might seem to promise at first sight. In coaxing it to give up its secrets, engagement with disciplines other than history is necessary, and the use of different approaches, such as historiographical and comparative ones, can be surprisingly effective.

Notes

1 Keynes and Lapidge.
2 Campbell, 'Asser's'.
3 Lerer.
4 Most recently in Smyth, *King*.
5 Anderson; Gellner. For an argument against the 'modernist' view, and that Christianity and the Church stimulated national identity see Hastings.
6 See Hamerow, Hinton and Crawford for a comprehensive survey of all the archaeological evidence.
7 Loveluck, *Rural*, 'Wealth'.
8 Audouy and Chapman; Boddington.
9 Bruce-Mitford and others.
10 Richards, 'Boundaries, 'Case', *Viking*.
11 Barrett; Woolf, *From*.

12 Barrett.
13 Graham-Campbell and Batey, for this and for archaeology of Scandinavian Scotland generally.
14 Carver, *Portmahomack*. For Pictish archaeology generally, Driscoll, 'Pictish'.
15 Arnold and J.L. Davies; Redknap, 'Viking'.
16 Redknap, *Vikings*.
17 Blackburn, 'Expansion'.
18 Graham-Campbell, 'Northern'.
19 For what follows, see Webster.
20 See Redknap, *Vikings* and 'Early'.
21 Redknap, *Vikings*.
22 Okasha, *Corpus*.
23 S. Turner.
24 Higgitt, 'Words'.
25 Nash-Williams. See also Sims-Williams, 'Five'.
26 Edwards, 'Viking-Age'.
27 Edwards, 'Rethinking'.
28 Translated slightly differently, based on differing reconstructions, in *ibid.* and Higham, *King*.
29 O.W. Jones.
30 Edwards, 'Rethinking'.
31 Higham, *King*.
32 Edwards, 'Celtic', 'Early-Medieval', 'Identifying', 'Monuments'.
33 Neuman de Vegvar.
34 Aitchison.
35 *Ibid.*
36 Driscoll, *Govan*.
37 Woolf, *From*.
38 Gneuss, 'King'.
39 *Ibid.*
40 Wormald, *Making*.
41 Breeze, 'Cornish', 'Cornwall'.
42 Dumville.
43 Giandrea.
44 Brown, *Book*.
45 Karkov, 'Frontispiece', *Ruler*.
46 Deshman.
47 Gittos, 'Is'; Pfaff.
48 W. Davies, *Wales*.
49 Forsyth (ed.).
50 I. Henderson, 'Understanding'; O'Loughlin.
51 Balchin; Padel, 'Place-Names'; Pearce.
52 Abrams and Parsons.
53 See Jennings and Kruse; Sharples and Smith; Woolf, *From*.
54 Redknap, *Vikings*.
55 Townend, *Language*.
56 *Ibid.*
57 *Ibid.*
58 Gneuss, 'Origin'.
59 M. Wood.
60 Gretsch, *Intellectual*.
61 See Crick, 'Edgar'; Keynes, 'Conspectus'.
62 S.D. Thompson.
63 See Dyer, *Making*; Hill, *Atlas*.

64 See e.g. Barrow, 'Chronology … forgery', 'Community'; King; Tinti, *Sustaining*; Wareham, 'St'.
65 For this last, Wormald, 'Charters', 'Handlist'.
66 Dyer, *Making*.
67 A. Reynolds, 'Burials'.
68 See Insley, 'Athelstan'; Pearce.
69 Insley, 'Athelstan'; Padel, *Slavery*.
70 Crick, 'Insular'.
71 *Ibid.*
72 Abrams, *Anglo-Saxon*.
73 Insley, 'Assemblies'; Pearce; S.D. Thompson.
74 Jankulak; Padel, *Slavery*.
75 Crick, 'Women'; Lees and Overing; Whitelock.
76 Helmholz; Wormald, *Making*.
77 S.D. Thompson.
78 Wormald, *Making*.
79 *Ibid.*
80 Foot, *Æthelstan*.
81 Wormald, 'Lex', *Making*.
82 Wormald, 'Archbishop … holiness', 'Archbishop … State-Builder', *Making*.
83 Cubitt, *Anglo-Saxon*; Keynes, *Councils*.
84 Barrow, 'Chronology … Benedictine' suggests earlier than 970.
85 Lapidge, 'Ælfric's'; Wilcox, *Ælfric's*.
86 Upchurch, *Ælfric's*, 'Homiletic'.
87 Tinti, 'England'.
88 Olson and Padel.
89 Toswell; Zacher.
90 Scheil.
91 Conner.
92 Foot, 'When'.
93 Salvador-Bello.
94 Scragg, 'Battle'.
95 S.J. Harris, *Race*.
96 See Schwab.
97 Woolf, *From*.
98 Rauer.
99 Marvin.
100 Damico.
101 See Anlezark.
102 *Ibid.*
103 Cramer.
104 *Ibid.*
105 Anlezark.
106 Dumville.
107 Bedingfield, *Dramatic*; Pfaff.
108 Gittos, 'Is'.
109 Warren and Stevenson.
110 Keynes and Lapidge: 126.
111 Godden and S. Irvine.
112 Lapidge, 'Æthelwold'.
113 Gatch.
114 Lapidge and Winterbottom.
115 Cameron. See also Pollington.
116 Extracts in *EHDI*.

117 Gerchow.
118 Woolf, *From*.
119 Macquarrie, *Saints*.
120 T.O. Clancy, 'Scottish'.
121 Woolf, *From*.
122 T.O. Clancy, 'Scottish'.
123 For a challenge to this view, Charles-Edwards, 'Picts'.
124 Challenged in *ibid.*
125 Hudson, 'Scottish'. See also Aitchison; Woolf, *From*.
126 Woolf, *From*.
127 Hudson, *Prophecy*.
128 T.O. Clancy, *Triumph*.
129 Broun, 'Property'; Forsyth, Broun and T. Clancy; Ó'Maolalaigh.
130 Identified in W. Davies, *Wales*.
131 Higham, *King*.
132 *Ibid.*
133 *Ibid.*; Charles-Edwards, *Wales*.
134 For translations, see J.P. Clancy.
135 W. Davies, *Wales*.
136 Charles-Edwards, *Wales*; Pryce, *Native*; Stacey.
137 W. Davies, *Early, Llandaff*. See also Charles-Edwards, *Wales*.
138 W. Davies, *Wales*.
139 Townend, *Language*.
140 Beckett.
141 Wallace-Hadrill.
142 Rosenwein, *Neighbor*.
143 Foot, *Veiled*.
144 Woolf, *From*.
145 For what follows, with full references, Redgate.
146 Keynes and Lapidge: 126.
147 Lapidge, 'Byzantium'.
148 Raw, *Trinity*.
149 Moore, *War*, www.rimoore.net.

Part II

Beginnings

Identities and communities

3 Kings

Christianity and control

Introduction

In all its aspects, from ideas to personnel, Christianity made important contributions to the creation and expression of political identities and communities. To identify them, we must consider several interrelated questions. One concerns the degree of control that kings had, and aspired to, over territories and people, and the involvement in it of a Christian ideology of kingship and a shared Christian identity. This in turn raises issues of the use of Christian imagery and ritual, such as in royal coronations, to strengthen kings' power, and of royal use of cults of saints and relics, and of pilgrimage. Patronage of particular cults could amount to annexation, of the subjects' lobbyists in Heaven and of the foci of subjects' loyalties, and so strengthen claims to over-lordship. In addition, their deliberate dissemination attempted some cultural unification. A fourth element is royal control of the Church itself.

The legitimation of dynasties or individual rulers was another major concern. This often involved alliance with particular religious groups, for example monastic communities, and promotion of the cults of royal saints. Saints were also used to legitimate war, and to generate national and international prestige. Furthermore, their cults helped to underpin social cohesion and community feeling, at a national as well as at, say, village or family, level, and to raise morale, both generally and in the face of sustained external pressure. For the Welsh, this pressure was predominantly Anglo-Saxon. For others it was Viking.

We have seen that Christian liturgy had political implications and the potential to contribute to a sense of national community. The institution of prayer for English kings encouraged senses of obligation to them and responsibility for their welfare. The *Regularis Concordia*, meant for reformed monasteries throughout Edgar's dominion, though there were none north of the Rivers Severn and Humber even by 1060,[1] gave such prayer special emphasis. The daily prayers it stipulated were not to be rushed, but chanted slowly enough for those chanting to understand them. Prayers for the king were also to be said outside the monastic context, as Aelfric's letter for the parochial clergy of Sherborne shows. The requirement was reiterated in the royal law-codes that Archbishop Wulfstan II worked on.[2] In one of 1009, everyone was to fast on the Monday, Tuesday and

Wednesday before Michaelmas, when, in every minster 'every priest is to say Mass for our lord and for all his people'.[3]

By 1009 such prayer was of quite long standing. The earliest known Anglo-Saxon legal ruling is in one of King Aethelstan's codes. 'Every Friday at every minster all the servants of God are to sing 50 psalms for the king and for all who desire what he desires'.[4] But Aethelstan may have been anticipated some fifty years before, by King Giric, who features, as we have seen, in the (Latin) Dunkeld Litany. Giric is a mysterious figure but may have been an important one. This is how he was remembered in Scotland, in the thirteenth century, as a powerful king who conquered much of England. His reality may, of course, have been more prosaic, raiding the Lothian area.[5] It is possible that it was Carolingian practice of prayer for kings that stimulated the English and northern ones, but they may have been parallel developments. There is nothing analogous in the sources for Wales.

This chapter will consider the mechanisms of royal control. The authoritarianism in the Anglo-Saxon regime, which was noted earlier, is especially visible in its legal tradition and in the representation of kings within it and in other media.

Self-representation and representation

Authorship: self-representation or representation?

To know how kings thought of themselves, their rights and their duties and how kings were represented is not, of course, to know how they were actually perceived throughout society, especially at its lower levels. But it does reveal what kings' subjects were encouraged to think, and how their government perceived and hence might have treated, their subjects. So it is relevant to the study of the world of the peasants as well as to that of the kings and their associates. The one was shaped by the other.

Texts and other media offer us both royal self-representation and the representation of royalty by others. Distinguishing between them is not always straightforward. Central rather than local responsibility certainly lies behind many instances. However, the extent of kings' personal involvement in this varied. Ecclesiastics contributed a great deal. Before analysing the import of royal images, we should consider the question of their authorship.

Excepting coinage, the earliest surviving representation of a king in Britain between 800 and 1066 may be that on the Pictish Dupplin Cross, if it was intended as a portrait (of Constantín I). The king about whose own views we can be most certain is Wessex's Alfred. Through his own work and that of his close associates, which together constitute almost all the textual evidence for his reign, Alfred has largely dictated how he has been perceived and left no doubt about how he wished to be. The knowledge, interests and concerns of the author of the *Anglo-Saxon Chronicle* suggest closeness to Alfred's circle.[6] Asser's biography was probably meant to please him,[7] and it emphasised concern with books, just as Alfred's self-representation did.[8] Furthermore, Asser's allusions to earlier texts gave his audience the means and opportunity to assess Alfred against other authors.[9] This is similar to Alfred's slightly earlier construction, in his *Pastoral Rule* preface, of a textual authority for himself by imitating Augustine's *Soliloquies* and Boethius' *Consolation of Philosophy*. He imitated them by recounting his thoughts as an internal dialogue.[10]

Other kings too have left some, though less personal, personal testimony. Viking rulers whose numerous coins represented them both explicitly and implicitly as Christian had surely approved their design, at least in general terms. The coins of Alfred's erstwhile foe, Guthrum, bore Guthrum's baptismal name (Aethelstan). Viking coinage in East Anglia came to be dominated by coins that honoured its King Edmund, killed by Vikings, as a saint. A little later, between about 905 and 925, coins inscribed as the money of St Peter predominated in the secular coinage of Scandinavian York.[11] Alfred's grandson Aethelstan was significantly involved with his own publicity.[12] Aethelstan had inscriptions and portraits added to manuscripts, both newly made and old, to record his gifts of them to the Church, and he was especially concerned about his coins, which likewise combined inscription and image. Laws about the coinage first appear in his codes. Mints were to be controlled and there was to be only one coinage. Aethelstan's use of different types of coins in different regions may signify a concern for which images circulated where, and hence remarkable awareness of the power of coins as communication. A possible precedent is his paternal aunt Aethelflaed, in Mercia, at whose court he was, probably, brought up.[13] Finally, since in many cases a royal chancery was involved in the production of his charters,[14] their royal titles and ideas must reflect the views and policies at least of his court and perhaps of himself. They would have been approved though not drafted by the king.

Other kings are much more elusive. Behind some of Edgar's charters is a figure termed by scholars 'Edgar A'. Some have thought that this was Bishop Aethelwold of Winchester.[15] Aethelwold is generally agreed to have composed the famous charter of 966 that records Edgar's refoundation, with Aethelwold's help, of Winchester's New Minster in 964. Additionally, in view of his other achievements, intellectual, ecclesiastical and political, it is likely that Aethelwold was the main contributor to the conception of two important pictures that featured Edgar, namely the 966 charter's frontispiece and another, now lost. This other is thought to lie behind the surviving c. 1050 frontispiece to a Canterbury copy of the *Regularis Concordia*.[16] We have already seen that in the law-codes of Edgar's son Aethelred II and his successor Cnut, these kings are the literary mouthpieces of Archbishop Wulfstan II of York. The case of Edgar's grandson, Edward the Confessor, is rather curious. Although, or perhaps because, his mother Emma and the family of his wife Edith had more real power than he did, he was, it has been argued, more concerned with his image, in all its forms, than any previous English king had been. Changes on his coins seem to demonstrate this. The traditional crowned bust in profile was followed by representations of power – the king bearded and helmeted in profile holding a fleur-de-lys in 1053, enthroned with staff and orb in 1056, crowned, jewelled and frontally facing in 1059. Edward apparently commissioned a new crown and, according to his biography, accepted Edith's garbing him with jewels and precious garments and providing gold-ornamented saddle- and horse-trappings that she herself commissioned.[17] Since Edith had commissioned the biography herself, shortly before Edward's death, and its purpose was to secure her position after it, its account of her qualifies as self-representation. The same applies to the *Encomium* and the portrait in its frontispiece, of Edith's mother-in-law Emma, written at Emma's command in 1041–1042. The one surviving copy was probably made for presentation to Emma herself and for a court audience.[18]

Two themes recur in the self-presentation and presentation of kings and queens. First, they were appointed and favoured by God. This could carry implications of the favour of the saints and of the Church, and that it was the duty of Church and people to support them. A consecrated king was the Lord's anointed. Rebellion or violence against him could be held to be sacrilege. Second, their people were equivalent to the Old Testament people of Israel, and the kings themselves to particular figures in biblical and early Christian history. Where the two themes most noticeably overlap and occur together is in the royal coronation ritual.

Divine favour

The anointing of Anglo-Saxon kings began in the first half of the ninth century and became the norm.[19] The ritual prescribed in the (Latin) text which scholars call the First Coronation *Ordo* was probably first used in 838/9, for Alfred's father, Aethelwulf. Some of its elements may be presumed to be Anglo-Saxon creations, meant to meet Anglo-Saxon requirements, since they have no Continental parallels. These original features are that all the *pontifices* (bishops) and *principes* (literally princes) hand the king a sceptre, and place a helmet on his head, the whole people acclaim him three times, and the aforesaid dignitaries kiss him. The coronation is a religious ceremony. That the acclamation is said three times evokes the Christian Trinity and the kiss evokes the kiss of peace in the Mass. The so-called Second *Ordo* survives in a manuscript made for Ratold, abbot of Corbie in Francia, who died in 986. An English source is thought to have been behind it, and most scholars have accepted that this *Ordo* was used in England. There has been disagreement as to when it was introduced, but the case for Aethelstan's coronation in 925 is the strongest. The ritual it describes, also a religious ceremony, with some Frankish elements, differs in some respects from the earlier one. A crown has replaced the helmet as the main item of regalia. Others are a ring, sword and rod. They signify religious and other responsibilities that are explicitly stated: to establish Christianity; to help widows and orphans and to restore things that have been left desolate; to soothe the righteous and terrify the reprobate. There is a prayer that the king remember to honour 'the clergy in due places, so that the mediator between God and men [Christ] may strengthen you as mediator between clergy and people in the throne of this kingdom'. The Virgin Mary, St Peter and Pope Gregory I feature as intercessors for divine protection for the new king. Coronation contributed to royal legitimacy and authority, and probably occurred soon after a king's accession.

It was regularly emphasised that kings enjoyed divine approval and patronage. The statement in the *Anglo-Saxon Chronicle*, for 853, that Alfred was consecrated king by the Pope in Rome, may reflect the young Alfred's misunderstanding of his ceremonial investiture as a Roman consul. It must represent what the adult Alfred wanted to be believed. A set of brief contemporary annals, for 902–924, is known as the Mercian Register or Annals of Aethelflaed, who ruled in Mercia after the death of her husband, Aethelred. They record that she built and took over *burh*s by the grace and with the help of God. Royal titles in charters routinely embody such ideas. Aethelstan's charters in the early 930s, for example, proclaimed him 'elevated by the right hand of the Almighty, which is Christ'.[20] In the *Regularis Concordia* Edgar is termed king by the grace of Christ. The Winchester New Minster's *Liber Vitae*, illuminated in 1031 though its core was probably written in Aethelred II's reign,[21] records pictorially the gift, of King Cnut and Queen Emma, of a gold altar cross. The picture signifies both their appointment by God and their assurance of future salvation.[22] An angel holds a crown over Cnut's head and points with his other hand to Christ. Another holds a veil above Emma. Edward the Confessor is claimed by his biographer to have been proclaimed as king by God, whilst still in Emma's womb.

Word play and timing reiterated points made more explicitly in words and pictures. The Latin for 'the English' was *Angli*, and for 'angels', *angeli*. Pope Gregory I had been reported as saying, to persons who told him that they were Angles, 'Angels of God', a pleasantry which could have been construed as a statement of truth. It must have stimulated the word play and implications of parallels that are detectible in later centuries.[23] For example in the 966 New Minster charter, the angels' creation and fall, and their fellowship are mentioned, as well as Edgar's reform of the Winchester community. Its frontispiece depicts angels as well as Edgar. At the end Edgar is titled king of the Angles. Such word play seems to have been most pronounced with regard to Edward the Confessor. The *Anglo-Saxon Chronicle*'s verse obituary refers to England and claims that its king's soul was taken to Heaven by angels (*englas*).

Kings' links with God were regularly advertised by the juxtaposition of royal events and religious festivals. The coronations of Alfred's son Edward and of Edgar and his wife in 973 (which probably repeated a timely though less grandiose coronation in late 960[24]) were at Pentecost. Pentecost commemorates both God's giving the Ten Commandments to Moses and the descent of the Holy Spirit to the apostles that gave them the gift of tongues. Edward the Confessor's coronation, in 1043, was on Easter Sunday. This was the most important festival of the year, marking the Resurrection of Christ. Coronations were not, of course, frequent events. Assemblies, where business, including law-making, was transacted, were. In the ninth century, Cenwulf of Mercia and Egbert of Wessex began holding assemblies at Christmas (the celebration of the birth of Christ), Easter and Pentecost. Four of the extant twenty-two royal law-codes are associated with these festivals. Of the ninety-nine councils held between 900 and 1066 whose dates are known, twelve were at Easter, two each at Christmas and Pentecost and one on Palm Sunday (a week before Easter, celebrating Christ's arrival in Jerusalem).[25]

Equivalence

The association between Moses, Pentecost and law-making, the liturgy's encouragement of sympathetic identification with biblical figures, and some manuscript illustration are all aspects of the representation and perception of the Anglo-Saxons as a new Israel. It was an all-pervasive theme. Vernacular scriptural poetry generally presents the biblical past in a Germanic light and Anglo-Saxon historical works often had biblical resonances.[26] Examples of the former include the casting of the great Flood (which was survived only by Noah's family and the creatures with them in Noah's Ark) in the battle idiom of heroic poetry, and the Hebrews in *Daniel.* Another is *Exodus'* use of typically Anglo-Saxon imagery in its presentation of the Israelites' exodus from Egypt to the Promised Land. Conversely, in what they thought of and recorded as their own history, the Anglo-Saxons' migration from the Continent to Britain echoes the Israelites' exodus,[27] and the poem about Aethelstan's victory at Brunanburh uses the same language as *Judith* in recounting hunting the enemy.

The biblical image of the chosen people, a nation-state whose king, ideally, was strong and cognisant of God's will, all of whose members should follow the path of righteousness, was inspirational for the West Saxon kings. Alfred's translations show that he believed that royal government should and did have divine guidance.[28] The image of the English in the work of 'Edgar A' is of a holy people, with a good king, part of whose goodness is the securing of his and their salvation.[29] The 966 New Minster charter's text presents its reformed community as a chosen people. Its frontispiece evokes the ceremony of dedication of a church, the rite for which establishes celebrants and congregation as a people, who, as the Israelites did, had a covenant with God.[30] Edgar's final law-code, c. 973, associates the king's will with God's will even more than earlier codes do.[31] In it, Edgar claimed to have realised, by analogy with earthly lords, that continuing failure to pay to God the tribute (church dues) that He was owed would endanger the possessions and life of the defaulters. Hence he commanded that God's dues be paid and that his reeves punish non-payment, the reeves' punishment for non-compliance to be loss of Edgar's friendship and of all their property. Offence against God had become punishable as crime against the king. Conversely, and even more significantly with regard to state-building, crime, an offence against the king, came to be regarded as an outrage against God, liable to provoke His anger.[32] This view was anticipated in Cynewulf's *Elene.* Here the Roman emperor and God have the same title, and resistance to the state and resistance to God are conflated.[33]

Though much more limited, the evidence for Scotland and Wales points towards similar ideas. The Picts and Irish were regarded as descendants of biblical peoples though not of the Israelites. According to Bede, the Picts were from Scythia (in central Asia) and had intermarried with the Irish. According to Nennius, Irish scholars believed the Irish to be descendants of a Scythian nobleman who had married a daughter of the Egyptian Pharaoh at the time of the Israelites' exodus from Egypt. In this tale the Scythian aristocrat seems, from his rectitude and experience, like an honorary Israelite: expelled both from his original home and from Egypt, he did not join the Egyptians' pursuit of the Israelites. Scottia (Ireland) was apparently named after his wife Scotta, the Irish having reached it after forty-two years of wandering through Africa and 960 years of living in Spain. Ninth-century kings were probably inaugurated at Dunning, near Forteviot, but it was at Scone that Constantín II's kingship (c. 900–943) was proclaimed, and validated by his bishop, in 906.[34] The Davidic content of Pictish sculpture may have been meant to signify that the Picts were equivalent to the Israelites. The scene of David dealing with a lion that crops up several times, for example on Constantín I's Dupplin Cross, may be a statement that David's protection of his flock is like the kings' protection of their people.[35]

The Davidic motif is one of a number that recur. The Anglo-Saxons too looked to David, as kingly role model and equivalent. Alfred made subtle changes, in his translation, to the first fifty of the Psalms, which suggest that he identified himself with David, in his capacity as a besieged, wise and teaching king, and wished to encourage others to do likewise.[36] Asser certainly portrays Alfred as a king who was like David.[37] A tenth-century pre-battle prayer for an Anglo-Saxon king asks that his enemies will fall before him like Goliath before David, and one in the Second Coronation *Ordo* entreats God that the new king will have the humility of David. The other commonly invoked Old Testament figure was Moses. This parallel is implicit in the choice of Pentecost as an occasion for law-making, and conspicuous in the battle prayer, *Ordo*, and in Alfred's law-code, finished probably in 893. The code uses both number symbolism and words to signify Alfred's and his people's equivalence with Moses and the Israelites. Its chapters number 120, the age that Moses reached, according to the Bible. Its preface offers a history of law that reads like an intellectual genealogy, beginning with Moses' reception of the Ten Commandments directly from God, and ending with Alfred's own legislative activity.[38] The battle prayer entreats that the king's enemies fall like 'the Pharaoh's people before Moses' and the coronation prayer asks that the king have Moses' meekness. It also hopes for the faithfulness, fortitude and wisdom of Abraham, Joshua and Solomon. These were, respectively, the patriarch with whom God had made His covenant; the military leader who, after Moses' death, had continued the progress to the Promised Land and conquered tribes and cities with divine assistance; and David's son, the archetypal wise and glorious king. Solomon too was one of Alfred's role models, and someone to whom he was compared.[39]

A century earlier, in Gwynedd, Nennius had given the Welsh both a Moses and a Joshua figure in their history. He had stated that (the fourth-century British) Patrick, who had preached to the Irish, was like Moses. He had implied that Arthur was like Joshua, by calling him 'leader of battles', which is reminiscent of the Latin version of the Bible's introduction of Joshua's leadership. Nennius had probably hoped that his work would suggest that Gwynedd's current king might prove to be an Arthur equivalent.[40] Thus in turn might suggest that Welsh kings too were perceived by some contemporaries as equivalent to Old Testament leaders. The thrust of Nennius' message is certainly that British history should be interpreted by reference to the Old Testament: the sinfulness of their fifth-century leader Vortigern had merited God's disfavour and hence caused the defeat of the Britons by the English: but the Britons were not inherently sinful; they had in fact subsequently generated a virtuous and victorious leader, the (invented) Joshua-equivalent Arthur: as it had happened in the past, so it could again.[41]

A likening of king to Christ, stressing Christ as mediator (for humanity with God the Father) and Christ in Majesty in Heaven and as judge, is most marked in the case of the English Edgar, but it was not unprecedented. Nennius had implied that Arthur was Christ-like, by reporting that his victories numbered twelve, since twelve was the number of Christ's disciples. Alfred's history of law interposes Christ and His apostles, as well as Church synods, between Moses and Alfred: all being law-makers they are all implicitly paralleled.[42] Alfred and Christ were also paralleled by Asser and in the Alfred Jewel.[43] Asser seems to have made a mistake in telling a story of Alfred as a child winning from his mother a book of Saxon poetry, which she had promised to whichever of her sons learnt the contents most quickly. The position of this tale in the text, after a reference to Alfred's twelfth year (860), implies that these events occurred then, or later. Yet by 860, Alfred's father and stepmother had been married for four years, his mother presumably dead. The mistake may, however, have been deliberate, to imply that the young Alfred resembled the young Christ. Christ had been twelve when, according to the Gospel of Luke, He conversed with the learned doctors of the Temple in Jerusalem, and told his mother, when she found him there, that he was about his Father's (meaning God's) business.[44] Asser's technique, using a few words to conjure up a biblical image rather than referring to it explicitly, was the same that his compatriot Nennius had used for Arthur and Joshua. The Alfred Jewel may have been making the same point, likewise obliquely. The pose of its figure, Christ, is one associated with judgement, He wears royal robes and He is a visual reminder of Alfred's order to read the book with which the jewel was associated. The jewel fuses wise ruler, Christ and Alfred.[45]

In Edgar's reign kingship's Christ-like element appears developed and very pronounced. In the 966 New Minster charter's frontispiece, some elements have resonances of Christ's Ascension to Heaven, and Edgar appears as mediator between Heaven and earth. That the king is bigger than Mary and Peter and indeed Christ is not artistic clumsiness but a statement of his role and status. The purple of the background symbolises both kingship and Christ's sacrificial blood.[46] The manuscript was probably displayed, open at the picture, upon the church's altar, where, of course, the offering of Christ's body and blood was made when the Eucharist was celebrated.[47] The Christ–Edgar equation is obvious too in one version of the *Anglo-Saxon Chronicle*'s account of the 973 coronation. This stresses that Edgar was in his thirtieth year. Thirty was the canonical age for ordination to the priesthood, because Christ, according to Luke, began his ministry when He was about thirty. Other versions of the *Chronicle* recount the coronation in verse, probably roughly contemporary. This equates Christ and Edgar by using ambiguous earthly/heavenly terms for both.[48]

These representations of Edgar's coronation have close links with Aethelwold's Benedictional. Here Aethelwold made Christ, as also St Benedict, seem like kings, making them appear to be exemplars for Edgar, and thereby legitimating Edgar's authority over the reformed, monasticised, Church. Aethelwold did the same for Edgar's queen and her supervision of nunneries, using St Aethelthryth and the Virgin Mary as her models.[49] Mary was characterised as Queen of Heaven, and Marian iconography was used in reference to the queen. The Mary–queen equation is also noticeable in the later case of Emma.[50] Emma heads the lists, in its *Liber Vitae*, of people that the New Minster community would pray for. This may have been due to her association with Mary, one of its patron saints. Emma's *Encomium* presents her son Alfred, who had died after being captured by Earl Godwine in 1036–1037, as a martyr, thereby implicitly paralleling Alfred and Emma, as grieving mother, with Christ and Mary, and its frontispiece uses maternal Marian imagery.[51]

Royal role models, equivalents and reference points were not limited to biblical figures. It was not their historical reality that was influential of course, but how they were perceived. The first Christian Roman emperor, Constantine I, was an important referent. In Scotland the Dupplin Cross represents King Constantín I holding a banner of Christ, evoking his namesake's vision that he would conquer using the sign of the cross and the fact that he did.[52] King Constantín II is recorded as having legislated for the Church and this too was to follow the example set by the emperor. The name Constantín was frequently used in Cinaed mac Alpín's family.[53]

Rome was very important to Alfred of Wessex.[54] Most of the texts in his literary programme were connected with Rome, through their content or authorship.[55] In a series of new coin types, he copied directly from Roman coin prototypes.[56] Most strikingly, he applied to his own kingship the teaching of Pope Gregory I. Gregory's importance is also apparent from Asser's biography, which not only portrays Alfred as becoming in stages a ruler on the Gregorian model but also implies a personal similarity. Asser's references to Alfred's ill-health are reminiscent of Gregory's own lamentations. Each had to cope with both illness and invaders.[57] The suggestion that the role of king is equivalent to that of certain ecclesiastics was repeated for Edgar, in the presentation of his authority as similar to that of abbots and bishops.[58]

Characteristics and attributes

The ideal of kingship emphasised piety. This could take very different forms, including Edward the Confessor's virginity, Edgar's enthusiasm for monastic reform, and Alfred's Gregorianism, and wisdom. Other desirable qualities were expertise in hunting, concern with books, generosity, wealth, having international contacts, and maintaining peace.

That the king was pious is explicitly suggested in various representations, as we have already seen. In 1052, according to a twelfth-century source, there was an attempt to establish Edgar as a saint. His grave, in Glastonbury, was opened by

Glastonbury's abbot. His body was found to be incorrupt, which was taken as a sign of sanctity. A cult resulted, but remained very local.[59] In Edward the Confessor's biography, piety is the dominant motif. His marriage was holy in its celibacy, and this gave Queen Edith too a saintly aspect. Wisdom was an integral element of Gregorian rulership and has been termed one of Alfred's voices. It recurs in the Alfred Jewel, Asser's biography, Alfred's *Pastoral Rule* preface and most markedly in the choice of Boethius' *Consolation of Philosophy* for translation and in its translator's changing Boethius' female personification of philosophy to a male one.[60]

Both Alfred and Asser connected wisdom to hunting, which in eastern Christendom certainly and Pictland probably had royal and religious overtones. The Alfredian Boethius and *Pastoral Rule* use hunting imagery in connection with intellectual discovery and the search for wisdom. Asser described Alfred as an enthusiastic huntsman who worked to incomparable effect in every branch of hunting. The positioning of this claim in an account of Alfred's education in texts and literacy implies that Asser had learning and kingship as well as animal life in mind as Alfred's prey.[61] Both symbolically and in actuality hunting was an important aspect of kingship. It offered proof of kings' and their followers' ability and virtue, provided practice for war, and required and demonstrated leadership and co-operation. This must be why Asser emphasised that Alfred pursued all manner of hunting whatever concerns and distractions he had to deal with and included hunting in the education of his children. In this last Alfred followed Charlemagne's example.[62]

In Edward the Confessor's reign, the image of the enthroned king, and the symbols of sword and sceptre, became important in royal representation.[63] Before then, beginning in Alfred's reign, a common motif was an intimate association with books, mostly overtly Christian ones, as both texts and artefacts.[64] This was not a motif copied from the Continent, but original. Its deliberate novelty suggests that it was important. Alfred appears as reader, writer, translator and distributor of books, and as encouraging reading. Aethelstan's surviving and lost portraits showed him presenting a book (Bede's prose and verse accounts of St Cuthbert and a Gospel Book respectively), as a record of his donations to the community of St Cuthbert. Edgar is recorded, by Aethelwold, as requesting his translation of the Benedictine *Rule*, is depicted in the 966 New Minster charter frontispiece holding it, and, in the Canterbury *Regularis Concordia* manuscript, holding jointly with Dunstan and Aethelwold a scroll that represents its text, for whose composition Edgar, as king, was responsible. Emma is shown in the frontispiece of her *Encomium* receiving the book, which she herself had commissioned and which, as it were, states her case.

Generosity to the Church was thought to be desirable in kings. Asser exaggerated Alfred's, saying that half of his annual disposable income was reserved for God, when in fact it was one-eighth.[65] His gifts to the Church in his will, and his endowment of two religious houses, at Shaftesbury and Athelney, were limited. Gifts were normally represented as items rather than lands, a famous exception being the 'Decimations' of Alfred's father, King Aethelwulf of Wessex. According to the *Anglo-Saxon Chronicle*, in 855 Aethelwulf granted by charter one-tenth of his land throughout his kingdom to the praise of God and his own salvation. What exactly this meant has been debated.[66] It need not have been a gift of lands. It may have granted freedom from taxation and royal service; or converted royal land into royally possessed bookland, that is, land that could be given away; or granted bookland to thegns, so that, and perhaps on the understanding that, they could subsequently bequeath it to religious houses.

Generosity displays and implies wealth, another ideal royal attribute. Treasure, including precious clothing, was used as gifts and rewards, to establish a social hierarchy. It also signalled the status of a royal household, with valuable table-ware for the feasts where alliances were made and social cohesion generated.[67] According to Asser, Alfred's activities even in wartime included instructing his goldsmiths and craftsmen. The same was probably true later. Aethelstan's gifts to St Cuthbert's community are reported to have included items of ecclesiastical attire – a stole, maniple and girdle. Three such items, probably these very gifts, were found when Cuthbert's tomb was opened in the nineteenth century. Apart from tiny fragments, they are the only surviving embroidered textiles that are certainly Anglo-Saxon. They must have been very costly to produce, in both time and money. Gold thread, that is, silk thread with gold wound around it, was used in the embroidery. Two of them have an embroidered inscription, stating that 'Aelfflaed had [this] made' 'for the pious bishop Frithestan'. They may never have reached him. Aelfflaed was probably the Aelfflaed who was the second wife of King Edward the Elder.[68] A king might suggest his wealth through his personal appearance. Edward's namesake, the Confessor, was decked by his wife with gold and jewels so that, apparently, not even Solomon was thus arrayed.[69]

The most striking aspects of the presentation of kings all had an overtly religious dimension. Some others did not, though they were not necessarily unconnected with religion. One of these is international contacts. Asser refers to foreign visitors of all races at Alfred's court, and lists Franks, Frisians, Gauls, Vikings, Welshmen, Irishmen and Bretons. Aethelstan seems to have perceived himself, and been perceived by western Continental contemporaries, as a member of the Carolingian dynasty, partly because of his involvement in their politics and his numerous Continental marriage alliances and kinship links.[70] In a letter of 1027 Cnut informed the people of England of his international prestige and contacts by way of reporting that he had been well received by the Pope and emperor and various princes at an assembly in Rome. On the other hand, Archbishop Wulf-stan II's obituary for Edgar, in the D Version of the *Anglo-Saxon Chronicle* under Edgar's accession year, 959, contains a negative criticism: Edgar loved evil foreign customs, imported heathen manners and attracted foreigners and harmful people to England. This has been explained as referring to an un- or ill-attested hiring of Scandinavian mercenaries and favouring of Scandinavian merchants. Some of Edgar's moneyers in York had Scandinavian names.[71] Peace was represented as one of Edgar's greatest achievements. Cnut too was represented as a king who bestowed peace. The preface to his 1018 law-code stresses that permanent peace had been established between English and Danes, and in a 1019–1020 letter

Cnut explains his absence in Denmark on the grounds of removing a potential foreign threat to peace and security. Both kings secured peace by might. In his portrait, Cnut wears a sword.[72]

There is, finally, the question of the importance for kings of association with particular Christian sites. Repton was important for Mercia. The royal mausoleum was there. The Viking army's use of it in the 870s has been interpreted as a political statement, perhaps a legitimation, of its conquest.[73] For the West Saxons, association with Winchester was important though not consistently so. Most of the known burials of their kings before 800 were there, in its cathedral church, the Old Minster.[74] In 901 Edward the Elder founded the adjacent New Minster, whither he had Alfred's remains moved and had Alfred's Mercian wife Ealhswith buried (902). This was perhaps to symbolise the new, united, kingdom that Alfred had created from Wessex and Mercia.[75] It was twice as long as the bishop's church, the Old Minster. Edward joined them, in 924, and his son Aelfweard too. Aethelstan, however, preferred Malmesbury, where he had two of his cousins buried and was interred himself. His half-brother and successor Edmund was buried at Glastonbury. Behind this lack of consistency might lie family rivalries and differing relationships with the leaders of the churches concerned.[76] The New Minster nevertheless retained and resumed importance. Edmund's son King Eadwig (955–959) was buried there.

Winchester's ecclesiastical community was more thoroughly integrated when the west-work was added to the Old Minster between 974 and 980. It may have incorporated a royal throne. If so, the king would have faced the bishop, whose throne was in the east end. The west end itself faced the royal palace and, built over the cemetery that contained royal burials, thereby incorporated them.[77] The symbolic importance of Winchester is suggested too by Edward the Confessor's biography, which seems to appropriate it for Edith and her family. It omits Edward's own patronage but exaggerates that of his in-laws, and sets Edward's coronation not, as the *Anglo-Saxon Chronicle* reports, at Winchester, but in Canterbury.[78]

Strong kingship and control of the Church

The strength of late-ninth-century and tenth-century Anglo-Saxon royal government sometimes involved exploitation of the Church, though to think in terms of Church and State is anachronistic. Contemporaries thought of one Christian society in which different people had different tasks and responsibilities, in whose discharge, of course, they might disagree. When Alfred reflected on the three orders of society, those who fought, prayed and laboured, he put the king above, and outside, them all. Aelfric, later, did the same. Kings were at the head of society, almost a fourth order.[79] Alfred took upon himself the revitalisation of minster life, as well as of learning, and the instruction of bishops. In pursuit of these aims he recruited foreign ecclesiastics. In Edgar's reign, the monastic reformation was both an act of state, for the whole kingdom, and an instrument of it. It has been seen as an alliance of king and monks against the aristocracy, whose grip had been tightening on two sorts of estates.[80] One was minster land, which lay aristocrats controlled through their relatives who were heads of religious houses. The other was land that was supposed to support royal appointees to administrative posts and subsequently revert to the king. The reform ended hereditary abbacies and ensured a supply, for the royal administration, of competent monks whose calling and celibacy meant that the lands associated with their posts were likely to be returned.

However, the reformation's reach into the north was certainly limited and in the far south-west never reached beyond Tavistock and Exeter. The extent of royal control there is debatable. In the early ninth century the Cornish were still independent, but in 838, though allied with Vikings, they were defeated by Egbert of Wessex. The *Welsh Annals*' reference to Dungarth, king of Cornwall, in 875, suggests that some native kings continued, but the word used there for Cornwall may really mean south-west Wales.[81] The Burghal Hidage, which relates to Alfred's building and fortifying *burh*s for defence, does not include anywhere in Cornwall, but Cornish estates may have contributed to the costs of *burh*s in Devon.[82] Royal itinerations did include Cornwall in the tenth century: Edmund, Edgar and Aethelred II attested manumissions in the Bodmin Gospels. The hundred system likewise seems to be attested there. Two of the manumissions refer to a hundredsman, meaning, presumably, the headman of the hundred. The system may have been indigenous, rooted in folk-regions, or alternatively been deliberately organised and artificially imposed. The evidence is very scanty indeed, but two facts may suggest the latter. Two of the post-Conquest Stratton hundred's three subdivisions (Trigg and Lesnewth) each had about 100 settlements with *tre* place-names. The district of Kerrier had approximately 228 and so looks like a double hundred. Such neat distribution seems unlikely to have arisen naturally.[83]

As for the Cornish Church, a high proportion of its estates are recorded in Domesday Book as exempt from tax, while Cornish estates owned by English ecclesiastical landowners were not exempt. This suggests that in many cases the Anglo-Saxons had allowed their original owners to retain their lands. On the other hand, the estates of St Keverne and St Neot were certainly broken up in the tenth century. St Neot owned only 3 hides in 1066, having lost lands after Fawton was established as centre of the hundred. The Cornish churches' increased use of crosses and inscribed stones as boundary markers suggests that there was felt to be a new danger to their estates, from land-hungry neighbours, and a need to fight it.[84] The same applies to inscribed Welsh stones.

In Wales, Christianity seems less to have increased Welsh kings' control than to have facilitated control over them, by Welsh ecclesiastics and by the Anglo-Saxons. War, as opposed to raiding, against the Anglo-Saxons, declined overall, though it resumed in the mid-eleventh century. The southern Welsh kingdoms sought Alfred's protection against Gwynedd. Anarawd of Gwynedd abandoned his alliance with the Viking kingdom of York and had Alfred as his sponsor at his confirmation, thereby establishing a spiritual son–father relationship with him. Asser represented these events as complete submission to Alfred. Welsh kings witnessed some of Aethelstan's charters. Intellectually, however, the

Welsh held their own. Asser was not the only Welshman to contribute to Anglo-Saxon scholarship. The 'Liber Commonei' (a sort of intellectual scrapbook), in the manuscript known as (Archbishop) Saint Dunstan's Classbook, is of Welsh origin. Written (at some time between 817 and 835) mainly by one scribe, with glosses in Old Welsh and notes in both that and Latin, it contains some Latin and some Greek items, computistical, alphabetical, exegetical, biblical and liturgical material. Another section, also with Latin and Welsh glosses, comprises Book 1 of the *Ars Amatoria* (The Art of Love) of the Roman poet Ovid (43 BC–AD 18). Most of this was penned by a Welsh scribe, but its final twenty-six lines were by Dunstan himself.

Unlike their Anglo-Saxon counterparts, Welsh kings seem not to have had control over the Church, either in theory or in practice, not to have legislated for its benefit and not to have been exalted by it. The law-code of Hywel Dda, insofar as it is recoverable, does show some signs of English influence, in some names and regarding distribution of compensation for homicide.[85] Of course, the lack of texts indicative of royal powers does not in itself mean that such powers were lacking. But some evidence suggests that royal power was actually limited, even controlled, by the Church. Welsh kings did not constitute a fourth order of society. Whilst Aethelstan headed lists of witnesses to his charters, charters in south-east Wales put their king at the head of the lay witnesses, after the ecclesiastical ones.[86] The Llandaff charters contain instances of kings being held responsible if members of their households violated the sanctuary of ecclesiastical territory. In law, proprietors had a right to protect people on their land, and during the tenth century this seems to have turned into a right of exemption from political dues and demands and of exclusion of royal officials. Anyone who breached this right thereby insulted the proprietor. The financial penalty could be considerable. A charter of c. 905 records that for an unspecified insult to the bishop, King Brochfael, who was responsible, should compensate the bishop in gold. Llandaff, probably while Bishop Joseph was in office, 1022–1045, claimed that it had the right of private jurisdiction within its lands and exemption from demands of king and royal officers (military service, tax and distraint, which was seizure of property in default of payments that were owed).[87] Finally, positions in the Welsh Church and churches themselves were hereditary, which meant both that royal influence, through patronage, was limited, and that churchmen, and houses, could build powerbases that rivalled those of kings.[88]

As in Anglo-Saxon England so in the Christian north strong kingship and unification involved a relationship with the Church.[89] If there was indeed a change in the character of royal sites, this might suggest that the king–Church relationship became closer too, in more than just physical proximity. Davidic royal imagery in ecclesiastically produced sculpture suggests both a general rapprochement regarding the meaning of kingship and co-operation in particular instances. Constantín I, praised in *The Prophecy of Berchán*, probably founded Dunkeld, but Cinaed mac Alpín strengthened it and made it into a religious capital. The Dunkeld Litany suggests an ecclesiastical alliance with Giric, being something that could engender loyalty and obtain divine favour for him. Constantín II made St

Andrews the centre of religious power instead of Dunkeld, and at Scone in 905 or 906 he somehow reformed the Church at a meeting, and presumably as part of an agreement, with Bishop Cellach. Each, apparently, swore to keep the laws and disciplines of the faith and the rights of the Church and Gospels along with, or in, the manner of the Irish, a problematic phrase that has prompted different interpretations.

The decline of the former church-settlements was probably due partly and directly, and possibly also indirectly, to the Viking threat. A likely royal response to both was to appropriate church lands, to endow military men, as Alfred of Wessex and his successors did. Céli Dé (Friends of God) imagery on the ninth- or tenth-century Dunkeld slab suggests that there was a Céli Dé community there then. The Céli Dé were celibate ascetics in Ireland, Wales and Scotland. It is possible that the kings were favouring them in return for greater freedom to exploit churches' wealth.[90] In Alba and Anglo-Saxon England, it is likely that lands of absent or defunct religious communities could have been seized without them protesting or the despoiler offering any excuse. A thriving house too could be despoiled, legally, by, for example, forcing it to loan land, in a theoretically temporary land grant, to the king's nominees, or to exchange lands, or by confiscating an estate as a fine or compensation for some alleged misdemeanour or default. Alfred almost certainly despoiled the Church.[91] One charter records that he gave some land that belonged to Malmesbury to one of his thegns. This was purportedly with Malmesbury's consent and on condition that the property would revert to Malmesbury.[92] He was stigmatised in a twelfth-century Abingdon chronicle as like Judas (who betrayed Christ), because he had seized the vill in which Abingdon's minster was situated. Many of the lands mentioned in his will are thought to be former minster sites.[93] By the tenth century much that had belonged to Kentish royal minsters was part of Wessex's royal estate. The appropriated properties probably included some that had belonged to minsters associated with rival lineages within his dynasty.[94]

Alfred's successors continued in the same vein.[95] Edward ensured an income for his New Minster by forcing the bishop of Winchester to lease some cathedral lands to him to fund it. In its agreement the cathedral community pleaded that Edward ask for no more of their lands.[96] Another example is Evesham's loss of lands around 940. Given to a 'wicked prince' and passing subsequently to a layman and to the bishop of Ramsbury, they were recovered at a 969 synod. In Aethelred II's reign, alienation of ecclesiastical estates, directly by the king or with his approval, may have been indirectly caused by renewed Viking pressure. Around 1000, for example, the bishop of Sherborne lost an estate to Ealdorman Eadric in payment of a debt that he owed for defence. But some losses may have been part of a backlash against Edgar's strictness. In the 990s Aethelred complained in charters that false councillors had taken advantage of his youth and inexperience and thereby obtained from him lands that rightly belonged to churches. One of these was the episcopal church of Rochester, whose diocese, according to the *Anglo-Saxon Chronicle*, Aethelred had laid waste in 986 and whose bishop disappears from the charter record between 984 and 987. Aethelred attempted to restore alienated property or some of it. Rochester for example recovered lands in Kent in 995.[97] But by the eleventh century some of the wealthiest thegns held lands that had once belonged to minsters, and in the cases of Deerhurst and Shrewsbury, it is clear that the communities were not defunct when they were deprived of their property.[98] Deerhurst minster had a long history: founded in the eighth century but first referred to in 804, it was a community of secular clerks in the eleventh. Whether it had been, temporarily, reformed in the tenth is unknown.

Where kings were strong their power was underpinned by the Church and its ideological and economic resources. The concept of the ideal king had Christian elements and biblical resonances and the image of the real king was in most cases shaped and propagated by ecclesiastics, directly or indirectly. Strong kings did not impoverish themselves when rewarding their followers with lands but used the Church's estates instead. In England, the king was at the head of society and could deal with the Church as a department of state. Whether this was true in Scotland is unclear, but it was not in Wales.

Notes

1 Hill, *Atlas.*
2 Barrow, 'Clergy'.
3 *EHDI*: 410.
4 *EHDI*: 387.
5 Woolf, *From.*
6 Scharer.
7 Campbell, 'Asser's'.
8 Karkov, *Ruler.*
9 Lerer.
10 *Ibid.*
11 Blackburn, 'Expansion'.
12 Karkov, *Ruler.*
13 Foot, *Æthelstan*, 'When'; Karkov, *Ruler.*
14 Foot, *Æthelstan*; S.D. Thompson.
15 See Keynes, 'Edgar'.
16 Karkov, *Ruler.*
17 *Ibid.*
18 *Ibid.*
19 For what follows, Nelson, 'First'; also Wormald, *Making.*
20 Foot, *Æthelstan*, 'When'.
21 Keynes, '*Liber*'.
22 Karkov, *Ruler.*
23 *Ibid.*
24 *Ibid.*
25 Wormald, *Making.*
26 Howe, *Migration.*
27 *Ibid.*
28 Pratt, *Political.*
29 Keynes, 'Edgar'.
30 Karkov, 'Frontispiece'.
31 Karkov, *Ruler.*

32 Wormald, *Making*.
33 Damon.
34 Woolf, *From*.
35 G. Henderson and I. Henderson; I. Henderson, 'David'; Woolf, *From*.
36 Keynes and Lapidge; Stanton.
37 Karkov, *Ruler*.
38 Wormald, *Making*.
39 Kempshall; Scharer.
40 Higham, *King*.
41 *Ibid.*
42 Karkov, *Ruler*.
43 *Ibid.*
44 *Ibid.*
45 *Ibid.*
46 Karkov, 'Frontispiece'.
47 *Ibid.*
48 Salvador-Bello.
49 Deshman.
50 Karkov, *Ruler*.
51 *Ibid.*
52 G. Henderson and I. Henderson.
53 Woolf, *From*.
54 S. Irvine.
55 Howe, 'Rome'.
56 Blackburn, 'Alfred's'; Karkov, *Ruler*; Kempshall.
57 Campbell, 'Asser's'.
58 Karkov, 'Frontispiece', *Ruler*.
59 Karkov, *Ruler*.
60 Karkov, *Ruler*; Lerer.
61 Karkov, *Ruler*; Lerer; Marvin.
62 Marvin.
63 Karkov, *Ruler*.
64 For what follows, *ibid.*
65 Wormald, '*On*'.
66 Abrams, *Anglo-Saxon*.
67 Hardt.
68 Coatsworth.
69 Karkov, *Ruler*.
70 Foot, 'Dynastic'; Ortenberg.
71 Abrams, 'King'; Keynes, 'Edgar'.
72 Karkov, *Ruler*.
73 Biddle and Kjølbye-Biddle; Richards, 'Case', 'Boundaries'.
74 Thacker, 'Dynastic'.
75 Keynes, 'Edward'.
76 Thacker, 'Dynastic'; Yorke, *Nunneries*.
77 Karkov, *Ruler*.
78 *Ibid.*
79 Damon; T.E. Powell.
80 John, 'King'.
81 Pearce.
82 *Ibid.*
83 *Ibid.*; S. Turner.
84 S. Turner. See also Insley, 'Aethelstan'.
85 Charles-Edwards, *Wales*.

86 *Ibid.*
87 W. Davies, 'Adding', *Early, Wales.*
88 W. David, *Wales.*
89 For what follows, Woolf, *From.*
90 *Ibid.*
91 Fleming, 'Monastic'.
92 Blair, *Church.*
93 Yorke, *Nunneries.*
94 Thacker, 'Dynastic'.
95 Blair, *Church.*
96 Rumble, 'Edward'.
97 A. Williams, *Æthelred.*
98 A. Williams, 'Thegnly'.

4 Kings

Christianity and acceptance

Unification

Conversion of the Vikings

As the fate of some ecclesiastical lands, described at the end of the last chapter, shows, Vikings offered opportunities as well as a threat to kings. Some fell. Others, as Alfred, profited both from the Vikings' elimination of their rivals and from proclaiming themselves victors over ferocious pagans, defenders of Christians and the faith, favoured by God. It is a measure of the West Saxon kings' grasp of this opportunity that their ninth- and tenth-century acquisition of Scandinavian-held territories, namely Mercia, East Anglia and Northumbria, has often been referred to as a reconquest, from Scandinavians. Since the original ninth-century rulers of these territories had been independent kings, and their people no more desirous than those of Cornwall to be subject to Wessex, the West Saxon take-over was in fact a second conquest.

One method of dealing with Scandinavians, both effective in itself and befitting kings' Christian images, was to convert them to Christianity. In England, this seems to have been effected by the second quarter of the tenth century.[1] Indeed, Viking coinage and rapid adoption of indigenous burial practice suggest conversion by around 900.[2] In northern and midland England enthusiasm for it was manifested in a flourishing of religious sculpture. This was not a Scandinavian tradition, and there are more sites with such sculpture and many more pieces than in the preceding period.[3]

Unfortunately, except for references in the *Anglo-Saxon Chronicle* to royal baptisms, the evidence for methods, speed, ease, sincerity, understanding and adoption of Christian practices in this conversion is of the very slightest. Its explanation, though much discussed, is therefore elusive. But explanation in terms of a generalised Christian influence exerted by indigenous inhabitants on newcomers, or of co-operation by local clergy with new rulers, is very unlikely to be correct.[4] Debate about the Vikings' effects on the Church continues, but there are many indications that institutionalised Christianity suffered greatly in the territories that they conquered. Minsters' losses of estates were more marked there than in Wessex, though some such lands may have been leased rather than lost.[5]

The great minsters ceased to be, and books and charters were lost on a large scale. In the north, one of the three Anglo-Saxon bishoprics, Hexham, disappeared in the 820s and the British Whithorn lapsed in the 830s. The latter may have had a bishop again by the tenth century,[6] or may not have been restored until the twelfth. In Mercia and East Anglia, the sees of Leicester, Dunwich, Elmham and Lindsey disappeared between 869 and 888, though Elmham and Lindsey were revived in the tenth century. London was vacant c. 867–897. Scandinavian confiscation (for settlement) of churches' lands would have deprived them of economic resources, imperilling their effectiveness.[7]

Conversion of the newcomers, even if only partial and temporary, would have required significant effort. For Christianity cannot initially have seemed attractive to them, whatever the strength and self-consciousness of Viking paganism in England. The introduction of Christianity to non-Christian societies has historically and recurrently posed problems and encountered difficulties in every aspect of their lives: it is not just that, as it were, the package as a whole has been problematic, but that every component of it has been. Christianity offered a significant culture-shock.[8] Emphasis on a single god; complex doctrine (for example about the nature of Christ, both human and divine); the stress on personal belief and individual responsibility (instead of behaviour and group responsibility); and the rejection of images were alien to many societies. Conversion provoked fear of being punished by the rejected gods, who were thought to be demons rather than figments of the imagination. It entailed disloyalty to ancestors. Besides intellectual and psychological difficulties, there were lifestyle differences. Christian rules about sex and marriage limited the creation and reinforcement of political and economic alliances, from village to kingly levels. The Christian calendar, with obligatory church attendance, festivals and fasting, was disruptive of agriculture, whose rhythms and patterns of work were quite different. Traditional mourning customs were decried because they were associated with worship of the spirits of the dead. Minstrels, the publicists and the guardians of memory and identity in societies whose culture was more oral than written, were disapproved of because of their association with funerals and banquets (and hence drunkenness and sexual licence) and their tales of pagan gods. Finally, conversion often had political disadvantages, implying or involving subordination to a foreign power or a despised subjugated group.

Almost all of these reasons for resisting conversion must have applied to the Scandinavians. It must have been necessary to convince them, as it has been other potential converts, of Christianity's advantages. Historically, these have outweighed its drawbacks, and ultimately explain conversions. It is sometimes thought that Christianity offered more satisfying explanations than paganism did to the questions 'why are we here?' and 'what is it all for?', and that its teaching of eternal life after death was attractive. Its historical associations with cultures that had superior knowledge and technology meant that it promised greater control of the natural world, for example in more productive agriculture and better health. As a book-based religion it entailed writing and literacy, which brought more control and profit in government and administration. And a shared Christianity could lessen tensions between different groups within a society, give rulers greater prestige on the international stage, and, as we have seen, strengthen kings.

It is difficult to imagine a continuing presence, over several decades, of local clergy and vibrant congregations in Scandinavian England, who, despite being deprived of resources and cut off from the Church in non-Scandinavian England, nevertheless had sufficient manpower and vigour to accomplish the Vikings' conversion. The impulse more probably came from outside. That it was not episcopal initiative is suggested by a rebuke of Pope Formosus (891–896), in a letter addressed to the bishops of England. They had kept silent, he complained, against 'the abominable rites of the pagans' and had only recently 'at length awakened' to renew Christianity.[9]

What is clear is that conversion was a royal policy, espoused by Alfred and regarded later as one that should be pursued, even if churchmen did not always agree. The *Anglo-Saxon Chronicle* represents Wessex's wars against the Vikings as wars of Christians against pagans. King Edmund of East Anglia, killed by Vikings in 869, was represented in the tenth century as having, unsuccessfully, offered his submission to the Vikings in return for their conversion.[10] Alfred's victory over the Vikings at the battle of Edington in 878 was followed by the baptism of the Viking king, Guthrum, with Alfred as his godfather, or sponsor. A twelfth-century tradition about St Edith of Polesworth, probably the sister of King Aethelstan who married King Sihtric of York in 926, held that Aethelstan made Sihtric's conversion a condition of their marriage. The catechumenate (training and instruction in Christianity before baptism or admission to Communion) was revived, to deal with Vikings. This was an indigenous development, neither stimulated nor paralleled by Continental practice. So was the creation of sponsorship at the catechumenate and at confirmation. Like god-parenthood, this created spiritual kinship, which was thought to be as binding as blood kinship.[11] In 943, King Edmund sponsored King Olaf (Óláfr) of York at his baptism and King Raegnald (Rögnvaldr) at his confirmation. He drove them both out in 944.

Similarly, during the second wave of Viking aggression that began in the 980s, Aethelred II, after several years of defeats, sponsored King Olaf at his confirmation, in 994, after paying him £16,000 for peace. All this, plus gifts, gained Olaf's promise, never to return to England in hostility, which he kept. There are, however, hints that there was disagreement about this strategy of tribute and conversion instead of continuing resistance. A major theme of Aelfric's *Lives of the Saints* was that defensive warfare was justified.[12] He felt that those whom God had placed in the social order of those who fight should do exactly that. And if Cynewulf's poems date to the later tenth century, then *Elene*'s treatment of the Emperor Constantine's defensive war against invading pagans is in part a contribution to the debate. It presents defensive war as divinely blessed and in some sense holy.[13]

As for the conversion of Vikings in Scotland, the 130 or so burials that are regarded as pagan Scandinavian seem to date to the years 850–950, and Scandinavian Christian sculpture appears around 1000. This suggests significant conversion in the mid-tenth century.[14] We can only guess how it came about.

Saints' cults

It is likely that Christian kings in Scotland took an interest in Viking conversion, for there had been some ninth-century attempts to unify the Christian regions by sharing saints' cults. A Dál Riatan saint, Constantine, was imported into Strathclyde.[15] The lost *Life* of the Strathclyde saint Kentigern tried to connect Kentigern with saints Serf and Columba, whose associations lay north of the Forth.[16] As Dál Riatan saint and apostle of the Picts, Columba was a particularly appropriate saint for a united Pictland and (Scottish) Dál Riata and his cult was promoted by its kings. The doves on the Pictish Constantín I's Dupplin Cross were probably references to it, the Latin for dove being *columba*.[17] In 849, some of Columba's relics were transferred from Iona to Dunkeld, where Cinaed mac Alpín had built a church for them, the rest going to Kells in Ireland. The first person known to bear the name Mael Coluim, which means devotee of Columba, was the king who was born probably 889–900 and ruled 943–954.[18]

In England, West Saxon rulers between Alfred and Edgar nurtured, and associated themselves with, Mercian cults, and those of the seventh-century Northumbrian King Oswald and Bishop Cuthbert. Oswald's had a Mercian dimension too. He had been slain by Mercia's pagan King Penda, in 641, and his bones had been moved by Mercia's queen, his own niece, to Bardney in Lindsey, which was subordinate to Mercia, in c. 679. His cult had been favoured by King Offa. More generally, Oswald was a figure of over-lordship and unification. In Bede's pages he had dominion over all the nations and provinces of Britain, and he was a model king. In 909, Lindsey, then held by the Danes, was ravaged by a West Saxon and Mercian army, and Oswald's bones taken to Gloucester, to a church built some ten years earlier by King Edward the Elder's sister, Aethelflaed, with whom he worked closely, and her Mercian husband. Oswald was added to its dedication, which originally had been to St Peter. This transfer symbolised the West Saxon regime's rescue of Oswald from the heathens, and implied that Oswald, reciprocally, would protect it. Athelflaed also established Mercian cults in the *burh*s whose foundation, along their north-west frontier, was part of her and Edward's military strategy. Thus in 907 relics of St Werburh were moved from Hanbury to Chester.[19]

King Aethelstan continued this approach. He too was a patron of St Oswald's, Gloucester. Surviving grave-covers there may have been commissioned by him, for his aunt's and uncle's graves.[20] More remarkably, he harnessed Cuthbert, who had likewise been presented by Bede as an exemplary and a unifying figure,[21] and his community at Chester-le-Street, which was one of the richest, most powerful and influential religious communities, as saint and support for the whole of his dominion. Aethelstan presented himself as Cuthbert's devotee, worthy, because of his generosity to them, of Cuthbert's and his community's support. When he visited Chester-le-Street in 934, on his way to Scotland with a great army, he offered, apparently, many gifts and estates, perhaps including the garments and books considered in the previous chapter. Or he may have given the manuscript, now in Cambridge, which contains a collection of Cuthbertian material, with liturgical as well as Bedan texts, just before or after the 937 battle of Brunanburh, in the hope of, or in thanks for, victory. His name was added, at the head, to the list of royal and aristocratic donors for whom Cuthbert's community prayed.[22] Furthermore, Aethelstan brought the cult to Wessex, giving northern and southern England another element of shared culture. It was probably under his patronage there that the Cambridge manuscript's material had been collected. One of its liturgical pieces had been made for use in the royal chapel. Cuthbert's cult was spread to Winchester's New Minster, and to Worcester and Peterborough in Mercia.[23] Finally, the *History of Saint Cuthbert* also testifies to the cult's annexation by and usefulness to the West Saxon kings. It asserts that Cuthbert appeared to Alfred in a dream, prophesying that his descendants would be kings of all Britain; that Alfred had told Edward to be faithful to Cuthbert; and that Edward had told Aethelstan to honour Cuthbert above all saints. The story of the dream may have been composed at Aethelstan's court, or perhaps in the mid-tenth century, in the context of his half-brother King Edmund's subjugation of Northumbria.[24] Edmund, like Aethelstan, visited Cuthbert's shrine.

No attempts to import Anglo-Saxon cults into Cornwall are discernible.[25] There were, however, some Anglo-Saxon attempts to annex Cornish saints. According to Asser, Alfred once, in his youth, prayed at the church of St Gueriir in Cornwall that the illness from which he suffered be replaced by one less severe. His prayer was granted. Since this was an important episode in Alfred's life, it is hard to imagine that Gueriir got no credit for it, though he is otherwise unknown. He was surely regarded as an Alfredian supporter. So too was St Neot, whose anonymous early-eleventh-century *Life* asserts that Alfred sought him out, saw him in dreams, and owed his victory at Edington to him. The similarity of the Alfred–Neot story to the Alfred–Cuthbert one may mean that the two had a common origin. Neot's relics were transferred from St Neot, Cornwall, to St Neots in Huntingdonshire, probably in the late tenth century.[26]

During the tenth-century reformation the saint whose cult expanded most noticeably was the Virgin Mary.[27] This was in association with Winchester and with royal policy, as exemplified by Bishop Aethelwold's making Mary a model for Edgar's queen. To the four Marian feasts that were already in the Church's calendar by about 900 some additions were made from the mid-tenth century onwards, attested mainly in texts from centres of reformed monasticism. The *Regularis Concordia*, for example, prescribes a Mass in her honour on Saturdays. Around 1030 two further feasts, which were celebrated in the Byzantine Church, were introduced. Almost all the known church dedications of tenth-century monastic foundations and refoundations, and half of the nunneries honour Mary, alone or in combination with another saint or saints. This is a much higher proportion than that of tenth-century cathedrals (one out of five) or earlier minsters (never more than half). Mary was perceived in England, as elsewhere, as Queen in Heaven and mediator for mankind.[28] The political potential of her cult was two-fold. It offered disparate groups and regions something in common. Her association with the royal regime proclaimed its authority over local communities, paralleling her own superiority over local saints, its power and the rectitude of acquiescence.

Dynasties and legitimacy

Kings and saints

In England, Christianity was used to legitimate both the office of kingship and particular dynasties and rulers, to justify and strengthen their hold on their subjects, sometimes recently acquired, and sometimes reluctant to meet their demands. This is most obvious in the case of Aethelstan's patronage of Chester-le-Street. His donor portrait implied that his relationship with St Cuthbert was one of mutual support, that his prayers, for victory and dominion in this life and salvation in the next, would be granted.[29] It thereby also proclaimed that Cuthbert's favour was unavailable to Aethelstan's northern opponents, whether Scandinavian or rulers of Alba. They may well have hoped for it themselves. The former had a late-ninth-century alliance with St Cuthbert's community as a precedent. The latter ruled territory in which the community had owned property and Cuthbert himself had worked, and two of their Pictish predecessors were remembered in the community's *Liber Vitae*. They might have expected to be perceived as its natural ally. The community's later patrons included King Cnut, whose gifts of lands, like Aethelstan's, are identified in the *History of Saint Cuthbert*, and Edward the Confessor's brother-in-law Tostig, earl of Northumbria and Tostig's wife.

Aethelstan's saintly strategy had been anticipated not only by his aunt, the Lady of the Mercians, but also by the Vikings in England and kings in Alba. By their coinage, the Viking rulers of East Anglia and Northumbria had associated themselves with, respectively, St Edmund, and St Peter. King Guthfrith had been chosen as king (at some time between 880 and 885–895) of the Danish army in Northumbria apparently through Cuthbert's intervention, as well as the help of Abbot Eadred of Carlisle and Bishop Eardwulf of Lindisfarne. This favour was in return for the territory between the Rivers Tyne and Wear and a right of sanctuary. At Guthfrith's inauguration ceremony, or ceremonies, Eadred invested him with the gold armlet of Scandinavian kingship and Eardwulf oversaw his and his whole army's swearing peace and fidelity, on Cuthbert's body. The deal was reported a success. How it was represented was that Cuthbert had appeared to the abbot in a dream, telling him to find Guthfrith, engineer his election and then secure the grant. In Alba too there were close connections between kings and saints as well as the ninth-century one between the Alpinid kings and the cult of Columba. In the tenth century two rival segments of the family were associated with different saints and rival religious foundations. One grouping was that of Constantín II and his line, based in or near Fife, with St Andrew and St Andrews. Columba and Dunkeld were associated with Cinaed II (971–995) and his line, based in Atholl and Strathearn.[30]

The nearest Welsh analogy to Cuthbert's prophecies relates to Powys, in a claim that differs from that made on the Pillar of Elise. Nennius reports that, in the fifth century, St Germanus had prophesied to Cadell, a servant of a wicked king of Powys, that Cadell would be king and his line of kings never fail. This,

Nennius notes, had proved true. The work that Nennius was drawing on may have been composed during the reign of Cadell's namesake, King Cadell of Powys, who had died in 808.[31]

War

To its blessing of kingly office, dynasty and in many cases, individual, the Church added the legitimating of warfare. Yet again this is particularly obvious of Aethelstan. In the *History of the Kings* the report of Aethelstan's gifts to St Cuthbert is immediately followed by one of his subjugation of his enemies, laying waste Scotland with an army and ravaging with a naval force. The juxtaposition implies cause and effect, and approval. The poem that celebrates Aethelstan's victory at Brunanburh was, probably, written by a bishop (Cenwald of Worcester).[32] Furthermore, there was intimate ecclesiastical involvement in the very conduct of war.[33] As Aethelstan's relationship with Cuthbert implies, prayer could be used as a weapon. In Bede's *History*, the early-seventh-century Northumbrian pagan King Aethelfrith, facing the Britons, says of their priests who had come to pray for their soldiers, that they were fighting against him.[34] King Oswald's victory at Heaven-field was preceded by Oswald and his army praying. Since Alfred, his successors, and their ecclesiastical advisers will have known these stories, they might have attempted to emulate them. According to Asser, Alfred and his men reached the battlefield of Ashdown in 871 sooner and in better order than his brother King Aethelred, who stayed in his tent hearing Mass. Their victory, which followed, showed, Asser says, that the king's faith counted for much with the Lord. Reported preparation for battle in Alba in 904 involved both laymen and clergy fasting and praying to God and Columba.[35]

Such behaviour was predicated on the belief that both the saints and God Himself were willing and able to take part in battle. The concern to demonstrate the army's worthiness of divine help, and to invoke it, was shared with post-Carolingian Continental western Europe, where it also often entailed demonstrating that the enemy was, by contrast, unworthy of such assistance. It is probably this rather than a real difference in conduct that lies behind the twelfth-century William of Malmesbury's assertion that before the battle of Hastings the English army spent the night in drunken revelry, in contrast to the proper behaviour of William the Conqueror's men.[36]

In Europe armies routinely took holy objects – relics and flags or banners that had been blessed – into battle.[37] Since such items were perceived as channels through which supernatural power worked, they may, like prayer, be considered as weapons, not merely morale boosters. It seems unlikely that these views and practices were not shared, though there is much less direct evidence. Aethelstan collected relics, and among the gifts he received was that of the Holy Lance (used at the Crucifixion to pierce Christ's side). He probably took this into battle. In Alba in 904 it was decided that the battle standard in the van of every battle would be Columba's crozier (staff of office), whence it was called Cathbuaid (battle triumph). Victory ensued. It and others were attributed to the crozier.[38]

The *Welsh Annals*, hereby telling us what its tenth-century author thought appropriate for a great warrior rather than details of fifth- and sixth-century armour, asserts that at the battle of Badon, Arthur had the Cross of Christ on his shoulders (or upper arms). The author may have meant either the image or a relic of the Cross, on Arthur's shield.

The holy objects that went to war were accompanied by live ecclesiastics.[39] Their presence is obvious from the anecdotes involving Mass, which cannot be celebrated without a priest. There is no direct indication of their numbers, but Continental evidence is more explicit and permits calculation for armies in Francia. There, it was decided in 742 that each military unit was to have one priest, for confession and penance, supplementing the one or two bishops with their chaplains who accompanied the army commander. A letter from Pope Hadrian I, written to Charlemagne between 784 and 791, and late-eighth- and early-ninth-century sermons show that the army was routinely accompanied by bishops and priests, and that preaching, confession and acceptance of penance were part of the routine preparation for battle. Reception of the Eucharist (to strengthen the men) was added in the tenth century. Similar preparation happened, apparently, in Alba in 904, when the men gave alms, received the Eucharist and promised to do what their clergy urged them.[40] Confession is revealing about the numbers of priests. It has been calculated that if each penitent was seen on his own and allowed three minutes, and each priest worked for ten hours without a break, hardly good pastoral or working conditions, twenty-five priests would have sufficed for 5,000 men.[41] Based on these figures there would have been 125 priests with the English army at Hastings in 1066.

The rites for individuals, the services for groups and the holy objects will all have raised individuals' morale and group cohesion in armies. Furthermore, as well as all this, there was the Continental view, of which Alfred, his successors and their circles were surely aware, that their acceptance of penance as part of preparation for battle against pagans and infidels assured eternal life to those who fell in it, even though the penance had not yet been performed. Pope John VIII, a correspondent of Alfred's brother-in-law Burgred, king of Mercia, and of the archbishops of York and Canterbury, had stated this in 879 in a letter to some Frankish bishops.[42] Alfredian and later presentation of the West Saxon struggle against the Vikings as one of Christians against pagans was therefore not simply a matter of legitimising it or maintaining morale and commitment. It was to offer to Christian warriors the chance of salvation, which might otherwise have been thought difficult to attain. Centuries later, the Crusades were to show that this could be a very potent aid in recruitment.

Royal saints

Contemporaries, including allies, rivals and enemies, will have supposed that kings who had saints among their kin had by the same token some special patronage in the court of Heaven. If kings demonstrated that they had such kin, they were claiming and probably obtaining, greater respect. The late-ninth-century Dunkeld

Litany includes three royal saints, two of them quite recent if they are indeed the Constantíns who died in 820 and 876.[43] In eighth-century Anglo-Saxon England, royal cults had been housed in double monasteries, whose inmates often included relatives of both saint and founder. These cults subsequently declined significantly. Probably some were suppressed by the West Saxon royal house.[44] In striking contrast to Mercia's, none of Wessex's early rulers had cults, and only two of its early members did.[45]

This deficiency was remedied in the tenth century. Aethelred II's half-brother and immediate predecessor as king, Edward (975–978), was promoted as a martyr, with the report of miracles, beginning in 989–990.[46] This may have been by Aethelred himself, to strengthen his own kingship, at the time of renewed Viking attacks. But it may have been by Aethelred's opponents, including Cnut, to discredit Aethelred and legitimise first their opposition and then his replacement, for at least some people blamed Aethelred for Edward's murder. The *Life of St Oswald* explicitly blames Aethelred's household. Edward's relics were translated in 1001, and in 1008 observation of his festival was made compulsory throughout the kingdom. Aethelred's half-sister Edith, daughter of King Edgar, who had been a nun, was also promoted as a saint, by both Aethelred and Cnut.[47]

Genealogy

History was another means of establishing individual and dynastic authority. One aspect of this was genealogy, and in a number of instances this too contained an explicitly Christian element. One, very innovative, example of West Saxon fusion of traditional Germanic with Christian elements, is the lineage of King Aethel-wulf. Though recorded in the *Anglo-Saxon Chronicle* with his death, it was produced nearly forty years later, in about 892. The royal line was traced, as was normal, to the pagan god Woden, herein deemed a man, not a god, and then beyond Woden to biblical ancestors; to a son of Noah, born in Noah's Ark, and beyond him again, to 'Adam the first man and our father, *i.e.* Christ'.[48] Since, according to the Old Testament, only Noah and his family survived the Flood, everybody shared a Noah–Adam ancestry. But it was only the West Saxon dynasty that claimed it – or at least, whose claim has survived.[49]

Further, its claim added an ark-born son for whom there was no biblical authority.[50] There may have been a Syrian tradition of such a son, brought by Theodore of Tarsus, who, appointed archbishop of Canterbury by the Pope, took up his position in 669. Aethelwulf's genealogy called this son Sceaf. In the later-tenth-century West Saxon Aethelweard's chronicle, Sceaf is someone who appeared from nowhere as a child in a ship. Nowadays he is considered to be a figure from West Saxon folk-tradition. Aethelweard's Sceaf gave the West Saxon dynasty and people a valuable similarity to two famous and historically significant groups, because their origins too lay with abandoned children. One was the Jews of Exodus, whose leader, Moses, had been found in a basket among bulrushes. The other was the Romans, whose founders, Romulus and Remus, had been raised by a wolf. The ark-born Sceaf by contrast offered the West Saxons a particularly prestigious place among Noah's descendants, since their origin lay in the saved world of the ark, rather than in the sinful world that preceded it and into which Noah's other three sons had been born. This might have been interpreted, by extension, as suggesting that they had greater authority and claim to rule the lands occupied by the descendants of Noah's other sons, which, of course, included their neighbours. The claim that Sceaf was Noah's son was not, however, universally accepted, even by West Saxons. Some hundred years later Aelfric clearly, though implicitly, contradicted it, by stressing, whenever he discussed the Flood, that Noah had only three sons. He must have known of the claim to an ark-born son. His decision not to challenge it directly was probably to avoid drawing attention to it, as well as to himself.

Among the mid-tenth-century Welsh genealogies, the maternal and paternal lineages composed for King Owain of Dyfed make different though similarly glorious claims. The maternal goes back to the Emperor Constantine I and his mother Helena who found the True Cross, and the paternal to Anna, whom it states was reputed to be cousin to the Virgin Mary.[51] The other genealogies claim Roman and biblical ancestors for the other major Welsh kingdoms.[52] As the texts of the Pillar of Elise and Nennius show, more recent and more local figures were also important. Lack of evidence and the questionability of the saga material make it difficult to identify the foundations of authority for the rulers of Scandinavian Scotland, but since the *Orkneyinga saga* starts with the ancestors of the earls of Orkney we may surmise that genealogy was important for them too.

Other methods of control and unification

Kings used, of course, other methods and mechanisms to control and unify their people and territory. The most important, behind which lay good judgement and planning, were: the written word in historical and contemporary reports; ceremonial; marriage strategy, the use of women, and manipulation of the system of succession; land strategy and administration; and law. Since these mechanisms are not overtly religious, which is not to say that they had no religious dimension at all, they will be considered only briefly.

The written and the painted portraits of kings emphasise history.[53] The books in which the painted pictures survive all deal with the past, sometimes the very recent past. The history related in Edgar's 966 Winchester New Minster charter is cast as his own account. His commissioning of the work and his role in the events that it records make him seem like its author. The same is true of the later case of Emma and her *Encomium*. To present an image of ruler as historian was to follow the example of Alfred's historical accounts, in his *Pastoral Rule* and law-code prefaces, and his claim to have been inspired by the past. In the first, Alfred represented English unity as related to a shared language and texts written in it, in the second as arising out of Christian history, shared law following a common faith that followed conversion. Alfred thus used texts to construct not only his own image, but also a nation and a future. In absolutely every sense, he made history.[54] Later, Cnut and Emma appealed to Edgar's memory and claimed to follow in his footsteps. The Winchester *Liber Vitae* containing their donation portrait would probably have been displayed on the altar next to Edgar's 966 charter. The portrait's message was continuity, analogous to the statement in Cnut's law-code that Edgar's laws would be adhered to.

Whether remote, recent or contemporary, what was reported in an historical work was often distorted in some way for political ends. The representation of English history in Alfred's *Pastoral Rule* is very inaccurate.[55] The *Anglo-Saxon Chronicle*'s representation made the rise of Wessex, over many centuries, its major theme. Its continuing references to the Vikings of East Anglia, even after they had legitimised themselves and integrated there, as armies, stigmatising them as aggressive aliens, reflects the West Saxon ambition to conquer. The continuation that was composed in Edward the Elder's Wessex reports Alfred's nephew Aethelwold's challenge (901–903) for the kingship misleadingly. It omits to state that Aethelwold was accepted by the Danes in Northumbria as their king.[56] All the continuations say that, without the king's (Edward) or bishop's permission, Aethelwold had taken a nun, thereby implying sinful lust on his part. But it may be that he had simply contracted a close-kin marriage, possibly to Alfred's daughter Aethelgifu, to strengthen his claim. It was not unusual for women who had rights of inheritance, or who could transmit such rights to their children, to be left unmarried by their families and placed in nunneries, to keep the field clear for those male kin whom the families favoured as heirs. Attempts to circumvent such arrangements may have lain behind the complaints of Pope John VIII and Archbishop Fulco of Reims in 874 and 890 about Anglo-Saxon men marrying and defiling nuns.[57]

Given the paucity of textual evidence relating to Scotland and the disagreement of scholars about why it is lacking, it is impossible to assess whether in Alba too there were predilections for a royal image of bookishness and historical authorship, and for using historical texts to buttress regimes and shape a future. The tenth-century *Chronicle of the Kings of Alba* has been thought to bear a message, that Alba was a new kingdom, not a continuation of either the Dál Riatan or the Pictish.[58] But this chronicle was not continued, and the exact significance of the name Alba remains elusive. Successive interpretations have differed greatly.[59] Having no coinage, rulers in Alba, as in Wales, lacked the opportunity of visual propaganda that Anglo-Saxon and Scandinavian rulers in England exploited on their coins. The Welsh, however, did produce some politically charged texts. As we shall see later, Nennius' *History* implicitly exalted Merfyn of Gwynedd, who may have come from the Isle of Man and seized power violently in c. 825,[60] while, as we have seen, denigrating the dynasty of Powys.[61] Nennius' work was exceptional. It is in genealogy, with their claims to descent from heroes, that Welsh kings seem to have been most directly involved with history.

There were several ceremonies of submission to Anglo-Saxon kings, though they may have been misreported and their apparently subordinate participants may actually have interpreted the proceedings quite differently. According to the *Anglo-Saxon Chronicle*, the rulers and peoples of the Scots, of Northumbria and of the Strathclyde Welsh chose King Edward as father and lord while he was at

Bakewell, in 920. At Eamont in 927, Aethelstan established peace with all the kings in 'this island' whom he had, the chronicler claims, 'brought under his rule', naming them as the West Welsh Hywel, Owain of Gwent, and the Scots' Constantine, and Ealdred of Bamburgh.[62] Further ceremonies followed in 935 at Cirencester and at Dorchester. Aethelstan may have been trying to appear like a Roman emperor in these ceremonies. All three places had structures that were, or were probably thought to be, Roman amphitheatres. Edgar's 973 coronation in Bath was followed by a ceremony at Chester, another place with a Roman amphitheatre, which is reported differently in different sources. Six, or eight, kings, including Cinaed of Alba, Mael Coluim of Strathclyde, Magnus of Man and the Isles, and other kings both Welsh and Norse, promised to be his 'even-workers', or, possibly, submitted to his rule. They perhaps symbolised this submission by rowing a boat along the River Dee with Edgar at the prow.[63]

Another method of control is to keep magnates close, thereby emphasising their subordination, establishing their loyalty and limiting their capacity to make trouble unexpectedly. The witness lists of some of Aethelstan's charters show this in respect of the Welsh: Hywel, Morgan and Idwal, for example, all designated as sub-king, witnessed a grant to the Church of York.

In this period the rule of succession by primogeniture lay far in the future, and kings could attempt to manage the succession and to ease the way for those whom they preferred as their heirs. Alfred's father Aethelwulf had planned that his sons succeed in turn. Alfred himself tried to ensure that his son Edward would be preferred to Aethelwold, the son of Alfred's brother Aethelred, whose bid for the kingship nevertheless very nearly succeeded. Alfred gave Edward more experience and land, and may even have had him anointed, in the capacity of sub-king of Kent.[64] As usual in history, kings had marriage strategies. One was to forge links with Continental powers, as Aethelwulf did in his marriage to the Emperor Charles the Bald's daughter Judith, and as Aethelstan did through his sisters.[65] West Saxon strategy included marrying into the Mercian ruling house, as Alfred, his sister and his daughter Aethelflaed did, and into leading noble families.[66] Unusually for a king, Aethelstan remained unmarried. One suggestion is that he had agreed with his stepmother Eadgifu, who belonged to a powerful Kentish family, that if she supported him, he would allow her sons, his half-brothers, to be his heirs. Another is that a marriage to Aethelflaed's daughter, Aelfwyn of Mercia, had once been intended, but had been abandoned because close-kin marriages were increasingly viewed by the Church as illegitimate.[67] Pope John in 874 and in 877 or 878, and Fulco of Reims twice in 890 expressed concern in letters to Anglo-Saxon England about marriage with kin. King Edmund's son King Eadwig's marriage to Aelfgifu fell foul of this and was dissolved on these grounds in 957. His wife was probably a descendant of Alfred's brother Aethelred. His marriage might have been meant to neutralise Aelfgifu's kin-group, excluded from the throne by Alfred's descendants.[68] His failure to remarry may have been meant to facilitate the succession of his brother Edgar, then king of Mercia, to Wessex: it has been suggested that the division of the kingdom into two in 955 had been with the intention that Edgar would eventually have both.[69] Edgar's three marriages have been seen as successive alliances with leading families in order to keep a balance of power between rival groups.[70]

Royal wives brought dowries in land as well as new kinship links to their husbands. Through their wives, therefore, kings' wealth was increased and royal power and influence were extended in the regions.[71] The West Saxon kings' property strategy was to keep a tight hold on their lands, to acquire more, to reward and stimulate service, to position loyal men throughout their kingdom by granting estates without losing resources, and to supervise their subordinates' grants.[72] Alfred's father, his brothers who preceded him on the throne, and Alfred himself all tried, largely successfully, to limit dissipation of their family's landed assets and to restrict them to kinsmen who were in a position to bid for the throne. Moreover, their success was long lasting. By 1066, according to Domesday Book, barely 15 per cent of Alfred's estates had been lost. In some instances land had been lost, but had been regained, in the tenth century. Alfred's concern for stability of landholding is also evident from some of his legislation. He allowed a kin-group to confine disposal of its bookland to itself, and stipulated that anyone who alienated bookland was to satisfy the king and the bishop as well as their kin of their right to do so.

Kings acquired lands in a number of ways. Exploitation of church lands has already been mentioned. Before he began his conquests, Edward encouraged purchasing land from Danes. Land taken from them was used to endow the new ealdordoms by which the kings governed what they had conquered. Dispossession and forfeiture were part of the legal process, for theft and other offences, and their use increased during the tenth century.[73] This affected not only the offender but also anyone who would have expected to inherit the confiscated property. Bookland may have been more liable to forfeiture than family land that was subject to inheritance by customary rules. This probably contributed to the disputes that occurred about whether an estate was bookland or folkland. Edward wanted such disputes to be settled quickly, and established that jurisdiction in these cases belonged to the king and his officers.[74] In any new reign, the previous regime's supporters could be targeted. Edgar's reign was peaceful in part because he was ruthless. He dispossessed Wulfric, a Berkshire landowner, a thegn of King Eadwig's, and exacted a large sum as the price of restitution in 960.[75]

In their reorganisation of administrative regions Alfred and his successors worked predominantly with pre-existing boundaries. Their shires mostly conformed to previous provincial boundaries, their hundreds to shire and *burh* boundaries.[76] Alfred attempted, however, to create a new elite: the school funded out of his annual income took boys not of noble birth as well as noble ones. Aethelred II's charters and appointments suggest that he chose advisers from, and endowed his supporters throughout, the whole of his kingdom, as a deliberate policy.[77] Whether Alba developed a strong royal administrative system is still debatable but recent work has made it seem unlikely.[78] Unlike the Anglo-Saxon, its system seems not to have used writing in administration, perhaps because it was not needed. The Alpiníd kings seem to have introduced a change to the succession system. From c. 889 the kingship alternated, though not entirely peacefully, between two branches of the family. There was no father–son succession in the ninth and tenth centuries. Until 971 a king from the senior segment would be succeeded by a member of the same generation from the junior segment.[79]

There is, finally, the matter of Anglo-Saxon law and legislation. In Anglo-Saxon England, law and justice were associated with kings, in the coronation ceremony as well as in the law-codes. The First Coronation *Ordo* includes prayers for justice and equity for all under the new king, who is to forbid robberies and injustice and to offer equity and mercy in all judgements. In the second, God is asked to crown the king with the honour of justice, and the king admonished to correct the wicked, give peace to the just and help them to keep to the just path.[80] Furthermore, the requirements of royal law encouraged the people towards loyalty and rectitude. Alfred's legislation against disloyalty has been described as having almost Stalinist zeal.[81] Aethelstan made theft a felony, as we have seen, and thieves were a target of Edgar too, according to Lantfred of Winchester, writing around 975. He says that in a law of great severity Edgar required any thief or robber to be comprehensively mutilated. That Edgar did not flinch from severe punishment is clear. According to one version of the *Anglo-Saxon Chronicle*, in 969 he ordered all Thanet to be ravaged. According to a later source this was because merchants of York had been mistreated there. And the so-called anti-monastic reaction after Edgar's death may have stemmed partly from what some scholars think were seething frustrations that had been dormant for most of his reign.[82]

There is little sign of any of this in Wales. Some kings made advantageous marriages. Merfyn's to Nest of Powys and Hywel Dda's to Elen of Dyfed brought both these kingdoms to Gwynedd's dynasty, though Dyfed's kingship remained distinct[83] and it is possible that Merfyn's marriage was an invented tradition, to legitimise Gwynedd's take-over.[84] Succession was expected to be from father to son, though joint kingship could occur and in the tenth century alternation of kingship between different branches of the family came into vogue in Gwynedd and Dyfed. Neither land acquisition nor ecclesiastical reform functioned as methods of extending royal control. Kings who acquired dominion over other Welsh kingdoms did not also acquire estates there.[85] There is no evidence of alliance between kings and Céli Dé adherents. Hywel, one of Aethelstan's sub-kings and charter witnesses, may have tried to introduce some aspects of English kingship. The Chester-minted coin bearing his name, and his issuing, perhaps, of a law-code may suggest this. But Welsh kings had little to do with the law.[86] Though the legal system did include local courts, it also had forms of dispute settlement that lay outside them. There were official judges but they could act by private arbitration. Policing was by kin and community. A powerful figure with regard to obligations created by contract was the contract's chief witness, the *mach*. Originally its chief enforcer, regarded as the living symbol of the bond between the parties, he was symbolically identified with the contract. Defendant and plaintiff were obliged to deal with him rather than directly with each other.

Law in Alba is more of a puzzle. There is only one surviving legal text.[87] There is one report of a king engaging in law-making, in the mid-ninth-century at

Forteviot,[88] though without any indication of what the law-making was. So, whether kings issued written law-codes is questionable. Comparison with England and western Europe makes their apparent failure to do so surprising and perhaps unlikely. Comparison with Armenia, whose kings certainly did not, makes it less so. For ambitious kings, a written code, following Roman practice, did have certain advantages, as the Anglo-Saxon case demonstrates. But it might also have had disadvantages. In some circumstances, imitating the Romans may not have been palatable. The fact that the Picts were in origin non-Romanised Britons may be relevant to their lack of law-codes. In Alba, written law might have seemed a particularly Anglo-Saxon practice, and its emulation distasteful. Anglicisation of the identity of Alba was perhaps felt to be something that should be avoided.

This is speculative, but other possible explanations are far from certain. A lack of intellectual figures and centres may be part of the answer. Yet the sculpture, though declining in quantity and quality during our period, shows that learning did not entirely die out, and Dunkeld and St Andrews were associated with the kings. It might be that Alba's was a more strongly and persistently oral culture than that of Wessex, so that law and the legal system were entirely oral, analogous to the situation in Iceland where, apparently, until about AD 1000 law was memorised. Or it might be that what is lacking is not production of law-codes but their survival, as has been suggested for written texts generally.[89]

In England alone is royal involvement in Christianising Scandinavians clear. Plain there too, and discernible in Alba, are the patronage and spreading of certain saintly cults in order to gain the favour of dead saint and live community, particularly as a sanction for the rule and deeds of king and dynasty and to unite the people who shared in their devotion. So too are the claiming of saints' support in war and the inclusion of holy objects and ecclesiastics in armies. Claiming saints in the family, remotely or recently, was common to kingship in England, Alba and Wales. The use of history as propaganda may too have been, though variably. Other tools used by or for kings are not very visible outside England.

Notes

1 Abrams, 'Conversion ... Danelaw'.
2 Richards, 'Case'.
3 Hadley, 'Burial'; Richards, *Viking*.
4 For what follows, Abrams, 'Conversion ... Danelaw'.
5 Pestell.
6 Driscoll, *Alba*.
7 Abrams, 'Conversion ... Danelaw'.
8 See for example Mayr-Harting, *Two*.
9 *EHD I*: 820–821.
10 Blackburn, 'Expansion'; Damon.
11 Lynch.
12 Damon.
13 *Ibid*.
14 Woolf, *From*. See also Abrams, 'Conversion ... Church'.
15 Macquarrie, *Saints*.

16 *Ibid.*
17 G. Henderson and I. Henderson.
18 Woolf, *From.*
19 D. Griffiths.
20 Heighway; V. Thompson, *Dying.*
21 See Thacker, '*Peculiaris*'.
22 Karkov, *Ruler.*
23 Coatsworth; Foot, *Æthelstan*; Karkov, *Ruler*; Rollason, 'St Cuthbert'.
24 Johnson South; Simpson.
25 Pearce.
26 John, 'Annals'.
27 Clayton, *Cult.*
28 *Ibid.*
29 Karkov, *Ruler.*
30 Grant; Woolf, *From.*
31 Higham, *King.* See also O.W. Jones.
32 Foot, 'When'.
33 Bachrach.
34 *Ibid.*
35 Woolf, *From.*
36 Bachrach.
37 *Ibid.*
38 Airlie; Woolf, *From.*
39 For what follows, Bachrach.
40 Woolf, *From.*
41 Bachrach.
42 *Ibid.*
43 T.O. Clancy, 'Scottish'.
44 Thacker, 'Dynastic'.
45 Yorke, *Nunneries.*
46 Thacker, 'Saint-making'; Yorke, *Nunneries.*
47 Yorke, *Nunneries.*
48 *EHDI*: 175.
49 Karkov, *Ruler.*
50 For what follows, Anlezark.
51 Higham, *King.*
52 W. Davies, *Wales.*
53 For what follows, Karkov, *Ruler.*
54 See also Foot, 'Making'.
55 Davis, 'National', 'Performance'.
56 Campbell, 'What'.
57 Woolf, 'View'.
58 Hudson, 'Scottish'; Woolf, *From.*
59 Broun, 'Origin', '*Alba*'.
60 Charles-Edwards, *Wales.*
61 Higham, *King.*
62 Davison; *EHDI*: 199, 200; Foot, *Æthelstan*, 'When'; Woolf, *From.*
63 Keynes, 'Edgar'. For a short summary of different interpretations of this meeting and
    identifications of those attending, Breeze, 'Edgar'.
64 Yorke, 'Edward'.
65 Foot, 'Dynastic'.
66 Sharp.
67 Woolf, 'View'.
68 Sharp.

69 Biggs.
70 Yorke, 'Women'.
71 Stafford, *Queen Emma, Unification*.
72 For what follows, Wormald, '*On*'.
73 Wormald, *Making*.
74 *Ibid.*
75 Jayakumar.
76 Bassett, 'Administrative'.
77 Campbell, 'Aspects'; A. Williams, *Æthelred*.
78 Broun, 'Property'. For the different, earlier view, Grant. See also Driscoll, *Alba*, 'Formalising'.
79 Woolf, *From*.
80 Wormald, *Making*.
81 Burghart, 'Review'.
82 Jayakumar; Keynes, 'Edgar'; Salvador-Bello.
83 W. Davies, *Wales*.
84 O.W. Jones.
85 W. Davies, *Wales*.
86 For what follows, Stacey.
87 Woolf, *From*.
88 Hudson, 'Scottish'.
89 Hughes.

5 Churches

Boundaries and aspirations

Introduction

The Christian Church is the community of all Christians, living and dead. In the case of the former, it comprises various sub-groups and administrative units. The boundaries of those groups, and the power and authority of the units and their heads, have been sometimes personal, including particular people, and sometimes territorial, limited to particular geographical areas, and subject to disagreement and competition. The exercise of authority within them and the establishment of boundaries around them have both contributed to groups' sense of community. In early medieval Britain, ecclesiastical institutions and communities were those of archbishoprics, bishoprics, minsters, reformed monasteries (including nunneries), local churches and proprietary churches, and parishes. They involved issues of lordship (royal and lay and the lordship of greater over lesser churches), dues and revenues, and of rights thereto. There is also a question whether there was anything approaching a national Church.

Archbishoprics and bishoprics

In 800, the archdiocese of York corresponded roughly with the political sway and independence of the kingdom of Northumbria, to which it contributed. In the late ninth century, after Northumbria had splintered, Vikings held York itself, and York's archbishops co-operated with their kings. The archbishopric's political significance is probably one reason for what was effectively its annexation by the West Saxon kings, in the 970s. Another is that Scandinavian activity had left it financially unsustainable. For nearly fifty years York was held in tandem with the see of Worcester, by incumbents who were closely associated with the English kings. The first of these was the reform leader Oswald, the third and last, Wulfstan (II). York aspired, at least sometimes, to authority over northern bishoprics that lay outside Anglo-Saxon territory. It seems to have retained contacts with the see of Whithorn.[1] That of Orkney was established in the eleventh century. Since Orkney was dominated from Norway, its see became subject to rivalry between York and Hamburg-Bremen. Archbishops, whether of York or Canterbury, had limited means to control their subordinate bishops. They depended on exhortation at church councils, whose agreed decrees and aspirations bishops were supposed to implement.

No other see claimed archiepiscopal authority in Scotland. The title of archbishop does seem to be implied with respect to Dunkeld in 865, and to have been used for St Andrews several times in the tenth and eleventh centuries, but it was probably a mark of respect rather than an indication of constitutional authority.[2] It is possible though that this respect might have encouraged its recipient to behave and be regarded like an Anglo-Saxon archbishop, or even that it was actually prompted by such behaviour. Much the same seems to have been true among the Welsh. The *Welsh Annals'* 809 entry terms Elfoddw 'archbishop' in Gwynedd. He had clearly been a very influential figure. He had been responsible for the changing of Easter 'among the Britons' in 768, and was Nennius' teacher. Asser uses 'archbishop' as an honorific, of his kinsman Nobis of St David's, who, according to the *Annals*, was merely a bishop (840–873). There is no evidence for any Welsh see having jurisdiction over others.[3] It is, however, possible that Canterbury attempted some control of the Welsh in the tenth century. Such an aspiration was perhaps inspired as much by Pope Gregory I's having given Augustine of Canterbury authority over all the bishops of Britain, in a letter of 601 which was quoted by Bede, as by English kings' expansionism. According to the later *Book of Llandaff*, King Edgar decided the bounds of the diocese and kingdom of Morgannwg, bishops of Llandaff were consecrated by archbishops of Canterbury from 972, and so too were some bishops of St David's, from 995.[4]

In practice, bishops were appointed by kings. The location of their bases, that is, their cathedrals (so called because they were the churches where the bishops' *cathedra*s, thrones, were situated), and the boundaries of their sees were also subject to royal influence. There were several changes between 800 and 1066. These were due, ultimately, to two causes. One was Scandinavian activity, which brought great disruption, directly or indirectly, to sees in northern and eastern England. For example, Hexham disappeared and Lindisfarne was abandoned in 875, its community re-established first in Chester-le-Street in 883, and finally in Durham in 995. The other cause was West Saxon reorganisation and aspiration. Some changes of boundaries or estates may have been due to questions of financial viability, sees needing to be self-supporting. But restoration of bishoprics in the early tenth century helped to cement West Saxon political control, perhaps intentionally so.

Wessex played an important part in the reorganisation of episcopal provision in three respects. Some sees were made smaller and new ones established. In 909 Archbishop Plegmund (archbishop of Canterbury 890–923) was involved in carving out the diocese of Ramsbury from that of Winchester, and those of Wells and Crediton from that of Sherborne (which acquired Ramsbury in 1058). A guiding principle in the reorganisation was that each shire should have its own bishop.[5] Second, West Saxon bishops may have been assigned to areas that Wessex had conquered from Scandinavians.[6] Third, the West Saxon centre of Dorchester-on-Thames played an important role in the revival of bishoprics. Leicester's had been relocated there by 888. Lindsey's was merged with it, though allowed a separate existence from about 915 to 950 and again for a few years before and after 1000. London's was briefly held in conjunction with it, in about 900.[7] Additionally, Elmham and Dunwich were merged and put under London, though Elmham was revived by 956. Except in Winchester, cathedrals in Wessex were not located in *burhs*, which implies that Alfred and Edward the Elder wanted to avoid churchmen being influential in towns. It is possibly this and their desire to weaken the Danish–Church alliance that lay behind the delay in appointing bishops to the disrupted East Anglian and east Mercian sees, rather than Scandinavian destruction.[8]

The history of episcopal provision for Cornwall is far less transparent, except that its direction and regularisation by Wessex is clear.[9] The crucial evidence is a letter purportedly from Archbishop Dunstan to King Aethelred II. Cornwall was part of the see of Sherborne until that of Crediton was created. Yet some time between 833 and 870 someone called Kenstec sent a profession of faith to the archbishop of Canterbury, describing himself as holding an episcopal see among the Cornish in the monastery Dinurrin. The exact status of this see seems unclear. Dinurrin (near Bodmin) may have been subordinate to the monastery of St Petroc. Petroc's main church was originally at Padstow, but in the second half of the eleventh century was at Bodmin. The date of its move is unknown. It might have been a prompt reaction to King Egbert of Wessex (died 839) disrupting its landholding when he granted three estates around Padstow to Sherborne. One of them probably belonged to St Petroc's, and its loss will have made Bodmin seem a more convenient administrative base for the community than Padstow. Curiously, when Crediton was divided and King Aethelstan established Bishop Conan in Cornwall, this was perceived as a restoration of liberties to a pre-existing see that was associated not with Bodmin, but with St Germans. It is conceivable that Kenstec's see had moved there in the interim. Conan's successor Daniel was given the same three estates that Egbert had given to Sherborne and had then passed to Crediton. They seem therefore to have been earmarked to support whatever see took care of Cornwall. Aethelred II confirmed the liberties of the see of Cornwall in a charter of 994. This may have entailed full diocesan status (as opposed to the bishop having the status of *chorepiscopus*, that is, local, assistant bishop). Alternatively it may have been meant merely to strengthen Cornwall's bishop's control over St Petroc's. It is quite likely that St Petroc's had been making claims over the defunct see of Dinurrin-Bodmin. In c. 1027, however, the Cornish see was reabsorbed by Crediton. In 1050 Crediton moved to Exeter, taking both saints, Germanus and Petroc, as its patrons.

As at Dinurrin, a number of Anglo-Saxon sees were based in minsters, and minster and see might act together. Modern interpretation of the southwards moves of St Cuthbert's monks, from Lindisfarne, is that they were in implementation of episcopal policy, and chiefly motivated, like St Petroc's relocation, by a desire for more control of the community's estates, rather than a flight for personal safety from Viking aggression.[10] The leaders of the tenth-century reform movement hoped not only to turn minsters into fully Benedictine monasteries and nunneries. They also wanted bishops to be based in such monasteries. In this their success was limited. At Winchester, Bishop Aethelwold and King Edgar famously monasticised the Old and New Minsters. At Archbishop Dunstan's Canterbury, change at the cathedral, Christ Church was by contrast very slow.[11] At Bishop Oswald's Worcester, the situation is a little less clear. The view that he tried to reform its cathedral community, St Peter's, purging it in 964 and abolishing the system whereby shares of its resources were allocated to individual members, as prebends, so that its property was held in common instead,[12] has been vigorously disputed.[13] Worcester's episcopal leases make it unlikely, partly because they were normally witnessed by members of the community and the witness lists do not suggest mass redundancy. Furthermore, the fact that some were in favour of members of the cathedral clergy suggests that Oswald did not require them to give up private property. The building of St Mary's, a monastic church, next to St Peter's in 966, may not have been because St Peter's clerics refused to change their ways. A later account states that it was to provide more space for people who wished to hear Oswald preach. St Mary's was usable by 977 and perhaps nearly finished by 980. The bishop's throne was moved there at some time after c. 991, but the monasticisation of the community was only completed during the episcopate of Bishop Wulfstan II (1062–1095), though it was normal for its head to be a monk.

Overall, reformers' rhetoric probably over-emphasised the drift towards their ideal. Sherborne's was the only other cathedral community that was monasticised. Non-episcopal establishments' reform was slow or disrupted. Benedictine communities were installed at Evesham, Pershore and Winchcombe, but were dispersed in 975, in the so-called anti-monastic reaction. Evesham and Pershore were re-monasticised in the episcopate of Wulfstan I. Winchcombe had an abbot in the 990s but afterwards none until the 1040s. St Peter's at Gloucester did not adopt the *Rule* until 1022.[14]

As the Cornish bishopric's 994 charter may illustrate, bishops were concerned about their rights, and about their infringement, both inside and from outside their sees. Yet this did not, as on the Continent, involve aspiration to freedom from royal jurisdiction and officials.[15] The outsiders who were to be excluded were other bishops. The case of the see of Selsey is instructive.[16] It was vacant from some time after c. 900 until 963. A charter of 957 restored to Selsey's minster estates that had been taken by Aelfsige, bishop of Winchester 951–958, and stipulated that they were to be inherited for the use of Selsey's bishops. It also invoked a clause of the early Church's Council of Nicaea, which forbade the invasion of another bishop's see. This all suggests that Winchester had not merely 'invaded' Selsey but tried to abolish it. The phenomenon of episcopal interference is also suggested by the *Law of the Northumbrian Priests*, one of the codes associated with Archbishop Wulfstan II. It stipulates fines for priests and deacons who obtained ordination outside the diocese.

Unfortunately, the boundaries of the dioceses before the tenth-century reform are very unclear. Our knowledge of bishoprics is defective in other ways too. Similarities, idiosyncrasies, change and continuity are elusive.[17] The number of diocesan priests must have varied.[18] The suites of priests accompanying the bishops who attended the 803 Council of Clovesho varied in number from three to ten. In the swearing of oaths that confirmed the settlement, in 824, of a dispute involving the bishop of Worcester, fifty Mass priests and 180 clerics were involved. This may have been the entirety of Worcester's personnel, for the nature of the occasion would have made its deployment appropriate. Smaller, less wealthy and important sees probably had far fewer. There was no significant increase in the number of Worcester's clergy until the eleventh century.[19] What did change, in the tenth century, was priests' residence and status. Before then, they lived mostly in communities (in the households of royalty and of bishops, and, possibly, in lay lords', and in minsters) and were of noble origin. Later, many priests were isolated in local churches and some were unfree.[20] Another variable was property and income. One manifestation of concern about these was the forging of charters. The Worcester archive has revealed three forging phases there: in the early ninth century, in the 890s, and in the early eleventh century, when a cartulary (collection of charters) was put together. About one-sixth (twenty-five out of 155) of its texts are forged or contain interpolations, and it is possible that some of them were forged especially for it.[21] Worcester's estates were distributed widely over the diocese. This was probably deliberate, to have access to different economic resources and hence more self-sufficiency, and so that the bishop could visit and stay in all of its parts, to rule it.[22]

Bishops aspired in their dioceses to control, and to remove others' control over, lay behaviour, priests, churches and minsters, and to receive and maximise the various dues to which they were entitled. According to the 786 Legatine Synod, bishops were to tour their sees annually, correcting errors in lay religious observance. In the poem *Elene*, the heroine teaches the people of Jerusalem that they should obey their bishop. As for minsters, episcopal lordship sometimes originated from a minster's having been founded by a bishop and endowed from his private property, and sometimes from settlement following dispute. The eighth-century reformers of the Frankish Church tried to establish episcopal control over all ecclesiastical institutions and property, and their example may have inspired Anglo-Saxon bishops to do the same.[23] The Council of Clovesho of 747 decided that bishops should go into minsters and admonish their heads about proper behaviour. That of 803 decreed that laymen and seculars were not to be chosen as lords over minsters. In 816 the Council at Chelsea decided that bishops should be involved in the appointment of heads of minsters, forbidding laymen to appoint abbots and abbesses. It also anticipated that minsters might become impoverished, and decreed that bishops could take over their property in such cases, to prevent them from coming under lay control. Prudently, however, it also forbade bishops to take over a minster out of greed.[24] Regarding later local churches, Aethelred II's laws forbid anyone to subject a church, to traffic illegally with a church or to expel a minister of the church without the bishop's consent. It is of course possible that in such cases episcopal control was fictional. A church's owner could have observed the proprieties but retained real control.[25]

Episcopal aspirations over minsters were certainly resisted. King Cenwulf of Mercia (796–821) acquired a Papal privilege for his minsters and fought the attempts of Archbishop Wulfred to exert his authority over them. Wulfred eventually won their dispute, focused on Minster-in-Thanet and Reculver. Under King Egbert of Wessex (802–839), however, free monasteries, their locations unidentified but either in Wessex or in areas under Wessex's domination, apparently chose Egbert and his son Aethelwulf for protection and lordship, and bishops as their spiritual lords.[26] There are also signs that episcopal control in the localities, even later when local priests were common, failed to turn ideal into reality. For example, according to Aelfric not only laity but also clergy behaved inappropriately at funerals. The *Law of the Northumbrian Priests* lists a variety of priestly misdemeanours and shortcomings, including failures to maintain proper standards in the celebration of Mass (for example, use of a wooden chalice, and failure to use wine). In some cases fines were stipulated. They were presumably to go to the bishop. Bishops were probably also entitled to a share of dues that lesser churches collected.

The means whereby bishops could exercise control were several. Candidates for the priesthood were examined before they were ordained. Priests were supposed to attend synods, where their bishop would be.[27] Priests of new churches would meet their bishop at the consecration of their church. The 816 Council stated that bishops had the exclusive right to consecrate churches within their dioceses. The rite that was used would certainly have made an impression on onlookers, being both time-consuming and dramatic. The bishop and his entourage walked round the outside of the church three times, then through its interior and then round the outside again, purifying and blessing its parts and the objects that would be used inside it. Relics were enclosed in, or underneath, its altar, while the sanctuary was veiled from the nave, and finally its first Mass would be celebrated.[28] This consecration rite was probably a once in a lifetime experience for local priests and people, and many may never have experienced it at all. The same may have been true for Wales and Scotland. There is no known surviving consecration rite from either, but the Anglo-Saxon ceremonial seems to have been fairly standard in Christendom.

There were bishoprics north of Anglo-Saxon ones but they are less easily discernible. Some major churches whose early role was episcopal are detectible within Scotland's early-twelfth-century sees, and there are some tantalising fragments of evidence. The signatories of a Council held in Rome in 721 include Sedulius, an Irish bishop of Britain. This may mean Dumbarton, or possibly Wales.[29] Glasgow seems to have been a see in the early period. Who established Govan, which by c. 1000 was more important than Glasgow, and whether it had an organised community, is unknown. The royal foundation of St Andrews was established between 729 and 747. Its first recorded bishop is Cellach, in 906. Like Dunkeld, Dunblane and Brechin, it held lands in other dioceses in the twelfth century. When Brechin became a bishopric is uncertain. It is first referred to in connection with King Cinaed II (971–995). Abernethy, a seventh-century royal foundation, had a bishop and was active in the tenth century.[30] Whithorn of course lapsed in the Viking period, possibly for a long time. Lindisfarne's sphere of influence had included parts of southern Scotland, so its community's move south diminished episcopal provision there. Orkney's see was established only in the eleventh century.

The aspirations and powers of tenth- and eleventh-century Welsh bishops are better known. They had administrative and visitation powers and some power to enforce their rulings.[31]

Monasteries, minsters and parishes

A major question for minsters was that of freedom. This could be difficult if freedom from one party's control came through another's protection, for such protection might tend to turn into control and certainly did so on the Continent.[32] There were dangers from, and of, both episcopal and lay control, though not simultaneously for the same institution. A way out of this dilemma that had been used in previous centuries was for a minster to be under the protection of the Papacy.

In Anglo-Saxon England the trend was towards royal control and protection,[33] though not without episcopal opposition, as we have seen. King Cenwulf of Mercia's Papal privilege allowed him to give, to whomever he wished, all the minsters that he had legitimately obtained, though it may be that the heirs envisaged were heads of houses, not future kings. At Winchcombe, where Cenwulf was buried, his heirs seem to have been the abbesses.[34] Free monasteries apparently chose King Alfred's grandfather and father as protectors. Alfred himself refers in his will to the community at Cheddar having agreed to choose his son Edward. This probably means that the community there, to which Edward gave estates, had agreed to choose him as lord and patron, or even as abbot.[35] In the tenth century, however, the leaders of the reform movement decried *secularium prioratus* (lay over-lordship of monasteries). This lay leadership may have entailed the appointment of heads of houses by lay members of their founding families or the actual rule of lay persons as abbots and abbesses. *Secularium prioratus* may also have occurred in Alba. Some scholars think that the involvement of abbots of Dunkeld in war and politics means that they were lay administrators of Dunkeld's estates rather than abbots, but they may have been examples of *secularium prioratus*.[36] Communities' choice or acquiescence in such arrangements might or might not have been genuinely free.

The English remedy, found in the *Regularis Concordia*, was for male and female houses to be put under the protection and lordship of, respectively, the king and queen. This seems to have been effective, for there is no evidence that the heirs of the founders of the five non-royal lay foundations of the reform period (the 970s to 1005) retained any control over them.[37] In Alba some reform may have been brought by the Céli Dé movement. Apart from the probable Céli Dé community at late-ninth- or early-tenth-century Dunkeld, there was one at St Andrews by the mid-tenth, to which King Constantín II retired, and probably one at Brechin too. A few others, of very uncertain origin have also been suggested (Abernethy, Dunblane, Loch Leven, Monifeith, Monymusk and Muthill).[38] Unfortunately we know nothing about these communities' relationships with bishops, or their functions.

The rhetoric of the English reform movement was that in every respect reformed monasteries were superior to what there had been before. This rhetoric was often similar, probably deliberately, to Bede's, both in his *Ecclesiastical History* and in the criticisms that he made in a letter in 734 to Egbert, archbishop of York. According to Aethelwold, only Glastonbury, where Dunstan had become a monk, was respectable before the reform.[39] Glastonbury's history is unclear. It may have been a royal proprietary church in King Alfred's time, as Dunstan's biographer implies, and revived later, but some charters suggest that some sort of community had continued there through the Viking period.[40] Despite the rhetoric, however, unreformed establishments, both major and minor, enjoyed lay support until late in the eleventh century. St Peter's, Worcester, for example, despite losing the episcopal throne to St Mary's, continued to attract lay patronage and its presbytery was enlarged in the 1030s.[41] One estimate is that there were hundreds of small, un-reformed, minsters in the later tenth and the early eleventh centuries.[42]

Religious houses were always concerned about property and revenue. Property comprised land and movables, including precious objects of various kinds. Among them were relics, about which there could be competition between establishments. The keeping, collecting together and sometimes forging of business records, as at eleventh-century Worcester, Durham and Ely and twelfth-century Deer are one testament to the importance of land. Another is the litigation and other efforts undertaken by, or on behalf of, some houses to restore or protect their property rights. Bishop Aethelwold was a vigorous litigant on behalf of Ely. Carved stones that are interpreted as probably or certainly boundary markers occur in Cornwall, Wales and Pictland, and some crosses in Wessex may have served the same purpose. Welsh examples include two surviving tenth-century crosses from Penmon in south-east Anglesey and two eleventh-century ones near Merthyr Mawr (Bridgend) that actually record donations, in words reminiscent of charters.[43] Churches were concerned about the boundaries not only of their estates, but also of the areas that owed them dues, which may not have coincided. Some of the stones were marking the latter. There is for example a frequent correlation, especially in Aberdeenshire, of early churches with Pictish symbol stones, which are mostly at the boundaries of later parishes.[44]

The modern meaning of the word 'parish' is a geographical sub-unit of a diocese, a locality with its own church and priest. The development of this system, everywhere in western Christian Europe, is very obscure. It began as early as the seventh century but was not completed until the thirteenth. The word *parrochia* (now meaning parish) had originally been used of dioceses themselves. In ninth-century Europe 'parish' meant simply a(ny) church's jurisdiction and rights, over its lands and the area and people that it served. That the pastoral functions of England's later parishes were, as the 'minster hypothesis' holds, once performed by at least some minsters is clear from studies of the diocese of Worcester, in which original parishes of, for example, Beckford, Bredon, Bishop's Cleeve and Ripple are partially identifiable.[45] In tenth-century England 'parish' could still signify a minster-territory even while, and although, parishes in the later sense were developing. These new parishes were smaller than the old minster-territories. Their development threatened the old minsters' financial viability, because the newer, more local churches increasingly took the dues that the people owed the minsters. Kings gave them some protection, with partial success, since royal officials could compel payments of dues.[46] Minsters nevertheless lost estates, to the predation of both bishops and kings. The parish of Deerhurst for example was once huge, including almost all the area later served by Tewkesbury. Tewkesbury itself was probably originally a daughter-church of Deerhurst, possibly founded by Odda of Deerhurst.[47]

The definition and marking of churches' boundaries stemmed from the concerns of would-be recipients of dues and of those who had to pay them. Each needed to know who had to pay whom. Several dues were owed.[48] In Anglo-Saxon England before the tenth century, the churches depended on churchscot, not, as in the Carolingian domains, tithe, which became compulsory there in the early ninth century.[49] Churchscot is first mentioned in Ine's law-code, as payable by Martinmas (11 November), with a 60-shilling fine and twelve-fold payment for failure so to do. It was meant as a payment for spiritual care and perhaps especially for penitential arrangements.[50] It was assessed on the hide, and payable in grain. Tithe, one-tenth of one's income or produce, was originally for the support of all the church's activities, and its payment regarded as a moral, not a legal, obligation. In Anglo-Saxon England, the decrees of the 786 Legatine Council encouraged it and there may have been some choice about who one paid it to, as is implied in what is preserved of the penitential teaching of the late-seventh-century Archbishop Theodore.[51] It became compulsory early in the tenth century, first appearing as such in Aethelstan's first law-code. Bishops received some of the proceeds, though less than their counterparts on the Continent where, theoretically, a bishop received a substantial percentage.[52]

Other dues too appear in royal laws.[53] Penalties for non-payment appear in Edgar's: of churchscot, a substantial fine, based on the amount due; of tithe, forfeiture of 10 per cent of the offender's property to the minster, and 40 per cent each to the bishop and to the lord of the estate. Churchbot, assessed on land and payable annually as a maintenance charge for the church, is first mentioned in a lease of 902 and subsequently in eleventh-century laws. Dues are listed in Aethelred II's laws of 1008. The tithe of young animals was payable by Pentecost and that of the fruits of the earth by All Saints' Day. Plough-alms, a penny for each plough, first referred to in Aethelstan's laws but probably of much earlier origin, was payable by fifteen days after Easter. Lightscot, a halfpenny's worth of wax, was due from every hide three times a year. Romescot, payable by St Peter's Day, was meant for the Papacy, not the local church. These laws also stipulate that soulscot, a payment for burial, first referred to in two late-ninth-century leases, should preferably be paid at the open grave. Other ecclesiastical revenues were gifts, including bequests, offerings at Sunday Masses and on feast days, of which there were a number besides the major ones of Easter, Whitsun (Pentecost) and Christmas, and perhaps penitential offerings in Lent. In some cases churches enjoyed rents and profits from their lands.[54]

As the proliferating local churches usurped the functions and the revenues of the old minsters, rulings were made about their respective entitlements. Aethelstan decreed that churchscot should be paid to the place to which it properly belonged. In Edgar's legislation all churchscot and soulscot were to go to the old minster. Aethelred II's added that this applied to soulscot even when a body was buried elsewhere, outside the proper parish. Tithe, from thegns and their tenants, was also to go to the old minster, except that any thegn who had a church with a graveyard on his own bookland was to pay only two-thirds of his tithe to the minster. The remainder was supposed to go to his own church, though there was no provision for ensuring that this third was actually paid. A local church and its priest were thus very much at the mercy of their lord. By 1066, tithes that were paid in villages went mostly to those villages' churches, and the boundaries of the local churches' parishes often coincided with those of their lords' estates.[55]

On the Continent, an important element in the financial rights of a church was baptism. Tithe was to be paid to the church where one had been baptised, and there was regulation about where people should be baptised.[56] In Anglo-Saxon England, however, although baptism was certainly required, of infants before they were thirty days old, and administered, it had no such legal significance. There is indeed some question about where baptisms were performed. For a parish church to have a fixed font inside it was neither standard, nor earlier than around 1050.[57] It was burial that was crucial to churches' rights. Edgar stipulated that churches without grave-yards were not to be financed out of tithes. In some parts of Europe in the mid-ninth century, there was a perception of the church building and its surrounding cemetery as the physical expression of the church community, uniting the living and the dead.[58] This is discernible too in England in Aethelstan's reign. It was expressed in his law that oath-breakers, who as such had left the Christian community, were not to be buried in a consecrated churchyard. Rites for churchyard consecration first appear a little before this, in the very early tenth century and it is possible that such consecration was something completely new. Unfortunately it is not clear whether the intention was to consecrate all cemeteries, or only new ones that accompanied new churches, or new cemetery boundaries.[59] Consecration of a place made it one of sanctuary and protection against violence. The *Law of the Northumbrian Priests* states that any violation of sanctuary is to be compensated for, in proportion to the status of the church, and according to what its right of protection is. As community areas and safe places, grave-yards were attractive as locations for community events, and they were often used for markets.[60]

Because of the lack of evidence, the best that can be done for Scotland is simply to try to distinguish major and minor ecclesiastical centres, whose ecclesiastical communities may have been monastic, clerical or mixed, and their territories. It is not texts, but the number and sophistication of their carved stones that identify some of the major ones. There were several of these between 800 and 1066, though not all continuously, quite apart from those which have been associated with bishoprics. Deer's community was probably mother-church and equivalent of a minster for the area that, later, was partly the parish of Deer (about 6 square miles) and partly the parish of Peterugie (modern Peterhead) to the east. This large area contains all except one of the lands that are both early grants and identifiable, and Deer parish church is sited centrally within it. Its foundation legend associates it with the sixth-century St Columba. This was probably a tenth- or eleventh-century invention, meant to attract patronage from the Gaelic nobility who were then taking part in the Gaelic take-over of Pictland.[61] Deer's property records certainly suggest a close relationship with the local aristocracy, including entertaining them at feasts at Easter and Christmas.[62]

Govan probably enjoyed royal patronage. Its proximity, across the River Clyde, to the royal residence of Partick, suggests this, as does its sculpture, the earliest piece of which is a hogback of c. 900. It includes a sarcophagus bearing a hunt scene. Govan may have become the political centre of the kingdom of Cumbria after the Vikings destroyed Dumbarton in 870.[63] Lay patronage at Meigle is suggested by the burial there of a Pictish king who died c. 842, and by the numerous ninth- and tenth-century tombstones. St Vigeans, whence an inscription that may refer to Drust son of Ferat (died c. 849) survives, was probably once an important church too.[64] Others were Hodden, Inchcolm, Kineddar, Kingarth, which lost its relics of St Bláán (Blane) to Dunblane in the mid-ninth century, Portmahomack and Whithorn.[65] These centres' economic resources must have been their own estates, gifts and whatever church dues were paid. As in the case of Wales, there is no known legislation about such dues.

Parishes, local churches and secular lordship

The parish system emerged in Scotland in the twelfth century. It had begun in Alba in the second half of the eleventh. Before that, the population had been cared for by the major churches and also, probably, in what may have been a proto-parish structure, by small local churches. Many of these may have been instituted by or co-ordinated from a major church. In north-east Scotland by about 900, some forty such small churches are detectable, dedicated to local saints of varying degrees of obscurity. Woloch, Talorcan and Gartnait, for example, whose names are Pictish, had six sites between them.[66]

Pre-Norman conquest church sites in Wales are indicated both in texts and also, probably, by curved churchyards and villages that cluster round churchyards.[67] Wales seems to have had at least as many churches as north-east Scotland before 1066, the best provision being in the south-east by the eleventh century. The numbers recently suggested for confirmed and suspected motherchurches or ecclesiastical sites in the early medieval period in the north-east,[68] north-west, where they were regularly spaced,[69] and south-west[70] are, respectively, some twenty, fourteen and thirty. Holy wells and cemeteries also seem to have been foci of lay devotion. As in Scotland's case, these involved small-scale local cults and may signify a proto-parish system, providing priests for villages.

There is evidence for early proto-parishes in Cornwall too, first in the implication of the tenth-century Vatican list that the named local churches each had a sphere of influence.[71] Second, active planning is implied in the foundations of two groups of churches, one in western and one in eastern Cornwall.[72] Their lack of earlier sculpture, the rectilinear shape of their churchyards and the form of their place-names date them to the late Anglo-Saxon period. In the western, Padstow, area, secular settlements with names incorporating the Cornish element *tre* (settlement) were regularly spaced over the countryside, and the ecclesiastical landscape matched this, each ecclesiastical site being surrounded by an estate. In 1066, most of these manors belonged to St Petroc's. It was probably St Petroc's that had founded most of the churches, for their dedications are almost all to Celtic saints. The eastern churches betray more Anglo-Saxon influence, both in their location, where other evidence shows it was strongest and in the dedication of all except one to a universal saint.

Whether there were any parishes before the tenth century is to a degree conjectural. Since parishes could not have existed without churches, the existence of the churches makes them a possibility. Yet the foundation of a church was not necessarily the same as that of a parish, with its duties, rights and boundaries. Parishes could be established around pre-existing, perhaps even long-standing churches. Whether this happened is a particular puzzle in the study of England's urban parishes, especially those of Worcester, which may have begun as early as the tenth century or as late as the twelfth.[73] By 1100 Worcester probably had ten churches. It had acquired seven since the 890s: one by 909, another by the mid-tenth century, another by 1003–1023, a fourth by 1050, two others by the mid-eleventh century and a seventh that is difficult to date. By the mid-eleventh century baptism, but not burial, was being performed at the lesser ones. Worcester's later parochial boundaries seem to be related to its tenth-century layout. For example two of them, with large rural parishes, lay outside the Anglo-Saxon defences. Overall, its parochial geography seems to fit the hypothesis that parish boundaries were rationally decided, in this case on the principle that the town's inhabitants should each be attached to the church that was nearest to them. Unfortunately no dating is available for the use of this method.

The same principle is discernible in Winchester and in London, the latter more certainly a place where the provision of pastoral care and establishment of boundaries were planned, at the end of the ninth century. This was in the context of restoration and fortification, which, like Worcester, London underwent then. Wards were created, each with a gate and a new minster, in the eastern part. London's later parochial geography indicates that some of its parishes originated in property-owners' wanting their own church, as seems to have been true in Nottingham too.[74] Such parishes were carved out of earlier ones. These had included land outside the town and had natural features as their boundaries, whereas the new ones were entirely inside the town and their boundaries abutted property boundaries. Other parishes, also to be found in London, were, seemingly, founded by communities of craftsmen. Each was a neighbourhood parish with a major road running through it. Gloucester's is another case where deliberate Anglo-Saxon pastoral provision almost certainly lies behind two parishes. They seem to have been designed in relation to the planned eastern half of the late Anglo-Saxon *burh*. One of them seems once to have been an estate of

Deerhurst. Gloucester probably had several lesser churches in the tenth century as well as the minster that was founded there at the end of the ninth century, and a total of ten by 1100.

Uncertain dating is only one obstacle to understanding the origins of urban parishes. There does not seem to have been a common pattern of development. In eastern towns small churches had burial rights and sites as soon as they were founded much more often than their western counterparts.[75] 'Parishes' will have been attached to churches and grave-yards that were short-lived, are undocumented and possibly mostly still undiscovered. A previously unknown church, which had been demolished soon after the Norman Conquest, was discovered in Norwich in 1979. It had been used for a maximum of seventy-five years, so it may have been founded in the last years of the tenth century. Burials discovered at another site in Norwich suggest another unknown, destroyed and undiscovered 'parish' church nearby.[76]

In the countryside, some local, parish, churches were founded by minsters, to facilitate their pastoral work, and others by lay lords, possibly for reasons of status. In the case of the former, the founding minsters might be expected to have tried to ensure that their foundations were effective, supporting the new churches, both financially and intellectually, out of the dues that they themselves received. That the same applies to lay lords is far less certain. These lords' churches' buildings, contents, equipment, lands and the lands' stock were the lords' property, and were treated as such.[77] There are a few references to the sale of churches. They include Domesday Book's revelations about St Mary's, Huntingdon. This had been sold by two of Edward the Confessor's priests to his chamberlain. Edward in turn had sold it to another two priests. It had previously been pledged by the abbot of Thorney to some burgesses. Domesday Book also reports ownership of fractions of churches, mostly in East Anglia and Lincolnshire.[78] Such fractions were probably the result of joint foundations in which both the costs of land, building, equipment and staff, and the subsequent profits were shared. Another possibility is that some churches had been divided between their founder's or founders' heirs. Thus for example a church in Norwich was shared between twelve burgesses, and two and a half churches in Lincoln belonged to one person. Little is known about urban churches' finances. They are thought to have had only small landed endowments, if any, and to have depended on gifts and offerings. Local rural churches were probably more, though not very, generously endowed. The counties' records in Domesday Book normally do not indicate church lands. Suffolk's, however, does. Local churches' holdings there varied, from 1 or 2 acres to 2 or 3 hides.[79]

Notwithstanding their niggardly endowments, there is no evidence that lay lords took for themselves the dues or offerings paid to their new churches, as their Continental counterparts certainly did. Nor is it easy to generalise about the financial circumstances of local priests. Some priests apparently owned their churches, whether by purchase, gift or inheritance.[80] Aelfric's strictures against selling and taking money for a church, and the *Northumbrian Priests' Law*'s against trafficking in churches may each refer to lords requiring priests to pay fees on taking up appointment, rather than their actually selling churches. If so, it might suggest that priests had hereditary tenure. Other evidence too suggests this. All Saints in Lincoln was the inheritance of its successive priests but could not be given out of the city or out of the kin. Three churches of Archenfield owed 20 shillings upon the death of their incumbents, who in life owed the king messenger service into Wales and the saying of two Masses a week.[81]

Some priests, however, may have been merely tenants, enjoying the property and its revenue, and possibly paying rent, as suggested by certain wills. In one dating from between 980 and 990, a certain Aethelgifu gave half a hide to a church and a man to the priest, who was to hold the church for life, provided he kept it in repair. This priest was clearly a slave, for she stipulated too that he was to be freed. The phenomenon of unfree priests may have been common, as it had become on the Continent by 818. On the other hand Aelfric's and Archbishop Wulfstan II's concerns and the *Northumbrian Priests' Law* imply that priests were independent. In one text associated with Wulfstan, Mass priests actually have the same wergeld as secular thegns and their oaths are equally valuable.[82]

National Churches?

A national Church might be said to have one or all of the following attributes: its people have a sense of a national identity; it aspires to be a national Church; it is perceived by contemporaries as, or potentially as, a national Church; it is a collective of units functioning as one unit; it has a hierarchical or centralised structure for governance and leadership; the units that make up the whole resemble each other, in general, in their values, practices and institutions.

There was not, in any meaningful sense, a Celtic Church, though the idea has had, and indeed still has, a popular and romantic appeal. The Churches in Scotland, Wales, Cornwall, Ireland and Brittany certainly had elements in common that differentiated them from those in Germanic lands. But they also had things in common with other Churches, and differed from each other. Furthermore, there was no organisational structure that linked, let alone united, them.[83] In Wales and Alba the Church lacked hierarchy and centralisation. Nor did it have the close relationship with kings, including protection in legislation, that Anglo-Saxon ones did.

In Anglo-Saxon England by contrast, the Church was usually closely linked to the most dominant, or single, ruling dynasty, and had both a hierarchical structure and active leadership and direction from Canterbury. Examples abound. Aethelstan's new coronation ritual was probably written, especially for him, by Archbishop Athelm.[84] The Church functioned and tried to function as a single organisation, as for instance in synods. Liturgical manuscripts suggest that Canterbury was a major source of reform, in culture and liturgy, in the 920s and mid-tenth-century.[85] The later-tenth-century monastic reform movement was led by Archbishop Dunstan, as well as Bishops Oswald and Aethelwold, in partnership with King Edgar. Over one-third of the surviving episcopal books, that is, books needed by bishops to perform their episcopal role in services, originated in

Canterbury.[86] Both Canterbury and York seem normally to have made a new Pontifical for a new archbishop and given his predecessor's book to another bishop in the archdiocese. Aelfric sent everything that he wrote, including revised versions, to Canterbury. There, copies were made, though sometimes with alterations, and then distributed.[87] As a result, his homilies circulated throughout England. There are thirty-five surviving copies and there is evidence that fifty more once existed. These will have contributed significantly to a sense of English identity.[88] By Aelfric's own account, the saints whose lives were commemorated in his *Catholic Homilies* were those venerated by all the English people, whereas his *Lives of Saints*, which likewise functioned as sermons, were concerned with saints who were commemorated only in monastic houses.

Specialisation in production of manuscripts is discernible by 1000, even though the origins of nearly one-third of those surviving are unknown.[89] This may be indicative of deliberate co-ordination, if not also of central direction. Hymnals were a speciality of Canterbury's cathedral. Canterbury also produced copies of works by the Anglo-Saxon author Aldhelm and the Continental Boethius, Prosper and Prudentius: their multiplicity suggests that they were intended for distribution. Glossed Psalters were a speciality of Winchester, which also produced liturgical texts.[90] That there was a reasonably widespread co-operation is clear from the improvement made to the see of Exeter's library by its last pre-Conquest bishop, Leofric. Of his additions (sixty-six in total), some were from Canterbury cathedral, one from Worcester and one from Dorchester, and of the exemplars that he obtained for copying, one was from Winchester and one from Ramsbury.

Finally, tenth-century ecclesiastical policy may have been in part inspired by the history and characteristics of the English Church as recounted and advocated by Bede in his *Ecclesiastical History of the People* [singular] *of the English* [plural]. This is hardly surprising. One of the reasons that Bede wrote it was precisely to provide models for policy and conduct, which he did very effectively. The work was known, both through its late-ninth-century Old English translation, and in its original Latin. The late-seventh-century Church of Bede's pages was not, naturally, the Church as it had actually existed. In Bede's presentation, the time was a Golden Age. Its Church was a monastic Church; united under Canterbury and ultimately Rome; coterminous or destined to be coterminous with the rule of English kings severally and of a single English over-lord; identified with a single English people, in whose ethnogenesis Bede himself, through his writing, played an important role.

Bede's influence in the tenth century has been detected in matters little and big. The draftsman of the Latin document detailing the reorganisation of the West Saxon sees in 909 may have been influenced by the *Ecclesiastical History*.[91] Winchester's mid-tenth-century attempt to terminate the see of Selsey was perhaps inspired by Bede's account that when it was created it was subject to Winchester.[92] Despite being heavily influenced by Continental reform and reformed houses the late-tenth-century English reform had several idiosyncrasies, the most notable its unparalleled attempt to monasticise cathedrals.[93] The tenth-century English Church's model was the Church of the *Ecclesiastical History*. That Church was a national Church.

Changes in ecclesiastical organisation and financing, often with royal involvement, are partially discernible in England, but only with difficulty to its north and west, though there is some evidence of ecclesiastical centres and effective ministry there. The minster system was undermined by increasing episcopal power, and by the rise of local churches and the beginnings of modern parishes, which presented Church and churchmen with problems as well as opportunities. Monastic reform was embraced by the elite, its leaders finding inspiration in the past. They overstated its necessity and achievements, but it undeniably strengthened the monarchy.

Notes

1 See Driscoll, *Alba*; Rollason, *Northumbria*; Woolf, *From*.
2 W. Davies, 'Myth'.
3 *Ibid.*, *Wales*.
4 J.R. Davies, 'Book'.
5 Keynes, 'Edward'; Heighway; Rumble, 'Edward'.
6 Abrams, 'Conversion … Danelaw'.
7 *Ibid.*
8 Barrow, 'Churches'.
9 For what follows, Jankulak.
10 Rollason, *Northumbria*.
11 Giandrea.
12 John, 'Church'.
13 For what follows, Barrow, 'Chronology … Benedictine', 'Community', 'Wulfstan'.
14 Barrow, 'Wulfstan'.
15 Rosenwein, *Negotiating*; Wormald, 'Lordship', 'Oswaldslow'.
16 For this, Wormald, 'Strange'.
17 Giandrea.
18 See Barrow, 'Clergy'.
19 For Councils, Cubitt, *Anglo-Saxon*; Keynes, *Councils*. For Worcester, Barrow, 'Community', 'Wulfstan'; Tinti, *Sustaining*.
20 S. Wood.
21 Barrow, 'Chronology … Forgery'.
22 Dyer, 'Bishop'.
23 S. Wood. Rosenwein, *Negotiating*. See also Foot, *Monastic*; Yorke, *Nunneries*.
24 Foot, *Monastic*; Yorke, *Nunneries*.
25 S. Wood.
26 *Ibid.*
27 Giandrea.
28 Rollason, *Two*.
29 T.O. Clancy, 'Deer'.
30 Macquarrie, 'Early'.
31 W. Davies, *Early*, 'Myth', *Wales*.
32 Rosenwein, *Negotiating*.
33 Blair, *Church*.
34 S. Wood.
35 *Ibid.*
36 Macquarrie, 'Early'.
37 S. Wood.
38 T.O. Clancy, 'Deer'; Driscoll, *Alba*; Macquarrie, 'Early'.
39 Foot, *Monastic*.

40 Abrams, *Anglo-Saxon.*
41 Tinti, *Sustaining.*
42 Foot, *Veiled* I.
43 See Edwards, 'Early-Medieval', Handley; Higgitt, 'Words'.
44 Forsyth, 'Stones'.
45 Bassett, 'Origins'; Tinti, *Sustaining.*
46 Blair, *Church*; S. Wood.
47 Bassett, *Origins.*
48 Blair, *Church*; Giandrea; S. Wood.
49 Blair, *Church.*
50 *Ibid.*
51 S. Wood.
52 *Ibid.*
53 For these, Blair, *Church*; Giandrea.
54 S. Wood.
55 *Ibid.*
56 Moore, *First.*
57 Blair, *Church*; C.A. Jones, 'Old'.
58 S. Wood.
59 Gittos, 'Creating'.
60 Genicot; S. Wood.
61 T.O. Clancy, 'Deer'; Taylor, 'Toponymic'.
62 Macquarrie, 'Early'.
63 Driscoll, *Alba, Govan.*
64 Macquarrie, 'Early'.
65 Driscoll, *Alba.*
66 T.O. Clancy, 'Deer'.
67 Silvester.
68 Silvester and Evans.
69 Davidson.
70 Ludlow.
71 Olson and Padel.
72 For what follows, Preston-Jones.
73 For what follows, Baker and Holt, and for Worcester's churches, Holt.
74 For what follows, Baker and Holt.
75 Barrow, 'Churches'.
76 S. Wood.
77 For what follows, *ibid.*
78 See also Blair, *Church.*
79 S. Wood.
80 *Ibid.*
81 *Ibid.*
82 *Ibid.*
83 W. Davies, 'Myth'.
84 Nelson, 'First'.
85 Dumville.
86 *Ibid.*
87 Teresi.
88 Wilcox, 'Ælfric', *Ælfric's.*
89 For what follows, Giandrea.
90 Gretsch, 'Junius'.
91 Rumble, 'Edward'.
92 Wormald, 'Strange'.
93 Wormald, 'Æthelwold'.

6   Social cohesion

Introduction

Quite apart from stimulating a sense of English national identity, Christianity and the Church, in their various aspects, made a major contribution to the social cohesion of the communities of Britain. These comprised mixed lay–religious ones, those of the (questionable) nation, dioceses, towns, villages and rural communities, and, within them, specialised ecclesiastical ones, of monks, nuns and cathedral clergy. Among the things that gave them community identity were, in England, activities within dioceses (including the workings of ecclesiastical estates), monastic landholding and monastic timetables, the beginnings of parishes, saints' cults, spiritual kinship, penance and pilgrimage. These operated simultaneously with royal policy, popular assemblies and institutions of local government and law and order, works of literature and of history which themselves had a strongly Christian element, and the propagation of ideals and aspirations by various means.

Christians, nations and kingdoms

An important question about tenth- and eleventh-century England is whether Danish, Mercian and Northumbrian identities were separate from and conflicted with English identity, and involved aspirations to separate rule. Opinions have differed. Currently, however, the weight of the evidence is against separatism.[1] With the exception of differing burial practice in the 870s, when the barrow cemetery at Heath Wood was created,[2] Scandinavian regimes and settlers worked within and with the structures and practices of indigenous society. For example, they used burial practice and sculpted monuments to establish a position and status of dominance, and to advertise it to their Anglo-Saxon neighbours and subordinates. Conversion to Christianity strengthened both rulers' and settlers' positions, and became widespread. The cult of East Anglia's King Edmund as a voluntary martyr, evidenced on East Anglian coins around 895 and continuing through the tenth century, made amicable native–incomer cohesion there possible. The Anglo-Saxon East Anglians were spared humiliation by Edmund's military defeat and the Danish ones needed only to convert, not to be defeated, to be acceptable.[3] Perhaps the most famous example of integration is that one of the leaders of the ecclesiastical reform, Bishop Oswald, was of Danish origin. This has been deduced from the facts that his family held land in East Anglia, that his grandfather and his parents were perceived as Danes, and that two of his kinsmen had Scandinavian names. The family's assimilation is demonstrable by the ecclesiastical careers, as bishops and as abbots, of several of its members besides Oswald himself, including his uncle Oda, who had been archbishop of Canterbury (941–958).[4]

Naturally, such integration sometimes involved differentiation from Wessex. Wessex's view of Edmund was that he had been defeated rather than martyred. The East Anglians only partly imitated Alfred in their coinage, using the weight standard of Offa of Mercia of the 790s rather than Alfred's.[5] In Northumbria, Scandinavian rule enjoyed the support not only of St Cuthbert's community, but also that of archbishops in York, especially Wulfstan I (931–956). His policy has been seen as an expression of regionalism, which is also detectible in sculpture.[6] Northumbrian Anglo-Scandinavian sculpture includes some pieces that featured allusions to Norse myth, which are probably indicative of genuine internalisation of Christianity. Much Anglo-Scandinavian sculpture is obviously funerary, and associated with the foundation of local churches, which itself symbolised and proclaimed the founders' legitimacy, status and power, as lords and landholders.[7] The distribution of pieces made in York stone may be an indication that in the north the archbishop himself was involved in, and authorised, the founding and equipping of such churches.[8] Both the geographical and chronological distribution of the sculpture suggest that it was an expression of a regional identity, the 'others' against which this was defined being, certainly, southern English, but also Scandinavian.[9] The sculpture was a northern and eastern phenomenon rather than a southern one and there was no tradition of stone carving in Scandinavia.

People of Danish origin were not isolated from the English either by their religion or, as we have seen, by their language.[10] Nor were these people perceived as separate and problematic groups. In the late Anglo-Saxon sources, what is meant by Danes, who were indeed troublesome, is Scandinavians who had arrived recently, not descendants of ninth-century settlers.[11] The legal autonomy of the Danelaw, suggested by some references in law-codes including one of Edgar's, probably dating to the 970s, may be more apparent than real, a regional rather than an ethnic legal tradition. Certainly Edgar simultaneously imposed some laws explicitly on all people. Aethelred's code promulgated at Wantage in, possibly, 997, extended his earlier laws to previously Scandinavian territory and specifically the Five Boroughs.[12] Furthermore, the individuals and groups who submitted, in his reign, to Danish invaders were not acting out of a sense of Danishness. Not all their motives are known, but personal factors and local rivalries were very important in some cases.[13] When Archbishop Wulfstan II of York addressed the English people in his calls for repentance, he envisaged them as including baptised and settled Danes, as well as persons of indigenous origin.[14]

Whether there was a 'Danish issue' during the reign of the Danish King Cnut is more uncertain. That Cnut is praised in Old Norse but not in Old English poetry may indicate alienation. It has been suggested that in Winchester a Danish elite revelled in memories of Cnut's conquest, and his victory over King Edmund at the battle of Ashingdon (1016), even twelve years after the event, in a manner likely to have been painful to the English.[15] Promises in Cnut's 1027 letter to the English, that henceforth his councillors and officials would not consent to injustice or use unjust force, and that he himself would repair anything that had been done 'contrary to what is right', rather imply that hitherto injustice had indeed occurred and been tolerated, despite earlier agreements and promises.[16] In 1018, one year after Cnut's accession to Wessex, two after his accession to Mercia, an agreement between Danes and English had been made at Oxford and a law-code, attributable to Archbishop Wulfstan II, produced. In a letter of 1019–1020 Cnut had promised to be a gracious lord and observe just law. One explanation of the dearth of documents for his reign is that it was too traumatic for documents to be produced, or preserved, or both. Another, however, is that since trauma tends to stimulate production of texts (for example complaints and manifestos), the lack of texts signifies lack of trauma.

Whichever is correct, Cnut allowed Archbishop Wulfstan II to mould him and his image. A major architect of the continuity that marked Cnut's reign, Wulfstan worked to establish an integrated society that was pleasing to God by its peace and justice, and he encouraged and supported Cnut to become a good Christian king.[17] The legislation and letter of 1019–1020 that were written in Cnut's name signified that Edgar's laws were the regime's gold standard. In 1020, Wulfstan, with many bishops, consecrated a minster for Cnut at Ashingdon, thereby commemorating, as if in thanksgiving, the victory that had given him England.[18] The law-code of 1020 drew very heavily on Wulfstan's earlier works, and has been described as effectively weaving Cnut's kingship into the legal and ecclesiastical fabric of England, offering a programme for a regenerated English people under the new regime.[19] As his wife, Aethelred's widow Queen Emma also contributed to Cnut's legitimation. Their success is indicated not only by Cnut's success in retaining England, but also by the unprecedented level of his commemoration in English obituary lists.[20]

Except for language, names and terminology, the respects in which the so-called Danelaw territories differed from the English may have been due not to Scandinavian settlers and innovations but to earlier inheritances. Regional identity may lie behind the fact that in some Irish and English sources the Anglo-Saxon rulers of Bamburgh in Northumbria are referred to as kings despite, and after, according to the *Anglo-Saxon Chronicle*, King Aethelstan's having succeeded to the kingdom of the Northumbrians. Mercia too retained a regional identity and there may have been some fragility in its union with Wessex. The two were united in 886, after what the *Anglo-Saxon Chronicle* called the submission to Alfred of all the English people who were not subject to the Danes. Aethelred, the former ruler of Mercia, was demoted to ealdorman. His wife Aethelflaed, Alfred's daughter, is termed queen in the *Welsh Annals*, and their charters represent them as acting independently of Wessex.[21] The fact that the Mercians accepted Aethelflaed's rule even after she was widowed has been interpreted as indicative of a desire for some independence.[22] So too has the fact that the innovative crowned-bust design that was used on King Aethelstan's coins from the early 930s never appears on those minted in Mercia, as if its ideological implications were unpalatable there.[23] Separatism might also be implied by succession disputes and by the separation of the two kingdoms in 955. After King Eadred died, his nephews Eadwig and Edgar succeeded, respectively, to Wessex and Mercia.

On the other hand, Alfred's daughter and son-in-law neither issued coins of their own nor used royal titles in their charters. When Alfred's nephew Aethelwold unsuccessfully contested the succession of Edward the Elder, his supporters included one of the families who had a claim to the Mercian throne, as well as the Northumbrian Danes who accepted him as king. Since Aethelwold also had influence in East Anglia his challenge was not separatist.[24] It was for rule of the whole. Later, coins suggest that the division between Eadwig and Edgar may have been only partial. Eadwig retained and exercised authority in Mercia, minting coins there even after Edgar took up its kingship in 957. The division may have been meant merely as a temporary expedient[25] or, possibly, as following West Saxon precedents for joint kingship.[26] In the ninth century, Kent had been entrusted to the king of Wessex's intended successor. The disputes that followed Edgar's death were personal and about the royal succession, though entangled with attempts to recover property that the Church had gained during his reign. They were not a Mercian reaction against Wessex.[27]

Multiple identities, which did not conflict with each other, were possible for individuals and for groups, and people with different identities could work together. Both Cornish and Anglo-Saxon names appear within each category of individuals in the manumissions in the Bodmin Gospels, namely manumittees, manumitters and witnesses, though in varying proportions.[28] Some people had both a Cornish and an English name. The different continuations of the *Anglo-Saxon Chronicle* combine local content and interests with an English perspective, even in the complaint about Aethelred II's reign that no shire would help others.[29] In the account of Cnut's victory at Ashingdon the dead who are named came from different areas, and all the English nation and all the nobility of England are referred to.[30] Localities were well connected to the royal centre, through local people who served in the royal household, the dowries and entourages of kings' brides, royal itinerations,[31] hunting expeditions that gave participants experience of collective action and reward and a demonstration of the virtues of collaboration, and by the national character of the Church. Alfred and the tenth-century reformers espoused and propagated belief in a lost (shared) Golden Age. Such a belief is one element, according to some theorists, of national identity.[32]

Ruling elites not only desired, but also took steps to encourage, the cohesion of new political units. Changes in political vocabulary that were coined and spread suggest this.[33] Alfred's traditional title was 'king of the West Saxons', but after his acquisition of Mercia he used the title 'king of the English' in some charters and in others, 'king of the Anglosaxons'. This last was also used of him by Asser, and sometimes by Edward the Elder and Aethelstan for themselves.[34] Alfred's circle also used *Angelcynn* (Anglekin), previously very little used, to signify the totality of his people and as an equivalent of the *gens Anglorum* of Bede's *Ecclesiastical History*.[35] All except two of Edward's coins that were minted in Mercia call him, simply, 'king'.[36] After Aethelstan, 'king of the English' was a norm, though until Wessex and Mercia were divided Eadwig appeared in some charters as 'king of the Anglosaxons'.[37] By the eleventh century, *Engla lond* and *Englisc* were being used much as 'England' and 'English' are today. These creative developments suggest a growing and increasingly strong sense of an English identity.[38] By the same token, the lack of a new term to signify 'state' has been suggested to indicate that this sense of identity did not include the concept of a state.[39]

Other titles were also developed, embodying a different aspiration which, by contrast, was unsuccessful, namely to rule over all Britain. This aim may have been underpinned by Canterbury's earlier claiming such authority. Dedicating his work to Alfred, Asser terms him *rector* of all Christians of the island of Britain, though king only of the Angles and Saxons. Kingship of all Britain was claimed in reign after reign in the tenth century, though the form of words varied. Thus from around 927 Aethelstan used on coins and in some charters the title 'king of the whole of Britain', and in the early 930s his charters made him 'king of the English elevated by Christ to the throne of the whole kingdom of *Britannia*' (Britain).[40] Another name used for Britain and claims to its dominion was 'Albion'. This usage too seems to have had an ecclesiastical stimulus and a special association with the reformers of the Church. Bede had pointed out that Britain had once been called Albion. In the Second Coronation *Ordo* the new king is to care for 'the church of all Albion' with the peoples annexed to it. The charters of the early 950s that were produced by a scribe or drafter known to scholars as Dunstan B use the title 'king of Albion'. Eadred's and Eadwig's charters use 'king of the whole of Britain'; Eadwig's corpus also includes 'king of Albion'.[41]

The claim to dominion over more than England is especially marked in Edgar's reign. In the opening of the *Regularis Concordia* Aethelwold terms Edgar king both of the English and of the other peoples dwelling within the boundaries of the island of Britain. In a text written in the 990s and possibly reflecting the reformers' usage, Byrhtferth of Ramsey refers to the king's subordinates as the nobility of all Albion. Edgar's claim to Albion is particularly evident in the corpus of the charters. One-third of the 151 apparently pre-1066 charters that refer to Albion are his. They contain three times as many references as any other king's. Interestingly, the grandiose titles appear in the section where Edgar is described as granting the land. In the witness lists, 'king of the English' is preferred.[42]

Another motif that recurs is that of the Jews, though there were none living in Britain, and its inhabitants knew Jews only through the Bible and other texts. This was to foster cohesion among the English. The English Church's liturgy, texts and pictures encouraged its members to identify themselves as a new people of Israel, which in the Old Testament was God's chosen people.[43] Additionally, the history of the Jews was used to understand the relationship between past and present and Jews themselves in the construction of English identity.[44] Some were represented as good examples to follow, others as the reverse. At a time of Viking attacks Aelfric presented the Maccabees as models. They had rebelled against foreign rule and persecution of Jews, in the second century BC. Aelfric even accorded Judas Maccabeus the right to be considered a saint. He translated Judith to serve as an example so that 'our land' should be protected, with weapons, against an invading army. In the Vercelli and Blickling homilies Jews are used, in one scholar's analysis, as a vehicle for the shared hate that some people think is involved in communal bonding. And *Elene*, one of the poems in the Vercelli manuscript, contains explicitly anti-Jewish sentiment, blaming the Jews for the Crucifixion.[45] The only other groups used as 'other' in Anglo-Saxon identity construction were the Britons and the pagans from the north.

English cohesion did not, naturally, preclude internal disagreements. Aelfric's *About the People of Israel*, composed between 998 and 1005, focuses on rebellion and teaches that Christians should be submissive to those whose authority derives from God, as did that of bishops and priests. Many people, he claims, had said that they did not wish to listen to the teaching of God. This suggests some degree of social or political tension, though he does not reveal what was at issue.[46] It might have been related to his statement elsewhere, in connection with the three orders of society, that those who fought should not compel those who prayed to engage in worldly fighting.

Yet the fact that English kings exerted power beyond what their coercive resources could have supported presupposes a level of collective solidarity that it makes sense to call national, implying participation or consent across a wide social span.[47] This 'political nation' interacted with kings in the shires, and acted, both there and in the hundreds, in community meetings. Behind at least four tenth-century law-codes, of Aethelstan, lies co-operation between the king, great men and local elites. After 956, assemblies and the issuing of charters are closely connected.[48] The charters, and possibly the law-codes too, will have created communities united in acceptance not merely of particular texts but of particular interpretations of them. That boundary clauses in (the otherwise Latin) charters are in the vernacular suggests that they were meant to be read aloud, perhaps in the estates to which they related as well as in assemblies.[49] People could participate in the grants by their very presence, even if they did not understand the language in which they were recorded.[50]

Assemblies were probably regular, even common, occurrences, part of the mental landscape just as their locations were part of the physical one. Place-names that include an element meaning 'assembly', often combined with one for 'mound', suggest that large numbers, perhaps thousands, attended, often at what they thought was an ancestral burial mound.[51] Edgar's laws state that the shire assembly, or court, which would hear legal cases and distribute its taxation burden across its hundreds, was to meet twice a year. The shire's peace-time responsibilities may have developed only in the tenth century but its military ones were ancient. The hundred courts first appear in the mid-tenth-century Hundred Ordinance, but the place-names suggest that their meetings had a long history.[52] Hundred courts were supposed to meet every four weeks, *burh* courts three times a year, and they too transacted a variety of business. Individuals had responsibility for more than just their own conduct. Aethelstan's and Aethelred's laws show that localities and lords were made responsible for bringing offenders to justice, one incentive being a share of the profits (forfeited property or fines) where the accused were found guilty.[53] Surety-ship, whereby one or more persons guaranteed the good behaviour of another, developed to the point that Edgar decreed that every man was to be under surety. He also enjoined that every *burh* and hundred have a permanent body of sworn witnesses, to provide two or three witnesses for every purchase or sale.[54]

Assemblies were one of the vehicles whereby kings and ecclesiastics disseminated their messages of royal dominion and national identity to very large numbers of people. There were at least five others, in all of which the Church and Christianity were directly involved. Aelfric's sermons and other texts show that the laity participated in the liturgy, especially at Christmas, Easter and Rogationtide (when God's blessing on the spring crops was invoked). Other church rites and ceremonies buttressed the army's sense of community and morale. A third stimulus to collective identity was provided by the exhortation to give alms, which recurs in surviving sermons, and by the teaching that the poor, as recipients of charity, were essential to the salvation of the rich, implying that rich and poor made up a single community. The plentiful evidence of charitable bequests suggests that this ideal was at least partially realised. Fourth, there was the teaching that the sins of individuals brought collective punishment from God, and, conversely, that He rewarded personal reform and virtue with collective well-being. Fifth, imagination of community and national identity were encouraged, less directly, through texts. The purposeful circulation of Aelfric's works has already been mentioned. There is some evidence that from the time of Alfred the *Anglo-Saxon Chronicle* was not only updated but also displayed in major churches in Wessex, and it is possible that Alfred's laws too were displayed, at least at Winchester.[55] In Edgar's reign, however, the *Anglo-Saxon Chronicle* was not maintained. Its continuation seems to have stopped being an interest of a community and fallen to a series of individual scribes.[56]

Finally, poetry, declaimed in the halls of royalty and nobility, offered the elite laity not merely entertainment but also instruction, in values and rules of conduct and in messages about the past that were relevant to present and imminent concerns.[57] This may be why learning Saxon poems was one of Alfred's enthusiasms. Almost all that survives has, as we have seen, some religious content. *Beowulf* can be considered as belonging to the 'mirror for princes' genre of literature. Some poems offered a New Israel self-image. Lessons were sometimes spelt out, sometimes left for the audience to deduce. *Juliana* and *Judith* for example carry the messages that the good Christian should have martial as well as sexual virtue, that Vikings and paganism (the contemporary equivalents of the villains of the poems) should be resisted, and that Christianity is worth dying for. The *Battle of Maldon* contains sentiments of Englishness and patriotism and a concern for honour, glory and loyalty. It may have been intended as the literary memorial to its fallen hero, Ealdorman Byrhtnoth.[58] A shared past was constructed and disseminated not only in poetry and historical works, but also in what look like far less exciting texts, including lists, for example of kings and of bishops. Lists and collections of lists brought together people, places and times, pointing up and implying inter-connections.[59] There are several in the manuscript that King Aethelstan gave to the Cuthbert community.[60]

Scotland's lack of textual evidence makes it almost impossible to assess the extent and the methods of propagation of any national feeling there. The apparent lack of an accomplished indigenous historian must have retarded the creation of the imagined community of the nation. Physical and political geography, and the potential for resentments following the union of the Pictish and Gaelic polities, in the mid-ninth century, would also have hindered such development. Ninety per cent of the place-names that include the Pictish element *pet* or *pit*, meaning a landholding unit, have a Gaelic second element and are found in the best agricultural land. They may represent Pictish estates taken over by Gaelic people. If so, they suggest extensive high-level dispossession.[61] The eventual displacement of the Pictish language (British) by Gaelic may also suggest disruption, though we do not know how long it took. British language may have lasted until the eleventh century.[62] The extent of displacement and suffering caused by Scandinavian settlement in the second half of the century is debatable, but may have been very significant.

On the other hand there are some positive indications and parallels to English phenomena. Govan's sculpture implies a significant, integrated, Norse presence, at least at the royal centre of the kingdom of Strathclyde.[63] Cinaed mac Alpín's dynasty may have been Pictish, not Gaelic. Exactly what happened when he took over Pictland, and the degree of resistance, remains opaque, as does the question of whether after c. 900 Alba had a new identity, or a predominantly Pictish one, or a predominantly Gaelic one. According to the view that Alba developed as a state with a royal administrative structure, later political conflicts most likely involved attempts to take over royal resources and the whole kingdom rather than to break away from it.[64] In the eleventh century, the pilgrimages to Rome, of Mael Coluim II, leaving Macbethad as ruler in his absence, of Macbethad when king himself, and of Earl Thorfinnr of Orkney in 1050, could mean that these rulers felt that their rule was secure enough to survive their absence.[65]

The English creation of new political terminology was anticipated in Scotland. England's *Albion* derived from the same Latin word as Scotland's *Alba*. The name Alba was first used in Irish sources, for the kingdom of Cinaed mac Alpín and his successors, c. 900 and thereafter consistently. It was a usage that originated in Alba itself. The name emphasised territory rather than people, and it, and the *Chronicle of the Kings of Alba*, may have been meant to signify that Alba was a new, unified polity.[66] The promotion of St Andrew, ultimately to be Scotland's patron saint, may have been part of the same ideology. Andrew had no historical connection with either Picts or Irish, though there were traditions both that he had been to Scythia and that the Picts and Irish originated there.[67] He could have been considered a neutral figure. Whether the English adopted *Albion* coincidentally, rather than in imitation of, or as a reaction and counter-claim to practice in Alba is unknown. But English writers' continued use of the term 'king of the Scots' suggests that they perceived a northern *Alba* as somehow unacceptable, or threatening, since it is unlikely that they were ignorant of the new practice.

As in England so in Scotland royal authority was exercised in a context of popular assemblies. Some of the prominent standing stones may, among other things, have marked regional assembly places. The large, low, oval, flat-topped mound Moot Hill at Scone, close to the Hill of Faith where a meeting is reported for 906, and which is referred to as a royal city, is artificial. Its building, and Scone's importance, seem to be linked to the adoption of the name Alba, since there is no evidence for earlier royal activity there. And the use of the now emotive Stone of Destiny in coronation ceremonies may have begun at the same time.[68] At Govan, a road linked the church to the large mound known as Doomster Hill, which was certainly a place of assembly and legal proceedings after the medieval period. It might have functioned likewise then.[69]

In Wales such developments were far less marked. The Pillar of Elise was erected on a mound, and it has been suggested that the site may have been an assembly place, and possibly where kings of Powys were inaugurated.[70] It was the continuously threatening Anglo-Saxons, not the Vikings, whose attacks began in 852 and continued until the 1080s, who functioned as the 'other' in expressions of identity, which remained British rather than Welsh. Nennius' *History* attempted to forge a people, as Bede's had for the English, offering them a shared history, from their coming to Britain up to the end of the fifth century.[71] Though in reality Britain had been a land of multiple kingships before the Roman conquest, and was mostly organised into Roman provinces after it, Nennius reported that in AD 167 the Britons had had one king and some underkings, all of whom converted that year to Christianity.[72] He represented the (fictitious) leadership of Arthur, in the later fifth century, as a time of victories over the Anglo-Saxons. He seems also to have thought that according to prophecies the time for their expulsion was at hand, and implied that King Merfyn of Gwynedd was being positioned as offering a chance of Arthurian-type success and reconquest in the future.[73] The immediate enemy other was the Mercians. *The Gododdin* and poems about Urien of Rheged likewise offered a vision of a lost Golden Age, claiming for British history the territories (in northern England and southern Scotland) wherein the events they recounted occurred. They too could have stimulated a sense of national identity and functioned as encouragement to claim these northern lands for, and in, the future.[74]

Nevertheless, the Britons differed among themselves about both history and the geography of Britishness. As we have seen, Nennius and the near-contemporary Pillar of Elise offered very different views of the early-fifth-century Vortigern of Powys. The tenth century offers another contrast. The author of *Armes Prydein* envisaged an alliance of all the Britons, from Manaw (the Stirling region) to Brittany, to recover all of Britain, despite the contemporary alliances between England and both Dyfed and Brittany. For him, the Britons were Britain's rightful owners and their dispossession by the English, begun in the fifth century and its unacceptability compounded by Aethelstan's taxation, illegitimate. A few years later, the compiler of the St David's annals conceived the Britons as a chosen people of God, but, probably because Owain of Dyfed needed English support, was not anti-English. Nor did he claim the whole island of Britain. His Arthur is less Joshua-like and militant than Nennius'.[75]

Texts were often read aloud. The Elise Pillar's inscription in fact invites its reader to do so.[76] This means that ideas that appear in texts could have been far more widespread than restricted literacy would suggest. Nennius probably had an audience at the court of King Merfyn that was capable of understanding his biblical allusions. Royal courts and monasteries were probably exposed to the poetry. But in the absence of frequent church-going, which would have meant exposure to liturgy and sermons, of royal coinage and of public assemblies, it is not safe to infer that their ideas would have reached a wider audience. Nor was there much movement towards political unity. There were only two short spells of near-unity or unity: one, in the north, under Rhodri Mawr in the 870s, another under Gruffudd between 1055 and 1063.

Dioceses, towns, villages and localities

In some cases it is demonstrable, and in others somewhat hypothetical, though plausible by analogy, that there was significant social cohesion and sense of community within cathedral communities, between them and their wider diocesan communities, and within each diocese as a whole.[77] The great reform monasticised only four cathedrals, to varying degrees, but the non-monastic cathedrals (of canons) may have resembled them in significant respects. Like monks, canons were meant to follow a Rule. Theirs was a version of one composed by the eighth-century Chrodegang of Metz. Except for allowing private property, it was very similar to the monks' *Regularis Concordia*. Unfortunately, the evidence for its observance is sketchy, mostly mid-eleventh century, and may reveal aspiration rather than practice. The wide availability of basic educational texts, and others, across England, warrants the inference that at least some cathedrals had schools, and the facilities to improve pastoral care as the reformers wanted. Any canons that did observe their rule would have acted as a community every day. Like monks, canons had Divine Office and the daily Chapter Office, meant for administration and the confession of faults. Unfortunately, the numbers of individuals involved are not clear. The attestations to Bishop Oswald of Worcester's leases (961–992) show an increase between 970 and 977, with about twenty-five witnesses per lease in 977–978, and a decline in the late 980s, when the average number of witnesses was sixteen to eighteen. Under Bishop Wulfstan I, numbers were much smaller. Under Bishop Lyfing (1038–1040 and 1041–1046) the largest number recorded is twelve.[78] At Winchester, the New Minster community comprised seventeen priests, eleven deacons and nine *pueri* (boys) in 1031. At Hereford, according to Domesday Book, the number living in the cathedral was two.[79] At St Petroc's in Cornwall never more than eight, and normally between three and four were recorded as witnessing a manumission.[80]

Cathedral communities forged bonds with people outside.[81] Burial linked them with the kin of the dead and with others who hoped in future to be buried there, since people often made donations to their intended resting places. As Chrodegang had, they may have invited priests from outside to attend their Chapter on Sundays and feast days. The bishop may have entertained diocesan priests and lay people. The clergy engaged in ceremonial foot-washing of the congregation in Lent. In Worcester, Bishop Oswald washed the feet of twelve poor men in Lent every day, which was more than was required.[82] Guesthouses, like schools, should have been open all year. Not only did local people go to cathedrals: cathedral staff reached out to the people. Local priests were probably cathedral trained. Bishops, in theory, regularly travelled throughout their sees to perform confirmation, which every Christian was meant to receive. And in practice they did, though perhaps only episodically. Aethelwold of Winchester and Wulfstan II of Worcester are attested as doing so, and the confirmation ritual is included in full or in part in some tenth- and eleventh-century Pontificals. The ceremony was brief, though its length depended on how many people had to be confirmed. Bishops also consecrated new churches in their dioceses. In this rite, the aspirations for the individual church were the same as for the nation as a whole. The celebrants were established as a covenant people of God, with Christ, Mary, the angels and saints as witnesses.[83]

Another mechanism that contributed to diocesan cohesion was lay donation.[84] It linked donors and their families with God, the saint to whom the gift was, officially, given, and the ecclesiastical community that represented him or her. Since donors were prayed for by name, their gifts both preserved their memory after their deaths and contributed to their families' continued power and authority, which partly depended on having illustrious ancestors. Surviving requests for prayers include specifying Masses and the singing of fifty psalms on the anniversary of death, thirty psalms and a Mass every Saturday, a Mass daily. Disputes about land tenure offered opportunities of reaffirming, at intervals, the relationships that the original donations had established. Giving precious objects that would be displayed on the altar promised that reminders of such relationships would be ever-present. Kings did this and so too did ealdormen and thegns.

That the activities of bishops went beyond the spiritual and pastoral also points towards senses of diocesan community. They were asked, as recorded in a number of wills, to act as executors or guardians, safeguarding property and the rights of heirs. There are cases of bishops providing, effectively, mortgages to landholders. Bishops had rights over tenants on their estates, and over retainers to whom they were both landlord and lord. Tenants would be involved in bishoprics' fulfilling their obligations to the king of the common dues of army service, bridgework and fortification, and in some cases provision of ships. Thus, for example, tenth-century bishops of Durham leased land to men both great and small in return for their allegiance and services and rent, and in the late tenth and early eleventh centuries London's military obligations were the responsibility of forty-five men from thirty-two estates in shires around London. The greatest episcopal lord was Stigand, archbishop of Canterbury 1052–1070, who was lord of more than 1,000 thegns and freemen in East Anglia and more than a hundred elsewhere.

Finally, the working of a bishop's estates would have created a consciousness of the landlord and some sense of a diocesan community. According to a charter of Edward the Elder, peasants who lived on the estates of Winchester cathedral owed it, among other things, 3 acres of ploughing and sowing, in their own time and with their own seed, and washing and shearing its sheep.[85] About 10,000 people worked the lands that supported Bishop Oswald of Worcester and Worcester's tenants and dependants.[86] Manors within Worcester's estates averaged about fifty tenant families who provided labour services.[87] This aspect of social cohesion will have been much more marked in episcopal manors than in smaller, recently formed, lay ones. The latter had a smaller proportion of peasants and so probably did not use their labour services as much as a bishop did. Each manor was a mixed farm, mostly self-supporting but engaging in some exchange with other manors, for example of timber and salt, with some buildings, including a residence, at its centre. Here the bishop and his household would stay on visits, probably lasting two or three weeks. One purpose of these was simply to feed the episcopal household, consuming the produce that had been gathered. Many paupers were also fed on these occasions. Bishop Wulfstan II is known to have travelled around his diocese every year.

Just as the Church stimulated a diocesan sense of community in various ways, so too it contributed to social cohesion in towns and in rural communities. Bishops had rights and properties in towns, including a place to stay when they were there on shire court business.[88] Urban churches bound different groups together. Those that were founded by groups, of neighbours or merchants, for example, both testified to and helped maintain that group's solidarity. Some churches were so tiny that there cannot have been in any respect a sense of distance between priest and congregation, or within it.[89] Large-scale ecclesiastical building plans and activity in a town could affect all its residents. The first record of those of Winchester acting as a corporate body is as witnesses in an exchange of land, at sometime between 975 and 978, whereby Bishop Aethelwold acquired 2 acres with a stream for the Old Minster.[90] Ecclesiastical sites were used for markets. Saints' cults likewise contributed to cohesion. This is probably partly why Aethelred and Aethelflaed of Mercia moved Oswald of Northumbria's relics to Gloucester, founded St Alkhmund's church in Shrewsbury and refounded and rededicated St Werburh's in Chester.[91]

Of course, the Church was not the only thing that contributed to urban cohesion. Another was governmental town planning, and regulation of minting and buying and selling. For example, Edward the Elder and Edgar stipulated that there was to be one coinage over all the king's dominion and Edgar fixed a minimum price for wool.[92] There were also the guilds. These voluntary associations were modelled on (ideal) sibling and monastic relationships, their members' cohesion buttressed by oaths and by collective action in ceremonies and feasting.[93] The regulations of five, varying in length and content, survive. Guilds offered mutual support at and after death, providing burial ceremonies, Masses and prayers,[94] and also in life, with prayers and various other services and supportive activities. Thus Alfred's law-code envisages members acting as kin if a kinless member perpetrated, or was victim of, a homicide. The Cambridge thegns' guild required this, except if the accused guild-brother had killed someone foolishly and wantonly. For a deceased member, London guild-brothers were to provide a loaf with suitable accompaniment and fifty psalms within thirty days, the Cambridge guild half the provisions of the funeral feast, Exeter guild-brothers six Masses or six Psalters each, and Bedwyn ones five, plus some provisions on the thirtieth day. The guilds' reach extended beyond the towns. Exeter's members might live up to fifteen or sixteen miles away, and Bedwyn's dead might be collected from up to fifty.

In rural communities, parishes would eventually become a cohesive force, as they did on the Continent.[95] As aristocrats established their own churches to serve, and be supported by, their own subordinates, they stimulated communities to act collectively, to safeguard their own interests.[96] Individuals worshipped near the land that they worked, and did both with their neighbours. They had identical obligations towards their church, whose territory had known boundaries. Many of their activities centred on their church, which acted as town hall, community centre and market place, its churchyard being regarded as community property. The community was assembled on Sundays and feast days, at Mass. The evidence of such parish cohesion is later than our period.[97] Perhaps the reality is too, but it was at least beginning in late Anglo-Saxon England. Churches became more numerous and more local, anxiety was expressed about the standards of care provided by local priests and attempts made to improve them. Rogationtide's three days of processions involved large numbers of lay people, across the whole spectrum of society, hearing Gospel readings at stations in the countryside, though not, as was the case later, on the parish boundaries.[98] Many manors ultimately became parishes, and there is some correlation between this and labour-intensive arable (as opposed to less labour-intensive pastoral) estates with a large population. Many, however, did not, and some parishes will have contained more than one settlement.[99]

Village cohesion also owed something to landlords and economic necessity.[100] The origins of many of the villages of the central belt of England, where arable farming was practised, lie in the tenth and eleventh centuries. Such things as identically sized and shaped house plots, laid out in rows, indicate planning and imply foundation by a lord's decision. But some villages may have arisen from the decisions of communities, as appreciative as lords were of the advantages of larger settlements. The village system of open fields, over which families' holdings were evenly distributed, gave each household an equal opportunity for prosperity. It also necessitated commitment to common rules, in order to manage the fields efficiently. The measuring and allocation of land that this new settlement pattern required was probably, since it needed local knowledge, done by the villagers themselves. Some elements of the open-field system were certainly in place in the tenth century. Many tenth-century field boundaries coincide with those of later parishes.

Monasticism, penance, pilgrimage, saints, spiritual kinship and prayer

By the ninth century many minsters were communities whose members included secular clergy as well as monks (some of whom might have been ordained). Their standards and achievements had not become uniformly low before the great tenth-century reform, despite the accusations of its leaders. Glastonbury, favoured by King Alfred's grandfather and father, was stable and strong in his own reign, and its abbot, Dunstan, led the reform party. Chester-le-Street and St Augustine's, Canterbury, had enjoyed King Aethelstan's patronage. Winchester had not abandoned the Divine Office. At Ely, despite late-ninth-century Viking attacks, religious life had continued for most of the tenth century. There were certainly some priests there in the 940s, guarding the relics and probably providing pastoral care in the region.[101] Nor was reform necessary for ecclesiastical vitality later. By 1066 only about half (thirty-five monasteries and nine nunneries), of the existing religious houses were reformed, the most northerly being Stow and Alkborough.[102] Their communities were not very large. There were twelve monks at Winchester in 958 and at Evesham in 1020. The richest houses, Christ Church, Canterbury, which had mustered seventeen witnesses to a charter in 805, Ely and Glastonbury, which may have been as small as six in 744, had the most monks, about forty each. Most may have had between twelve and twenty-five.[103]

Nevertheless, reformed monasticism had the potential to undermine social cohesion. In some respects it divided and emphasised distinction between monastic, clerical and lay. Aelfric's ideal, promoted in works that reached the laity as well as ecclesiastics, was a monastic-style, learned and celibate priesthood, whose daily concerns and experiences were very different from those of their flock. By stigmatising married clergy and ignorant local priests he may have blurred the distinction between pious married priests and pious laymen, and undermined secular priests' authority.[104] Other churchmen, for example the author of one of the Blickling homilies, were more inclusive, emphasising not priests' sexual chastity but a broader moral purity.[105] Ecclesiastical legislation required priests and men and women in monastic orders to be physically distinguishable from the laity and from each other, through their attire and the monks' tonsure. Furthermore, the sites of new establishments may have been more isolated than many Middle Saxon minsters.

Yet in other respects reformed monasticism was unifying: within each house, between houses, between the living and the dead, between monastic and lay communities and by contributing to a sense of national identity. Inmates observed one rule, obeying their abbot or abbess, sharing daily life for nineteen hours a day. Their prayers included prayer for their own community's dead and for the dead of other houses, which, of course, they believed to be following the same timetable and procedures as themselves. Very little is known about minster routine before the reform, except that houses would have done similar work but had different timetables and different versions of the liturgy, although Councils encouraged consistency and uniformity.[106] They will nevertheless have felt part of a wider community. The early-ninth-century Book of Cerne suggests this, in offering a meditation on the communion of saints (all the baptised), and engagement with it. By reading it, its reader invokes the prayers of all the faithful for himself, and contributes his own to the common good.[107]

Links with the lay community were strong. It was not just that benefactors, both live and dead, were prayed for frequently.[108] According to the *Regularis Concordia*, the king and queen were prayed for several times a day, charity to the poor was undertaken, washing the feet of the poor in Lent was a requirement, and some references indicate that laity attended Mass in the monastery. Donations and redonations, claims, temporary land grants and grants with reservations were all, of course, means of making or renewing relationships between families, saints and monastic houses.[109] Perhaps because their relic collections were more impressive, monasteries enjoyed more lay patronage than secular cathedral communities.[110] They thereby played a role in regional, if not diocesan, cohesion and identity. The refounded Ely and the new Ramsey Abbeys, for example, enjoyed the patronage of aristocratic families for whom association with these religious houses was a means of acquiring and retaining status and power in East Anglia.[111]

Donation has, historically, often been an act of penance, which if widely practised could itself be cohesive. Rebuke, the threat and the reality of a penance which had a public dimension, and excommunication could all be used to implement the wishes of bishops, to curb anti-social behaviour both of a general and of a political kind, and to solve disputes. The rite of reconciliation took place in the grave-yard, which, of course, was both a public place and a symbol of the community. It involved intercessors who had, presumably, negotiated an agreement earlier.[112] Pilgrimage likewise could have a penitential dimension. Though in some societies and circumstances it might be divisive, if perceived as ostentatious and self-centred, it too was a force for social cohesion, in at least two respects. Travel, and experience of different communities, can reinforce individuals' sense of, and commitment to, their own. Second, the shared experience of pilgrims, namely the difficulties of the journey, the delight at reaching the shrine, the miracles that occur there, together with the equality that obtains between them whilst the pilgrimage is in train, can promote a sense of community within the group which cuts across different social classes.[113] A few cases of travel to Rome and to Jerusalem, both pilgrim-sites, by members of the Anglo-Saxon elite are known. In some of them, pilgrimage may have been subordinate or incidental to some other purpose. More important is pilgrimage within England. The evidence for 800–1066 is very slight, and better for the eleventh than for the ninth and tenth centuries[114] but pilgrimage is well attested for the eighth century and seems unlikely to have fallen out of favour in the ninth. Pilgrimage may also be legitimately inferred from evidence for saints' cults, which is rather more plentiful, and from reports of miracles.

Major cults did suffer disruption in the second half of the ninth century. Aethelthryth's shrine at Ely was destroyed in 860. Cuthbert's community moved about in Northumbria. But the tenth century saw stability and expansion. Relics of the martyred King Edmund of East Anglia were moved in about 915 to Bury St Edmunds, where, in the eleventh century, Edmund and his new community were visited by kings (Cnut, Edward the Confessor and Harold II) and by many people from various parts of Britain. Cuthbert was settled at Durham in 995. Bishop Aethelwold encouraged reformed monasteries to rehouse their own relics, and also to acquire relics from unreformed houses.[115] In addition he particularly promoted the existing cults of the royal saints Eadburh and Aethelthryth and a new one, of Bishop Swithun of Winchester, who had died in 862. Aethelwold translated (moved) the remains of Eadburh, who had died at Winchester's Nunnaminster in 960, to a new shrine where she performed miracles of healing. He restored Aethelthryth's Ely, originally a double house, as a reformed, male one, in 970, and, as we have seen, made her a role model for the queen's supervision of nunneries. That cult sites attracted pilgrims is clear from an account of Swithun's, written between 971, when his remains were moved, and 973. For about five months after his translation there was rarely a day without a cure in the church that housed him, and there were crowds of invalids around the monastery. Not all the visitors were locals. They included people from Abingdon, London and the Isle of Wight.[116]

There were some other notable cults of recent saints. King Edgar's mother, Aelfgifu, cured many sick people at her tomb in Shaftesbury. Another tomb at Shaftesbury where many miracles occurred was that of King Edward, murdered in 978, whose relics were moved there in 979. Edward's cult was first promoted by the ealdorman Aelfhere, who may have been implicated in his murder, and later by his half-brother King Aethelred II.[117] It was promoted too, very early, at Ramsey. Another Ramsey cult began in about 1001 with the discovery of relics of Ivo, believed then to have been a Persian bishop, which subsequently worked miracles.[118] Canterbury had Dunstan, who around 1020 was healing sick people who went to his tomb, and in the middle of the eleventh century was being visited by poor people from all parts. At that time it also had Archbishop Aelfheah (1005–1012), martyred by the Danes, whose remains had been moved, with Cnut's consent, from London to Canterbury, and Mildred moved from Minster-in-Thanet.[119]

The unifying effect of pilgrimage and cult is confirmed in these and other cases by the nature of the miracles that are recorded: healing miracles and in some cases liberation from iron chains that had been fitted as punishments for crime. Such stories have implications of reacceptance into the community after exclusion. There is also an instructive tale about a mid-eleventh-century noble priest. He successfully sought healing from Dunstan but afterwards was smitten by a stroke in punishment for complaining about being reckoned 'as one of those paupers'.[120] This story testifies to a shared recognition of the cohesive potential of pilgrimage.

Major cults were controlled by kings and highly placed ecclesiastics, who used their saints to stimulate and to reinforce senses of community at various levels. The promotion of the unifying figure of Cuthbert is the most obvious case at the highest (national) level. The intermediate level was the province or diocese.

Oswald, simultaneously bishop of Worcester and archbishop of York, used Cuthbert's contemporary, Bishop Wilfrid, and other saints of Ripon as sources for gifts of relics. When he himself was promoted as a saint his biographer modelled him on Cuthbert. His relationship with the monastery of Ramsey was made, implicitly, analogous to that which had been recorded between Cuthbert and the minster of Whitby. Oswald's translation to Worcester in 1002 was a major diocesan event, the ceremony attended by bishops, abbots and eminent laymen.[121] In Anglo-Saxon-dominated Cornwall, the continental St Germanus was annexed as a Cornish equivalent of Augustine of Canterbury. A Mass text calls him the lamp and support of Cornwall, sent from Rome by Pope Gregory I. Since Germanus died over 150 years before Gregory, this connection is unhistorical.[122]

Finally, social cohesion was created and safeguarded through spiritual kinship, at all levels of society.[123] At baptism, infants had to have god-parents, who were not their biological parents. Their relationship to the child was conceived as kinship, as adoption, not just as surety-ship, with God, for its adherence to God's teaching. Obligations, authority and rights were involved in the god-parent–god-child relationship, for example in respect of bloodfeud and patronage. Deterioration of such relationships, to the point of killing each other, was one of the aspects of social breakdown and sin that Archbishop Wulfstan II's *Sermon of the Wolf*, in 1014, blamed for divine punishment in the shape of Vikings. In addition to god-parenthood there was sponsorship at confirmation (when the child was a near-adult). The Anglo-Saxons seem to have been pioneers of this relationship, which also created a spiritual parent–child bond. Even more important, these spiritual relationships also created another, co-parenthood, between the individual's biological and spiritual parents. This seems to have been a late development, for marriage between co-parents was forbidden on the Continent much earlier than in England. Its English prohibition is associated with Wulfstan. It is possible that co-parenthood had developed as a response both to the social disruption caused by Vikings and to the development of kingship that this had stimulated, to strengthen the horizontal, as opposed to the vertical, bonds in society.

Communities and cohesion are recurrently linked with prayer, seen in tangible form in the Durham and Winchester *Libri Vitae*, the only two that survive. The prime community was the communion of saints, continually brought to the attention of all the laity and professional religious. According to one of the Blickling homilies, bishops and priests should say Mass at least weekly 'for all Christian people who have ever been born', 'and those that are in heaven shall intercede for those' who do this, and they themselves 'shall be in the prayers of all earthly folk, who have been Christians, or yet may be'.[124] Sub-communities and their leaders were likewise strengthened by prayer. Prayer for the king is only one example. In the early eleventh century, bishops were meant to sing a special Mass, weekly, for fellow-bishops, and after their ordinations a priest was to celebrate thirty Masses for his bishop, and a deacon sing thirty psalms. Both were to pray zealously for the bishop for their whole lifetime. The laity, according to Wulfstan, were to pray for their parents, their confessors and all Christian people.

Scots and Welsh communities and their bonds

The social bonds and activities of settlements in Scotland and Wales, like the internal organisation and daily life of their religious communities, are elusive. Céli Dé groups would have been unmarried and celibate, and we may infer that communities spent time on worship, learning and the production of manuscripts, works of art and sculpture. Engagement with the regional community, at least at Deer, is suggested by the Book of Deer's smallness and hence portability, and by aspects of its content. Deer probably housed mobile priests who travelled to undertake pastoral care, and it regularly hosted feasts. Scotland's priests may have been married and hereditary, and not especially distinct from the laity.[125] In Wales, bishops did less than their Anglo-Saxon counterparts. They seem not to have been involved in confirmations. Monastic communities seem to have been small, though to have increased in size in the tenth century, and from the middle of it to have been composed mostly of secular clergy.[126] An important church probably had four officials under its head, and a late-eleventh-century text's statement that St Cadog established thirty-six canons implies that this was then a realisable ideal.[127] Clerics were allowed to marry. Until the eleventh century, the only festivals whose celebration is attested are Easter and Whitsun. There may have been others. Festivals for local saints were celebrated then, and may have begun earlier.[128] The working of ecclesiastical estates may not have contributed to community feeling since the smaller estates into which the great estates fragmented from the ninth century onwards seem not to have required labour services from dependent peasants. Wealth was conceptualised as movable non-essential goods, such as gold and jewels and attire. Though the idea of exchange was developing by the tenth century, its most important mechanism was still gift-exchange.[129] Since this involves, or creates, personal rather than impersonal relationships, it contributes to social cohesion.

Perhaps the most important thing that did so in Wales was the system of compensation and sureties. In the Laws of Hywel Dda, compensation was to be paid and received by the offender's and victim's kindreds, which included fifth cousins. Apart from stimulating people to put pressure on their relatives not to generate liability, this must have promoted group consultations, for the sums were complicated. Thus, of the compensation for murder, one-third was to be paid by the offender or his parents or his siblings, women paying half of what men paid, two-thirds of the remaining two-thirds by the offender's father's kin and the rest by his mother's kin. An individual nearer than another to the offender by one degree of kinship paid twice what that other kinsman did and so on. The compensation was distributed according to the same principles.[130] As for the formal surety-ship, Welsh custom was for only one surety, whereas the Anglo-Saxons had several. Yet since contracts were made in a public ritual, to inform the community of what was being agreed, neighbours were effectively sureties, entitled to use force against their social equals to enforce the contract.[131]

As in England, dead saints focused loyalties and were manipulated by churchmen. In the tenth century the *Armes Prydein* prophesied that the Britons would raise the standard of (the Welsh) St David, and that through his intercession and that of the saints of Britain the Anglo-Saxons would be put to flight. By the eleventh century, saints' relics were largely housed in churches. There were many highly localised cults of saints who were thought, whether correctly or not, to have been active in that place many centuries before. Their status arose from popular feeling.[132] Pilgrimage was not very significant, though Nennius' *History* includes fourteen Wonders of Britain, mostly in Wales, with anecdotes and comments that suggest that they were objects of curiosity and tourism when he wrote. One features a church, built by St Illtud in Gower that contained an altar suspended by the will of God. Two, in Ergyng and Ceredigion, each had a tomb whose length was variable when measured. Others involved wonderfully behaving natural features, such as springs. The evidence for popular pilgrimage to Welsh sites is, however, both very slight and very late.[133]

Despite difficulties and traumas England attained a national identity and political unification that accommodated regional pride and differences and some local self-government, in which Christianity was an integral part, and whose construction was often self-conscious. The most important contributions were those of Alfred, Aethelstan, the tenth-century reformers, Aelfric and Archbishop Wulfstan II. There are signs that similar developments were significantly under way in Alba. 'Britain' was part of the ideological landscape for both, and probably the main element of national identity in Wales. Anglo-Saxon communities of professional religious were often small, and reformed monasticism could be divisive, but in general religious communities united people both very locally and more distantly, as did the rhythm and practices of the laity's religious life. Wales and Alba may have had some similar experiences on a smaller scale.

Notes

1 E.g. Abrams, 'Edward', 'King'; Barrow, 'Survival'; Hadley, '"Cockle … Wheat" … Settlement', 'Conquest', *Northern*, 'Viking', *Vikings*; Richards, 'Finding', *Viking*; Townend, *Language*.
2 Richards, 'Boundaries'.
3 Blackburn, 'Expansion'; Damon.
4 Wareham, 'St'.
5 Blackburn, 'Expansion'.
6 Hadley, *Vikings*.
7 Hadley, 'Negotiating'. See also Stocker; Stocker and Everson.
8 Hadley, *Vikings*.
9 *Ibid.*
10 Townend, *Language*.
11 Hadley, '"Cockle … Wheat" … Settlement'.
12 Abrams, 'King'.
13 For these events, Higham, *Death*; A. Williams, *Æthelred*.
14 Wilcox, 'Wulfstan's'.
15 Treharne, *Living*.
16 *EHDI*: 418.
17 Wormald, 'Archbishop … Holiness', 'Archbishop … State-Builder', *Making*.
18 Higham, *Death*.

19 Wormald, 'Archbishop … State-Builder'.
20 Giandrea.
21 Keynes, 'Edward'.
22 Stafford, *Queen Emma*.
23 Foot, *Æthelstan*.
24 Campbell, 'What'.
25 Lewis.
26 Biggs.
27 Keynes, 'Edgar'.
28 Jankulak.
29 Stafford, *Unification*.
30 *Ibid.*; *EHDI*: 227.
31 Stafford, *Queen Emma*. For marriage, also Woolf, 'View'.
32 A.D. Smith.
33 Foot, 'Historiography'.
34 Foot, *Æthelstan*, 'Making'; Keynes, 'Edward'.
35 Foot, 'Making'.
36 Lewis.
37 Keynes, 'Edgar'.
38 Wormald, *'Engla'*.
39 Foot, 'Historiography', disagreeing with Campbell, 'United'.
40 Foot, *Æthelstan*, 'Dynastic', 'When'. See also Woolf, *From*.
41 Crick, 'Edgar'; Keynes, 'Edgar'.
42 Crick, 'Edgar'.
43 Bedingfield, *Dramatic*.
44 For what follows, Scheil.
45 Damon.
46 Scheil. See also Damon; T.E. Powell.
47 Wormald, 'Germanic'.
48 Insley, 'Assemblies'.
49 Howe, *Writing*.
50 Insley, 'Assemblies'.
51 Wormald, 'Germanic'.
52 *Ibid.* See also Pearce.
53 Wormald, 'Lordship'.
54 Abrams, 'King'; Wormald, *Making*.
55 Campbell, 'What'.
56 Barrow, 'Chronology … Benedictine'.
57 Campbell, 'Aspects'.
58 See e.g. Scragg, 'Battle'; Schwab; S.J. Harris, *Race*.
59 Howe, *Writing*.
60 Karkov, *Ruler*.
61 Driscoll, *Alba*; Taylor, 'Toponymic'; Woolf, *From*.
62 Woolf, *From*.
63 Driscoll, *Alba*, *Govan*.
64 Grant.
65 Duncan.
66 Hudson, 'Scottish'; Woolf, *From*.
67 Fraser, 'Rochester'.
68 Driscoll, *Alba*, 'Formalising', *Govan*.
69 Driscoll, *Govan*.
70 Edwards, 'Rethinking'.
71 Higham, *King*.
72 Charles-Edwards, *Wales*.

73 Higham, *King*. Charles-Edwards, *Wales*, takes a very different view but mentions neither Higham's (in *King*) nor the Arthurian material in his discussion.
74 Higham, *King*.
75 *Ibid.*
76 Higgitt, 'Words'. See also Edwards, 'Rethinking'.
77 For what follows, Giandrea.
78 Barrow, 'Community'; Tinti, *Sustaining*.
79 Giandrea.
80 Padel, *Slavery*.
81 For what follows, *ibid.*
82 Bullough, 'St'.
83 Karkov, 'Frontispiece', *Ruler*.
84 For what follows, Giandrea.
85 Foot, *Monastic*.
86 Dyer, 'St'.
87 For what follows, Dyer, 'Bishop'.
88 Giandrea.
89 Campbell, 'Church'; S. Wood.
90 Rumble, 'Laity', *Property*.
91 Barrow, 'Churches'.
92 Hill, *Atlas*.
93 S. Reynolds, *Kingdoms*. See also Conner.
94 V. Thompson, *Dying*.
95 S. Reynolds, *Kingdoms*.
96 For what follows, Genicot.
97 S. Reynolds, *Kingdoms*.
98 Bedingfield, *Dramatic*; Blair, *Church*; Harte.
99 Faith, 'Cola's'.
100 For what follows, Dyer, *Making*.
101 Fairweather.
102 Hill, *Atlas*.
103 Foot, *Monastic*; Giandrea.
104 Cubitt, 'Virginity'; Upchurch, *Ælfric's*.
105 Wright.
106 Foot, *Monastic*; Pfaff.
107 Brown, *Book*.
108 For the importance of prayer for the dead, Geary, *Living*; McLaughlin.
109 Rosenwein, *Negotiating, Neighbor*; S. Wood.
110 Giandrea.
111 Wareham, *Lords*.
112 Hamilton.
113 V. Turner and E. Turner.
114 For what follows, Webb, *Pilgrimage*.
115 Thacker, 'Saint-making'.
116 Gretsch, *Ælfric*; Webb, *Pilgrimage*.
117 Thacker, 'Saint-making'.
118 *Ibid.*
119 Webb, *Pilgrimage*.
120 *Ibid.*
121 Thacker, 'Saint-making'.
122 Warren and Stevenson.
123 For what follows, Lynch.
124 Transl. R. Morris.
125 T.O. Clancy, 'Deer'.

126 W. Davies, *Wales*.
127 Charles-Edwards, *Wales*.
128 W. Davies, *Wales*.
129 W. Davies, *Early, Wales*.
130 Hywel.
131 Stacey; Pryce, *Native*.
132 W. Davies, *Wales*.
133 *Ibid.*

Part III

Ends

The structuring of society

7

The Church in society

Introduction

Identities and cohesion were not the only aspects of the structuring of Anglo-Saxon society that Christianity contributed to. Others were the theory and practice of government, including its legal system, taxation, war and diplomacy, and the role of women. Exploring their role involves issues of power and property rights, of nuns and abbesses and of female saints, of marriage, and of rules and ideas about virginity and celibacy. Finally, the Church was important in the physical, social and economic landscapes of society. King Alfred's and Abbot Aelfric's views about the three orders of society, which have already been discussed, are relevant to all of these questions except perhaps to that of women.

Political theory and engagement

The most significant people in the development of Anglo-Saxon political philosophy between the ninth and the eleventh centuries are kings Alfred and Edgar and their circles and Archbishop Wulfstan II. Wulfstan, probably the most important of the advisers of kings Aethelred II and Cnut, was one of the major builders of the English state.

Alfred's reign laid down ideas and a model of kingship that were subsequently modified and elaborated whilst remaining fundamentally unchanged. Those changes that did occur were due to circumstances and to developments in theory. Throughout the period, political theory involved intertwining, not separating, government and religion.

Alfred's concept, and perhaps his practice, of kingship were particularly indebted to the Old Testament's account of King Solomon.[1] Asser explicitly compares the two. Some of Alfred's achievements, as represented by himself and others, parallel those of Solomon. Both, apparently, were writers and teachers, acted as judges, imposed administrative districts in place of tribal ones, rebuilt cities as fortified centres and economic stores, built ships, recruited craftsmen from other kingdoms and constructed lights.[2] Another inspiring figure was Pope Gregory I.[3] Alfred applied Gregory's ideas about bishops to kingship. Thus, his people owed him obedience, he himself had to be able to inspire fear, but he was also duty bound to try, through contemplation, to avoid becoming proud. To Alfred's exemplars Bishop Aethelwold added, or perhaps in Christ's case rather brought into higher relief,[4] regalised versions of Christ and St Benedict for the king and the Virgin Mary, and Aethelthryth, both saint and queen, for the queen.[5] Ecclesiastical writers also developed a preference for single kingship, disapproving of the early Anglo-Saxon phenomenon of joint kingship. It is possible that in 955 Eadwig and Edgar had used joint kingship to ensure that Edgar should eventually succeed to the whole. But this appears in one version of the *Anglo-Saxon Chronicle* as an actual division of the kingdom in 957, and as a criticism of Eadwig. Aethelwold recorded it in the same terms.[6]

Perhaps the most important of the ideas that obtained about tenth- and eleventh-century Anglo-Saxon kingship was, as on the Continent, that kings had a ministry to and office over their people.[7] Kingly power was effectively limited only at the time of a king's accession. For in practice kings gained their positions by seizing power, or from nomination by their predecessor and from powerful support. Succession disputes, and fears that they would occur, were common. It could therefore be said, as Aelfric did in one of his sermons, that the people had a choice. In tenth-century coronations, kings promised good government before they were consecrated. But once consecrated they had something of a sacred character. Aelfric also preached that the people cannot shake from their necks the yoke imposed by a consecrated king. It was unusual, and shocking, for a king to be killed by his subjects. What consecration gave kings included a quasi-priestly authority, for royal coronation resembled ecclesiastical consecration, especially of abbots and bishops. The parallel between king and bishop will have been regularly affirmed, whenever a coronation or a council was at Pentecost. Some images in Aethelwold's Benedictional and in the Tiberius Psalter of c. 1050, another Winchester production, emphasise that episcopal authority originated at Pentecost: it derives from the authority of the apostles, who had received it then, directly from Christ and from the descent of the Holy Ghost.[8]

Kings' authority extended over both laity and ecclesiastics, and both secular and spiritual matters. Kings were supposedly charged by God to work for their people's prosperity both in this world and the next, and accountable to God concerning this responsibility. In its discharge they had the right and duty of correction. The people's spiritual health was relevant to their own eventual salvation and to their king's, and also to their earthly welfare. For the Old Testament showed that God would punish sin with earthly disasters and miseries, which might include the end of the royal dynasty and the people's loss of their land, whereas keeping His laws and paying His dues would result in His favour, and, consequently, in success.[9] These attitudes are exemplified in Edgar's association with the *Regularis Concordia*, and particularly clearly expounded by Wulfstan. Throughout all his literary works, royal law-codes as well as sermons, Wulfstan strove for reform, to create a society that was sufficiently holy to merit God's favour, to resist Antichrist and to do well at the Last Judgement. He exhorted righteousness in general terms and he provided, with particular laws and penalties and in their collection together, a series of guide-books for a Christian society.[10] In Wulfstan's view 'a Christian king is Christ's deputy in a Christian people, and he must avenge very zealously offences against Christ'.[11]

Wulfstan's remark referred to violation of the sanctuary of the Church or defrauding or killing a man in holy orders or a foreigner. But it was capable of broader application. Every crime was regarded as an outrage against God, liable to result in divine punishment. Not only did kings have a priest-like and Christ-like dimension, but also Christ had come to be regarded as both priest and king, as a miniature in Aethelwold's Benedictional that depicts angels crowning Him with royal regalia at His baptism suggests.[12] In Wulfstan's assessment of Edgar, he juxtaposed praise for Edgar's zealous labour for peace, his exaltation of God's praise far and wide, his love of God's law, and his improvement of the peace of the people, with assertion that God supported him.[13] He thereby implied cause and effect. The king's laws and sanctions were perceived as an extension of God's law in the Bible. They and those of the Church were to be applied in tandem and not kept separate. Thus sentences imposed on people who violated the laws of God or man included both secular and ecclesiastical penalties, for example the payment of compensation and the performance of penance for the same offence.[14]

Some people felt that part of the maintenance of society's law and order and something that would contribute to its holiness was preservation of the three-fold God-given structure of society, keeping those who prayed, fought and laboured distinct from each other. Thegns, as Aelfric emphasised, were supposed to offer armed resistance to an enemy. By contrast, cloistered monks were not to participate in their kinsmen's demands for, or payment of, compensation in the case of feud. Nor were minsters to be involved in warfare. In Aethelred II's 1008 laws, what the professional religious should do (bishops, abbots, monks, cloistered women, priests and vowesses) was submit to their duty, live according to their rule, and pray for all Christian people. In Wulfstan's *Institutes of Polity* it was to live rightly and set the laity a good example. Yet the perceived purpose of kingship meant that the duties of ecclesiastics also included royal service, acting as instruments, for example bishops being involved in shire meetings, as well as publicists and advisers.[15] Furthermore, kings had to take particular account of bishops since bishops had the power to bar people from Heaven, by excommunicating them. As Aelfric pointed out, a king's duties included heeding his counsellors.

Theory, rhetoric and imagery thus encouraged and emphasised mutual engagement. Kings were like bishops and abbots, bishops were like kings, all worked together for the good of the people of God. This perception is explicit in the picture, derived from a tenth-century model that the eleventh-century *Regularis Concordia* manuscript contains, of Edgar with Archbishop Dunstan and Bishop Aethelwold. The king is in the centre and dressed as an abbot. All three hold part of a single scroll that signifies the text that the manuscript contained.[16]

How much of all this was true in Alba and among the Welsh is not clear. There is evidence of familiarity in Wales and Scotland with contemporary west European scholarship and with the earlier traditions on which it drew, all of which lay behind some Anglo-Saxon ideas. It is therefore plausible that these same ideas were at least known. Some further deductions can be made about Welsh perceptions. Since Asser's depiction of Alfred was almost certainly addressed to a Welsh audience, with a wish to impress them,[17] the Welsh elite probably shared the values with which it was imbued. From other sources scholars have concluded that: kings would ideally be militarily capable and wealthy; would have warbands, which changed little over the centuries; and would levy (in kind) tribute from subject kingdoms and taxes from their subjects. They were often perceived as plunderers, but were restrained by the practical and psychological powers of ecclesiastics, as well as by insufficiencies of resources, ambitious kin and the corporate will of their people. Only by the late eleventh century was there any suggestion that kingship involved responsibility beyond the military.[18] The Welsh experienced dynastic struggles and king–king hostility but not, it seems, the killing of kings by their own people. In Alba, however, such a fate seems not to have been uncommon.[19]

The Church and gender

The role and status of Anglo-Saxon women has been much studied and differently interpreted. The higher the social class of women, the more evidence is available about them. Queens are the most knowable, yet even they can be known only obliquely. The most extensive textual depictions of queens are of ancient and foreign queens, rather than Anglo-Saxon ones, though domesticated both by the addition of Anglo-Saxon details and characteristics, such as dress, and by the omission of those of their original setting. Such domestication is particularly striking in Aelfric's works. Queens were not, of course, typical of Anglo-Saxon women. However, the Old English word for queen was used for women of varying status, and the Church does not seem to have developed a particular definition of the role of queens. Anglo-Saxons' representations of royal women may therefore offer some useful insight into their society's ideals concerning women.[20] Yet other problems remain. Authors wanted to offer audiences examples that would both stimulate emulation and inspire respect for anyone who emulated them successfully. They offer us ideals, not realities. Second, the successful and general enforcement of regulations in law-codes and pastoral letters is not demonstrable and must not be assumed. These sources indicate what their authors' ideals were and what they believed were common or potential problems and deviations. Third, elements in poetry and in accounts of saints' lives were symbolic, in some cases possibly to the exclusion of their literal significance.[21] Fourth, how their audiences interpreted them may have varied. The lessons they drew from them might have been exactly, partially or not at all what their authors intended, whether or not the intended meaning was explained.

Finally, the effects of an idea or policy might have been very different from its intended purpose. The most obvious examples are the Church's restrictive rules about sexual intercourse and about remarriage of widowed persons, and its exaltation of virginity. The early Church had designed these for the spiritual health of both men and women and of society and, in the opinion of some scholars, to maximise the Church's chance of receiving bequests from childless individuals. Yet, given the dangers of pregnancy and childbirth, the effects of following them must have included better physical health and longer life expectancy for women and opportunities for widows of economic independence and choice of lifestyle (religious or secular, remarriage or not).

Images, attitudes, and power

The two most important women in Christian history were Eve and the Virgin Mary. In the Bible, Eve, the first woman, takes part in the Fall of mankind and its expulsion from Paradise. She succumbs to the persuasion of Satan to eat the fruit that God had forbidden, and to persuade Adam, the first man, to do so too. Mary is very different. She agrees to motherhood of Jesus, as God wishes. This was perceived as essential to mankind's salvation, and Mary's humility and obedience as counter-balancing Eve's pride and disobedience. By the ninth century, Mary was regarded as Queen of Heaven, and as both a model for, and a source of, earthly rule.[22] Eve by contrast has often been perceived and used as an awful warning of female folly and of the advisability of restraining female power. Yet according to a recent interpretation, *Genesis B*, a tenth-century version of a Continental, Old Saxon, poem, stresses Eve's good intention, rather than, as the early Church Fathers had, her pride. In this version, the tempter plays on Eve's desire to be a responsible wife and mother, promising that her family would benefit if she and Adam ate the fruit, but suffer if they did not. He claims to be sent by God and is so plausible that Eve's task of discerning the truth looks virtually impossible. The poet may have been encouraging his audience to feel that most of mankind, always facing temptation, trying but failing to be virtuous, are like Eve rather than Adam.[23]

Both Eve and Mary had meaning for all Christians, not just female ones. Neither, therefore, offers us a straightforward insight into Anglo-Saxon attitudes to women. The same difficulty, that what looks at first sight to be about women might in fact not be, attends the women in translations of biblical books and saints' *Lives*. Thus, for example, it may be that it is anxieties about poor counsel being offered to and taken by Aethelred II, and about royal power generally, that lie behind Aelfric's treatment of the biblical queen Jezebel. In his version of the Book of Kings, done between 992 and 1002, Jezebel's idolatry, tyranny and counsel of her husband caused failure, shame and punishment. Yet Aelfric then had no reason to be negative about contemporary queenship or any particular queen. Aethelred's mother had been an ally of his teacher, Aethelwold, and Aethelred's wife probably did not attend councils, for she is not included in charter witness lists. He was not critical of female advisers in other works. He may instead have been trying to teach that counsel should be followed only if those who gave it were pious, and that it should not be secret but open.[24] He might also have been seeing queenly power not as an issue about women, but as an aspect and an expression of an extension of royal power generally, which was unwelcome. This sentiment has also been detected in *Beowulf*.[25] The same concerns might explain Aelfric's omission of the queen from the injunction that psalms be said for king, queen and benefactors, in the version of the *Regularis Concordia* that he wrote in 1005 for the monks of Eynsham.[26]

The figure of a queen was sometimes used very positively. In a homily for a dedication of a church, Aelfric symbolised the Church as an elaborately adorned queen, seeing it as a spiritual queen, adorned with the precious ornaments and varied colours of good habits and virtues.[27] This raises the possibility that some queens in other texts may have an element of ecclesiastical symbolism about them. When the queen in *Beowulf* passes the mead cup around the royal hall, her role is a social one. Her action reinforces both hierarchy and the king–retainer bond, and reminds her audience, both within and outside the poem, that the king can and will reward retainers of different backgrounds with items from his store of treasures.[28] She might also be symbolising the Church working in the earthly world for the Heavenly king, namely God. The heroine of *Elene* has also been seen as symbolic of the Church. Her subservience to her son, Emperor Constantine, is more marked here than in the poem's source, and may be being presented as an aspect of her place in the hierarchy, not her gender. In *Elene*, subservience to authority and being part of a community are presented as integral to a Christian life. In Aelfric's version of the biblical Esther, done between 1002 and 1005, he probably meant the queen as a model for the English people. Turning to prayer and fasting at a time of danger, Esther foreshadowed the national penance enjoined by King Aethelred in 1009, after the arrival of the Scandinavian 'great army'. Yet she is, and probably was, also perceptible as an exemplar for real queens and especially for Aethelred's second wife, Emma. Aelfric chose to emphasise Esther's personal piety, her conversion of others, and her intercession, both between her lord and people and between God and the people, not her controlling lands and attending royal councils, though both she and Emma did these things. His decision may have been provoked by the massacre of 'Danes' on St Brice's Day in November 1002, if indeed he was writing after this. Aethelred had ordered it. Aelfric's Esther could have been construed as a model of how Emma ought to have prevented it.[29]

The tradition of the Church had emphasised the role of saints as symbolic and representative of believers rather than as individuals. Aelfric did the same in his provision of gender-neutral models of piety, in both male and female form, in the collection of Latin saints' *Lives* that he translated, no later than 998. He produced this work for his patrons Ealdorman Aethelweard (died 998) and his son (and successor as ealdorman) Aethelmaer (died 1005), both of whom were royal counsellors.[30] Yet as his preface shows, he intended it to reach a wider audience, outside the monastic setting and including women. In this text, the martyred virgins and the saints who practised chastity within marriage exemplified at least three virtues: adherence to the Church's ideals concerning sexual activity, constancy and resistance to various pressures to sin. Furthermore, it equated moral purity with orthodox belief. The married virgins symbolised the Church, wedded to Christ. They shunned idolatry, which included disobedience to God, and which was equated with adultery. Their marriages produced offspring, not biological but spiritual children, that is new Christians, through their teaching and example. Thus they were models not only for clerics but also for lay adults, who were supposed to teach their children and god-children the Lord's Prayer and the Creed.[31] Similarly, one of the married virgins, Cecilia, functioned in an eleventh-century private prayer from Canterbury as a model for the mortification of the body and for contemplation.[32]

It would seem that in the view of, and as represented by, the Church, the highest ideals, and the qualifications to be counsellors and to be revered, were attainable, and had been attained, by women as well as by men. However, according to some scholars, its emphasis in the reform period on sexual purity turned out to be disadvantageous for women. This was because women became associated with impurity, and the separation of the sexes came to be seen as desirable.[33] Yet apart from women being barred from ordination as priests, and hence denied the influential position of bishop, there are very few indications of overt, explicit expression or discussion of the unsuitability of women for power or influence.[34] One of the Vercelli homilies states that women are by their nature sick, because of their soft indoor lives without strenuous activity, their frequent washing and other luxuries.[35] There were at least three debates in ninth-century Wessex about queenship.[36] According to Asser, in 802 all the inhabitants decided to exclude kings' wives from royal power, in response to the misdeeds of the wicked Mercian-born queen Eadburh. Yet in 856, without any apparent disagreement, Alfred's Carolingian stepmother Judith, who had been consecrated as queen on the Continent, was given the title of queen and commanded by her husband to sit beside him on his throne. After being widowed she married her stepson King Aethelbald, and is recorded in a surviving charter witness list as queen. So too is Wulfthryth, wife of Aethelwulf's second successor, Aethelbert. Policy was clearly reversed again some time before 886, for Asser saw the king's wife being treated as just that and not as queen. He regarded this as peculiar, wrong and detestable and states that it was disputed. These serial changes may have been due to concerns about influencing the succession, not queenship as such.[37] A candidate whose mother was a consecrated queen probably had more prestige than one whose mother was not. It is possible that when Wulfthryth's and Aethelbert's son Aethelwold challenged his cousin Edward, Alfred's son, for the throne, one of the things that gained him support was her queenly status.

The best-known examples of royal women wielding power are Queens Emma and Edith,[38] in the late tenth and the eleventh century, but there were instances before them. The notable tenth-century ones are Alfred's daughter Aethelflaed, Lady of the Mercians; Edward's third wife, Eadgifu; and Edgar's third wife, Aelfthryth. Aethelflaed worked with her husband and, after his death, in co-operation with her brother Edward. Her activities included building and capturing *burhs*, sending an army into Wales, and persuading the people of York, shortly before her death in June 918, to promise to be under her direction. Because of this, it has been suggested that the poem *Judith* was written for her, perhaps as a tribute, since Judith's and Aethelflaed's character and activities had similarities.[39] Her daughter Aelfwyn was deprived of authority in Mercia, by Edward, in December 918, probably because he wanted to rule Mercia directly.[40] Queen Eadgifu seems to have been more influential in her long widowhood than in her husband Edward's lifetime. Her stepson King Aethelstan did not marry, conceivably because she offered her support in return for his allowing his half-brothers, her sons, to be his heirs.[41] She probably attended Edmund's and Eadred's councils, for she appears in the witness lists of their charters. She was a patron both of the future archbishop Dunstan, though he went into exile in the reign of Edmund's son Eadwig, and of the future bishop Aethelwold, who subsequently worked closely with Queen Aelfthryth.[42]

Aelfthryth's support of Aethelwold's foundations began before she was queen, jointly with her first husband, with the refoundation of the monastery of Ely. Thereafter, it continued, often jointly with Edgar. Aelfthryth attended royal councils and witnessed charters and was most powerful from 979 to 984 whilst her son, Aethelred II, was king but a minor. She favoured her birth family and supporters and she intervened in disputes about land, many of which arose after Edgar's death. They sprang from resentment, which Edgar's severity had repressed, about loss of lands to the reformed Church. In the 990s she seems to have been entrusted with the care of Aethelred's sons. It was in her time, and to her benefit, that the status of queen was much enhanced. This was mostly the work of her friend Bishop Aethelwold, but Archbishop Dunstan must have consented, since it began about 964, the date of her marriage to Edgar. No queen before her, since Wulfthryth, had had the title of queen, but she did, and it was used in charter witness lists. She was the first reigning, as opposed to dowager, queen to attest charters.[43] The *Regularis Concordia* made her protector of female religious houses, Aethelwold's Benedictional gave her St Aethelthryth and the Virgin Mary as models, making her position equivalent to the king's, whose models were St Benedict and Christ, over male houses.[44]

The duty and right of protection of religious houses inevitably carried with it authority and control over them. Aelfthryth seems to have exercised this during King Aethelred's minority. She engineered the expulsion of Abbess Wulfhild from Barking. Wulfhild had once been courted by Edgar and was a cousin of his second wife, Wulfthryth. Aelfthryth's motive may have been political, to strengthen Aethelred's position. One of its weaknesses was that the validity of the marriage of his parents, Aelfthryth and Edgar, was questionable. Another was what was thought about the murder of his half-brother Edward, the son of Edgar's first wife, who had briefly preceded him on the throne. Edward's family did not avenge him, and late-eleventh-century texts involve Aelfthryth in his fate, possibly reflecting tenth-century views. In these circumstances, Aethelred's half-sister Edith, Wulfthryth's daughter, a nun at Wilton with her mother, was a danger, as a potential claimant to the throne. To expel Wulfhild was to discredit and weaken her family. Whatever the truth about the murder, its later association with Aelfthryth suggests that at the houses of Barking, Shaftesbury, Wherwell and Wilton she was remembered as dangerous and unpleasant. Their attitude can be interpreted as a sign that she had interfered in their affairs.[45]

Queens were probably the only women who were significantly active in the public sphere. Otherwise it seems that such activity was exceptional and regarded as, normally, inappropriate, though not impossible. Thus abbesses attended eighth- and ninth-century church councils less regularly than abbots did. Yet they did attend when they were particularly involved in items of a council's business. The granting of charters was a public event, involving performance, announcements and acceptance at meetings. Abbesses very rarely appear in the witness lists. Aelfwyn of Mercia did, but after the mid-tenth century no women are known to have done so, apart from queens. Law courts too were public occasions. Land disputes are the cases best recorded, and it seems from them that women usually had a male representative when they litigated. The case of Wynflaed versus Leofwine, about 990–992, is very unusual. Wynflaed appeared herself at two meetings: the first attended by the king, some ealdormen and some ecclesiastics; the second a shire meeting. Women clearly had a legal capacity, as the list of witnesses to Wynflaed's ownership that she cited similarly shows. It included twelve women as well as the king's mother, Aelfthryth, and eleven men. Yet the witnesses recorded in the document attesting the settlement of the dispute are all male. Other public documents too show a gender bias. Far more men's than women's wills survive, though we know, from other texts as well as wills, that the ratio of male to female bequests was much more equal.[46] Of the surviving Anglo-Saxon inscriptions, including those from before 800, commemorating commissions, for example of churches, almost all relate to men. Yet other evidence reveals that women commissioned similar works. Of memorial inscriptions, some 75 per cent relate to men. By contrast, ownership inscriptions, except on weapons, attest male and female owners in roughly equal proportions.[47]

The high point of evidence for female learning and scholarship is in the seventh and early eighth centuries. Nothing in late Anglo-Saxon England bears comparison with it. Yet some education was available, for some women. Alfred's mother had owned a book of poetry, whose contents she knew, and which she had inspired him to win from her. Wilton, where Edgar's second wife, Wulfthryth, and her cousin Wulfhild were brought up, probably had some intellectual capacity then. Edward the Confessor's wife Edith was also brought up there and she was praised for her learning. The post-Conquest biographer of the Edith who was Wulfthryth's and Edgar's daughter, suggests that Wilton had recorded its own history, by claiming that written sources pertaining to his subject were available there.[48]

On these grounds some scholars argue that an asymmetry had developed in society, in which men dominated the written process whilst women operated through the oral.[49] This asymmetry may also be present in *Genesis B*. Another interpretation of this poem, apart from the one with which this discussion of gender began, is that it is teaching that oral culture is inferior to textual culture. The tempter lies to Adam and Eve, saying that God had changed His mind about the fruit that He had originally forbidden and now wanted them to eat it. Their acceptance of this oral report, despite remembering what God had told them directly, brought disaster. Since Eve was the more easily persuaded, and persuaded Adam, she represents orality.[50]

Sex and marriage

The English Church espoused ideals and rules about sexual activity that were common throughout early and early medieval Christendom, though details and emphases varied, as indeed they do in the corpus of Anglo-Saxon evidence. Recurring themes, in a variety of texts, are aspiration that the ideals and rules be adhered to, and worry that they are not.[51]

The ideal state was thought to be virginity. Christ Himself, His mother Mary and His favourite apostle, John, had all, according to the Church's teaching, retained theirs. Furthermore, virginity was more than emulation of these three. It was a sign of virtue, because to keep it demanded effort, and not just in extreme cases, as in those of the virgin martyrs and virgin spouses of late Antiquity, who suffered pressure to marry or to copulate. Virginity required mastery of the body's natural desire for sex. The early Church had developed the idea that virgins were not only a kind of martyr, but also superior to angels, because angels, though pure, did not have sexual urges that they needed to overcome. Consequently, virgins could be perceived as valuable intercessors. Such views permeated the English Church. Aelfric for example called virgin monks and nuns martyrs of Christ, and believed that virgins would not be judged at the Last Judgement but would join in the judging, alongside Christ.

The tenth-century reformers vigorously promoted virginity.[52] Other kinds of sexual purity, such as celibacy in widowhood, and restraint in marriage were also required. They were regarded as honourable but lesser states. Reformers required celibacy of all religious. Married clergy were excoriated and where possible, for example in Aethelwold's expulsion of the clerics of Winchester's Old Minster, expelled or pressed to reform. For the reformers, clerical marriage was a sort of concubinage. In earlier centuries, a man's concubine had had some privileges, including the eligibility of her children to inherit from their father if he so wished. But concubinage had been redefined as illegal and immoral, its offspring barred from inheritance.[53] During Dunstan's archiepiscopate the community at Canterbury gave special honour to the third-century Roman virgin spouses and martyrs Chrysanthus and Daria. Their feast appears in a calendar written there between 979 and 987 and prefacing Dunstan's sacramentary, ranking below the feasts of the apostles but above those of most saints. Dunstan may have perceived them as useful models for his cathedral, non-monastic, clergy.[54] Despite the efforts of the reformers clerical marriage did continue.[55] It was recognised as a fact in the eleventh-century *Northumbrian Priests' Law*'s stipulation that if a priest leaves a woman and takes another he should be anathema.

Virginity was often linked with intercession, and the importance attached to sexual purity was probably intensified at times of crisis. At such times both moral renewal and good-quality intercession were felt to be necessary, to regain God's favour. Thus in his law-code of 962–963, represented as a remedy for a calamitous pestilence, King Edgar required that servants of God who receive the payment of God's dues, 'are to live a pure [clean, chaste, celibate] life, that through that purity they may intercede for us to God'.[56] Edgar saw the pestilence as divine punishment for sins. Aelfric's *Lives of Saints* includes three pairs of virgin spouses and four female virgin martyrs from late Antiquity. It was finished late in the 990s. This was soon after Scandinavian attacks had resumed and perhaps connected to them. For twenty years England suffered attacks, expense and defeats. It was against this background that cults of native virgin saints who had lived very recently were promoted. Aethelred II's half-sister Edith was one. The *Lives* of the three reform leaders – Dunstan, Aethelwold and Oswald – were produced during these years.

It was only within marriage that sexual activity was approved, and both the approval and the activity were limited. It was taught that the married laity would receive a thirty-fold reward at the Last Judgement whilst celibate widows and others who were sexually experienced but chaste would receive a sixty-fold reward and virgins a 100-fold one. Married people were to indulge in sexual activity only for procreation, and only when they had no religious duties. Consequently, sex was forbidden to them for most of the year.[57] Aelfric, but not other writers, was explicit that couples should forego sexual activity after the wife's menopause. The prohibited times included during menstruation and pregnancy and for some time after childbirth, the forty-day fasts before Christmas and Easter and after Pentecost, every Sunday, Wednesday and Friday, and a three-night period before receiving the Eucharist. The choice of two biblical readings that are offered as alternatives in the Durham Collectar's marriage service illustrates this attitude. One warns the audience to shun fornication. The other implicitly recommends celibacy.[58] Sexual impurity was a public concern. It imperilled not only divine favour and effective intercession, but also good government. Pope Gregory I had taught that persons in authority should be free from lust. This might be why Alfred, according to Asser, prayed to be granted a disease that would free him from carnal sin, and, in part, why the married Edward the Confessor maintained his virginity.

The Church applied restrictions to marriage as well as to sex. A person was to consent to marriage, was not to marry close kin, the definition of which varied over time, was to have only one spouse at a time, had very limited grounds for divorce and was discouraged from remarriage. Women had the right to refuse an arranged marriage. This right may have been more theoretical than real, but without it they would have had less respect and been even more vulnerable to compulsion and a lack of support. The penitential teaching of the seventh-century Archbishop Theodore had provided for betrothed girls refusing to go through with the arrangements.[59] Girls were under the power of their parents until they were sixteen or seventeen, boys until they were fifteen. An early-eleventh-century text about betrothal, thought to be part of a handbook on procedures that local officials should oversee, refers to the consent of the woman, maiden or widow, before mentioning that of her kinsmen. This might imply that women had some say during, not only after, the negotiations about their marriages.[60] Archbishop Wulfstan II's teaching, in Cnut's laws, was that no woman was to be forced to marry a man whom she disliked. As to consanguinity, Theodore had ruled against marriages of individuals related in the third degree and applied this rule also to affines (in-laws). Cnut's laws forbade six degrees of relationship, likewise including affines, and also prohibited men from marrying their god-mothers, vowesses or deserted (divorced) women. The *Northumbrian*

Priests' Law forbids marriage to anyone related within the fourth degree or spiritually related, that is fellow-god-parents and god-parents of one's biological children.[61] Incest, that is, sexual relations with somebody who was too closely related for marriage, entailed payment of compensation. This might be the wergeld, a fine, or all of the perpetrator's possessions, depending on the closeness of the kinship.[62]

These rules applied equally to men and women, but the penalties for adultery and the grounds for divorce were unequal. In Cnut's laws, a male adulterer is to compensate not his own wife but the husband or family of his partner in adultery. Rape of a widow or maiden necessitated paying her wergeld. A female adulterer was to lose all her property to her husband and also her nose and ears, though this may have been an improvement on an earlier, pre-Christian, punishment of death.[63] According to Theodore, a man had grounds for divorce if his wife committed fornication, after five years if she deserted him, and after one year if she was taken captive. A woman had to prove her husband's impotence or, if she had not previously been married, she could obtain a divorce if her husband made himself a slave through theft, fornication or other sin.

Remarriage was disapproved of. Theodore taught that whereas a newly married couple in a first marriage were to absent themselves from church for thirty days and then do forty days penance, those who married a second time had a year's penance, and seven years' for any subsequent remarriage. Twice-married men, and men married to twice-married women, were not eligible to be ordained as priests. Later, Aelfric taught that priests should neither attend nor bless second marriages, and no man who had married a widow or divorced woman could become a deacon or priest. Penitentials required that widows wait one year before remarrying, and Aethelred's and Cnut's laws gave this rule royal sanction.[64] In Cnut's laws the penalty for infringing it was the widow's loss, to her first husband's kin, of all property that she had acquired through her first marriage, and her second husband had to pay her first husband's wergeld to the king. Any woman who claimed that she had been remarried by force had to leave her new husband in order to keep her property.

Society did not, of course, entirely live up to the Church's ideals. Marriage had political, social and economic consequences for all classes, so close-kin marriage, divorce, remarriage and illicit unions must often have been attractive, not necessarily for personal reasons. There are certainly plentiful examples and suggestions of them occurring. Alfred's brother King Aethelbald married his stepmother Judith. Edward the Elder married as his second wife a lady who was, as the granddaughter of his paternal uncle, within the prohibited degrees. He may have been trying to ensure that her branch of the family would not dispute the succession in the future. Edward put her aside. He then remarried again. King Eadwig married a relative and the couple were separated by Archbishop Oda. King Edgar married three times and his third wife, Aelfthryth, was a widow. It was perhaps because their marriage was questionable, that, later, the validity of Edgar's second marriage was undermined, with stories that Wulfthryth had been a vowed nun before it.[65] If it was invalid, then the marriage that apparently was the third was really the second. Aethelred II married twice. His widow Emma remarried, to his successor King Cnut, and Cnut already had an English wife.

Below the level of kings, the marital history of Earl Uhtred of Northumbria, who died in 1016, is notable.[66] He married three times. His first marriage ended in separation. His third was to a daughter of the king. His first wife also married three times. She divorced twice. Subsequent to her third wedding she embraced the religious life, though it is not known whether she was by then a widow. Yet she was the daughter of a bishop, of Chester-le-Street. He seems to have been using her to further his influence in Yorkshire. He deployed six estates that actually belonged to the Cuthbert community in her first and second dowries. Concerns about intercourse with, abduction of, or marriage to, nuns, recur in various texts, and the complaints about such illicit unions represent them as common. They might have been undertaken as political moves, given that in some cases women who chose the religious life, or had it chosen for them, would otherwise have played a role in building a dynasty or strengthening a claim in a succession dispute, and owned property.[67] Unfortunately the Wimborne nun with whom Alfred's nephew Aethelwold liaised in his bid for the throne is unidentifiable, and in the only one other particular case that is known, involving an abbess in 1046, the lady's background is not.[68]

The law-codes envisage the rules being broken and prescribe penalties for doing so. Cnut's laws, for example, envisage a man having both a lawful wife and a concubine. They prohibit any priest doing for him 'any of the offices which must be done for a Christian man, until he desists and atones ... as the bishop directs'.[69] The *Northumbrian Priests' Law* prescribes atonement for marrying within prohibited degrees and for abandoning a living legal wife and wrongly wedding another woman. Atonement carries the meaning of penance and desisting. It has, however, been suggested that since the primary meaning of the word for 'atone' is to pay compensation, we should conclude that, for the wealthy, divorce was not out of reach. But perhaps getting away with marital and sexual error and divorce was not confined to the upper classes. Wergelds, the basis for compensation payments, differed according to the status of the men concerned. Atonement for divorce might have done too. It is not impossible that the Church quietly derived considerable material profit from remarriages.

In Anglo-Saxon political theory, anointed kings headed society, their responsibilities and authority incorporating religious matters, but needed counsellors, who included ecclesiastics. The ultimate purpose of all involved in government was to make society pleasing to God. Such ideas were probably known to the elites in Alba and Wales. In Anglo-Saxon society queens could be powerful, though women generally lacked a public role, and the Church's restrictive rules about sexual activity, marriage and remarriage may often have been broken. Nevertheless, it is fair to conclude that women enjoyed more respect and their lives were less restricted than in many traditional societies, or in England for centuries after 1066.

Notes

1 Kempshall; Scharer.
2 Kempshall.
3 *Ibid.*
4 Karkov, *Ruler.*
5 Deshman.
6 Biggs.
7 Kempshall.
8 Dekker; Deshman.
9 Howe, *Migration.*
10 Wormald, 'Archbishop ... Holiness', 'Archbishop ... State-Builder', *Making.*
11 *EHDI*: 411.
12 Deshman.
13 *Anglo-Saxon Chronicle* for 959.
14 For Wulfstan's views see also Fletcher; A. Williams, *Æthelred.*
15 Giandrea; T.E. Powell.
16 Karkov, *Ruler.*
17 Keynes and Lapidge.
18 W. Davies, *Wales.*
19 Woolf, *From.*
20 For all these points, Klein.
21 Cubitt, 'Virginity'; Upchurch, *Aelfric's.*
22 Mayr-Harting, 'Idea'.
23 Buchelt.
24 Klein.
25 Marvin.
26 Klein.
27 *Ibid.*
28 *Ibid.*
29 For these points, Klein.
30 *Ibid.*
31 Upchurch, *Aelfric's*, 'Homiletic'.
32 Upchurch, 'Homiletic'.
33 Cubitt, 'Virginity'.
34 Klein.
35 Scheil.
36 Nelson, 'Reconstructing'.
37 *Ibid.*
38 Karkov, *Ruler*; Stafford, *Queen Emma.*
39 Stafford, 'Annals'.
40 Bailey.
41 Foot, *Æthelstan.*
42 Yorke, *Nunneries.*
43 Yorke, 'Women'.
44 Deshman.
45 Yorke, *Nunneries*, 'Women'.
46 For these points, Lees and Overing.
47 Okasha, 'Anglo-Saxon'.
48 Lees and Overing.
49 *Ibid.*
50 Buchelt.
51 McCarthy, *Love, Marriage.*
52 Cubitt, 'Virginity'.

53 Ross.
54 Upchurch, *Aelfric's.*
55 Cubitt, 'Virginity'; Helmholz.
56 *EHDI*: 399.
57 Payer.
58 K.W. Stevenson.
59 Gamer and McNeill.
60 Fell.
61 Helmholz.
62 For these topics, see also McCarthy, *Love, Marriage.*
63 Klinck; Payer.
64 Hollis.
65 Yorke, 'Women'.
66 Fletcher; Morris.
67 Woolf, 'View'.
68 Yorke, *Nunneries.*
69 *EHDI*: 427.

8 Women's agency

Misogyny and emancipation

Some scholars regard the importance that the reformers attached to virginity and chastity as misogynistic.[1] Unfortunately, the evidence leaves the matter uncertain. Certainly there is some that overtly suggests misogyny. The anonymous author of one, undated, vernacular homily, for example, was deliberately misogynist where his earlier, Latin source, was not. According to the New Testament, the first people to whom the Resurrection of Christ was revealed and to proclaim it were women. The Latin sermon taught that this reversed the condemnation of Eve and the reproach for the Fall that women had suffered ever since. The English omits this and instead implies that women must endure forever the scorn that Eve suffered from Adam for her mistake.[2]

Other evidence for misogyny is far less direct. Aelfric's recurring statements that virginity and monasticism are open to both genders, for example, have been regarded as mere lip-service. It has been argued that he intended his *Lives of Saints* primarily for monks, despite its preface anticipating a wider audience; that he associated virginity chiefly with men, seeing it as an attribute of male monasticism; and that he was suspicious of women.[3] However, in the tenth and eleventh centuries there were far fewer religious houses for women than for men. Women's enthusiasm for a religious life was often expressed through taking vows of chastity and to God and dressing like a female religious, whilst retaining their property and living where they would and could, including in their own homes with their own households or with other like-minded females. The Old English word for such a woman was *nunne* but since this is the same as the modern English word for a female monk (nun) some scholars avoid the term 'nuns' as confusing and refer instead to cloistered woman (Old English *mynecen*, female monk) and vowesses. Vowesses were often widows. They were seen as female equivalents of the secular clergy.[4] There may well have been many more male virgin religious than female ones, so Aelfric's association of virginity with men and his rarely referring to female houses could be interpreted as realistic rather than misogynistic. In some works he did deal with female virtue, considering widows and married women in a sermon about the Nativity of the Virgin Mary and presenting Judith in another as a model for vowesses. Nevertheless, within these texts his approval

of marital chastity seems muted and he warned of the danger for female virgins of
becoming proud. Some readers have therefore concluded that his view of female
spirituality and sexuality was negative. Another instance of ambiguous significance is that he addresses his admonitions against marital sex at the forbidden
times to men.[5] He may have supposed that women were less persuadable, or
incapable of thinking responsibly, in this matter. Or he may have been recognis-
ing an imbalance of power in the marriage bed. Regarding divorce, Aelfric's
teaching was even-handed: only death ends a marriage.

Yet whatever churchmen thought about them, it is likely that women benefited
from ecclesiastical teaching about marriage and sex. It was probably widely
known, Aelfric's sermons for example being widely circulated, and probably used
by local priests. It is possible that this teaching and the available female exemplars
emboldened some girls and women to resist marriage and sex, or increased their
families' and husbands' willingness to respect their preference for abstinence. It is
plausible that the rules about sexual activity were largely adhered to. The living
conditions of most couples would not have included privacy, so what they did
would have been subject to comment and report to a priest.[6] The arrangement of
a Continental Penitential suggests that in late-eighth-century Francia flouting
the rule about permitted times was perceived not as normal backsliding but as
startling, and akin to magical practices.[7]

The Church helped widows enormously, both theoretically and in practice. Its
disapproval of remarriage offered them justification for refusing to remarry, and it
seems that they were often subject to pressure to do so. A widow's remarriage
could benefit her own kin, through the marriage settlement, and also her affines.
They would regain her dower, namely, what her deceased husband had allowed
her for her maintenance as a widow, which was ultimately to pass to his children
or, if he were childless, to his kin. Other dangers were pressure to enter the religious life, if kinsmen saw profit in that, and harassment by kinsmen and kings
about bequests and dues. A passage in one version of the *Anglo-Saxon Chronicle*
includes the plundering of widows in the troubles of Edward the Martyr's reign.
Some charters reveal instances of estates being forcibly taken. In one case in the
late 990s, King Aethelred accused a deceased man of treason and wanted his
widow's inheritance as the penalty. Some wills seem to anticipate that the king
might not allow the will to be executed.[8] Sometimes bishops were appointed as
widows' protectors in wills. Cases of bishops performing this role effectively are
known, sometimes indeed to their own profit, but sometimes to their dis-
advantage. Archbishop Aelfric of Canterbury persuaded Aethelred to relent
towards the alleged traitor's widow, so that he required only that she give her
morning-gift (gift from her husband after their marriage) to Christ Church,
Canterbury, for the sake of his soul and his people. Archbishop Dunstan had
bought back property that King Eadwig had confiscated from a widow.[9]

Protection of widows (and orphans) was a topos of piety and good kingship,
stemming from the Bible. Curiously, it is absent both from Asser's praise of
Alfred's charity and from royal law-codes in which Archbishop Wulfstan II was
not involved. In texts associated with the reformers, just treatment of widows

recurs. In a homily that Archbishop Dunstan wrote for, and probably preached at, Aethelred II's coronation, defence and protection of widows, orphans and strangers is presented as the second most important of a king's duties, the first being not to judge falsely. The earliest datable laws associated with Wulfstan, those of 1008, introduced widows' remarriage into royal law, stipulating a year's delay before remarriage, that they were to choose for themselves what they wanted, and that widows who conducted themselves rightly were to have God's and the king's protection. Cnut's laws added harsh financial penalties that would have affected the widow herself, her own kin, and her illicit second husband. This may suggest that resistance to the new law had occurred and was anticipated. It must have been meant as a practical protection from pressure to remarry. Protection from financial harassment and from pressure to enter religious life came in the allowance of a year to pay the heriot (death duty), the prohibition of hasty consecration of widows and the emphasis on choice.[10]

Observance of the Church's teaching about sexual activity would have guaranteed women better health and longer lives by reducing their chances of conception. Pregnancy and childbirth have been the biggest killers of women in societies without modern medical practices. The life-enhancing aspect of abstinence will have been even greater if, as some scholars have argued, the early medieval diet was low in iron, though improvements appeared in the tenth and eleventh centuries. Dietary iron deficiency, which increases the risks of various illnesses and conditions, is more harmful to women than to men, because of their blood loss in menstruation and their bodies' needs in pregnancy. One estimate is that even if she escaped pregnancy, a woman would probably have been severely anaemic by the age of twenty-three. On average, unregulated sexual intercourse would probably have made a woman pregnant every two years. A woman who had had two pregnancies by twenty-three would have exhausted her body's iron stores and been at very serious risk in a third one. Other aspects of diet would also have militated against healthy pregnancy.[11] We lack precise figures for Anglo-Saxon mortality rates, but for the Middle Anglo-Saxon period the median life expectancy for women was 35.8 years as against 38.2 for men. Of the women in the mid-tenth- to mid-twelfth-century cemetery at Raunds 71per cent died between the ages of seventeen and thirty-five.[12] During their years of fertility, women's mortality rates were much higher than men's. It is hard not to conclude that women who chose virginity, wives who chose sexual abstinence or restraint, and pre-menopausal widows who chose celibacy over remarriage were wise to do so.

Property

The subject of widows raises questions of whether women themselves were treated as property, of women as property-owners, and of women's use of property for religious purposes, including the religious duties of their families, with which, historically, women have often been charged.

The Church's stress on consent to marriage implies that women should never have been treated as property, and by the eleventh century practice may have coincided with ideal. Cnut's laws enjoined that no woman was to be given for money, though the bridegroom could choose to give something if he wished. What he paid was, according to the text about betrothal, for the upbringing of his bride. On the other hand, the law might merely have been strengthening buyer against seller, and payment for upbringing a more acceptable term for price.[13] Certainly a succession of earlier law-codes imply that women had, in previous years, been seen as property. They were under the protection of men – kinsmen or powerful figures such as bishops – and injury to them was perceived as injury to these men's property. In addition, women were to obey their husbands. Thus Alfred's laws stipulate that the permission of the king or bishop is necessary to bring a nun, the necessity of whose own consent is not stated, out of a nunnery. Anyone who did so without permission was to pay a fine, half to the king and half to the bishop and the lord of the church that had the nun. Neither such a nun nor any children of the union were to inherit from the man. If the children happened to be killed, the share of the compensation normally payable to the victim's maternal kin was to go to the king. A man who had sexual intercourse with someone else's wife was to compensate her husband. If a betrothed woman had sexual intercourse, her family was to pay compensation to the surety, presumably to be passed to her fiancé or his family. As for wifely obedience, Ine's laws had stated that because she owed him obedience, a wife did not share the guilt of a husband who stole cattle and brought it to his house. Cnut's laws similarly cleared wives of complicity in thefts by their husbands unless stolen objects were found in the wife's storeroom, chest or coffer, whose keys it was her duty to look after.[14]

It is nevertheless clear that women had rights to, and control over, property independently of their husbands. A letter to Edward the Elder, about disputed land at Fonthill, states that the land had been sold by a lady, who had told the purchaser that her entitlement to sell it was that it was her morning-gift. In the eleventh century, a prospective bridegroom was not only supposed to pledge to maintain his lady properly. He was also to announce what he granted her in return for accepting his suit, and what as a dower. Two betrothal agreements survive. One, datable to 1014–1016, concerns Archbishop Wulfstan II's sister and the other, datable to 1016–1020, a lady from Kent. Neither lady's family received anything. They themselves received estates, gold, animals, and men or slaves.

Some estates, however, were temporary grants, for a lifetime or on a lease of three lives, rather than lands that the lady could dispose of as she chose. Whichever spouse outlived the other was to succeed to everything. In the general text concerning betrothals, a widow is entitled to half the couple's goods if they were childless, and to all of them if they had children, unless and until she remarried. Domesday Book too suggests that a widow's share was half. In Nottinghamshire, the wife of a thief was entitled to half of his property, the rest going to the king and lord. Earlier, West Saxon widows had been entitled to only one-third. In Ine's laws, the wife of a cattle-thief whose property was forfeit could keep one-third, provided that she could swear that she had not eaten any of the stolen meat. Aethelstan's laws allowed a third to an innocent wife of an executed thief. Of course, we do not know how often what was supposed to happen actually did, for example whether testators' wishes were realised. But since women inherited property, from both female and male kin, either outright or with the provision that it would ultimately pass to another beneficiary, it may not have been only widows who were financially independent female landowners. It is possible that some women who had never been married were too.[15]

According to charters and wills, women disposed of property freely, often for religious purposes, but it is likely that the freedom with which they could do so was in fact more limited than it appears. Their bequests may have been implementing family strategies that had been designed earlier, to apply to several generations and to provide for kin both by lifetime grants and by ultimate gift to a church.[16] A church's expectation of ownership will have resulted in its community praying for the family and supporting the implementation of the bequests. Such a strategy is demonstrable in the religious patronage in East Anglia of two (widowed) daughters of Aelfgar, ealdorman of Essex from 946 to 951, all three of whose wills survive. Many of the bequests of the daughters were of estates that their father had left them only for their lifetime, and to beneficiaries that he had designated.[17] But only one daughter referred in her own will (c. 1002) to her father's. If her sister's (c. 975) had been the only one of the three to survive, it would have implied, erroneously, her complete control over the property. Women were probably most often the channel rather than the source of the bequests made in their wills, though it was not only women who were given temporary ownership of property. Of the forty-seven recorded male bequests, eighteen included reversionary grants to men as opposed to twenty-five to women. Women were sometimes named as the second holder in three-lifetime leases. It is not certain whether married women needed their husbands' consent to make a bequest, but the surviving records of female bequests suggest that the women who made wills were widows, or childless wives. In sixteen of the twenty cases of joint bequests by a couple they are certainly married, and in only one (datable to between 1042 and 1066) are any children mentioned. Of the twenty-six women who are known to have made bequests acting alone, twenty were definitely or probably widows.[18]

Gifts to churches, whether bequests or not, were made in the hope that their donors would somehow be rewarded. Thus for example a Bodmin manumission of, probably, the early eleventh century, records the freeing of a slave by a woman for her and her husband's souls. One function of gifts to religious communities was to finance or reward those communities' care for the souls of the donors' deceased kin, for example saying Mass, reciting psalms and praying for them. Another was to forge links that would benefit the living kin as well as the dead. This too has been illuminated by studies of Aelfgar's family.[19] Aelfgar gave to his twice-widowed elder daughter, Aethelflaed, who in her first marriage had been King Edmund's second wife, nearly twice as many estates as his younger daughter, Aelfflaed, widow of Ealdorman Byrhtnoth, the hero of the battle of Maldon. It was to Aethelflaed that he entrusted the care of her ancestors' souls. She left thirteen estates to religious houses in East Anglia. Eight of these were new bequests rather than her father's, and the houses that she favoured included two new to her family. But in total, her bequests and gifts were spread evenly between houses associated with her natal family and houses associated with her affines. Aelfflaed's patronage was similar. In addition, between c. 950 and c. 1002, the sisters gave East Anglian churches more than their father had done, the number of donated estates increasing from nine to twenty-five. This suggests that some of their patronage was their own decision, and that they chose to reorient their kinsfolk's values and concerns. They also, of course, underline the importance of widows in the laity's economic support of the Church, which itself has been described as being fundamental to social unity.[20]

Vowesses, cloistered women and saints

In later Anglo-Saxon England, the women who had most control over property were widows. But before c. 800 those who controlled lands had included abbesses, female heads of female or double minster houses, some of whom had exercised great influence in politics and society. One theory about the lack of such women later is that the Church failed to promote or significantly provide for the religious life for women; that any account that it did take of this life was merely in order to control it; and that it was imbued with a misogyny that had been stimulated in part by developments on the Continent.[21] There, regard for abbesses and nuns started to decline in the late eighth century, as did their authority, power and influence.[22] Yet there are other possibilities. The decline of female and double houses began well before c. 800. It coincided with, and may be related to, other developments. The aristocracy was giving less land to minsters, whether old or new. Minsters were becoming less attractive as investments. Kings were trying to ensure that minsters fulfilled the fiscal and military obligations that went with landownership. Meanwhile bishops were weakening family control of minster endowments and of the appointments of abbots and abbesses. In the ninth century, kings' determination to levy dues will have increased in the face of the expense and difficulty of dealing with Viking attacks. Aristocrats may have needed to keep, or reclaim, their lands to pay what they themselves owed. The Vikings threatened minster treasures, estates and personnel. Some minsters were attacked. Some lands were seized. Some people must have been afraid of losses, including loss of life, and of atrocities, as suggested by the grant in 804 of an estate inside Canterbury as a refuge to the abbess of Lyminge. One interpretation of the poem *Judith*, in which the heroine is not, as in the original version, a widow, but a virgin, is that it was meant to be inspirational to nuns who feared rape and martyrdom. Such fears were not unreasonable. Vikings did attack places where there were female houses.[23]

After conditions had become safer, female religious life resumed. But the tenth-century reformation, and the ideals expressed in the *Regularis Concordia* were antipathetic to earlier norms,[24] comprising: close relationships between religious houses and their founders' families; married clerics; male and female inmates; the retention by individuals of estates and other property; the corporate pursuit simultaneously of both the contemplative life and pastoral care of the laity; and a lifestyle often resembling that of the lay aristocracy. Instead, a regular (that is, according to a rule, Latin *regula*) life, involving stricter seclusion, chastity and no private property was prescribed. No double houses are known after the early tenth century. The female religious vocation came to be expressed partly in and through cloistered houses, and predominantly through women becoming vowesses. The phenomenon of the vowess was quite long standing. In the late seventh century, Archbishop Theodore's penitential teaching had envisaged a woman vowing not to remarry after her husband's death. But the Old English linguistic distinction between cloistered woman and vowess is first seen in the reform period.

Taking vows was more economically advantageous for a woman's family than her entry to a cloistered house, which would have involved a gift of land to it. And although vowesses were effectively outside male and episcopal control, the phenomenon seems to have enjoyed some promotion by the late Anglo-Saxon Church. The Church thereby offered women an opportunity of self-determination and of the realisation of religious inclinations that their male relatives' economic concerns might otherwise have served to deny.

Unification under the West Saxon dynasty also contributed to the long-term decline in the number of female houses, though in some respects there was striking continuity.[25] For economic reasons the long lasting and most important minsters had always been royal, not aristocratic, foundations. By c. 735 there had been thirty-three royal female houses and only four non-royal. Yet royal religious houses were always susceptible to decline if and when the dynasty to which they were connected, and whose interests they promoted, itself declined. Thus Winchcombe, founded by King Cenwulf of Mercia, did not survive when Mercia was under direct West Saxon rule. Alfred's dynasty backed religious houses just as earlier ones had, in its own family territories. It has also been suggested that families which had once been royal felt that careers in the Church now offered the best opportunities for power and status, and consequently tended to make men rather than women the heads of their minsters.[26]

Though the history of the female religious life overall is susceptible to differing interpretations, most of its details are not.[27] Female religious consistently appear in laws and directives, as part of society, vulnerable to oppression, protected or oppressed. Alfred's laws suggest that women in late-ninth-century minsters enjoyed, or were exposed to, male attention. He anticipated that they might be brought out without royal or episcopal permission, or lewdly seized by clothes or breast without their own permission. Such possibilities were to reappear in a variety of other texts. Edmund's laws, issued one Easter between 941 and 946, stipulate that the holy orders, both male and female, maintain their chastity, and lay down a penalty for intercourse with a *nun*. This penalty was loss of the right to consecrated burial without making amends, the same as for a manslayer and an adulterer. The *Regularis Concordia* was supposed to apply to women as well as men and it claimed to offer female religious some special protection. Archbishop Dunstan added to it that no man of whatever rank should trespass in places that were set apart for them, nor should anyone with spiritual authority over them use their powers like a worldly tyrant. The problem remained a matter of concern.

Cnut's 1019/20 letter to the people of England forbade marriage to cloistered women and vowesses. Property was also an issue. Bishop Aethelwold, at the end of his account of Edgar's establishment of monasteries, exhorts both his (male) 'successors' and abbesses to observe the *Rule* and not diminish God's property. But he also warns abbesses, and only them, against giving estates to their kin or to great lay persons, for money or flattery.[28] This might signify that Aethelwold felt that abbesses were likely to have less sense and probity than their male counterparts or, less pejoratively, that he thought that religious women might have to suffer pressure that abbots did not, and was providing an authority for them to cite in their resistance.

Female religious are as visible as male ones in directives, but far less so in the charters and histories that record foundations and reformations. This makes tracing the history of female religious houses both individually and collectively very difficult.[29] Three things, nevertheless, seem certain about the period c. 800–1066. There were far fewer female than male religious houses. There were far fewer female houses than in the seventh and eighth centuries. Female houses in the tenth and eleventh centuries were closely connected to Alfred's dynasty.[30]

Scholars' estimates of the number of houses for women between the seventh century and the mid-ninth vary, though only slightly. According to one estimate there were forty-two, of which eighteen were certainly and four probably double houses, quite widely and evenly distributed across Anglo-Saxon terrain.[31] According to another, there were sixty-five female houses, nineteen of them demonstrably double.[32] Only a few are attested both before and in the ninth century. Three are for Northumbria, two for Mercia. By the late ninth century even these were defunct or almost so. Wessex's female houses fared a little better. Wareham, which may have been founded in the late seventh century, lasted until at least 982, though not necessarily continuously. Wimborne, where King Aethelred I (died 871) was buried, is not attested as a female house after 899, when King Alfred's nephew Aethelwold took one of its women in the course of his claim to the throne. Between c. 890 and 1066 there were fourteen houses for women that definitely or possibly dated back to pre-Viking years, but of these only two lasted until 1066. Three houses, all of which survived beyond the Norman Conquest, were founded before Edgar's reign: one at Shaftesbury by King Alfred, in about 888; the Nunnaminster (nuns' monastery) at Winchester by Alfred's widow; and Wilton, which was well established by the mid-tenth century. Only the Nunnaminster is recorded as having undergone reform in the tenth century, though in contrast to accounts of male houses, no account of the inmates' wickedness or their resistance survives. Aethelwold established cloistered women there, with an abbess. Eleven new female houses were established after the mid-tenth-century reform. In c. 1000 the total of surviving female houses was eight, nine or ten. The latest was Chatteris, founded by Eadnoth, abbot of Ramsey and bishop of Dorchester for his sister, between 1006 and 1016. Royal patronage was directed primarily to Shaftesbury, the Nunnaminster, Wilton, Romsey, which was almost certainly founded by Edgar, Amesbury, founded by Queen Aelfthryth, and Wherwell, probably also founded by Aelfthryth or by her brother. The only pre-Alfredian female house and the only one not in Wessex that was favoured was Barking. The geographical distribution of female houses was the same as that of reformed male ones.

The standards within female monasteries may have been a little more relaxed than in male ones, not, probably, because less was expected of or attained by women, but because some of them were royal. At Wilton, Edgar's daughter apparently dressed like a princess, though she wore a hair shirt undergarment. Almost all the female houses of the late ninth, tenth and eleventh centuries had associations with royal women. Princesses, discarded royal wives, and royal widows lived there. Not all of these widows took vows or became abbesses. It may have been Alfred who began the phenomenon of West Saxon royal women following the religious life, making his daughter Aethelgifu Shaftesbury's first abbess. However, according to a tradition recorded in the fifteenth century his grandfather, King Egbert, had converted Wilton into a nunnery for his widowed sister in 830, her husband having established the house in 800. Of the family of Edward the Elder, perhaps Wilton's real founder, one daughter, Eadburh lived at the Nunnaminster from the age of three. Two others, Eadflaed and Aethelhild, lived at Wilton, as did Edward's discarded second wife, Aelfflaed, possibly as a vowess. All three were buried there. His third wife, Eadgifu, who likewise may have become a vowess, spent some time at Shaftesbury, later the burial place of King Edmund's first wife, Aelfgifu, King Edgar's mother. Wilton was the abode and burial place of Edgar's discarded second wife, Wulfthryth, who was its abbess, and of their daughter (later saint) Edith, who was placed there as an infant. Wherwell, where Wulfthryth's aunt had once lived, was where Queen Aelfthryth retired. Royal wives were not invariably buried at a nunnery: Eadwig's separated wife was buried at Winchester's Old Minster, whither Queen Emma followed her husband, Cnut. Queen Edith joined Edward the Confessor at Westminster.

The lives and locations of vowesses too can be traced.[33] Some references in the sources require them to live according to rule, but no rule for vowesses survives. Perhaps a generally recognised standard, including chastity, was meant rather than a particular text.[34] Aelfric may have been trying to offer vowesses a role model in his version of the story of Judith. He stressed that she fasted and dressed plainly and combined humility with her chastity. Some scholars think that the woman to whom he addressed the text's epilogue was a virgin vowess; others that she was an abbess.[35] It is possible that in the late tenth century the number of widows choosing to become vowesses increased. Two Pontificals that were written about c. 1000 include a new prayer, for vowesses, with the rites of consecration into the religious life and blessing of widows. Formal profession offered vowesses respect and protection.[36]

Sixty places have been identified as possible locations of female religious life, of any kind but involving more than one woman, between 871 and 1066, and the majority were probably the abodes of vowesses.[37] If so, vowess sites outnumbered sites of cloistered houses by about five to one, and had a far wider geographical distribution. Hence it is likely that, below the level of the royal family, more women who had a religious vocation expressed it through becoming a vowess than by entering a convent. There are fifteen instances of vowesses, living alone or in a group, attached to male houses. How continuous such group arrangements were is unknown. Some endeavours were short-lived and perhaps meant to be so, to cater for particular individuals. Lone vowesses were not uncommon. King Edgar's widowed maternal grandmother Wynflaed, a benefactress of Shaftesbury, where she was buried, may have been a vowess, possibly the same Wynflaed, termed a 'religious woman', to whom King Edmund granted an estate in 942 and possibly the Wynflaed who refers in her will, c. 950, to her nun's clothing, and best holy veil. The individual 'religious women' who were the beneficiaries in seventeen mid-tenth-century surviving charters were probably vowesses. One, Aelfwyn, may have been the Aelfwyn who was the daughter of Aethelflaed of Mercia.

For an aristocratic family supporting a vowess was less expensive than funding a cloistered nun. But for kings and for society as a whole, cloistered women were not just an expense – they were a valuable asset.[38] Like cloistered men they acted as intercessors, and if they lived correctly they could be presumed to be effective. A king's giving a daughter to a convent was equivalent to giving a daughter in marriage to a man whose alliance and support would be beneficial, gaining God's instead. None of the known cases of royal infants being offered to monastic life involve boys.[39] It is possible that the spiritual duties and concerns of the royal dynasty collectively were predominantly devolved to its female members, to be discharged in and by the communities that they supervised. Until the mid-eighth century, in the western Church, recital of the Psalter was a favoured method of intercession, and the daily monastic prayer, in which beneficiaries were prayed for by name and particular services or prayers dedicated to their benefit, was perceived as an effective one.[40] Women were able to perform both. Furthermore, the Church seems to have regarded 'sisterly prayer' as more pure and more effective than men's.[41] This might be why in 932 King Aethelstan required, in return for a grant, that Shaftesbury sing fifty psalms and celebrate a Mass for his soul, every day until Judgement. This was a greater burden than he imposed on male communities. In 933 for example Sherborne was required only to sing the Psalter, once a year.[42]

Women's engagement in intercession may have declined after the tenth-century reform. The late-eighth-century Carolingian Church saw the offering of the Eucharist at Mass as the most effective method of intercession. To name beneficiaries during its celebration was to make Christ Himself an offering on the beneficiaries' behalf. A further attraction was that several Masses could be said in the time that a single recital of the Psalter took. There was consequently a demand for special Masses.[43] Unfortunately for women religious, the Eucharist required a (male) priest, and the sexual segregation imposed by the reformers probably meant that convents would have found it difficult to say Mass more often than the minimum requirement. A male house by contrast, especially since some monks were also priests, could do so easily. It could even, if it had more than one altar, offer Masses for different beneficiaries simultaneously.[44]

So male houses will have become more attractive to patrons than female ones. Nevertheless the old methods did not die out. The *Regularis Concordia*'s requirement, of all houses, for prayers for king, queen and benefactors, was for prayers after each office of the day, not for special Masses.

Intercession was not an activity that only the living engaged in. It was expected that those deceased family members who were saints would also offer intercession, in Heaven, unless their kin on earth displeased them. One function of the cult of royal saints was to encourage them to intercede for their earthly kin, and one function of royal women's minsters was to promote these royal cults.[45] The minsters offered and controlled physical access to the saints, via their remains, and attested and publicised the miracles that they worked. Thus in Mercia Winchcombe and Repton had promoted the cults of the martyred kings Cynehelm (Kenelm) and Wigstan. In Wessex, Shaftesbury developed that of King Edward the Martyr (died 978), receiving his remains from Wareham in 979. Edward apparently began working miracles in about 990, subsequently appeared in a vision to a male religious, telling him to tell the abbess to tell the king that he wished to be translated, and was translated in 1001. King Aethelred made grants to Shaftesbury in return for the promotion of Edward's cult and for intercession, stipulating that they were in honour of Edward and for the salvation of the whole lineage, past and future. At Wilton their half-sister Edith was promoted as a saint some time between 997 and 1000.

Royal female minsters generally were not burial sites for kings, though in ninth-century Mercia Winchcombe was for King Cenwulf and his son Cynehelm, and Repton for the kings Wiglaf and (St) Wigstan. In the tenth century almost all kings were interred at male houses. Winchester's New Minster received Alfred (and his wife), and Eadwig (died 959), its Old Minster Eadred (died 955), Cnut (died 1035) and Harthacnut (died 1042). Aethelstan, and two of his cousins who died at the battle of Brunanburh went to Malmesbury, Edmund (died 946), Edgar (died 975) and Edmund Ironside (died 1016) to Glastonbury, Aethelred II (died 1016) to St Paul's, London, and Edward the Confessor to Westminster.[46]

The various functions of royal female minsters all had political dimensions and they included an overt political role.[47] Some early-tenth-century charters were issued at Wilton suggesting that it hosted political assemblies. Even after the great reform Wilton had many lay visitors and was, according to the later *Life* of Edith, expected to participate in politics. Edith was, apparently, often visited, by petitioners, royal officials and foreign diplomats who sought her favour, presumably both respecting her advice and expecting that she had political influence. Any house that was associated with a royal wife contributed to the status of her natal family, attracted its patronage and might play a part in local politics. Such a house and family could sometimes have an important role in central politics, especially if the succession was disputed.

The functions of vowesses may not have been entirely dissimilar to those of cloistered women, though they would have been much more limited in extent. They could certainly have undertaken prayer, intercession and commemoration of the dead, which would have been valued by their families. And, like kings', their families' status would have benefited, since pious individuals were regarded as evidence that their lineage itself was holy.[48] Of course, women who had not taken any vows at all could also undertake commemoration of the dead. The tenth-century sculptures in northern England, many of which are adorned with hunting and/or warrior images, may have been foundation monuments for new churches. As funerary monuments they perhaps commemorated newly established, possibly Scandinavian, families not just individuals. Since at least some Scandinavian settlers married indigenous women, it has been suggested that at least some female patrons may be behind these monuments.[49]

The extent to which women religious were inspired by the images of female saints that were available, and, as we saw earlier, how the laity, both female and male, interpreted these saints is more difficult to imagine. Even if, for example, Aelfric did not intend his depictions of female saints to be taken as lessons and role models about and for women in particular, it is still possible that they sometimes were. He had not included any women in his homilies, but he did in his *Lives of Saints*, though they are a minority. Three of his women belong to pairs of early, foreign, virgin spouses. Their historical reality is doubtful but they had been regarded for several centuries as martyrs. All three appear in the ninth-century Old English Martyrology, and Aethelstan apparently gave some of their relics to Exeter.[50] Of Aelfric's other four female martyrs, one was the seventh-century Anglo-Saxon virgin married queen Aethelthryth. In Aelfric's text, it is the maintenance of their virginity that qualifies these women as saints, Aethelthryth being the only one who did not die in its cause. Thus female virginity, suffering, death and sanctity are linked here, just as they had been in some earlier Continental texts. Some scholars think that this had been done deliberately, in order to discourage women from choosing virginity, and hence to minimise their liberation from social restriction and threatening the ecclesiastical hierarchy. Virginity seemed to promise women these things, because it was so highly esteemed.[51] On the other hand, no surviving Anglo-Saxon account of any Anglo-Saxon saint uses the motif of the virgin resisting marriage. Where Aelfric does, it is with regard to foreign saints and because it was present in his sources.[52] Indeed he seems to tone down the violence.[53]

There were other Anglo-Saxon female saints besides Aethelthryth. Most were thought to be royal. In the tenth century, King Edgar's mother Aelfgifu and daughter Edith were added to those whom Bede had recorded.[54] The eleventh-century list of relics' resting places includes some dozen. One was Aethelthryth's contemporary, Balthild, a high-born Anglo-Saxon who had married a Frankish king, exercised much political power and ecclesiastical patronage, and, in widowhood, been cruelly put to death. Another royal, though foreign, female saint, who must have been well known, was Helena (Old English Elene, mother of the first Christian Roman emperor, Constantine I). Some account of her finding the True Cross would have been declaimed country-wide, annually, in churches, in celebration of the feast of the Invention of the Cross, and probably at that of the Exaltation of the Cross too.[55]

Anglo-Saxon Christians could therefore contemplate many female saints, whether or not this means that Church and society had a positive view of women or women religious. The prime saint of course was the Virgin Mary. She had the status of a martyr, that is, witness to the faith, because of her suffering at the Crucifixion and her obedience to God.[56] Her obedience, motherhood of God and virginity justified her exaltation as Queen of Heaven, ruler of angels. The Church taught that after her death she had been assumed (taken) into heaven. In the western Church, the official but not the only view was that this assumption was spiritual rather than bodily.[57] A miniature in Aethelwold's Benedictional, and some texts, show that some people, in later-tenth-century England, as on the Continent, including Aethelwold, accepted the story of her bodily assumption that was recounted in apocryphal texts. Aelfric seems to have been alone in England in his objection to this and other stories.[58] Mary was also characterised as the star of the sea: the sea is this world, the light of the star is Christ, the star helps all Christians to navigate, that is, to live rightly and gain salvation and eternal life.

Devotion to Mary had a sanctifying effect on the devotee. Consequently, as has been argued of the tenth-century German emperor Otto III, a monarch's devotion to her played a role in boosting the holiness of the state as an institution.[59] This may be one explanation of the expansion of her cult in England as part of the tenth-century reform of the Church, in both of which Winchester became the centre.[60] Mary is prominent in the picture that adorns King Edgar's New Minster charter of 966, and in the *Regularis Concordia*, which enjoined religious houses to celebrate a weekly Mass in her honour. Aelfric wrote five homilies for her feasts. The number and proportion of churches dedicated to Mary greatly increased. Mary featured in the dedication of the churches in seventeen out of seven new and fourteen refounded, monasteries. She was the sole dedicatee in seven, and shared the honour with another saint or saints in ten. By contrast, in twelve known eighth-century dedications she was involved only once. Female houses' dedications do not show so sharp a contrast. Mary featured in about half of the new foundations as compared to two out of five in the ninth century.

Mary's cult had first flourished in England in the late seventh and early eighth centuries, and it had never died out. In the Mercian Book of Cerne she is as important as St Peter: of its seventy-four prayers three are to Mary and three feature Peter. There are prayers to Mary too in the Book of Nunnaminster, which is possibly Northumbrian, and slightly earlier, namely c. 800. These prayers express confidence in her powers of intercession. Four Marian feasts – the Purification, Annunciation, Assumption and Nativity – were firmly established by 900. The surviving Old English versions of Latin Marian apocryphal gospels cannot be precisely dated or localised. But they are independent of the Winchester School, and were circulating at the time of Aelfric.[61] Byzantine influence, possibly via Italy, may explain the introduction, in about 1030, of two more Marian feasts, which were unknown elsewhere in the west, the Conception of the Virgin and the Presentation of the Virgin Mary in the Temple.[62] Finally, the Marian pilgrimage to Walsingham that flourished for several centuries may have begun in 1061. Mary's cult was certainly rooted in monastic circles, but it was far from unknown to the English outside them.

Women in British and Scots' societies

Women in Cornwall and Scotland are veiled in mystery. Something can be said about the Welsh, though it derives from the later legal sources and it is uncertain how far they reflect conditions of an earlier period; furthermore, the different tracts do not all say the same things.[63] The lowly status of kings' wives in late-ninth-century Wessex, of which Asser disapproved, contrasts with that of Welsh queens in the Welsh laws. A Welsh queen was, for example, entitled to one-third of the produce of her king's landed property, was to be attended by eight of the twenty-four royal officers, and was one of the three legal needles of the court, the others being those of the mediciner and the chief huntsman.[64] Sex and marriage are treated very differently in Welsh and English texts. Virginity is not empha-sised in the former, though brides were expected to be virgin. As in Anglo-Saxon England, marriages were arranged by families, the bride's family gave her a dowry and the bridegroom paid a fee, ostensibly in recognition and recompense for his bride's lord or father having protected her, and gave his wife a morning-gift. But the involvement of the Church was minimal, perhaps non-existent. Its forbidden degrees of kinship were not respected, marriage was not regarded as indissoluble, illegitimate sons were allowed to inherit from their fathers and cle-rical marriage was allowed. Unlike her English counterpart, a Welsh wife apparently had some rights against her husband and could expect that separation and subsequent remarriage might be permitted, and marriage had something of a trial period before it was fully fashioned. She was, for example, entitled to compensation if her husband committed adultery, provided that she caught him in the act, and to a divorce if she caught him a third time. Husbands' grounds for repudiation of their wives are not clear. A wife had property rights: for example she was entitled to half the couple's common chattels and also the chil-dren if she separated from her husband justifiably, provided that they had been married for no less than seven years. If they had not, she was entitled only to her dower, which was dependent on the status of her father. A wife who was repu-diated without injustice retained her morning-gift and dowry and received her honour price.[65]

Despite these rights women, as in England, normally played no public role. The hundreds of witnesses of property transactions that are recorded are almost all men. Later evidence suggests that before the thirteenth century women could not give sureties and so could only make contracts by using Godsurety-ship, that is, calling on God to guarantee their word. Nor were they legally competent to bear witness against a man. A woman's status and significance in kinship varied according to circumstances. Inheritance of land was through the male line but both male and female were important in alliances. An individual's maternal kin were involved in the payment of compensation for insult and homicide of which he was guilty, but a woman's honour price depended on the status of her husband, not her father. It seems likely that women were normally regarded as weak, and inferior to men. The cult of the Virgin Mary is attested from the tenth century, but it was not as prominent in Wales as in England.

Some of the teaching of Anglo-Saxon reformers can be interpreted as misogynistic, but it may not have been, either in intent or in its effects. Adherence to their ideals about sex and marriage would have been life-enhancing for women. The decline of female and double religious houses were consequences not of misogynism but of other factors. In the reform period women could realise religious vocations either as cloistered nuns or vowesses, they contributed to the godliness of society and the eternal salvation of their male kin, as well as to political life, and these contributions were valued. English women in general had rights to property, and some played an important role in implementing families' strategies for the transmission of land over generations. The lot of women in contemporary Alba, Wales and Cornwall, however, seems unknowable, which may suggest that it was less favourable and possibly very different in crucial respects, one of them the religious life. Thus only a few nuns are known in Wales in the early Middle Ages and there is no evidence for any female religious houses in Cornwall or Scotland before the Norman period.[66]

Notes

1 Cubitt, 'Virginity'.
2 Wright.
3 Cubitt, 'Virginity'; Lees and Overing.
4 Foot, *Monastic, Veiled* I.
5 For these subjects, Cubitt, 'Virginity'.
6 Thacker, 'Monks'.
7 Meens, 'Magic'.
8 For these issues, Hollis.
9 Giandrea; Hollis.
10 Hollis.
11 Bullough and Campbell; Lee.
12 Lee.
13 Hollis.
14 *Ibid.*; Klinck; Ross.
15 Foot, *Veiled* I. For women and property, Crick, 'Women'; Hollis; Klinck.
16 Crick, 'Women'.
17 *Ibid.*; Wareham, *Lords.*
18 Crick, 'Women'.
19 Wareham, *Lords.*
20 *Ibid.*
21 Cubitt, 'Virginity'; and see Foot, *Monastic, Veiled* I; Yorke, *Nunneries.*
22 Muschcol.
23 For these explanations, Foot, *Monastic, Veiled* I; Yorke, *Nunneries.*
24 For what follows, Foot, *Monastic, Veiled* I.
25 Yorke, *Nunneries.*
26 *Ibid.* and Foot, *Veiled* I.
27 For what follows, Foot, *Monastic, Veiled* I; Yorke, *Nunneries.*
28 Lees and Overing.

29 Foot, *Veiled*, I and II.
30 For what follows, Foot, *Veiled* I; Yorke, *Nunneries*.
31 Foot, *Veiled* I citing D.B. Schneider, 'Anglo-Saxon Women and the Religious Life: A Study of the Status and Position of Women in an Early Medieval Society', unpublished PhD. Diss., Cambridge University, 1985.
32 Yorke, *Nunneries*.
33 Foot, *Veiled* I.
34 *Ibid.*
35 *Ibid.*
36 Foot, *Veiled* I; Hollis; Yorke, *Nunneries*.
37 For what follows, Foot, *Veiled* I and see also Volume II.
38 Yorke, *Nunneries*.
39 *Ibid.*
40 *Ibid.*
41 Muschcol.
42 Yorke, *Nunneries*.
43 Muschcol; McLaughlin; Paxton.
44 Yorke, *Nunneries*.
45 For what follows, Yorke, *Nunneries*.
46 *Ibid.*
47 *Ibid.*
48 *Ibid.*
49 Hadley, 'Negotiating'.
50 Upchurch, *Ælfric's*.
51 See contributions in McInerney.
52 Yorke, *Nunneries*.
53 Lees and Overing.
54 Yorke, *Nunneries*.
55 Klein.
56 Cubitt, 'Virginity'.
57 Clayton, *Apocryphal*; Mayr-Harting, 'Idea'.
58 Clayton, *Apocryphal, Cult*.
59 Mayr-Harting, 'Idea'.
60 For what follows, Clayton, *Cult*.
61 Clayton, *Apocryphal*.
62 Clayton, *Cult*.
63 Pryce, *Native*.
64 Klein, citing Hywel Dda's laws.
65 For these subjects and what follows, Pryce, *Native*. See also W. Davies, *Wales*.
66 Foot, *Veiled* I.

9 The Church in the landscape

The Church was an important, and sometimes dominant, presence in the socio-economic landscape. Minsters and sees owned land and other property, including many slaves. In England, where it became an increasingly noticeable feature of the physical landscape, the Church also played a role in urban and other economic growth and, through this, contributed to social mobility, which caused anxiety for at least some churchmen.

The physical reality

There were significant regional variations but, overall, in England, the number of churches and the distinctiveness of many ecclesiastical buildings and sites increased, as did the disparities between them, and grave-yards associated with churches proliferated.[1]

Numbers and locations of minsters in the eighth and ninth centuries are uncertain because there is disagreement about identifying minster sites. Thus for example signs of central planning, an enclosure (often curved), more than one church, and axial arrangement of buildings have been regarded as indications, even when there is no documentary evidence.[2] But some such sites have also been interpreted differently, as royal or aristocratic ones.[3] Flixborough is one.[4] Furthermore, the sites of some documented minsters do not fit this model, and some minsters may have shared secular sites rather than had separate ones.[5]

There was variety in layout and in how minster sites were separated from the rest of society.[6] Some complexes had several churches as well as other buildings. In some, churches were arranged in a line, for instance at Lindisfarne. Some churches were prominent in the landscape, because of their location or appearance, as at Breedon-on-the-Hill and the seventh-century church at Escomb in Northumbria, in whose construction Roman material was reused. Many churches were built in stone, which distinguished them from secular buildings, which were in wood.[7] Standing stone crosses will also have been noticeable, some serving as locations for meetings for worship and preaching. The crosses were ornamented with sculpture and probably also painted.

In Cornwall, probably, there were churches early in our period at places whose names included the element *lann* and where there were oval sites, typically in valleys and close to water communications, the earlier churches being nearer the coast than later ones. Their buildings were small and insubstantial. Some had an outer enclosure. The sites varied in size from 0.05 hectares to over 0.9, the average being 0.3. The larger ones are probably the earlier foundations. Some of these retained a high status and importance. Others, such as Veryan and St Anthony-in-Meneage, did not. The sites of late churches in Cornwall were usually quite different. The churchyards of the St Petroc foundations, and of others in east Cornwall, were rectilinear. In the latter, the churchyards seem to have been designed around existing buildings. Typical locations are valley sides and hilltops. Late foundations often had the word, or element, *eglos* in their place-names, while place-names including *Merther* indicate relatively late chapels, with burial grounds, each in honour of a locally popular saint or martyr. These chapels were sometimes on enclosed farming settlements of the Romano-British period that are known as rounds, or on hills, enclosed by banks and ditches, and were usually curvilinear.[8]

By the tenth century, the isolation and enclosure of minsters had long been seen as desirable, and had sometimes been attained, and their importance was heightened by the reformers. Bishop Aethelwold enclosed, adjacent to each other, the three minster communities and the episcopal palace at Winchester, probably beginning in 970.[9] Bishop Oswald's Ramsey, which he established probably in 965,[10] though close to the hall of its lay founder, Ealdorman Aethelwine, was on an isthmus that was perceived as an island.[11] Monastic complexes and individual buildings within them could both be large. Wimborne's dormitory could apparently sleep fifty women.[12]

The number of churches began to increase in the middle of the tenth century, and in eastern before western England.[13] Five reform houses (Ramsey, Crowland, Ely, Peterborough and Thorney) were set up there, as new or refoundations, between 969 and 971.[14] The greatest growth, however, was in the number of minor churches that were not part of monastic complexes.[15] Some had graveyards and some did not. Their entitlement to fees appears, as we have seen, in royal law-codes. By 1086, according to Domesday Book, there were at least 2,000 churches in the area that its surviving text covers.[16] Such local churches were more numerous where fewer minsters survived. Thus the diocese of Worcester had 160 churches, located on the lands of its leaseholders and its monastic community. Many more minster churches survived there than in East Anglia. The diocese of Elmham had 700 churches. Staffordshire and Leicestershire were where the fewest minsters had survived.[17] There were many churches in towns: at least forty-nine in Norwich by 1086, for a population that by 1066 was at least 5,000, possibly even 10,000, and at least thirty-two in Lincoln.[18]

Local churches related to secular settlements or to aristocratic residences or both, as lords' and villages' and proto-parish churches, could be very small. Ketton Quarry's one-room church, in Rutland, was surrounded by seventy graves in neat rows, beside at least three wooden buildings that are datable to between 900 and 1100.[19] The terminology of Domesday Book suggests that its compilers did not find the churches of the see of Worcester impressive compared to those of

Elmham and in Lincolnshire. Worcester's churches may have been single-cell and wooden.[20] Though wood had sometimes been used for important churches, stone was more highly esteemed and desirable. Some major churches were replaced by stone buildings, from the later tenth century onwards.[21] Winchester's Nunnaminster's main church was one. Wilton's, the replacement financed by Queen Edith, was another. Yet another was the wooden church of the seventh-century saint Aidan, which the monks of St Cuthbert had taken from Lindisfarne and reconstructed in Chester-le-Street in the tenth century. It was replaced by Aethelric, bishop of Durham 1041–1056.[22]

What some churches looked like is partially known, from texts, material remains and archaeology.[23] Some of the eleventh-century ones, established by powerful and high-ranking aristocrats, were very large and impressive. The transepts at Stow, whose patrons were Earl Leofric and his wife, were 85 feet long.[24] The size of the cathedral at Canterbury is not known, but its huge westward extension done in the time of Wulfred, archbishop 805–832, or of Oda, archbishop 941–958 made it, apparently, one of the largest aisled churches of northern Europe of the time. By 1066 it had a splendid western apse. What York's cathedral was like remains mysterious, though we know something of its environment. Near it was a hostel or hospital. There was a large cemetery, for laity and ecclesiastics, on the city side of the cathedral precinct from the late ninth century onwards, which was associated with a church dedicated to St Michael.[25] In late-tenth- and early-eleventh-century Worcester the cathedral cemetery had a large bell-tower with an attached chapel, which was likewise dedicated to St Michael. The Worcester precinct also contained two large churches adjacent to each other, St Peter's, staffed by clerics, and St Mary's, by monks. One of them, though it is unclear which, had eighteen altars.[26] After about 970, a cruciform plan, no aisles, and a central tower recur in the design of churches. Major churches had several altars, each in a chapel, with the high (main) altar at the east end of the nave. In very small churches the altar was in an eastern porticus, or chancel, and the entrance, increasingly, on the north or south side rather than at the west end. Altars were normally wooden.[27]

Important churches would have been visually splendid, perhaps as buildings and certainly in their decoration and contents, despite depletions in the period of Scandinavian raids and wars. A limestone angel, probably from a panel on a shrine chest that in its entirety would have measured about 31½ inches by 25¾ inches high, carved c. 800, was found at Lichfield cathedral in 2003. Its hair and halo, possibly gilded on its outer edge, had been painted yellow, its garments yellow with folds picked out in red, its wings in red, yellow and white.[28] St Oswald's, Gloucester, founded between the mid-880s and 899, had carved door- and window-arches, was plastered inside and outside, had wall paintings and wall hangings, and decorated, probably brightly painted, grave-covers.[29] The manuscript picture of King Cnut and Queen Emma as patrons of Winchester's New Minster implies that there Christ, the Virgin Mary and St Peter were depicted in the apse. The many lay bequests and other donations, of precious objects, and of gold, suggest that a great deal of treasure was displayed in churches, both monastic and non-monastic.[30] The *Ely Book* records many items at Ely. In the eleventh century, several foundations possessed man-sized crosses. By 1066, Waltham Holy Cross owned over £6,000 worth of treasures.[31] There was a sense, not unique to this time or place, that the Church should not appear to be any less rich than lay lords, and that its appearance should be an indication of its ultimate superiority over them, which was spiritual. Furthermore, the Church was regarded as a symbol of Heaven. Both ideas imply that visual splendour in churches would have been normal. Each will have stimulated it.

At the lower end of the scale, an estate church, usually built of mortared rubble and comprising one or two cells, was a manifestation of its thegn's status, power and wealth. At Raunds, the mid-tenth-century, stone, one-cell church was extended slightly later by a chancel, making it about 26 feet long, not to accommodate more people but to be more impressive.[32] Estate churches often adjoined a thegn's house, as at Goltho in Lincolnshire. Many had grave-yards, which would contain gravestones and be, somehow, enclosed. Small churches that did not have grave-yards were probably not enclosed.

Churches were not the only physical manifestations of religion in the landscape of late Anglo-Saxon England. There were also pilgrimage sites, some of course being churches that had miracle-working relics. The name St Petroc's stow, recorded in the *Anglo-Saxon Chronicle*, for example, suggests that by c. 1000 this site was perceived as being significantly connected with Petroc. His relics are recorded in the early eleventh century as being at Padstow, and his cult is evidenced in the Bodmin Gospels.[33] Places without churches but associated with saints also attracted visitors. This was true in the cults of murdered royal saints, one being that of King Edmund of East Anglia in the tenth century.[34] Aelfric worried about devotion to holy stones and trees, which might have been very traditional, going back to pre-Christian religion. Crosses that had been erected in earlier centuries still stood, and new ones were erected, most notably in Wessex and further south-west. Their functions may now have included that of marking routes, particularly pilgrim routes, as well as assembly places and boundaries.[35]

The situation in Wales had points in common with that in south-west England. There may have been few churches outside monastic contexts before the mid-eleventh century. Probably most churches were very small, and the vast majority wooden. Some thirty-two sites in central east and south-east Wales have been identified as probably having had a church. Gwent was probably the area best provided for, with almost sixty churches attested in the Llandaff charters, though since most are referred to only once it is impossible to tell how many existed at any one time. For Glamorgan, by contrast, only some ten are attested.[36] Supplementing the churches were inscribed stones and crosses, which probably marked assembly sites for worship, praying stations along route-ways, and pilgrim routes, as well as signifying ownership, sometimes as boundary markers, sometimes bearing records of donations whose wording resembles that of charters. Datable standing crosses from the St David's area mostly belong to the period c. 1015–1115 and are contemporary with its chapels, cemeteries and wells.[37]

In Scotland too churches and other ecclesiastical constructions were integral to the landscape, though some are less obvious now than others. In the north-east, scholars have detected centres that served limited areas and tended cults of local saints, from the seventh century onwards.[38] Stones were very prominent: half of the landscape features that are referred to in the Deer property records are stones. Deer church itself was probably bounded, partly by an outer enclosure, and partly by a river.[39] Portmahomack monastery was on a peninsula, and enclosed. At Meigle, there was perhaps a group of churches within an enclosure.[40] Known churches are mostly small. The church built about AD 900 or later on the island of May was around 13 by 10 feet (internally). It was extended in about AD 1000.[41] At Govan, important in the tenth century, the church was the central element of the landscape, close to the huge assembly mound. Its churchyard was probably noticeable and impressive because of its sculptures, but their original locations are, unfortunately, unknown.[42]

Quite apart from their immediate visual impact, churches and their estates also affected the landscape through their estate-management and stimulation of the economy. Some English reformed monasteries are thought to have undertaken radical replanning of their estates. In the mid-tenth century, Glastonbury Abbey began to acquire lands in Wiltshire, and the development there of nucleated, planned villages, with open fields, may have begun then, and as a consequence.[43] Around 960, Bishop Aethelwold had part of the River Thames diverted to provide for the mill of Abingdon Abbey. His enclosure of Winchester's three religious communities took several years and involved closing streets, demolishing houses and diverting streams, displacing some inhabitants and monopolising most of the south-east of the town.[44] In the early eleventh century, monasteries managed the fenlands of East Anglia.[45]

The Church in the economy

The stone sculpture in Scotland not only makes its Church visible in the landscape but also testifies to its wealth, which must have derived from royal and aristocratic gifts. Aspects of the sculpture from Aberdeenshire may indicate a lack of wealthy mid-ranking laity there,[46] but Deer was not in any significant economic difficulty in the late ninth and early tenth century. Its Book shows no wish, or need, to be sparing in the use of parchment.[47] In Wales, Llandaff's estates are the best known. They were smaller and less consolidated than those of nearby English Worcester.[48] The Welsh thought that ecclesiastical lands should be exempt from tax. Welsh ecclesiastical income came from lands, cattle and crops, and gifts. As in England, there was concern about lay encroachment and fear of losses, which probably inspired the various collections of charters that have been identified as lying behind the Llandaff collection itself. There was one made in or after about 868, one after about 975, and one probably in south Glamorgan in the second quarter of the eleventh century. In the mid-ninth century, King Meurig had ordered all ecclesiastical property in lay hands to be released. It is not certain that there was ever a significant amount of Welsh ecclesiastical treasure. Welsh ecclesiastics may have lacked the resources, or desire, to produce it.[49]

In Anglo-Saxon England the Church was always a major part of the economy, most obviously with regard to landownership, though the fortunes of individual churches differed, and varied, over time, and were sometimes under significant pressure.[50] In some cases a chronology can be sketched. As well as lands, churches had property in towns, income from dues and fines and grants of rights to them, and treasures. Good management and gifts, many of them bequests, increased ecclesiastical wealth. Losses in land disputes, the predation of aristocracy and kings, and the various expenses that the Scandinavian threats generated diminished it.

Domesday Book and surviving charter archives have been well used in studies of landholding, and the episcopate has very recently been the object of detailed scrutiny.[51] In 1066 episcopal landed wealth was about 8 per cent of that of the entire kingdom. It was less than the monasteries', valued at £5,430, compared with £7,185. Its distribution between sees was uneven, both with regard to value and also taking into account the size of the sees. The richest, Canterbury, was more than eighteen times richer than the poorest, Lichfield. York, the fifth richest, was probably under-reported, but when it was held in plurality with Worcester, which was the sixth richest, the two together would have amounted to one of England's wealthiest landowners. York had about 630 hides in 1066, Worcester about 810 hides (worth about £625.00) in 1016 though only 610 (worth about £450.00) in 1086. By the late Anglo-Saxon period a hide was probably normally about 120 acres: the *Ely Book*, drawing on Bishop Aethelwold's book, gives this equivalent.

Most episcopal landed wealth derived from royal gifts made before about 900. Of the holdings of Canterbury, and of the second richest see, Winchester, about half were held by c. 909. These regions had probably been the most continuously favoured. The further that other sees were from Canterbury, Winchester and London, the fourth richest, the greater was the antiquity of their endowment. Selsey had acquired nearly all its lands by about 800. Worcester had about 90 per cent of its lands by about 900. There had not been many royal grants to episcopal churches after 900. Winchester had gained sixteen estates, valued at about £230.00, from tenth-century kings and eight, worth about £70.00, from eleventh-century ones. Aristocratic gifts, however, were not insignificant. They were the source, for instance, of nineteen Winchester estates, and of 10 per cent of Canterbury's 1066 wealth. Durham's holdings are unknown, but early-eleventh-century donations from local families are recorded in its archive. Bishoprics had, however, suffered losses and fear of more. At Worcester, Bishop Wulfstan I (Archbishop Wulfstan II of York) had the earliest surviving cartulary (collection of charters) in England compiled, in or soon after 1002. It combined charters and leases, and notes by Wulfstan that kept the record of Worcester's leases and tenants up to date. This was probably in the hope of preventing losses, through inadvertence or others' recalcitrance, and especially losses of leased lands when their leases expired, as many were about to. Losses over time were indeed mostly of leased rather than directly managed land. Worcester claimed to have lost about 200 hides in the eleventh century after 1016.[52] Ironically, at least some of this loss was due to Wulfstan himself: he kept some estates after giving up Worcester in 1016, as his 1017 lease of some Worcester land reveals.[53]

The Church was landlord to many tenants, and since diocesan lands were concentrated in the bishoprics' localities, it was a very dominant presence in some areas. About 200 hides of Worcester's, which was about one-third of its 1086 estate, were leased out between 957 and 996. By 1086, about 47 per cent, amounting to about 39 per cent of the gross value, of the estate was held by tenants, most of whom were laymen and held small estates.[54] The archive shows that some sort of annual rent was normal, but also that conditions of land tenure varied, which may suggest that service was a matter of negotiation.[55] Nearly half, or more, of four sees' estates – Winchester, Worcester, Dorchester and Lichfield – were in their home shire. Between one-fifth and one-third of all land in Yorkshire, Worcestershire, Hampshire, Kent and Middlesex was held by sees, but relatively little in Lincolnshire, Bedfordshire, Leicestershire and Cambridgeshire. In addition, the episcopal presence in towns was significant.[56] In 1066, for example, Canterbury had rights over 116 burgesses in the town of Canterbury whilst the king had fifty-one burgesses there, and a third landowner had fourteen. Canterbury also had a presence in other towns, in five shires altogether. Some thirteen other bishops had urban interests, including Durham in Durham and York, and Dorchester in six towns. Worcester's included one-third of the toll levied there on each horse-load of goods and the toll levied on market trading, granted by Edward the Confessor. Lichfield's enjoyed the fines paid in Chester by freemen for working on holy days, and by merchants who transacted business, without the approval of the bishop's officer, between Saturday noon and Monday, or on feast days.

Other sources of wealth were judicial rights, which could contribute significantly to bishops' income, just as they did in the case of lay lords (as well as being a conduit of their influence in the social landscape), beneficial hidation (assessment) and the personal wealth of the bishops. Thus the archbishop of York's rights included the king's custom of two pennies and the earl's third penny over his manors in Nottinghamshire and Derbyshire. Since the hide was a unit of productivity and of assessment for tax, artificially low hidage assessments for geld were actually exemptions from tax. The most obvious, and hence famous case, is that of the manor of Chilcomb and the monks of Winchester cathedral. Two pre-Conquest documents represent this estate as comprising 100 hides but assessed as only one hide. Its Domesday Book valuation was £73.10.[57] Winchester, Worcester, Sherborne and York all benefited from geld exemption. Some prelates were personally generous to their sees. Aelfsige I of Winchester, in his will of sometime between 955 and 956, granted several estates to friends and kinsfolk for their lifetimes, of which two were supposed subsequently to pass to Winchester's Old, and one to its New, Minster. Between 989 and 1066 Canterbury acquired seven estates from its archbishops. Wealthy bishops included Aelfwold of Crediton (998– c. 1008), whose bequests included a huge amount of gold as well as other items and estates, and Theodred of London (942–951), whose will refers to thirty-one estates. Unfortunately it is not possible to tell whether Theodred owned all these privately, or had previously leased some from the three East Anglian religious communities, including Bury St Edmunds, to which he was apparently making gifts.[58]

Finally, a see could be enriched through effective episcopal control of staff and churches within it. The *Northumbrian Priests' Law* sets out fines, presumably payable at least in part to the bishop, for priests' infringement of standards and correct behaviour. The Worcester archive's possession of old minster charters shows that by the mid-ninth century Worcester had taken over many establishments in its region. Some of them retained their churchscot in the late ninth century. But in the late tenth, Bishop Oswald's leases sometimes stipulated an estate's reversion to Worcester where predecessors had stipulated reversion to a minster. In fourteen out of the fifteen of these cases in which churchscot was mentioned, this was payable to the bishopric. That is, minsters were becoming episcopal estate churches. By the time of Domesday Book, nearly all of Worcester's manorial centres in Worcestershire, and some outside it, were former minster sites, and the payment of churchscot in Worcestershire was to Worcester as landowner, rather than for pastoral care in a particular parish.[59]

The main difference in 1066 between the lands of the bishoprics and those of the monasteries, which numbered over forty, was that those of the greatest houses were much more scattered than those of the sees.[60] Glastonbury, the richest, had estates in at least seven counties, and its archive of about 251 charters refers to over 200 places connected with it.[61] There was also considerable variation in endowment. Glastonbury held over 800 hides. Ely's holdings were valued, in Domesday Book, at £900.00 per calendar month. The gross income of Shaftesbury and Wilton, the two richest of the eight convents, was between a quarter and three-eighths of Glastonbury's. The poorest of these eight, Chatteris in Cambridgeshire, held only 30 hides. Its gross income was less than one-eighth of Glastonbury's, while the income of the very poorest houses was less than one-sixteenth of Glastonbury's.[62]

Like bishoprics, monasteries were a dominant presence in some areas. Place-names suggest that in Cornwall, the estate of the house of St Keverne, on the east coast of the Lizard peninsula, may originally have included all the northern part of the peninsula, running the length of the River Helford. This area is known as Meneage. The element '-in-Meneage' is, or has been, part of the names of the two churches and settlements at either end of the river, Mawgan and St Anthony, and of one in between and further inland, St Martin. Meneage means 'monks' land'.[63] Over half of Glastonbury's endowment was in Somerset, making it the second largest landowner there, after the king. Glastonbury also had substantial holdings in Wiltshire and some in Dorset. Some of its lands were managed directly, but 43 per cent of their hidage, amounting to about 40 per cent of the endowment's gross value, was held by tenants. In Somerset the ratio was about 50:50, in Wiltshire the proportion of tenants was low, in Dorset very high. Twenty-nine of its thirty-four known tenants were not ecclesiastics and they had modest holdings. Some cases in Somerset and Devon suggest that Glastonbury had a policy of reorganising the landscape there into nucleated villages and open fields,[64] as it may also have done in Wiltshire.[65] Ely's lands were widespread but concentrated in East Anglia. Some monasteries' lands were predominantly local. Thus Holm St Benet's endowment was centred in north-east Norfolk.[66]

Tracing the chronology of monastic landownership is very difficult. This is because the entire endowment of individual churches and of the Church collectively, at any one time, is visible only in Domesday Book, for much of it there is no other evidence, and charters tell only part of the history of the estates that they mention. Thus the apparent stability of Glastonbury's may be illusory.[67] Nevertheless, it is clear that the experiences of minsters collectively had differed significantly from those of the episcopate. In the early ninth century, minsters had varied in their wealth. Their founding families had controlled their lands and individual residents had had land, though perhaps only as a lifetime interest. Subsequently, some minsters suffered losses to their bishops and others to kings and aristocracy. Minsters had commonly leased lands to lay tenants for up to three lifetimes.[68] This had generated income but also a danger that the families of tenants might not return the lands when they should. It was perhaps because of this that the 816 Council of Chelsea forbade the leasing out of ecclesiastical estates for more than one life.[69] The West Saxon kings seem to have despoiled and exploited minsters from the 880s onwards[70] and much former minster land enriched eleventh-century thegns.[71] The kings did make grants to minsters, but the donations did not match the losses. In 854 King Aethelwulf gave a tenth part of his land to the Church, but how this was put into practice is not entirely clear. One suggestion is that the 854 grant was used as a template to create others that included details of the particular estates that were affected. Glastonbury Abbey's version suggests that at least some of these were existing, rather than new, holdings, and its case may have been typical. It received few (surviving) grants between 855 and 939, and again this may have been typical.[72]

The mid- and late-tenth-century by contrast saw many substantial grants. It may be that the pattern of royal grants was to lay recipients who were supposed subsequently to pass them on. This may explain why Glastonbury's archive preserved nearly three times as many charters granting land to laymen as to itself.[73] The financial exactions of Aethelred II, in his attempts to deal with renewed Scandinavian attacks, and of Cnut, subsequently caused some losses. The security of monastic estates may, however, have been strengthened by the reform of the Church, since, increasingly, houses owned their lands as permanent collectives, rather than depending on their inmates' lifetime interests. Grants to Shaftesbury were, for example, to the community, beginning in the 960s. Some grants permanently transferred lands that had previously been granted temporarily to a member or head of a house, as was one of 968 to Wilton.[74]

Patrons of monasteries included the greatest aristocrats and lesser, local figures besides royalty. Ely's wealth was built up first by Bishop Aethelwold, and later by the families of Ealdorman Byrhtnoth and Wulfstan of Dalham. Its royal grants between about 970 and 1066 amounted to twelve estates, six of which totalled 85.5 hides. Byrhtnoth bequeathed it fifteen estates, his kin twenty-seven between

991 and 1044, and Wulfstan and his kin thirteen estates, amounting to about 90 hides plus 70 acres, between about 955 and 983.[75] Ramsey was well endowed by Bishop Oswald and his family and Ealdorman Aethelwine. Royal grants, between about 965 and 1052, brought it ten estates, six of which totalled 18 hides. Aethelwine's, made between about 965 and 992, comprised seventeen, totalling at least 92.5 hides and 80 acres. Those of his kin, made between about 969 and 990, amounted to nine estates.[76] In the mid-eleventh century mid-ranking thegns became more significant both as donors to and as lease-holders of churches. Of the eleven wills in the Bury St Edmunds archive, eight were of persons of middle rank. They record small bequests to East Anglian churches, including parish churches.[77] Some of the lands with which laymen endowed churches, both reformed and non-monastic, were actually former minster lands. This was true of the two monasteries in which Aelfric made his career, Cerne (987) and Eynsham (refounded 1005), founded, respectively, by Ealdorman Aethelweard and his son Aethelmaer, and by Aethelmaer himself.[78] Conversely some widows and daughters of royal officials seem to have entered royal convents and offered them the estates that were supposed to support their kinsmen's office.[79]

Monasteries were as concerned as bishops about their holdings and income. Unfortunately, it is normally very difficult not only to distinguish between the monastic and the episcopal holdings in those cases where cathedrals and monasteries were located in the same place, but also to perceive a distinction being made at the time. Many bishops of the reform and post-reform period were monks. They would act as abbots of their monastic cathedral communities. Formal division of the endowment of a see, between its bishop and its cathedral monks was a very late development. Worcester's archive reveals that a separate monastic estate had been created there before 1066, but only in the eleventh century. One of the leases of Ealdred, bishop 1046–1062, refers to the existence of estates set apart for the cathedral monastic community. The monks' property was concentrated near the town, and less of it was loaned out than the bishop's.[80]

Just as in earlier centuries minsters had been vulnerable to bishops, so in the reform period unreformed communities were vulnerable to the reformers. Reformers could claim their lands by alleging that they had neglected the saints to whom they were dedicated, and that those saints wanted the change. For the saints were the ultimate owners of the lands. Many grants indeed named a saint, or saints, as the beneficiary, even if they were dead. Thus the *Ely Book* records gifts of land as being to God and St Aethelthryth. This partly explains why the possession of relics of saints was so important, and why there were disputes about them: the relics were effectively both landowners and title deeds. In the case of Ramsey, its discovery of remains of St Ivo, in 1001/1002 in its manor of Slepe, and their transfer to Ramsey, were connected with a dispute between the monastery and the kin of Slepe's original owner. The outcome was that Ramsey kept both the relics and the manor. The opposition of the monks of Ely to Ramsey's slightly later acquisition of relics of St Felix, from Soham, was likewise connected to a dispute, between the two monasteries, about ownership of an estate.[81]

Disputes between monastic houses and laity rose after the death of King Edgar, as some laymen who had lost lands to monasteries during his lifetime attempted to recover them. The *Ely Book* documents a number of lawsuits concerning its estates.[82] It was often claimed that land had been granted under pressure, or that the donor had not had the right to alienate it. Aelfric may have been thinking of, and trying to prompt his audience to condemn, the seizure of monastic lands when he portrayed the wicked Old Testament queen Jezebel's reaction to the refusal of a God-fearing vineyard owner to cede his vineyard to the king. Jezebel acquired it by producing a fraudulent letter.[83]

How ecclesiastical land was managed is only fragmentarily known. Monks probably did not do much themselves, because their timetable was full and demanding. Two Glastonbury officials, each termed *praepositus* (overseer), are referred to in the *Life* of Dunstan.[84] Ely had a monk overseer until, in 1029, Abbot Leofsige established an office to deal with estate management.[85] Two surviving texts that relate to this subject attest officials, including the estate reeve, for whose use one, the *Gerefa* (Reeve), was composed. The other, known now as the *Rectitudines Singularum Personarum* may be a work of the mid-tenth century or later, and connected to somewhere in the south-west, possibly Bath or Glastonbury, though another theory is that it is describing peasant conditions on the Worcester estate in the late tenth century. Its author seems to have anticipated that his work would be used in different places, for he recognises that there were differences between communities.[86] Since they were meant to be self-sufficient but also needed coin, to buy what could not be produced and to pay tax, monastic houses will have tried to generate variety through direct production and levying rents in kind as well as in cash and selling surplus produce.[87] Some particular arrangements are known, for example herring renders[88] and a list surviving from Ely's Abbot Leofsige's organisation of the church's annual food supply states the number of weeks or days that each estate on the list was responsible for.[89]

The wealth of Anglo-Saxon monasteries derived from the same sources as that of sees, including interests of various kinds in towns. And profiting from rights there was the only involvement that monasteries and sees had with urban life.

The Church and socio-economic change

In the origins of Anglo-Saxon towns and in their growth in the tenth and early eleventh centuries kings and aristocracy, at various levels, played a role, and so did churches.[90] Churches whose sites seemed to have potential for economic profit, for instance at a harbour, were likely to attract settlement. Furthermore, churches could attract both visitors and settlement regardless of their location. After all, they held services, administered the sacraments and housed relics, in some cases miracle-working ones.[91] Alms-giving and burial also contributed to urban growth. Alms-giving was regarded as meritorious and spiritually profitable, so it was ideologically appealing to the rich. Both rich and poor were therefore attracted to towns, the rich because there were more people to give to there than in the countryside, the poor because there were more alms to receive.[92] This process became self-perpetuating. Alms-giving provided by lay bequests was administered by churches, and churches gave alms on their own account. One example lies in an early-ninth-century bequest to Christ Church, Canterbury, which required annual alms-giving on the anniversary of the testators' death, and its confirmation by Archbishop Wulfred.[93] He stipulated that the minster was itself to provide 120 *gesufl* (possibly loaves with a filling) for distribution 'as is done at the anniversaries of lords', a remark which suggests that such events were common, and its land at Bourne 1,000 loaves.[94] As for burial, urban funerals may have seemed more desirable to the aristocracy than rural ones, since they would have offered a larger and wider audience for the deceased's family to impress, as well as proximity to more, and more prestigious, relics.[95] Gravestones for wealthy dead have been found in Cambridge, Gloucester, London, Lincoln and York.[96]

In addition, church sites and sanctuaries attracted markets,[97] partly because violence was forbidden there, and partly because large numbers of people went there, predictably, often and regularly. The royal law-codes contain repeated strictures against Sunday markets, which implies that such markets were common. It seems logical to suppose that they were near churches, to target people as they went to and from Mass.[98] Kenelmstow, the place of St Kenelm's martyrdom, eventually became the site of an annual pilgrimage and fair.[99] Archbishop Ealdred had a fair at Beverley on the feast of John the Baptist, which had been granted by Edward the Confessor.[100] Four of Domesday Book's six Cornish markets were on ecclesiastical sites.[101] The traditional view of York is that it was first a royal and later a Viking centre, and that its merchants, trade and urban growth are related to its Scandinavian lords' stimuli and control. Another is that it was actually dominated by the Church, which was both politically and militarily independent. York's Christian Viking coins may be evidence of the Church's control of both the city and the Viking kings. York's archbishops may have employed Viking military forces as, centuries earlier, Roman emperors and their officials had used barbarian federates. It may have been the archbishops who imposed York's town planning.[102] They were certainly involved in regulating northern economic life in the eleventh century. The *Northumbrian Priests' Law* forbids trade and travel on Sundays but allows that travel on the eves of feasts – presumably for markets – is permissible within a certain radius of York in times of hostility.[103]

Trading opportunities seem sometimes to have influenced the choice, or acquisition, of a site for a church. One instance is in Mercia, where the western half of tenth-century Worcester was dominated by a riverside site which the bishop had leased from Aethelred and Aethelflaed of Mercia and their daughter Aelfwyn in 904.[104] In East Anglia, Ely enjoyed the coastal Holland-on-Sea, which Bishop Aethelwold had received from Queen Aelfthryth, and also the estate of Sudbourne, which controlled an inlet, his reward, from her and King Edgar, for his English translation of the *Rule* of St Benedict.

Urban growth and the vibrancy of the economy of which it was a part facilitated tenth- and eleventh-century social mobility and change, in both of which the Church participated.[105] Aethelwold's own family was an urban one, in

Winchester, and, to judge by what is reported in the *Ely Book* of his expenditure in acquiring lands for Ely, a rich one. He came from, and signifies, what has been called a new social group, of thegn-burgesses.[106] Stigand, the last pre-Conquest archbishop of Canterbury, the second or third richest subject in England in 1066, with a net worth of £750.00, probably came from Norwich.[107] Change came also to the countryside, as large estates were broken up into smaller units, held by more owners, and nucleated villages began to form. Leasehold was used in the periods of Scandinavian threat, probably to raise money to deal (directly or indirectly) with it, though the connection is almost never mentioned in the texts. Some scholars think that leasehold may have helped to loosen property relationships, that there was an unrecorded norm of short leases involving quite small estates, possibly by the eleventh century, for less than one life in some places. One Worcester lease is for only three years. Short leases might well have stimulated productivity and hence the wealth of individual landholders.[108] Changes in place-names, some names consisting of a personal name plus *tun*, have been connected to changes in estate ownership and structure.[109] The demand for skilled and knowledgeable craftsmen, to build estate and proprietary churches, will also have contributed to social mobility.

All these developments are part of the growth of a lesser nobility, owners of a few, small, estates perhaps purchased with money. Their possible origins are illuminated by several short texts concerned with status that occur in one of the manuscripts associated with Archbishop Wulfstan II, and may have been collected by him. One refers, as if to conditions in the past, to traders who had crossed the open sea three times at their own expense being entitled to the rights of a thegn; to *ceorls* who owned 5 hides of land, a bell, *burh*-gate (castle-gate), seat and office in the king's hall being entitled to thegns' rights; and to thegns' prospering, becoming earls and entitled to earls' rights. In another, the 5-hide *ceorl* has the same wergeld as a Mass thegn and secular thegn. Thus royal service, prosperity and living correctly as a priest or canon seem to have been routes to thegnly status.[110] Wealth did, however, have to be translated into landownership, at least in theory. In practice social status seems to have followed lifestyle and behaviour.[111]

The culture of thegns was expensive and it included some elements that had no explicitly religious dimensions, such as loyalty and bravery in battle, and participating in and behaving honourably at shire meetings. But some of its elements did. Having one's own church and giving gifts to it and to other churches were exercises in self-promotion, with a competitive element. Aristocrats of varying wealth behaved in similar ways but on varying scales.[112] Thus both lesser and greater nobles established close relationships with monasteries and other churches. In East Anglia some of those who had attained nobility through royal service are visible in Edward the Confessor's reign as founding or refounding minor religious houses. This class thereby contributed to an intensification of regionalism.[113] Lastly, insofar as some education was necessary for service in the royal bureaucracy, the Church contributed to the social mobility which men in that service attained, since it was the Church that provided education.[114]

As for the peasants, we can turn to the *Rectitudines*. Whatever estate its author had in mind was a self-contained one. On it, slave labour was important, *geburs*, holding 30 acres, owed it half of their working time, as labour service, and *cotsletas*, with five acres, owed it a quarter of theirs. The peasants thus had time to work for themselves and hence the opportunity to profit from the economic change and growth that was happening, and might have taken it. This may have contributed to the rise of nucleated villages with open fields. The Avon valley and the Cotswolds are thought to have been dotted with nucleated villages by, or in, the time that Oswald was bishop of Worcester.[115]

There is, finally, the question of the decline of slavery in England.[116] The Church's active discouragement of slavery was limited. It merely deprecated the sale of Christians abroad and encouraged kings to prohibit it in their laws. Such traffic happened certainly at Bristol and probably at Lewes, York and Chester. Yet indirectly it undermined slavery, in several ways. First, the freeing of slaves by an individual ecclesiastical or lay person was regarded as an act that was pleasing to God and beneficial for his or her soul. The 816 Council of Chelsea ordained that after the death of a bishop all those English men of his who had been enslaved during his lifetime should be freed. Tenth- and eleventh-century episcopal wills contain bequests of freedom, perhaps in honour of this requirement. A late-tenth-century ordinance states that following the death of a fellow-bishop every bishop should free a man. As for the laity, many wills and manumissions testify to lay owners freeing slaves, likewise in the tenth and eleventh centuries. The cumulative effect was probably very significant. In addition, there was a trend in the eleventh century towards lay manumission of all, not just some, slaves on estates, especially in East Anglia.

Second, both the tenth-century exaction of tithes, one portion of which was for the relief of the poor, and the Church's continuous teaching that alms-giving was a pious action were beneficial for slaves, because they were among the recipients of poor-relief and alms. Alfred's laws allowed them to keep anything that they were given in God's name, as well as anything that they acquired in their spare time, and to sell such things on the Wednesday of each Ember week (a week designated by the western Church as a period of fasting; there was one each in spring, summer, autumn and winter). Some slaves may have been able to accumulate enough to buy their freedom. A Welsh document of 840, written in the Lichfield Gospels, refers to a man buying his freedom, though it may be that he was paying compensation for an offence to avoid the penalty of enslavement. The price was about nine times what seems later to have been the usual price of a slave.[117] Third, the Church taught that in God's sight slaves were equal to their masters, it safeguarded the spiritual interests of slaves and it required them to observe the same rules that it imposed on free people. For example, the code VII Aethelred (one of those authored by Wulfstan) required everybody to fast on the Monday, Tuesday and Wednesday before Michaelmas, stipulating that slaves were to be exempted from work for these three days so that they could comply. Masters who forced slaves to work when they were not supposed to work were to be punished. The early texts imposed a fine; Cnut's laws imposed the freeing of the slave as well.

Such ecclesiastical teaching, treatment and requirements contributed to a blur-ring of the distinction between slave and free just as economic and social develop-ments were doing the same thing. Co-operative farming, manorial custom and the growth of lordship had a levelling effect, one aspect of which was that many people who were legally free did not have the right to leave their holdings. Ironi-cally, the decline of slavery was most dramatic with regard to secular landholders, between the Norman Conquest and 1086, and slowest and least dramatic with regard to slave ownership by churches. This was probably because churches were not supposed to alienate their property permanently. In 1086, according to Domesday Book, many churches owned many slaves, and a high proportion of slaves were owned by churches.[118] In Worcestershire, nearly 44 per cent of the slaves were on one or other church's demesne lands – nearly 30 per cent on Wor-cester's, nearly 14 per cent on those of the monasteries of Evesham, Pershore and the more distant Westminster. Only 15.6 per cent of its recorded population, but 20.5 per cent of the population of its ecclesiastical estates were slaves. Cornwall did not fit the general pattern. In Cornwall, 21 per cent of the recorded population were slaves, and the major slave owners were the king and the Count of Mortain. The proportion of slaves on ecclesiastical estates there was much lower.

Socio-economic change is seldom comfortable for everybody involved. It can undermine social cohesion and cause insecurity and anxiety. Some Anglo-Saxon thegns may have felt threatened, as new men joined the class and disparities of wealth within it increased. However, the period also saw two developments that may have seemed to offer stability, in each of which the Church played a part. One was the lineage. The other was spiritual kinship. It is usually held, though now controversially, that a shift in kinship identity from what has been described as a loose, horizontal (siblings and cousins) group to that of a lineage, in which father–son–grandson relationships were what mattered, was a west-European-wide phenomenon.[119] One of the contributing factors was the commemoration of kin and ancestors, in calendars and prayers, by ecclesiastics and descendants. One example of this happening is at Ely, where Byrhtnoth and his descendants were commemorated in return for lands that they gave for this very purpose. Such commemorations must have increased individuals' consciousness of their own and others' descent through several generations rather than of their living relatives.[120] As for spiritual kinship, this, and especially the increasing importance of co-parenthood, which tied adults, rather than two generations, together, may have been a response to social mobility as well as to stresses caused by Vikings, lordship and kingship.[121] It created social bonds. Guilds, whose regulations had a strongly religious dimension, had the same function.

Some social anxiety and discomfort is detectable in law-codes and in the works of Aelfric and Archbishop Wulfstan II. The increasing number of local churches engendered concerns about the rights of minsters to tithes and about the standard of local priests. There was some concern that marks of, and qualifications for, status could simply be bought, rather than being part of a network of social relationships, as inheritances or rewards for service. Wulfstan's *Sermon of the Wolf* deplored social breakdown and failure to behave properly. Like Aelfric, he thought that there were three orders of society, that everybody should restrict themselves to and fulfil their proper function, and that all three orders were necessary for the good of society as a whole. This has been taken to signify that Wulfstan disapproved of social mobility generally, or perhaps that he had a more particular concern – about low-born men who had become rich from fighting against the Danish invaders but had not bought land and did not display social responsibility.[122] Certainly what we know about military pay in late Anglo-Saxon England implies that much of the huge amount of tax that was levied ended up in soldiers' hands.[123] But it has been suggested that what prompted these ideals of social stability was in fact a debate about whether or not ecclesiastics should engage in warfare as part of their service to the king. This debate will have involved citations of biblical authority and consideration of the religious status of kings and of their duty of protecting the Church. Both of these aspects of kingship were capable of being interpreted, and probably often were, as warranting the physical support of churchmen in a king's wars, especially those against non-Christians.[124] Social mobility in itself was probably not the cause of Aelfric's and Wulfstan's concern.

We can picture Anglo-Saxon and Cornish churches, recognise changes in their numbers and trace their fluctuating economic and ecclesiastical fortunes, and, in England, their sources, whilst those in Wales and Scotland are more elusive. The Church marked the landscape with both buildings and inscribed stones and crosses and, in southern England, changed it by its estate management. It was intimately involved with English towns, its patronage was one of the marks of English nobility and its teaching contributed to the decline of English slavery. Churchmen were not unfavourably disposed towards social mobility, but were anxious about social responsibility.

Notes

1 Blair, *Church*.
2 *Ibid.*
3 Pestell.
4 Loveluck, *Rural*, 'Wealth'.
5 Pestell.
6 Foot, *Monastic*.
7 *Ibid.*
8 Preston-Jones; S. Turner.
9 Foot, *Monastic*; Yorke, *Nunneries*.
10 Barrow, 'Chronology … Benedictine', 'Community'.
11 Pestell.
12 Foot, *Monastic*.
13 Barrow, 'Wulfstan'.
14 Pestell.
15 Blair, *Church*.
16 Dyer, *Making*; Loyn; Stafford, *Unification*.
17 Barrow, 'Wulfstan'.
18 For population, Campbell, 'Domesday'. For churches, Fleming, 'Rural'; Hadley, *Northern*, *Vikings*.

19 Pestell.
20 Barrow, 'Wulfstan'.
21 Yorke, *Nunneries*.
22 Foot, *Monastic*.
23 Gittos, 'Architecture'.
24 Fleming, 'New'.
25 Norton.
26 Barrow, 'Wulfstan'.
27 Gittos, 'Architecture'.
28 Rodwell et al.
29 Heighway; V. Thompson, *Dying*.
30 Gameson; Giandrea; A. Williams, 'Thegnly'.
31 Fleming, 'New'.
32 Audouy and Chapman; Boddington; Fleming, 'New'.
33 Jankulak.
34 Cubitt, 'Sites'.
35 Pearce; S. Turner.
36 W. Davies, *Early, Wales*; T.A. James.
37 Edwards, 'Early-Medieval', 'Identifying', 'Monuments'.
38 T.O. Clancy, 'Deer'.
39 Forsyth, 'Stones'.
40 Macquarrie, 'Early'.
41 Yeoman.
42 Driscoll, *Govan*.
43 Abrams, *Anglo-Saxon*.
44 Rumble, 'Laity', *Property*.
45 Wareham, *Lords*.
46 Forsyth, 'Stones'.
47 Henderson, 'Understanding'.
48 Hurley.
49 W. Davies, *Early, Llandaff, Wales*; Pryce, 'Ecclesiastical'.
50 Blair, *Church*.
51 What follows concerning episcopal wealth is largely a summary of the work of Giandrea.
52 For Worcester, see Barrow, 'Chronology ... Forgery', 'Wulfstan'; Baxter, 'Archbishop'; Dyer, *Making*; King.
53 Mason.
54 For these estates, see King; Wareham, 'St'.
55 Abrams, *Anglo-Saxon*.
56 See also Fleming, 'Rural'.
57 For Chilcomb see also Rumble, *Property*.
58 For Theodred, see Pestell.
59 Barrow, 'Wulfstan'; Tinti, *Sustaining*.
60 Giandrea.
61 For Glastonbury see Abrams, *Anglo-Saxon*.
62 For the nunneries, Yorke, *Nunneries*.
63 Pearce.
64 *Ibid*.
65 For Glastonbury, Abrams, *Anglo-Saxon*.
66 Pestell.
67 Abrams, *Anglo-Saxon*.
68 Foot, *Monastic*.
69 Burghart and Wareham.
70 Fleming, 'Monastic'.

71 A. Williams, 'Thegnly'.
72 Abrams, *Anglo-Saxon*.
73 *Ibid*.
74 Yorke, *Nunneries*.
75 Wareham, *Lords*.
76 Wareham, *Lords*, 'St'.
77 Wareham, *Lords*.
78 A. Williams, 'Thegnly'.
79 Yorke, *Nunneries*.
80 Tinti, *Sustaining*.
81 For these points, Thacker, 'Saint-making'.
82 Trans. Fairweather.
83 Klein.
84 Abrams, *Anglo-Saxon*.
85 E. Miller.
86 Dyer, 'St'; Burghart and Wareham.
87 Abrams, *Anglo-Saxon*.
88 Campbell, 'Domesday'.
89 Fairweather.
90 Fleming, 'Rural'; Foot, *Monastic*.
91 Foot, *Monastic*.
92 Fleming, 'Rural'.
93 *Ibid*.
94 Text and transl. (charter Sawyer Number 1188) at www.aschart.kcl.ac.uk.
95 Fleming, 'Rural'.
96 *Ibid*.
97 Barrow, 'Churches'.
98 Foot, *Monastic*.
99 Thacker, 'Saint-making'.
100 Giandrea.
101 Jankulak; Pearce.
102 Rollason, *Northumbria*.
103 *Ibid*.; Giandrea.
104 Baker and Holt. See also Barrow, 'Churches'.
105 Fleming, 'New'.
106 Fleming, 'Rural'.
107 Campbell, 'Aspects'; Giandrea.
108 Burghart and Wareham.
109 Stafford, *Unification*.
110 Campbell, 'Aspects'; Fleming, 'Rural'; Stafford, *Unification*.
111 Senecal.
112 Fleming, 'New'; Senecal.
113 Wareham, *Lords*.
114 Moore, *First*.
115 Dyer, 'St'.
116 What follows is based on Pelteret.
117 Padel, *Slavery*.
118 See also Foot, *Monastic*.
119 Moore, *First*.
120 Wareham, *Lords*.
121 Lynch.
122 Fletcher.
123 Campbell, 'Aspects'.
124 T.E. Powell.

Part IV

Means

Order and individuals

10 Government, law and administration

Ecclesiastical personnel and Christian concerns were intimately involved in the routine and everyday workings of politics and society, and in the lives of individual Christians. The second of these issues raises questions of the provision of pastoral care, and of Christian ritual, explanations of evil and misfortune, definitions of sin, ideas about how to attain salvation, and provision for the afterlife. The first, the subject of this chapter, involves questions of taxation, the raising of troops and diplomacy, as well as government, law and other aspects of the administration of the late Anglo-Saxon kingdom. At the highest level of government, churchmen were prominent among royalty's advisers throughout the period, and among the leading political players. Close scrutiny of charters, of episcopal careers, of aspects of the administrative-legal structure, of people and status and of areas and places, shows that they were important at all the lower levels too. So were Christian objects, ordeals and sanctuary.

High politics and government

The importance in Anglo-Saxon government of bishops in particular, and of ecclesiastics in general, is easily demonstrable from Alfred's reign onwards. According to Asser, Alfred yearned for divine wisdom and the liberal arts, and his desire was increased and fulfilled by the men whom he summoned from Mercia: Bishop Waerferth, who translated Pope Gregory I's *Dialogues* for him, Archbishop Plegmund, and two learned 'priests and chaplains'.[1] Alfred subsequently recruited Asser himself and Grimbald, from St Bertin, both of whom helped with his translation of Gregory's *Pastoral Rule*. This text, though intended by Gregory specifically for bishops, was perceived as a guide for anyone in a position of authority. Alfred sent a copy of his translation to each of his bishops. Asser does not mention bishops in his account of Alfred's looking into 'nearly all the judgements which were passed in his absence anywhere in his realm', only ealdormen and reeves.[2] Episcopal involvement in judgement was, however, to become very marked.

In the tenth century, the West Saxon kings worked closely with archbishops of Canterbury and with bishops of Winchester. There are some indications that this co-operation was long standing and carefully nurtured. A high proportion of the archbishops had previously been bishops of Wells, in central Somerset, or

Ramsbury, in west Berkshire, areas where royal demesne lands, that is centres of royal power, were concentrated.[3] The three monk-bishop leaders of the great reform – Dunstan, Aethelwold and Oswald – had, like other bishops, been educated at court. After the reform and until c. 1030, almost all the bishops came from the reformed monasteries, a phenomenon symbolised by the depiction in Aethelwold's Benedictional of the monk-abbot St Benedict wearing a *pallium*, the sign of an archbishop's office. Thus between 970 and 1066 about 90 per cent of episcopal appointees were monks. All six of the archbishops of Canterbury between 988 and 1038 had been monks at Glastonbury.[4]

The recruitment of these monastic bishops enabled kings to exercise control throughout the kingdom. This was because Edgar and his successors had authority over, and protected, the reformed monasteries, and entrusted the bishops with significant power and authority in the shires, especially in the shire courts. These transacted a variety of business. Writs announcing royal decisions were sent to the shire courts for communication to the shire community. The bishops worked in the shires with the local ealdormen and had the same status.[5] This last is clear from, for example, Alfred's laws about breach of the peace and forcible entry into someone's house, and Cnut's about violation of surety. Bishops' superiors, the archbishops, were equated with the *aetheling* (the presumed heir to the throne), their subordinates, chaste Mass priests, with thegns. It is likely that the shire and hundred system was developed by the kings in the tenth century. The earliest certain example of the shire as a legal forum is mid-tenth century, and the best ones are from the reigns of Aethelred II and Cnut.[6] In his treatise about episcopal duties Archbishop Wulfstan II included participation in secular justice, to avoid injustice.

The overlap between Church and society, each helping to run the other, does not imply corruption or lack of commitment, and it was ubiquitous. Several ecclesiastics were formidable influences, as brief summaries of their careers and work make plain. Archbishop Dunstan was first influential as a supporter of King Eadred. One indication of his importance lies in the history of royal charters. In Eadred's reign Dunstan's monastery, Glastonbury, seems to have taken over production of the king's charters. The mid-tenth-century collection of charters known now as the Dunstan B charters, the earliest datable one written in 951, consistently lack Eadred's own attestation. After the accession of Eadwig, Dunstan went into exile and very few Dunstan B charters were produced, though three were for Edgar, as king of Mercia, in 957.[7] Dunstan was a leader of the reform movement, and a major figure in Edgar's reign. The number of royal charters that include a claim to rule Albion peaks then, coinciding with the peak of Dunstan's influence as revealed by our other sources.[8] After Edgar died Dunstan remained influential. He was an ally of Queen Eadgifu and, when the succession was disputed, a supporter of Edward (the Martyr) against his half-brother Aethelred. It was only after Aethelred's accession that Dunstan's influence declined. Nevertheless, within a generation of his death Dunstan was remembered as someone who had visions and was willing to excommunicate and to curse people. This may have been an accurate recollection of how he had behaved, or a fabrication, whose purpose was to strengthen Dunstan's successors' armoury of persuasion in their disputes with others.[9] Or it may have been both.

The high standing and special influence of Dunstan's younger contemporary and co-reformer, Aethelwold, is also clear. While he was an abbot, Aethelwold was included in most charter witness lists between 959 and 963, the only abbot to be so.[10] Aethelwold was close to King Edgar and developed the image and theory of kingship and queenship. He was also active in succession disputes or negotiations. He seems to have supported Eadwig rather than Edgar when the two of them succeeded their uncle, and after Edgar's death he favoured Aethelred, who was the son of his own close associate, Queen Aelfthryth, rather than Dunstan's choice, Edward. Thereafter he was an adviser to both Aelfthryth and Aethelred.[11]

The towering ecclesiastical figure from Aethelred's rule as an adult is that of Wulfstan, a monk, and bishop of London, bishop of Worcester and archbishop of York.[12] His importance, as for example in fashioning royal law-codes and contributing to the continuity that marks Cnut's reign, has been indicated in previous chapters. Like Aethelwold, Wulfstan appears in charter witness lists and attended royal councils. His influence can be seen, for example, in 1008, in Aethelred's response to Scandinavian threat, which had several symbolic elements. The council met at Pentecost, and at Enham, whose name means 'the place where lambs are bred'. Its name is significant because the lamb was, and is, symbolic of Christ. Aethelred also issued coins with a new design. This had the Lamb of God where the royal portrait normally was, and on the coin's other side a dove, whose symbolism includes devotion to God.[13] From Aethelred's son Edward the Confessor's reign, Archbishop Stigand is the most remarkable ecclesiastic. Before becoming archbishop Stigand had supported Edward's mother Queen Emma against Edward, and had mediated between Edward and his rebellious and troublesome in-laws, the Godwinesons, in 1050 and in 1052, when he was appointed to Canterbury. It is possible that his elevation, as someone acceptable to both factions, was a reward for this service.[14]

Ecclesiastics also contributed to government less spectacularly. Charter witness lists imply that significant numbers of bishops and abbots attended meetings of the council, or Witan, which had both lay and ecclesiastical members, and met often though not at fixed or regular times. The charters of Aethelred II's reign suggest that his Witan usually met at least once a year.[15] The Witan, like the shire courts, dealt with a variety of business and its meetings are very likely the occasions at which charters were issued. After 964 only a few abbots, of whom between twenty and forty were in office at any one time, were normally included in the witness lists. There were usually at least four and in the early 970s sometimes twelve. But not everybody present at a meeting would be included in its lists. The Dunstan B charters for some reason excluded abbots and favoured bishops. The number of bishops who attended royal councils in the tenth and eleventh centuries varied between nine and nineteen.[16] When the Witan met at Christmas, Easter or Pentecost, as it often did, political messages about kingship and society could have been, and probably were, delivered in spectacle as well as words. Given the large numbers of ecclesiastics present, the religious services held during meetings of the Witan will have been impressive at whatever time of year.[17] It was to its meeting at York, in 1014, on or about the 16th of February, that Wulfstan preached his *Sermon of the Wolf*, which has been interpreted as condemnation of his fellow-councillors. In it, Wulfstan deprecates treachery to one's lord, and particularly murder, and the expulsion of one's lord from the land. These had been the fates of King Edward the Martyr, and of King Aethelred in 1013. This sermon was preparatory to the council's invitation to Aethelred to resume his kingship, stipulating that he should rule 'more justly'. The invitation was probably by letter, and probably written by Wulfstan.[18]

The conduct of ecclesiastical and governmental business at the same place, as seen at York in 1014, was normal in the tenth and eleventh centuries. In southwest England, except in Cornwall, minster churches were often near royal centres, and had links with hundredal administration. Almost two-thirds of the Devon hundreds had their own church, as did half of Somerset's.[19] There may also have been a close correspondence between governmental and some ecclesiastical sites in their character. Some excavated sites, including Flixborough, as we have seen, may have been aristocratic dwellings or royal palaces, but have been interpreted differently by some scholars, as minsters. Two such are Northampton and Cheddar. There is no textual evidence for a palace at Northampton, where an early-ninth-century stone hall was sited between two churches, though there is later evidence for a minster there. The hall may have been part of King Cenwulf of Mercia's palace or alternatively of the royal minster's social life, in which, according to some eighth-century criticisms, monks behaved like lay aristocrats.[20] At Cheddar, the minster was gradually taken over by a royal dwelling that was established to its north-west in the late ninth or early tenth century. In the mid-tenth century, assemblies were held there. It was referred to as a palace of the king in 956. Domesday Book referred to it as a royal manor. Such encroachment seems to have been common. Another example is Cookham, a major, and thus probably rich, religious establishment in the late eighth century, but a royal manor in Domesday Book.[21]

Law, law courts and the legal system

Generation, content and assumptions

Quite apart from Archbishop Wulfstan II's responsibility for the eleventh-century English royal law-codes in their extant forms, the making of law involved both ecclesiastics and laity, and distinction between religious and secular law was very blurred. The kings' laws were regarded as extensions of the laws of God that were set out in the Bible, and the decrees of Church Synods were regarded as laws. Alfred's reference to the laws of Offa of Mercia may not be to some lost text but to the surviving decrees of the 786 Church Council.[22] High-ranking laity routinely attended Church Councils. At the last meeting in the series that met at Clovesho and for which a record survives, were the king of Mercia, some Mercian ealdormen and others who were probably members of the king's household. This was in 825. The last Church Council that a Mercian king is recorded as having attended was in 836, at Croft. There was another Church Council in 845, in London, but thereafter there is no evidence for the holding of such councils, though of course this does not preclude the possibility.[23] The Church had a rule that synods be held regularly. It may be that the meetings of the Witan and royal councils on the occasions of religious festivals met this requirement.[24]

Certainly, the royal law-codes had no gaps that needed to be filled by separate ecclesiastical legislation. Their prefaces normally refer to the advice of the king's councillors, and often state that these were both lay and ecclesiastical. The law-code I Edmund, in the 940s, for instance, announces that the king called a great synod at Easter, both of ecclesiastical and secular people, and that at this meeting two archbishops and many other bishops enquired about the benefit of their (those attending) souls and of the souls of those that were subject to them. Wulf-stan was not the first churchman to play an authorial role in royal laws. I Edmund itself is thought to have been drafted by Archbishop Oda of Canterbury. Much of Aethelstan's legislation has been attributed to his archbishop of Canter-bury, and some of Edgar's to Bishop Aethelwold.[25] Within one and the same code, secular and religious laws intertwine, because the payment of God's dues, in every respect, was a public and governmental matter and so too was sin, since kings were supposed to correct it.[26] Royal law embraced, for instance, ecclesias-tical failings, and, throughout the period, the observance of Sundays as days free from labour, trade and public meetings, and of festivals and fasts. Reeves and ealdormen were to assist abbots and bishops to obtain God's rights. The codes include laws against adultery, the practice of witchcraft and of heathenism, which was defined in Cnut's code as sacrifice, divination, idol worship, the worship of heathen gods, sun, moon, fire, flood, wells, stones and any kind of forest trees. Late codes proclaimed the holding of one Christian faith as a key principle.

A second example of the intertwining of secular and religious law is the nature of the penalties. Some religious offences were apparently liable only to religious penalties. Thus Cnut's code stipulates that when a man has both a lawful wife and a concubine, 'no priest is to do for him any of the offices which must be done for a Christian man' until he atones 'as the bishop directs him'.[27] Some religious offences, however, were liable to secular punishments, from which kings could profit. In Alfred's code the compensation for stealing on Sundays, at Christmas, Easter, the Holy Thursday in Rogation Days and the Lenten fast is double that for stealing at other times. Sunday trading merited a fine and confiscation of goods in Aethelstan's laws. I Edmund decrees that those in holy orders who do not maintain their chastity are liable to forfeit worldly goods and consecrated burial if they do not make amends. Edgar prescribed that those who failed to pay tithe should forfeit almost all their property, that late payment of Romescot incurred a fine, to the king, and that a third refusal to pay it was punishable by forfeiture of all property. The *Northumbrian Priests' Law* states that the fine payable by a king's thegn who was guilty of heathen practice is to be divided between Christ and the king. Finally, royal laws often include instructions to bishops about ecclesiastical matters. Examples include Alfred's requirement that they depose priests who have been found guilty of homicide; Edmund's that they repair churches in their own property and cast out from the Church perjurers and practitioners of sorcery who do not do penance; and Aethelred's that monks or priests who become apostates are to be excommunicated.[28]

Nevertheless a little evidence indicates some significant legal separation between ecclesiastics and laity. Some people disapproved of churchmen's involvement in law courts. Aelfric thought that none should be involved in agreeing to anybody's death, whatever the offence, lest he destroy an innocent person. In Cnut's laws a man in holy orders who commits a capital crime is reserved for the bishop's judgement. The *Northumbrian Priests' Law* tantalisingly alludes to the possibility of a priest referring to a layman a case that he ought to refer to an ecclesiastic, in which eventuality he is to pay a fine.

Process: people, places and things

Royal law-codes not only required offenders to do penance. They also directed bishops to participate in the courts. Thus II Edmund decrees that slayers are not allowed to visit the royal court without having done penance, paid or undertaken to pay the due compensation and 'submitted to every legal obligation, as the bishop, in whose diocese it is, instructs'.[29] Bishops had been required by II Aethelstan to exact a fine for disobedience from any king's reeve in their diocese who would not carry out the code's ordinances. According to Edgar's laws, each bishop had to attend the twice-yearly shire court and the thrice-yearly *burh* court and, it is implied, the four-weekly hundred courts with the ealdorman, and there expound both ecclesiastical and secular law and exact compensation. The bishop was also to exact compensation, on the king's behalf, from any judge who pronounced a wrong judgement. In Cnut's laws, reeves are to give just judgement with the witness of the bishops. Such laws set out the aspirations of kings and of Archbishop Wulfstan II. Other, scattered, evidence, including case law preserved in some charters and other sources, shows that they were realised. The evidence is clear from Edgar's reign onwards and it may be that what it shows was actually happening earlier. It has been suggested that within their dioceses bishops' legal authority was virtually unrivalled, and that in some regions they were the only authority, in all matters.[30]

Just as wergelds varied according to individuals' status, so too did the value of oaths. Bishops and their oaths were therefore very desirable as allies and as witnesses to transactions. Thus in some ninth-, tenth- and eleventh-century wills, bishops are asked to act like guardians, to widows and children to protect their inheritance, and as executors, and appear as witnesses.[31] Furthermore, the status of wills gave ecclesiastics, priests as well as bishops, a great deal of influence over inheritance. A written will was merely evidence of the intention of the testator(s). It was not the actual act of disposition of the property. An oral will was equally valid, provided that it was reported by reliable witnesses. Oral wills might be made as deathbed declarations and probably often were. Priests were instructed (for example in Laud Misc. 482) that when they attended a lay deathbed they were to tell the person that he must bequeath his property as well as confess his sins.[32] To make an oral will was to revoke any earlier written one. There was thus scope after a death for considerable disagreement between would-be beneficiaries and for chicanery. Ecclesiastical witnesses to wills could have made a great difference to their execution. Deathbed wills, which were probably the majority, were particularly likely to have been witnessed by priests.

Surviving wills do not usually nominate executors. Rather, like charters, they explicitly rely on God, by invoking His anger and punishment for anybody who should ignore the stated wishes of the testator(s) and overturn the arrangements that have been made.[33] Much legal process was permeated by the supernatural. Sanctuary could be regarded as another instance of this, since it involved the concept of sacred space. But it may also, or instead, be regarded as a convention to encourage the resolution of disputes, and the prosecution of offenders, without an escalation of violence and with time for reflection and negotiation.[34] Additionally, nobody was supposed to breach the peace within somebody else's domain or to attack anyone under somebody else's protection. The fines for doing so varied according to the status of the person whose peace, or protection, had been breached, and were known, except that the compensation for breaching the king's peace was left to the king to decide. Fugitives in sanctuary were immune from violence. However, their immunity was not indefinite, and they were not to be given food.[35] These rules were in force throughout the period, though the details were subject to change. One of Aethelstan's codes allows a respite of nine days to thieves and robbers whose appeal was to king or bishop, but only three to those who went to an ealdorman, abbot or thegn, after which they are subject to the death penalty. Alfred's code had allowed three days, in any monastic house 'to which the king's food-rent belongs, or some other privileged community' and seven to those whose flight from feud had taken them to a consecrated church.[36] In a treatise by Archbishop Wulfstan II, seven days are allowed, and only the bishop, the ealdorman and a church of high rank were mentioned.

Some particular sanctuaries are referred to in late Anglo-Saxon and later sources. At York, Hexham, Ripon, Beverley and Tynemouth the sanctuaries were circular zones, 2 miles in diameter. Some late traditions attribute them to grants by King Aethelstan, like the sanctuary zones around St Buryan, Padstow, Probus and St Keverne, all in Cornwall.[37] York, Beverley, Hexham and Southwell each had a peace-seat. Such seats marked where sanctuary was available, and were for the use of those who claimed it, in their claim. At Hexham and Beverley they predated 800.[38] Compensation was payable for violation of sanctuary, except for homicide. The amount varied in proportion to the status of the church in question. Alfred had specified 120 shillings compensation to monastic houses. Aethelred II's laws specify four categories of churches: chief, rather smaller, and still smaller minsters – this last thought to be the category of local churches with a burial-place that appears in Edgar's laws – and field-churches. They were entitled to 5 pounds, 120 shillings, 60 shillings and 30 shillings respectively.

The legal system deployed other Christian sites, symbols and objects as well as the church buildings that were involved in sanctuary. Churchyards were meeting places for legal proceedings. The *Ely Book*'s accounts of land disputes after King Edgar's death include one of Ealdorman Aethelwine going to Ely and holding a meeting of the whole hundred within the churchyard at the northern gate of the monastery, where he adjudicated the suit. And long before this, apparently, Wulfstan of Dalham had gone to Ely with many men of rank and held a meeting at the entrance to the minster towards the north, with the people of two hundreds. There he had made gifts of land to St Aethelthryth. Charters contained pictorial invocation of Christ as well as Christian ideas and allusions and threats of divine punishment for anyone who, in future, infringed their terms. Until the 930s this was usually a simple cross, preceding the name of each witness. In the eleventh century it was usually the more elaborate chi-rho symbol, using the Greek letters chi and rho, the first two letters of Christ's name in Greek. The first known use of this symbol in England was in 956. Some late documents, nine surviving, were written without such pictorial invocation. This might conceivably indicate some move, shortly before the Norman Conquest, towards a secularisation of government.[39]

Some legal documents, though wills were not among them, were routinely copied into sacred books. This may have been to sanctify and thereby strengthen the content of the documents, and also to preserve them, from harm and for consultation. About one-third of Gospel Books and liturgical manuscripts from the early tenth century onwards and from all over England have such additions, the earliest being in the vernacular. Contemporary statements that a record was to be kept in the 'Christ's Book' suggest that these additions were not copies made after the transaction, but rather at the time of it, as part of its ritual.[40] The most notable example is the series of manumissions at Petroc's stow, which were recorded in the Bodmin Gospel Book. These manumissions also reveal that the church was used for the proceedings. The manumissions were at the altar. Besides the Bodmin ones, forty are recorded in two books that are associated with Exeter, bringing the total known Cornish manumissions to approximately 120. Like royal councils, manumissions involved both laity and ecclesiastics. Ealdormen, bishops, abbots, priests and deacons attended them. The known witnesses include all the kings between 941 and 1016 except Edward the Martyr.[41] Some guild regulations have likewise survived because they were entered into Gospels. The Cambridge ones are on a detached leaf of a late-tenth-century Gospel Book that once belonged to Ely. Exeter's are written in an early-tenth-century hand in an eighth-century Gospel Book. Bedwyn's are in a Gospel Book written in or before the mid-tenth century. Other documents were entrusted to churches for safe-keeping without being copied into holy books. For example, at the end of a marriage agreement from Kent, written some time between 1016 and 1020, is the statement that there are three copies of the document. Two were entrusted to churches in Canterbury (Christ Church and St Augustine's), and one to the bride's father. This particular agreement involved very highly placed people, but lesser ones too had to make this kind of contract. By keeping such marriage, guild and manumission records the Church served the thegn and freemen classes too, not merely kings and ealdormen.[42]

Finally, some legal transactions involved relics. Like holy books, relics provided a safe haven for legal documents, though indirectly. The earliest reference to documents being kept with the king's relics is in a charter of the late 990s. But the practice may be much earlier. It certainly continued. A grant to Stow made by Earl Leofric and his wife in the 1050s refers to one of its three copies being kept by the bishop, another by the earl and one with the king's relics. The Bodmin manumissions contain explicit references to relics of St Petroc upon which the manumissions had been transacted. Since others refer only to the altar, it is likely that the relics were kept in the altar and that the manumissions were therefore all relic related.[43] A manumission had, in fact, a quality of an oath, and it is in connection with oaths that relics had their greatest legal significance.

Oaths and ordeals

Oath-breaking and false oaths were matters of great concern to law-makers and the punishment for perjury could be very severe. Alfred's code decrees 'first … what is most necessary, that each man keep carefully his oath and pledge'. Pledge-breaking entailed forty days in prison and penance prescribed by the bishop, and outlawry and excommunication if the offender escaped.[44] In Aethelstan's laws, the penalty for perjury is loss of the rights to clear oneself by oath if accused, and to burial in consecrated ground unless the perjurer's bishop bears witness that he had done penance. In Cnut's laws, proven perjury incurs loss of the hands or payment of half the wergeld.

The reliability of oaths was important because oaths were much used, by both the highly and the lesser placed. One purpose was promissory. The surviving text of the treaty between Alfred and the Danish king Guthrum states that it was 'confirmed with oaths', on both sides.[45] Alfred had three times extracted oaths of peace from the Vikings, in 876, 877 and 878, before King Guthrum was baptised. According to Edmund's laws, every free man had to swear an oath of fidelity to the king. This requirement, and practice, may have been in place some time before it was recorded.[46] In Cnut's laws, every man over the age of twelve is to swear that he will be neither a thief nor an accessory to theft. Another use of oaths was to establish a person's innocence when allegations were made against them. An accused person could use both his own oath and the oaths of other people to the same effect. Examples, in theory and practice, abound. According to Alfred's laws, someone accused of plotting against the king's life could clear himself by an oath that was equivalent to the king's wergeld. His treaty with Guthrum allows for a king's thegn who was accused of manslaughter to clear himself with twelve of his equals, and anyone below that rank to do so with twelve of his equals and one king's thegn. In Aethelstan's laws, someone who spares a thief or harbours one may clear himself with an oath of the amount of his wergeld. In a case from Cnut's reign, recorded in the records of Ramsey Abbey, a Danish nobleman's second wife was accused of murdering her stepson, and the nobleman failed to answer the bishop's summons three times. The king ordered the couple to appear at an ecclesiastical assembly with eleven oath-helpers each, male ones for him, female for her.[47] Conversely, some accusations necessitated oath-swearing by the plaintiffs. According to Alfred's laws, a preliminary oath had to be sworn in four churches if anyone wished to accuse somebody else of defaulting on 'a pledge sworn by God'.[48] Such a pledge was one that invoked God rather than a human as surety. The defendant in such a case could clear himself by an oath in twelve churches. Allowing this practice may have been meant to help people, such as traders, who had no family and friends in their vicinity, these being the normal source of sureties and oath-helpers.[49]

The use of oaths was not simply a resort to the supernatural. Honest oath-helpers were acting as witnesses and character referees. Nevertheless, it was common, perhaps usual, for oaths, like manumissions, to be sworn on relics. Cambridge guild-members swore loyalty to their fellows on relics. In Aethelred II's laws, a man is to 'come forward as witness [only] of what he dares to swear to on the relics which are placed in his hand'.[50] The oath of the twelve leading thegns and reeve charged with justice in each wapentake, to accuse no innocent man and conceal no guilty one, was to be sworn in the same way. Cnut's laws' fierce penalty for perjury was a punishment for swearing falsely 'on the relics'.[51] In the Ramsey case mentioned above, the bishop ordered the monastery's most precious relics to be placed on the site where, it was claimed, the murder victim had been buried. The text suggests that some sort of supernatural affirmation or denial of the truth of the oath was expected. What happened, apparently, was that the husband tried to stop his wife swearing, but swore himself, on his beard, to assert her innocence and his own ignorance of any crime. His beard then came away in his hands. This did not lead to any further prosecution, but the couple granted property to the bishop, who passed it to the monastery.[52] Relics were not the only holy things that were used in oath-swearing. Altars, crosses and ecclesiastical personnel were also deployed. An oath sworn on the hand of an ordained deacon had the same status as one sworn on an altar or consecrated cross.

Another use of the oath was in the ordeal, first mentioned in the laws of Ine.[53] In those of Edward the Elder, men who have been convincingly charged with perjury are not allowed to clear themselves with oaths but only by ordeal.[54] Its process can be reconstructed, from II Aethelstan, which offers the fullest statement about it in the law-codes, and from other texts, including ordeal rituals in the Pontificals and in the Red Book of Darley, which provide more details.[55] The accuser could choose the type of ordeal. The accused person was to go to the officiating priest three days beforehand, live off a minimal diet and attend Mass each day, go to Communion and swear innocence on the day itself. The plaintiff too was to fast. The number of supporters who attended was to be equal on each side, and neither side was to field more than twelve supporters. A fire might be lit. Ordeal by iron entailed carrying a hot iron (1 pound in weight, probably a little less than the modern pound) a specified distance. Ordeal by hot (boiling) water entailed putting one's hand, up to the wrist, into hot water, to extract a stone suspended therein at the required depth. In the ordeal by cold water, the accused was bound, attached to a rope that had a knot at the length of 1½ ells (probably about 4 feet 6 inches), and put into a receptacle of cold water to see if they would sink deep enough to wet the knot. An ordeal might be triple rather than single. The triple ordeal is prescribed in Aethelstan's laws for cases where the allegation was of treachery to one's lord, of breaking into a church, or of murder by witchcraft, sorcery or 'secret attempts on life'.[56] In Aethelred II's laws, it is prescribed for moneyers who are accused of coining false money. This is harsher than what Aethelstan's had prescribed for them. Cnut's laws prescribe the triple ordeal for a man accused of theft by three men together, who had previously been 'regarded with suspicion by the hundred' and frequently accused.[57] In the triple ordeal by iron, according to the mid-century so-called Hundred Ordinance, the weight had to be three times heavier than in the single ordeal and be carried 9 feet. Triple ordeal by hot water required immersion of the accused's arm up to the elbow.[58]

Contemporaries apparently perceived use of the ordeal as an appeal to non-human agencies to indicate the truth. In the cold water ordeal, the verdict was immediate. Failure to sink up to the required depth was interpreted as rejection by the water and hence proof of guilt. In hot water and iron ordeals the verdict was delayed. The scalded, or burnt, hand or arm was bound for three days. If after that its injuries were healing cleanly, that was regarded as proof of innocence. Conversely, their failure to do so signified guilt.[59] There was also a fourth type of ordeal, limited to priests, of the consecrated (barley) bread and cheese. This is prescribed in Aethelred II's laws, for an accused minister of the altar who has no friends and no oath-helpers, and its details are known from other texts. Though less dramatic and physically dangerous than the other ordeal processes, it too will have been unpleasant. The bread was plain and there was a lot of it, namely one-twelfth of a loaf which itself was large – there were several inscriptions on it. Vomiting, or failure to swallow the food, either of which could have been caused by toxins, terror or both in combination, signified guilt.[60]

Ordeals were thus both royal and ecclesiastical concerns. They involved ecclesiastics and churches and, like oaths, they were forbidden on feast days and other particular points in the Church's liturgical calendar. There are very few references to the right to hold ordeals but, considering the Hundred Ordinance's interest, it seems likely that ordeals were linked to the sites of hundredal justice and were part of the activities of each hundred's major church.[61] According to Aethelred II's laws, ordeals were to be held in king's *burhs*.

The ordeal, like the oath, did in fact, whatever contemporaries thought, have a natural and rational, as well as a supernatural, dimension. First, it must have been frightening for the accused. The preparation was long and tiring, the rite solemn and even threatening. The bread and cheese prayers, for example, allude to the gut cramping, choking and pain that the guilty will suffer. Terrified people might confess before the ordeal was completed. Second, and perhaps most significantly, the outcome of the ordeal process must almost always have been debatable, so that it was in fact human debate that decided the verdict. Indeed, modern understanding of the ordeal, based on the observations of social anthropologists, is that it was a device for mobilising and focusing public opinion. The knot that was crucial in the cold water ordeal could have got wet without being submerged and also might have been hard to see because of the water splashing. How well burns were healing would have been as questionable as how deep an individual had sunk. It would have been for the parties' witnesses and for the churchmen of the church concerned to decide.[62] The ordeal process thus gave the Church a central role in every respect in the determination of guilt or innocence. Third, there are further, though alternative, interpretations of ordeals as rational processes. One is that they have been useful in small communities that are isolated both from other communities and from central authority. They free the community of the responsibility of convicting the accused and also, crucially, the resentment that his kin would feel on his behalf, by transferring them to supernatural forces. They thereby preserve peace and social cohesion in such communities. On the other hand, the ordeal could provide a way for kings to impose order, and their authority, in cases where the nature of the offence meant that there were no witnesses, or where the accused was from outside the community and so had no friends or family to vouch for his character.

Dues, troops and war

As landowners, monastic communities (representing saints), bishoprics and other churches both levied and paid dues from their tenants and estates and to the king. Churches had their own officials to collect their dues. At Ely, for example, after Bishop Aethelwold had increased its landed wealth, a monk was put in charge of levying the food-rents.[63] But such officials may have needed support. Aethelred II's laws enjoin reeves and ealdormen to help abbots and bishops obtain their rights. As for paying dues to kings, the charters that grant exemptions to some churches may be interpreted as evidence that such payment had been normal there beforehand, and was perhaps normal for others not similarly exempted. There were very expensive obligations of hospitality in the 'servitude in secular affairs' from which King Ceolwulf I of Mercia (821–823) freed some land that he gave to the archbishop of Canterbury in a charter of 822. Entertainment of king, bishop, ealdormen, reeves, tax-gatherers, keepers of dogs or horses or hawks, and feeding or support of *faesting* men (those who had the right to lodging as they went about the king's business) are listed.[64] Exemptions were, naturally, not given for nothing. Many ninth-century ones were granted in return for gifts. For example, Ceolwulf's stated motives included the archbishop's 'acceptable money', namely a very valuable gold ring, and in 855 the bishop of Worcester paid 300 shillings for Blockley minster's freedom from huntsmen and 'mounted men'.[65]

One of the basic duties of landowners and subjects was to support their king in war.[66] Apart from not defining killing in war as a sin, the Church provided military support in several ways. It allowed kings to use ecclesiastical lands to reward their followers, by agreeing to leases, disadvantageous exchanges and suchlike, as the West Saxon kings did indeed press it to do. It legitimised war, or particular wars, especially through the use of saints' cults and the production of texts that would inspire martial effort, as some of Aelfric's works and some of the poetry seem to have been meant to do. It provided pastors to accompany armies into battle. In addition, churches rendered military service from their estates just as lay landowners did, ecclesiastics performed organisational and advisory tasks, some of which, like pastoral ones, entailed accompanying armies into battle, and some ecclesiastics actually fought.[67]

Church land, like the laity's bookland, was liable for *fyrd* (army) service, bridgework (bridges being necessary for troop movement) and *burh* service (for-tification work).[68] Charters that granted general exemptions from dues excluded these three. King Aethelwulf's 'decimation' in favour of the Church, in 855, may, however, have freed particular lands from military service, thereby reducing their owners' overall obligation.[69] There are many instances and indications of the fulfilment of ecclesiastical military obligations, some already considered in con-nection with social cohesion. Various churches were involved in naval defence. The London record, c. 1000, of the forty-five men due from thirty-two episcopal estates comprising 350 hides mentioned earlier, concerned *shipfyrd* service. In 1008, a general order was issued about the provision of ships. It seems that one ship was to be provided from every 300 or 320 hides, and a helmet and mail-shirt from every eight. Fulfilment of these requirements would have given each ship forty properly equipped men. Besides London's, the incumbents of the sees of Canterbury, Crediton and, by Edward the Confessor's reign, Worcester, and probably Dorchester, had to provide ships. Archbishop Aelfric, who died in 1005, left a sixty-oared ship to the king and Aelfwold, bishop of Crediton from some time after 986 until sometime between 1011 and 1015, left him a 64-oared one. The monastery of Ramsey too almost certainly owed a ship. Its holdings in Domesday Book were around 320 hides and it was left a warship some time between 975 and 1016 by a thegn. Since this bequest must have been meant to be useful, it suggests that a ship was part of Ramsey's military obligation.[70]

Ecclesiastics might also be associated with military forces personally, though it is not always known whether or not they fought themselves, or intended to, or simply acted as organisers and advisers. In 992, King Aethelred II entrusted a naval expedition to two bishops and two ealdormen, to trap the Danes. At the battle of Ashingdon in 1016, Bishop Eadnoth of Dorchester and Abbot Wulfsige of Ramsey were killed. Military equipment features in some episcopal wills. Bishop Aelfwold of Crediton, for example, left six mail-shirts and one helmet. Of course, the equipment in such cases might have been what bishops provided for their retainers.[71] Yet there are some indications that ecclesiastics did actually engage in fighting, one of them being that Aelfric disapproved of it. His concern that worldly soldiers should not compel 'those who pray' to worldly fighting, rather suggests that it was happening, or, at least, that he feared it as a real possibility. No churchman, he taught, should wield arms or go out to war, because the canons of the Church ruled that if such men died in warfare they should not be prayed for, though they should not be denied a grave. It is unclear whether Archbishop Wulfstan II thought the same.[72] Some ecclesias-tics certainly did wage worldly war, like many contemporary Continental bish-ops. The *Anglo-Saxon Chronicle* reports for 1056 that Leofgar, bishop of Hereford, forsook his spiritual weapons and took his spear and sword against Gruffudd of

Wales. He and the priests with him were killed, which suggests that he did not stay on the sidelines.

Diplomacy: embassies and letters

War, and other matters, entailed negotiation, diplomatic visits and correspondence. The *Anglo-Saxon Chronicle*'s entry for 889, that no journey was made to Rome, except by two (anonymous) couriers whom King Alfred sent with letters, is famous for implying that such journeys were routine. Normally this text names travellers to Rome, and they are kings, ealdormen, bishops and abbots. In 890, when alms were sent, it was an abbot who took them. The Church provided diplomatic personnel throughout the period, working with both ecclesiastical and secular authorities. Examples include a visit in 929 by Bishop Cenwald of Worcester, to monasteries in Germany with gifts from King Aethelstan. This, though not its purpose, was recorded at St Gall. Cenwald is thought to have combined the visit with Aethelstan's making a German alliance, escorting the king's two sisters to the royal court, where one subsequently married the future emperor Otto I.[73] In 1050, Edward the Confessor sent two abbots and a bishop to the great Papal council at Reims, to report to him whatever was decided there, and two further bishops to the Pope in Rome.[74] As was perhaps true of Cenwald, ecclesiastics acted as escorts to royal persons who left England. In the crisis of 1013, the bishop of London took King Aethelred II's sons, Edward and Alfred, to Normandy, for safety.[75] Ecclesiastics were also involved in making arrangements with Vikings. Their involvement was inescapable when treaties and agreements included baptism or confirmation, or oaths, but they worked in other contexts too. In 994, for example, Archbishop Sigeric, who had probably negotiated with Viking forces after the English defeat at Maldon in 991, and two ealdormen obtained the king's permission to purchase peace from the Vikings, for the districts that they ruled under him. The price is thought to have been 6,000 pounds between them.[76]

Ecclesiastics also both wrote and composed letters for kings. Furthermore, since lay literacy was limited, they must often have read letters aloud to their lay recipients, and been present at, and probably involved in, any immediate discussion that they generated. The letters that survive probably represent only a fraction of those that were sent. Those to Alfred from Jerusalem of which Asser tells us, for example, do not survive except partially and indirectly in the medical remedies in Bald's *Leechbook*. Many letters, however, will have contained little of substance, their purpose being to introduce the bearer, who was to deliver the important messages orally. Some surviving letters were subjected to textual revision. The sole copy of Cnut's first letter to the people of England, written in late 1019 or early 1020, apparently from Denmark, seems to owe a lot to Archbishop Wulfstan II. It uses his phraseology and laws that he drafted, and it is preserved with some Wulfstan texts in the York Gospels.[77] Cnut's second letter to England, of 1027, may represent the work of Abbot Lyfing of Tavistock.[78]

The Church also assisted in the care of ambassadors and messengers. Minsters were a normal source of hospitality for them. When the king of Mercia, in 848, exempted the community at Breedon-on-the-Hill from certain obligations, he excepted that of giving board to ambassadors from overseas and messengers to the king from Wessex and Northumbria. This suggests that this particular diplomatic duty was part of the common stock of ecclesiastical landowners' obligations.[79]

Scotland and Wales

Much less can be said about these matters with regard to Alba and the Welsh than for England, but it does seem that customs were broadly similar. The *Chronicle of the Kings of Alba*'s reference, to King Constantín II and Bishop Cellach pledging in 906 at Scone to keep the laws and disciplines of the faith and the rights of the Church and the Gospels[80] is our best evidence for the making or content of law in Alba. Priests did minister to the dying, as the Book of Deer makes plain and therefore could have functioned as witnesses to deathbed oral wills. It is likely that holy objects and oaths were used in and for judicial purposes, as was the case later.[81]

As for Wales, the pre-1066 Llandaff material suggests that in the tenth and eleventh centuries the major ecclesiastics asserted their right to protect people on their lands, that is, a type of sanctuary, and that they demanded and received compensation for its violation. It is probable that by the eleventh century the protected spaces of churches were physically marked. There were also protected times, that is, dates on which offences incurred extra penalties. There is evidence for the use, in the tenth and eleventh centuries, of *clamor*.[82] This was loud public complaint, and even insult, directed by ecclesiastics or lay people to a saint. It was a practice well known in northern Francia whereby the powerful (both individuals and institutions) could sometimes be shamed into better and less oppressive behaviour. Fasting was similarly an attempt to obtain God's approval and support, and to shame one's opponent into conciliation. This too was used by churchmen. Legal documents were written into holy books: the Lichfield Gospels contain some ninth-century ones. Ecclesiastical rituals confirmed land grants.

The Welsh laws are very much later than the Anglo-Saxon ones, but they offer a wealth of detail, and some may be reflective in general of the pre-1066 period. They indicate that the legal process incorporated the supernatural at every stage.[83] One example is the naming of God as a witness in two of the Lichfield Gospel charters.[84] Another is the surety-ship of God, which also occurs in Alfred's laws and may indeed have been borrowed by the Anglo-Saxons from earlier British law.[85] As in Anglo-Saxon England, relics and oaths were much used. Some Llandaff charters suggest that an oath might be enforced by the authorities of the church that owned the relics on which the oath had been sworn. Though there were three particular 'testimonies' that did not 'go to the relic', almost every oath was taken on relics, which were assumed to be easily available. Oaths were used throughout the surety procedure, which was a keystone of order. Oath-swearing by between 50 and 300 men was a method of denying murder and being accessory to murder. Legal judgements were not, however, supposed to involve ecclesiastics. People bound by holy orders or monastic rules could not legally pronounce judgements between litigants.[86]

The latest study of the legal documents in Scotland's Book of Deer concludes that the concern of ecclesiastics there was to gain exemption not from royal dues, but from dues that were imposed by local magnates on their own account, neither acting nor being perceived as royal officials.[87] In Wales the Church's lands seem often to have been exempt from royal taxes. Church and kings, or kings' stewards, collected renders from their own properties, and churchmen sometimes protested against the over-forceful exaction of the kings' dues. By the late eleventh century there was a general obligation to service in the army.[88] In Alba, the Church was involved in war in both personal and institutional capacities. The site of Dunkeld Abbey is strategically important and the fact that it is twice mentioned, with other, secular, strongholds, in the context of Viking raids has suggested that it had a military function. It may have been intended as such from its beginning. Two of its abbots were killed in battle.[89]

There are no surviving Welsh or Scottish letters and no allusions to them in the sources. References to (England's) King Aethelstan's meetings and agreements with other kings in the archipelago do not mention any ecclesiastics that accompanied them, though some surely did. The Welsh who appear in the witness lists of his charters are kings, not their ecclesiastics. There is, however, evidence for pilgrimage to Rome, by Wales' Hywel Dda in 928, and Scotland's Macbethad, Mael Coluim and Thorfinnr in the eleventh century. Elite pilgrimage could involve negotiations with foreign powers, as it did in the case of King Cnut's visit to Rome, and it seems unlikely that pilgrim kings and earls would have taken no priests with them. There is some evidence for ecclesiastical diplomacy in Wales itself. Bishops sometimes undertook a peace-keeping role. Protest on behalf of others might also be counted under this heading.

Anglo-Saxon political practice matched its theory: kings concerned themselves with the Church, ecclesiastics with secular government and law. Royal law-codes covered all aspects of society, types of offences and punishments. Legal business was often witnessed by ecclesiastics, sometimes recorded in sacred books, sometimes transacted in churchyards. The supernatural elements of the legal system, recourse to relics, sanctuary, oaths and ordeals, often had rational dimensions. Ecclesiastical landowners fulfilled the same obligations as secular ones. There is evidence that the legal process in Alba and Wales had significant elements in common with England's, but in other respects similarities are elusive.

Notes

1 Asser: 92–93.
2 Asser: 109.
3 Wormald, 'Strange'.
4 Cubitt, 'Virginity'; Giandrea.
5 *Ibid.*
6 Wormald, 'Handlist'.
7 Abrams, *Anglo-Saxon*.

8 Keynes, 'Edgar'.
9 Cubitt, 'Archbishop'.
10 Keynes, 'Edgar'.
11 Yorke, 'Æthelwold'.
12 J. Hill, 'Archbishop'; Wormald, 'Archbishop ... State-Builder'.
13 Fletcher; Giandrea; A. Williams, *Æthelred*.
14 Giandrea.
15 *Ibid.*; Insley, 'Assemblies'; A. Williams, *Æthelred*.
16 Keynes, 'Edgar'.
17 Giandrea.
18 *EHDI*: 224; Wilcox, 'Wulfstan's'.
19 Pearce; S. Turner.
20 Blair, *Church*.
21 *Ibid.*
22 Wormald, 'In Search', *Making*.
23 Cubitt, *Anglo-Saxon*; Keynes, *Councils*.
24 Giandrea.
25 Wormald, *Making*.
26 Kempshall; Meaney 'And', 'Old'; Wormald, *Making*.
27 *EHDI*: 427.
28 Helmholz.
29 *EHDI*: 392.
30 Giandrea.
31 *Ibid.*
32 V. Thompson, *Dying*.
33 Helmholz.
34 Riggs; Wormald, *Making*.
35 *EHDI*: 374–375.
36 *Ibid.*
37 Blair, *Church*; for Cornwall see also S. Turner.
38 Blair, *Church*; Foot, *Æthelstan*.
39 S.D. Thompson.
40 Dumville.
41 Jankulak; Pelteret.
42 Giandrea.
43 Jankulak.
44 *EHDI*: 374.
45 *EHDI*: 380.
46 For oaths see Wormald, *Making*.
47 Wareham, *Lords*.
48 *EHDI*: 378.
49 For Godsurety-ship, Pryce, *Native*; Wormald, *Making*.
50 *EHDI*: 403.
51 *EHDI*: 424.
52 Wareham, *Lords*.
53 Keefer, 'Ðonne'.
54 Campbell, 'What'.
55 Keefer, 'Ðonne'; Rollason, *Two*; Wormald, *Making*.
56 *EHDI*: 382–383.
57 *EHDI*: 422–423.
58 Keefer, 'Ðonne'; Rollason, *Two*.
59 Keefer, 'Ðonne'; Rollason, *Two*.
60 Keefer, 'Ut'; Niles, 'Trial'; Rollason, *Two*.
61 Blair, *Church*.

62 Rollason, *Two*.
63 E. Miller.
64 *EHDI*: 474–475.
65 *EHDI*: 486–487.
66 Giandrea; Halsall, *Warfare*.
67 Damon; Giandrea; T.E. Powell.
68 Halsall, *Warfare*.
69 Abrams, *Anglo-Saxon*.
70 Barrow, 'Chronology … Benedictine'; Damon; Giandrea; A. Williams, *Æthelred*.
71 Giandrea.
72 Damon; T.E. Powell.
73 Foot, *Æthelstan*; Tinti, *Sustaining*.
74 Giandrea.
75 *Ibid.*
76 *Ibid.*
77 Giandrea.
78 *Ibid.*
79 Keynes, *Councils*.
80 Woolf, *From*.
81 Grant.
82 W. Davies, 'Adding'.
83 Stacey.
84 Charles-Edwards, *Wales*.
85 Pryce, *Native*; Wormald, *Making*.
86 For Welsh law, W. Davies, *Wales*; Hywel Dda trans. M. Richards; Pryce, *Native*; Stacey.
87 Broun, 'Property'.
88 W. Davies, *Early*, *Wales*.
89 Macquarrie, 'Early'.

11 Pastoral care

Introduction

If there had been no effective provision for pastoral care, the impact of the rituals and ideas of the Church and of the efforts of kings and ecclesiastics to create a godly society would have been very limited. This chapter will attempt an over-view of provision in Anglo-Saxon England, without detailing either old or current debates, such as those about the 'minster hypothesis', the effects of the Vikings, and the frequency of penance, and without considering the lack of vernacular liturgy, which has already been discussed. Rather, it will address the provision of churches; the standards of bishops and priests; teaching, through preaching, texts and works of art; and the availability of the liturgy and of the sacraments of the Eucharist, baptism, penance and extreme unction (last rites, for the dying).

Pastoral care in England before the great reform

There is little direct evidence for pastoral provision in the early ninth century, but it can be supplemented by inferences drawn from earlier evidence.[1] Some priests and deacons resided in royal or aristocratic households – though according to the 747 decrees of the Council of Clovesho they ought not to have done – and others in bishops' households and the rest in minsters. Probably all minsters engaged in some sort of pastoral care. Official responsibility for pastoral care in each diocese lay with the bishop and the deacons and priests who lived there. The bishop was supposed not to ordain a priest without examining his way of life, behaviour and knowledge of the faith. In some cases, people will have visited a minster for ministry; in others, ministers will have travelled to offer it. Bishops seem to have assigned particular areas to particular priests and deacons, who were to restrict themselves to their designated areas and tasks.

Effective pastoral care was definitely an aspiration. Lay people were meant to be invited to churches on Sundays and major feast days to hear the Bible and sermons, bishops to tour their dioceses annually, in order to assemble their people and teach them. But these goals may have been only partially realised, and the availability of the sacraments limited. Many people for example may not have been baptised, not from lack of conviction but from lack of opportunity.[2]

This might be why when the 816 Council of Chelsea ruled that priests should not stray beyond their assigned tasks, it also ruled that they should never refuse to baptise. People who had not been baptised were not allowed to take Communion, and it may have been unusual even for the baptised laity to take it. The 747 decrees seem to require the people simply to be present at Mass on Sundays.[3] Earlier, Bede had lamented that many people were fit to take Communion every Sunday but did not do so through the carelessness of teachers. It is impossible to tell how often penance, which priests were supposed to impose, was imposed or performed. Penance involved fasting and the singing of psalms. Other people were allowed to perform it on behalf of the sinner, provided that no payment was involved. The author of one of the Vercelli homilies seems to envisage an annual confession and penance, for at least some people. He stated that true repentance in church at Rogationtide would obtain forgiveness for the past twelve months' sins.[4] The anointing of the sick and dying may, as in the Carolingian lands, have been provided for only a very few of the laity until the tenth century.[5] On the other hand, although minsters varied in size, resources and commitment, there were many of them. One estimate is that some hundreds were founded before the First Viking Age.[6] Some probably offered excellent training and support.[7] A mid-eighth-century text requires priests to have six books, which it names, including a missal (a service-book for Mass, for the whole year).[8] Priests would have used these books in and for services. Not all minsters were isolated, and proximity to secular sites would have made pastoral care easy to give and receive, and, perhaps, to revive after setbacks.[9]

The ninth century seems overall to have seen a decline in pastoral care, or at least a fear of decline, but also attempts to combat it. One indication of the decline of the minsters, which had several causes, is that the identities of many local saints, who had been venerated in them, seem not to have been known accurately in the tenth century.[10] Some interesting letters imply that there were allegations of a lack of priestly teaching, reveal unorthodox attempts to rectify it, and illuminate episcopal activity to suppress these attempts. One, from King Aethelwulf to the Carolingian emperor Louis the Pious (814–840), partially survives in the *Annals of St Bertin* and refers to an English priest who had been inspired by a vision. He taught that if the people did not immediately do penance for their various vices and crimes and did not observe Sundays more strictly, they would suffer great disaster as divine punishment. There would be three days and nights of fog and then sudden devastation by pagans. Another letter, from the bishop of Lindisfarne, to Wulfsige, archbishop of York 830–837, refers to the mendacious raving, and book, of someone called Pehtred. Pehtred claimed, apparently, among other things, that a certain Nial the deacon, who is known from the Irish annals to have died in 859, had come back to life after seven weeks. The bishop reveals that Wulfsige had previously warned him about Pehtred's teaching, and undertakes to extinguish these errors if they arise. He also advises Wulfsige that Pehtred's own bishop and 'the other servants of God dwelling in his neighbourhood' should be ordered to admonish him, in the hope both that Pehtred himself might be saved and that he might correct, so far as he could, those whom he had deceived.[11]

The evidence for pastoral care in the late ninth century is a little mixed. Penance was probably well known. Vernacular words for confessor and canonical penance were used in the translation of Pope Gregory I's *Pastoral Rule* and in Alfred's law-code. One of the three surviving Old English penitential collections, the *Scriftboc*, which includes instructions for confessors about how to question penitents and assign penances, may be Alfredian in date.[12] Public penance, required by Alfred's code for oath-breaking, was a matter for bishops, though private confession, imposition and performance of penance were matters for priests. By contrast, letters from foreign dignitaries suggest serious problems. Pope John VIII's letters complain about fornication, the marriage of nuns and consanguineous marriages. In one of 877 or early 878 he actually advised the archbishop of Canterbury to resist the king, and stated that hc himsclf had advised the king to be obedient.[13] Fulco, archbishop of Reims writing between 883 and about 890, agreed with Alfred that the ecclesiastical order had 'fallen in ruins in many respects', and he was critical again in 890 or soon after. Fulco was especially concerned about irregular marriages, concubines, and bishops and priests having women living near them.[14] Pope Formosus (891–896) admonished the bishops of England for allowing the faith to be violated, and the flock to wander and scatter due to lack of pastors.[15]

Fulco had, however, heard that Alfred was concerned to correct things, and Formosus, from Archbishop Plegmund, that the bishops had woken up. Attempts at improvement continued under the next two kings, Edward and Aethelstan. A recent suggestion is that the first component of the manuscript known as the Leofric Missal, usually thought to be a Frankish work that came to England in the early tenth century, was written in England for Plegmund. It may have been meant for use at the dedication of the cathedral of Wells, to which one of the prayers seems applicable. The manuscript's inclusion of prayers for dedications of churches to saints who were not associated with Wells suggests that its owner expected to be consecrating a number of churches.[16] This implies that within the Church there was vitality, a concern for pastoral care and an active engagement in it. The creation of four new sees (Wells, Crediton, Ramsbury and Sherborne) between 909 and 918 does likewise. In Aethelstan's reign, the acquisition of Breton liturgical books and Breton clergy may indicate some concern that English standards and resources needed improvement. Aethelstan's gifts to Christ Church and St Augustine's in Canterbury, and to Chester-le-Street, of Gospels that had been produced on the Continent may also reflect it.[17] Concern for pastoral care lies also behind his laws about the financing of the Church. His first law-code, dated to sometime between 926 and c. 930, requires his reeves to ensure that churchscot and soulscot are paid where they legally belong, and plough-alms yearly, 'on condition that those enjoy it at the holy places who are willing to attend to their churches and to deserve it … he … who is not willing is to forfeit that benefice or to revert to what is right'.[18] In the same period, priests undertook duties in the town guilds that were formed. The Exeter statutes, for instance, which date to the period sometime between 920 and 959, say that at each of the thrice-yearly meetings the Mass priest is to sing two Masses, one for the living friends and one for the dead ones.[19]

Since they are earlier than the manuscripts that preserve them, the Vercelli and Blickling homilies offer some illumination of early- or mid-tenth-century teaching and preaching, though scholars' opinions about them have varied considerably. They may actually have been preached to lay audiences.[20] That the Blickling compiler seems to have had limited resources on which to draw for his compilation may suggest that there was a lack of public preaching.[21] He collected together texts for some occasions in Lent, Easter and Pentecost, each of five saints' days (John the Baptist, Peter and Paul, Michael, Martin and Andrew), the Annunciation, and the Assumption of the Virgin, plus three fragmentary homilies probably meant for Rogationtide.[22] There seems to be more personal taste in the Vercelli collection so it offers less insight into the general availability of texts. It has homilies for Good Friday (one), Lent (one), Christmas (two), Rogationtide (six) and Epiphany (one), and seven others, concerned with catechetical and eschatological subjects.[23]

On the eve of the Benedictine reform, some time between 942 and 946, Archbishop Oda of Canterbury issued a set of ordinances that drew selectively on the decrees of the 786 Legatine Synod. If what he omitted was what he thought unnecessary, it implies, in most instances, that pastoral work was regular and effective. Oda was not, however, complacent: he added some material, for example in condemning wandering monks, and about the observance of fasts, Sundays and other holy days.[24] Considered objectively, the Church on the eve of the reform was not in desperate need of it. It was just very different from what the reformers wanted it to be.

Pastoral care in late Anglo-Saxon England: aspirations, complaints and concern

It is difficult to be confident about the extent and quality of pastoral care in later Anglo-Saxon England. One problem is that the legal and quasi-legal material is dominated by Archbishop Wulfstan II.[25] His work lies behind some texts that are presented as the responsibilities of other people. Besides royal law-codes, Wulfstan also put together the so-called *Canons of Edgar*, concerning secular clergy, some time in the first decade of the eleventh century, and the *Institutes of Polity*, concerned with proper behaviour and the ordering of authority. Tracing a chronology of pastoral care from them is hazardous, because he continuously revised his works. Another problem is that Wulfstan used Aelfric's works as sources. In the *Canons* he drew heavily on the pastoral letters that Aelfric had composed for Wulfsige of Sherborne, and for himself. In the *Institutes* he drew not only on Aelfric's work for Wulfsige, but also on his letter to Sigeweard and his *Catholic Homilies*. He also drew on Aelfric in composing his sermons.[26] Hence these two writers dominate our textual evidence. Nevertheless, since they belonged to different wings of the Church, Aelfric the monastic and Wulfstan the secular, and they worked in and presumably knew different regions, Aelfric only in the south and Wulfstan in the north as well, together they may, perhaps, offer us a balanced picture. They were similar in many of their ideas, and each was influential, so they have been regarded as both testifying and contributing to the national character of the English Church. Yet they had very different views about some matters. A third problem is that, as quarries for material for a negative view of the pastoral work of the late Anglo-Saxon Church, their writings might be taken as evidence of its inadequacy. They need not, however, be interpreted in this way. They may, rather, be evidence for a deep commitment to, active leadership in, and continuing expansion and improvement of, teaching. Furthermore, some of the clerics who attracted their disapproval may actually have been conscientious and held views that were well considered, rather than corrupt and self-indulgent.

There are certainly many implications that standards of local clergy and their effectiveness were perceived to be poor. If so, it may sometimes have been because lay landlords owned estate churches and had lordship over their priests.[27] Wulfstan's pastoral letters for example rule that without episcopal permission no priest should leave his church for another, or have two churches, and no unknown priest was to celebrate Mass or receive a church. Such misdemeanours could easily have been caused by lords' deployments and reorganisations of their staff. The greed for fees and participation in trade that were feared could have been generated by lords failing properly to resource their estate priests. The same applies to lack of equipment. Aelfric thought it necessary to stipulate, in one of the pastoral letters that he composed, that priests should be armed with sacred books (ten in total) for the spiritual battle, and have clean Mass vestments that were not worn out, a good quality altar-cloth, and a clean chalice and paten made of imperishable material. Priests' lack of equipment might also, or instead, have been a responsibility of their bishops, who themselves were not deemed faultless. It has been suggested that Aelfric meant the pastoral letter that he wrote for Wulfsige to be as much for Wulfsige's instruction about what he, as bishop, should require of his priests, as for theirs. In its preface Aelfric advised Wulfsige to speak more often to his clergy and to point out their negligence.

In a private letter to Wulfstan, Aelfric explicitly criticised bishops, saying for example that they did not attend to divine scripture or teach pupils who would be bishops in the future, and did not love justice. Wulfstan too articulated concern. The subject of episcopal duties recurs in his works, including short texts that could have functioned as sermons or letters, or both, to bishops.[28] He stipulated prayer, study, observance of the liturgy, distribution of alms, and administration. He regretted that some bishops indulged in hunting and drinking and the flattery of noblemen, and he warned them not to be too eager for power or avaricious. He lamented that public penance was not sufficiently practised and that bishops did not sufficiently speak out against sin and shortcomings. Bishops, he taught, should preach boldly. In Cnut's law-code he termed bishops and priests God's heralds, who are to guard the people against the works of the Devil. Another of his texts stresses that the episcopate as a whole should be cohesive. Bishops were all to put right wrongs that were offered to any one of them; to defend, warn and help each other; and to solve disputes among themselves by the arbitration of their colleagues. They were all to join in excommunication of any sinner who did

not submit despite having been excommunicated by one of them. It may sometimes have been impossible for a bishop to do everything that he was supposed to,
which was a lot. For example, when a royal council was held at Easter, as many
were, many bishops would have been unable both to attend it and to reconcile
public penitents in their cathedrals on Maundy Thursday, because of the travelling involved. Wulfstan himself seems not to have toured his see of Worcester as
Bishop Oswald had and Bishop Wulfstan II was to do.[29]

The negative impressions of priests that Aelfric and Wulfstan offer us go beyond
implying that some were under-resourced and at the behest of their lay lords.
Aelfric thought it necessary to warn that priests should neither drink immoderately
nor compel any man to do so. He was especially concerned that priests be
unmarried and chaste. In his view, no women other than their sisters, mothers and
aunts by blood should be in their houses. He envisaged that among the diocesan
priests of Sherborne there would be men who saw no harm in a priest living like a
married man, with the services of a woman. He thought, too, that many priests
loved secular concerns, and wished to be reeves, rather than to live according to a
rule. Another concern was that some priests were poorly educated. Byrhtferth of
Ramsey remarked on priests' ignorance in comparison to monks, and justified his
use of English, as well as Latin, in his *Enchiridion*, by clerics' inability to understand
Latin.[30] Aelfric too refers to this, for example stigmatising his own first teacher for
it. He also criticises him for not understanding the difference between what was
right before, and since, the time of Christ and establishment of the Church.[31]
A text that is associated with Wulfstan concedes that it might be necessary to
ordain a man who was only partially educated. The teacher of such a man was to
be responsible for ensuring that his education continued. The *Canons of Edgar*
requires learned priests to help half-learned ones to improve.

In his English pastoral letter for Wulfsige, Aelfric spelt out some basic points,
including the seven canonical hours that Mass priests should sing in their churches, and the seven orders of the Church (doorkeepers, lectors, exorcists, acolytes,
sub-deacons, deacons and priests) and their duties. He may have been anticipating a clerical audience that was unfamiliar with them and trying to educate it.
He certainly shows what the conditions in local parishes should have been. Mass
priests were to pray for the king and bishop, those who did good to them and for
all Christian people; tell the people on Sundays and festivals the meaning of the
Gospel in English and about the Lord's Prayer and Creed as often as they could;
divide the tithes into three portions – for repairs to the church, for the poor and
for God's servants (the priests) who look after the church. They were not to
celebrate Mass in any house that was not consecrated, except in cases of great
necessity or if someone was ill. They were to baptise any child brought to them
suddenly for that purpose. They were not to ask for fees or attend on a corpse
without invitation. They were to impose penance; anoint the sick; require the
sick to confess before being anointed and give them the sacrament if, and only if,
they could swallow it. They were not to take part in secular suits, swear oaths,
carry weapons or drink in taverns. By implication they were to ensure that
Christian men went to church frequently and that whilst they were in church

they did not converse, eat or drink or play disgracefully. Aelfric's pastoral letters
for Wulfstan cover much the same ground, though with some additions and extra
emphases. A Mass priest was to celebrate Mass no more than once a day and to
attend the corpses only of the men who belonged to his parish at his church.
He was to have books, but only eight were required. He was not go to battle.
No cleric was to participate in sentencing any offender to death. Nor were clerics
to hunt or go hawking.

Wulfstan himself provides some further details. His *Canons of Edgar* offers extra
information about the celebration of Mass. For instance, a priest was to say Mass
with an open book before him; only when he had someone with him; he was to
use pure wine, pure water and a pure sacrificial wafer; there was to be a light
burning in church when Mass was sung. Dogs and horses were to be kept out of
churchyards as far as was possible. Pigs were not to be allowed in. The anonymous *Northumbrian Priests' Law* also implies priestly negligence and incompe-
tence. Its author warns against celebrating Mass despite the bishop's or
archdeacon's prohibition; refusing baptism or confession; celebrating Mass without wine; putting unsuitable things in churches; not ringing or singing the hours
at the proper times; bringing weapons into churches; performing services in
the wrong order; not conducting an ordeal properly; and failing to demand
the yearly dues. Aelfric and Wulfstan both stressed the duty of teaching the
people, in part by preaching. In one sermon, written after 1007, Aelfric laments
failure openly to condemn wrong-doing, and says that teachers should not cease
teaching however obstinate their listeners are. He also says that preachers who
accept the offerings of the people but do not preach are feeding on the sins of
the people. Of course, it is likely that ill-educated priests found the task of
preaching very difficult. Aelfric advised that those who could not teach should
set a good example by living well. Another remedy would have been for them to
use sermons that had been written by other people, perhaps for that very purpose, as Aelfric's were, or collected for it, as the Blickling texts may have been.[32]
Unfortunately, some of the material that was available to priests was deemed
unorthodox. Pehtred's book is a case in point, and Aelfric explicitly stated that
he felt that *gedwyld* (which means error, heresy) was widely current in contemporary thought and teaching and in English books. It was to combat this that
he wrote his own homilies.[33]

Lack of teaching and of good example would have encouraged sin and error
not to wither but to flourish. It is not unnatural that perception of such flowering
caused Aelfric and Wulfstan (and has encouraged some modern scholars) to suspect a pastoral deficiency behind it. One concern, in a late-tenth-century confessional text and in a number of Wulfstan texts, was about heathens, heathen
practices and heathenism.[34] In some cases the author had the religion of Scandinavian attackers, or settlers, in mind. In others, however, heathen seems to signify
people who were not baptised, or poor Christians, and heathenism anything that
stopped Anglo-Saxons from being good Christians.[35] Furthermore, the heathen
practices that are indicated may be traditional, possibly resurgent, Anglo-Saxon
folkloric customs.

Yet, in their complaints and exhortations, Aelfric and Wulfstan were literally practising what they preached: the duty to teach and to set a good example. They were setting a good example of teaching.

Pastoral care in late Anglo-Saxon England: an optimistic view

Teaching and standards

The optimistic view of pastoral care depends first of all on Aelfric's and Wulfstan's commitment to, and promotion of, teaching. This was both explicit and subtle. Aelfric stated that teachers would be more rewarded in the next life than the laity would, because of the difficulties of their office. In his choices and treatments of figures and materials that he used in his homilies, he put forward an active life of teaching as the ideal, not the contemplative and secluded life.[36] In this he was following in the footsteps of Bede, in whose pages it is monks who preach, do pastoral work and become bishops, and whose depiction had inspired the reformers to try to monasticise England's cathedrals. One example is Aelfric's interpretation, in his homily about the Assumption of the Virgin Mary, of Martha and Mary.[37] It was not in Aelfric's sources and seems to have been his own idea. According to the Bible, when Jesus visited them, Martha did all the work while her sister Mary listened to His teaching instead and Jesus praised Mary for her choice. Martha and Mary had often been regarded as symbolising the active and the contemplative religious lives, the story as teaching that it was the contemplative that was superior. Aelfric, however, presented Martha and Mary as symbolising, respectively, feeding and teaching. A prioritisation of teaching is apparent too in his omission of reclusive saints, including the Anglo-Saxon Guthlac. Furthermore, he only once refers to contemporary hermits, when he alludes in his letter to Sigefryth, to 'your anchorite at home'. This implies that Sigefryth was maintaining the anchorite on his estate. Only a few other late Anglo-Saxon hermits (three Evesham monks, and a Worcester monk) are known, from other sources. It is possible that hermits were more common than this suggests. What seems clear is that the reformers did not perceive hermits as good role models.[38]

Wulfstan's commitment to teaching is always explicit. He warned that at Judgement Day priests would be responsible for the souls of wicked men whom they do not attempt to convert. Wulfstan was heavily influenced by Carolingian ideas and texts, and his repeated legislation about pastoral care and lay Christian observance looks routine rather than exceptional when considered in a Carolingian context. Examples include Aethelred's law-codes' demands of attendance at church and, most strikingly in 1008, that everybody frequently confess, do penance and prepare themselves for Communion. Cnut's laws require that everybody learn the Lord's Prayer and Creed, and confess regularly.

Not everything that Aelfric excoriated need be perceived as he perceived it, or as indicative of degeneracy. His works contain indications that there were reasoned debates and disagreements within the Church. In his pastoral letters,

Aelfric anticipates that some people will cite biblical precedents to justify clerical marriage and clerical participation in war, and explains that they do not.[39] It is also clear that not only married priests disagreed with him about the legitimacy of clerical marriage. Sigefryth's anchorite taught that priests were allowed to marry. The author of the *Northumbrian Priests' Law* stipulates a penalty for a priest's leaving a woman and taking another, but not for having one in the first place, though he clearly disapproved.[40] Furthermore, there were also some significant differences of opinion between Aelfric and Wulfstan.[41] Aelfric limited the number of times a priest might say Mass to once a day; Wulfstan allowed it three times daily. In letters to and for Wulfstan, Aelfric stated that bishops were not appointed to be judges of thieves and robbers, and deprecated bishops' and priests' involvement in the legal system. But this censure does not appear in the Old English translation. It must have been either omitted by Aelfric or deleted by Wulfstan,[42] whose view was the opposite. Because a bishop was committed to elevate right and suppress wrong, he should 'always dictate judgements along with secular judges'. Furthermore, every law, of *burh* or country district, should go by the bishop's advice and witness, and every *burh* measure and weighing machine should be regulated according to the bishop's direction. Likewise a priest was to regulate measuring rods by his own, and to direct the regulation of all measures and weights in his parish.[43]

Behind what seem pastoral weaknesses there may actually have been aspiration and reverence. Aelfric explained the prohibition of immoderate drinking by the necessity that a priest be ready always to baptise or give the sacrament (of the Eucharist), that is, by his always being on call to serve the sick and dying. He envisaged that the Eucharist that was consecrated on Easter Day might be kept over the subsequent year, for use for the sick, and that it would in consequence be profaned by decay, loss or consumption by mice. He set seven or fourteen days as the limit for keeping it. Yet his words suggest that what lay behind this particular mistake (of keeping Easter-consecrated Eucharist for use later in the year) was not carelessness or lack of reverence, but rather a mistaken view, namely that the Eucharist that was consecrated on Easter Day, the day of Christ's Resurrection, was somehow more holy than that consecrated on other occasions.

The Church was committed to teaching, its aspirations were high and disagreements were reasoned rather than self-indulgent. These are grounds for inferring that the later Anglo-Saxon priesthood had a significant and positive impact on the laity. Others are that the Church targeted the entire population, that it made practical provision for the laity, and that there is evidence that ecclesiastics did indeed perform their pastoral duties and that priests were trained and monitored. Particularly notable with regard to the first of these is what Aelfric says about the duties of Mass priests, and his injunction that every Sunday be observed as a festival, from Saturday noon until Monday dawn. Other sorts of text, besides the quasi-legal, include anticipation that lay people would attend churches, monastic as well as non-monastic. For example, the *Regularis Concordia* refers to the laity (the people), assisting at the chief Mass on Sundays and feasts and holding candles, and Aelfric envisaged a mixed audience for his homilies. He anticipated, for example, that not everybody would be present at every homily. Since professional religious were not only supposed to be in church much more often than the laity but were also closely supervised, this suggests that Aelfric expected laity, not merely professional religious, to be in some of the congregations to which his homilies would be delivered.[44]

Furthermore, though the extent of lay attendance is still unknowable, and scholars vary in their judgements about it, lay exposure to liturgy was neither simply a matter of aspiration nor one of social class. There are signs that the common people were far from untouched by the Church and indeed had some incentives to engage with it. Anglo-Saxon medical texts show that local priests were involved, one way or another, in medical care. Remedies frequently require that the Mass be said over this or that potion or herb for this or that number of times. The most convenient way of complying with this instruction would have been to do it before the items were actually needed, perhaps having them under a church's altar while Mass was routinely said, and keeping them there afterwards.[45] Thus the local church may have functioned as a pharmacy. This may be one of the reasons, though there are others too, why Aelfric enjoined that people should seek healing from the Church. The dues that the people owed to the Church must also have stimulated lay engagement. Ecclesiastical demands for payment are likely to have stimulated a desire for some benefit in, and as a, return. That there should indeed be some return is occasionally stated in texts.[46] One of Edgar's law-codes requires those who receive the dues that are paid to God to live purely and intercede to God for those who pay the dues.

Churches and teaching methods

Practical provision of churches for the laity, and for the laity inside churches, was not lacking. 'Church' was generally accessible by the time of Domesday Book, the proliferation of small churches and grave-yards during the tenth and especially the eleventh centuries anticipating the parish system of later centuries. For many tenth- and eleventh-century lay people, 'Church' will have meant a local, proprietary, estate church. Some eleventh-century examples seem to have been named from the lords of the estates where they were located.[47] Many people, however, will have attended other types of churches, of which there were several, including unreformed minsters, reformed monastic churches, cathedrals, churches run by, or at, nunneries, and other churches that housed saints' shrines. There is post-Conquest evidence that the nunneries of Amesbury and Wherwell acted as mother-churches with dependent churches that provided pastoral care. Though the tenants of the Nunnaminster, in Winchester, had their own church, the public could attend the nuns' church, for it was there that the cult of St Eadburh was based. That must also have been true of other nunneries' churches that housed saints' shrines.[48] People living near Aelfric's first monastery, Cerne, may have attended its church, since they had no village church to attend. They may, however, have attended any one of several others nearby: Sherborne cathedral (some fifteen miles away), which had secular clergy until 998; perhaps as many as five minsters; and possibly two other churches, all of which may have been staffed by married clerics.[49]

Inside the churches, the liturgy might in itself have been appealing and it was certainly inclusive. In the liturgy, Christian history was re-enacted. Members of the congregation were not mere spectators. They participated actively, being encouraged to identify with particular biblical figures, for example the shepherds at Christmas, the Magi at Epiphany, and the three Maries at Easter. This is why in his sermon for Candlemas Aelfric discussed Anna as well as Symeon, who was the biblical model for recognition and proclamation of Christ. He was establishing Anna as the model with whom his female audience was to feel sympathetic identification. Some of the Church's proceedings literally went out to the community. According to the *Regularis Concordia*, there were several processions in Lent. In Canterbury one went on Palm Sunday from Christ Church, through the town and outside it. Since the liturgy for Palm Sunday gives a central place to the laity it is likely that many of the people of Canterbury took part, carrying palms and singing Hosanna, thereby joining themselves with the original palm-waving and singing crowd of Jerusalem.[50] Rogationtide was another time for public processions. Lay involvement then is indicated by the concern of some ecclesiastics that it was misinterpreted, as a festival and a time for indulgence in riding, hunting and gaming.[51]

Supplementing liturgy and processions were vernacular homilies. Many of these, Aelfric's in particular, which constitute over half of those that survive, seem to have been attempts to reach the common people through their local priests, to overcome the priests' problems of inadequate learning, isolation and lack of resources.[52] Aelfric provided orthodox, vernacular, book-learning that could simply be read out. He wanted, and, so far as we can judge, probably managed, to hold his audience's attention. This aspiration explains aspects of his literary style. He emphasises in his prefaces the importance of brevity, to avoid boring the audience. He developed a particular prose style that makes his sermons gripping and memorable as well as, incidentally, showing that he meant them to be read aloud rather than silently. This was a heightened rhythmical prose, including sound effects of words to emphasise their meaning. It is related to the form of Old English poetry.[53] Aelfric also wanted to provide for the whole of the Church's year. His eighty sermons cover most Sundays and almost all the major saints' and other festivals and special occasions. His preface to his first set, of forty pieces, states that they are sufficient for a year if recited in their entirety and that he was composing another book. This, he wrote, was so that one book could be read one year and the other in the following year. His homilies circulated very widely. This is indicated by the large number of surviving copies, in thirty-five manuscripts and nine fragments, and by the fact that they reached Durham as well as southern communities.[54] One of these was Wulfstan's Worcester. Wulfstan used at least thirteen of Aelfric's works apart from the five letters that Aelfric wrote to and for him.[55] It has been suggested that the circulation included booklets that were copied in local minsters and kept loose for years rather than being immediately sewn together into a binding, these booklets being meant for borrowing by monks and by local priests.[56] There is earlier evidence for such a practice, in the Blickling Book. Its scribe copied texts from different exemplars into seven booklets. Each was easily portable (the whole book's original size was about 7.5 x 11 inches), and signs of wear are indicative of use.[57] It may be that many more such booklets once existed, and that library loans were common.[58] As for Archbishop Wulfstan II's sermons, twenty-five of these survive, the manuscript evidence showing that they circulated at Canterbury, Winchester and Exeter as well as at Worcester and York.[59]

Aelfric intended his *Lives of Saints*, like his *Homilies*, for a wide audience, or at least wider than Ealdorman Aethelweard and his son and successor Aethelmaer, for whom he wrote them in the 990s. He used the *Lives* to provide political as well as spiritual teaching, and models whose application was quite broad. This sometimes meant reworking rather than simply reflecting his sources. Thus the virginal though married St Cecilia, who was perceived as a model for, and aid to, overcoming the challenges of the religious life, became a model for lay people. Lay people after all were supposed to teach Christianity in daily life, especially to their children and god-children, by example as well as explanation. Aelfric represented Cecilia as a begetter of spiritual children, through her conversion of others.[60] Another example is his inclusion of a story about a chaste and charitable married couple in his *Life* of the twice married but virgin queen Aethelthryth. Aelfric had found this tale in a much earlier Latin text and added it to the Bedan material that was his source, abbreviating it to highlight the marital chastity and making the wife more prominent. This suggests that Aelfric wanted married people to follow their example rather than Aethelthryth's, which was rather different. The marital chastity of Aethelthryth and her husbands was the result of her decision alone and made the marriages childless. In the non-Bedan case that Aelfric added it was by mutual consent and after procreation.[61]

Once Aelfric's works were available, priests, other professional religious, and devout literate lay people did not lack vernacular texts, written for the occasion, to study and use when observing Sundays and other holy days. Indeed, they had some choice.[62] In addition, much of the surviving vernacular poetry that was not explicitly about any Christian subject actually addressed Christian issues and attempted to convey particular ideas, ideals and lessons. Some of it seems to have been meant primarily for a professional religious audience, though it may have reached a lay audience too. Some, however, may have been meant originally for laity.[63] It may have been intended, and used, to stimulate meditation about its symbolism as well as its overt subject matter. Both the character and the possible history of the Vercelli Book suggest this. Vercelli, its current home, was on the pilgrim route to Rome and the manuscript may have arrived there in the luggage of an English pilgrim, as a reading programme for the journey. But the question of whose private study it was originally intended for has not been resolved. A monastic audience, a secular cleric, a nun or nuns and Archbishop Dunstan have all been suggested.[64]

Another medium for teaching must have been the various artistic works that adorned and were used in the churches. They were useful especially for the illiterate, but not only for them.[65] Art has been described as, like liturgy, an essential tool for bridging the gap between Man and the Divine: its content and its details teach both basics and nuances of faith and doctrine; it suggests what God is like, facilitates interaction with Him, and proclaims the importance of the objects that are used in ritual and worship.[66] Priests could have explained the meanings of the artworks that were in their churches. The works themselves, like poems, could have stimulated meditation and devotion. They included sculptures and frescoes (wall paintings). Frescoes were probably normal, though little survives and there is little written evidence that describes them. There were also church furnishings such as altars, and equipment such as chalices, reliquaries and vestments.

In addition, there were the pictures that decorated manuscripts. These often embodied important explanations and messages. At least some of the illuminated manuscripts would have been displayed and used in ceremonies.[67] They included biblical texts and bishops' books, like the Benedictional of Aethelwold, which he would have used on Sundays and feast days at Winchester, as its bishop, but were not limited to them. The New Minster, for example, displayed its foundation charter from Edgar and its *Liber Vitae*. The charter was probably on the altar, and it was supposed to be read out to the community at certain seasons, though the details of when were written on a part of the manuscript that is now missing. The *Liber Vitae* will have been taken to the altar during the celebration of Mass.[68] Of course, the pictures in manuscripts that were used in ceremonies were small, so only a few people could have seen them then. Yet they might have stimulated officiating clergy to comment on them to the congregation, whilst the impressive appearance of the actual books probably had an immediate impact.

Other ecclesiastical artwork was, by contrast, very large and highly visible. Earl Harold Godwineson apparently gave gold or gold-covered life-size figures of the twelve apostles and of two lions to Waltham.[69] A sculpted crucified Christ at Romsey is just over 6 feet high, and the two sculpted angels, probably originally part of a group that, possibly, attended a crucified Christ, at Bradford-on-Avon are each about 5 feet long. The greater and richer churches, which were usually reformed, Benedictine, houses, will, naturally, have offered their congregations much more art than the lesser and less well-off ones could dream of.[70] Nevertheless, since abbey churches and cathedrals served their local communities as well as their own residents and patrons, such visual teaching material was not socially exclusive.

There is throughout the work of the English reformers, like that of their Carolingian predecessors which inspired them, a concern that the people understand what they are doing in church and what they are subscribing to. Aelfric explained that he used plain English, not obscure words in his homilies, and repeatedly stressed his simplicity of style.[71] He was especially concerned to explain the meaning of the liturgy to the laity. For example, he emphasised the biblical models and explicitly instructed his audience to emulate them, increasing the sense of identification between these models and contemporary believers.[72] Wulfstan's *Canons of Edgar* stresses that the laity should teach their children the

Lord's Prayer and the Creed, knowledge of which was, as Cnut's laws reiterate, the qualification for being a sponsor at baptism or confirmation, for entitlement to the sacrament and for having a consecrated grave. Carolingian rulings that the laity was meant to know these two texts are often interpreted as meaning to know them in the vernacular, to which some rulings explicitly refer, and this was probably the case too in eleventh-century England. From the mid-tenth century onwards vernacular was used in some English liturgical manuscripts in places where lay understanding was particularly important. Its most frequent context is that of confession and penance.[73]

Performance of pastoral duties

Churchmen's concern for lay understanding bears on another reason for a favourable conclusion about pastoral provision for the late Anglo-Saxon laity. Further evidence, apart from the presence of Old English rubrics in some of the liturgical manuscripts, suggests that ecclesiastics did in fact perform their pastoral duties. Some manuscripts seem from their size and content to be designed for parish use or for use by travelling priests. The mid-eleventh-century Laud Misc. 428, probably made at Worcester, measures 8 x 3.625 inches. In it, there are long, detailed vernacular rubrics, in the context of visiting the sick and dying, including saying Mass in a sick person's house. There are also vernacular confession and penitential texts, including a formula for absolution after confession. Since the manuscript includes some theoretical material as well, it may have been meant for use in training priests. Another possibility, however, is that it was used in parish work, in the churches of the town.[74] The contemporary Red Book of Darley is also easily portable. It shows signs of having been heavily used, and it too includes Old English material. For example, in its visitation of the sick, the priest sometimes uses the vernacular, there are English translations of baptismal rubrics and two vernacular texts for use in the process of ordeal. One interpretation of this manuscript is that because it includes everything that a conscientious parish priest would have needed, apart from confessional and penitential material, it was actually designed for parish use. It was probably used by eleventh-century secular clergy at Darley in Derbyshire, where the manuscript was in the sixteenth century. Since there was no monastery in Darley until the middle of the twelfth century, its people would have needed a parish priest in the eleventh. An earlier theory, however, was that the manuscript was for a monk-priest to take around the villages he visited.[75]

Such usable and used manuscripts confirm the impression given by other evidence, that administration of the sacraments to the laity was usual. References to Bishop Oswald of Worcester touring his diocese and building his new church because the old one was too small for the numbers of people who came to hear him preach suggest that he discharged his pastoral duties effectively. The so-called Sidney Sussex Pontifical may have been written for him, at Ramsey, whilst he was bishop of Worcester but not yet archbishop of York, before 971. Whether or not it was for Oswald, the manuscript certainly suggests that its first owner was a conscientious bishop. It includes a small booklet, whose size, contents and dirtiness suggest that it was both usable and used. It contains the confirmation ritual for children, and its words, using plural forms and referring to both male and female, suggest that more than one candidate was expected at a ceremony, at least sometimes.[76]

Furthermore, recent studies have shown that penance was part of both religious and political culture, though exactly how often the laity generally confessed remains unknown.[77] Lay people were supposed to do so regularly, monks and canons weekly and every three weeks respectively. Confession is rarely mentioned in the narrative sources, but perhaps because it was simply taken for granted. That it did happen is indicated by the existence of vernacular vocabulary for penance in the Vercelli and Blickling homilies and in those of Aelfric and Wulfstan. Even more significantly, the authors of the homilies repeatedly urge their audience to confess and do penance, and assume in doing so that the only obstacle to it is the audience's reluctance. One of the Blickling homilies refers to priests' use of a penitential book; and this remark seems to be the author's own, not a quotation, suggesting that he thought it normal. Aelfric indeed regarded such a book as part of a priest's essential equipment. Our earliest penitential is possibly Alfredian, and the latest – the easiest for a priest to use – may have been revised by Wulfstan. In all three cases, Worcester's scriptorium played a major part in their transmission.[78]

The fact that only three English penitentials survive does not mean that there were never very many in existence. Very few manuscripts that were made for everyday use survive. One record of one parish church's books does, that of the eleventh-century Sherburn-in-Elmet in Yorkshire. This church had nine: two Gospel books, two Epistolaries, an Antiphonary, a Gradual, a Sacramentary, a hymn-book and a Psalter. We can infer, from Aelfric's identification of the eight or ten books that every priest should have possessed, that if practice matched theory, enormous numbers of parochial books have been lost. Something similar is true at a higher level. Every bishop will have used a Pontifical and a Benedictional. There were some 120 bishops between c. 960 and 1100 and yet only nineteen such manuscripts survive.[79] Even allowing for long use there must have been more.

The extent to which public penance (which involved a bishop excommunicating and dismissing the offender from the Church on Ash Wednesday and reconciling them on Maundy Thursday) was practised is also unknown, though a variety of evidence undermines Archbishop Wulfstan II's complaint that it was infrequent.[80] Nearly half of the surviving tenth- and eleventh-century episcopal books include material for use in its ritual. Royal law-codes stipulate episcopally directed penance for a number of offences, including oath-breaking, refusal to pay tithes, marrying a nun, sorcery and murder. They thereby suggest that public penance was perceived as something that was for sins that were publicly committed, contrary to the public good, and carried the danger of imitation if they were not publicly punished.[81] Such penance was probably a great spectacle. Its performance will have been politically advantageous for the bishop who imposed it, since it was an acknowledgement of his authority.[82] It will also have been politically advantageous for the penitent. Humility before Christ, whose representatives bishops were thought to be, was regarded as a very great virtue, and one which gave earthly authority to those who possessed it. This is probably why Archbishop Dunstan was portrayed in the 'Saint Dunstan's Classbook' manuscript as prostrate before Christ.[83] With kings he was authoritative rather than humble, and in his picture in the frontispiece of a copy of the *Regularis Concordia* he shares authority with Bishop Aethelwold and King Edgar.[84]

The training and monitoring of priests

Regular synods, meetings of priests and attempts at their instruction are not recorded. There are nevertheless some indications not only that they were supposed to happen but also that they actually did.[85] The *Regularis Concordia* assumes that monasteries normally had schools. Such schools provided education for priests and future priests, as Byrhtferth of Ramsey's remarks about ignorant clerics illustrate. Aelfric wrote three texts for use in teaching Latin: a *Grammar* and *Glossary* and a *Colloquy*, that is, a set of conversations in Latin. His pupil Aelfric Bata wrote his own *Colloquies* in about 1000, possibly at Canterbury. Since the conversations are set in the context of a monastic school, they throw a little light on monastic education in general as well as on the teaching of Latin in particular. Pupils learnt reading and writing, chants, prayers and biblical texts for the Office, and to speak Latin. They learnt by memorising and from question and answer sessions with their teacher, and they were subjected to corporal punishment. Breaches of the monastic *Rule*, by both monks and pupils, in both letter and spirit, feature in Aelfric Bata's work. Examples are drinking to excess and owning private property, which Aelfric would have deprecated. This has sometimes been interpreted as evidence for poor or declining standards in monasteries.[86] But such depiction of corruption may have been a teaching device, both to make the conversation more gripping and to stimulate recollection and discussion of proper standards. The two teachers were certainly capable of sophistication in their pedagogical approach. They have been described as anticipating pedagogic theory about the teaching of speaking a foreign language by a thousand years or so.[87]

Priests were supposed to be examined before ordination, bishops to meet regularly and to supervise their diocesan priests. Candidates for ordination were to have a month's period of examination, which included doctrine and liturgy.[88] Several texts imply that meetings of bishops did take place. The pastoral letter composed by Aelfric for Wulfsige of Sherborne refers to the bishops having made decisions when they were together, about national fasting before the festivals of Mary and of the Apostles, and about the singing of a particular Mass every Wednesday in every minster and by every Mass priest in his church. Wulfstan requires bishops to have a book of canons in synod. Bishops were together at the Witan and the consecration of fellow-bishops. The *Canons of Edgar*, requiring priests to announce certain things in diocesan synods, assumes their presence there. If, for example, priests knew people in their parish who were disobedient to God and whom they could not turn to repentance, or dared not because of their worldly power, they were to proclaim it. This text is based on foreign sources but others too imply that diocesan synods happened. Bishops' pastoral letters may have been read out there, instead of, or as well as, being circulated to their priests. Certainly some, like Wulfsige's, which Wulfstan knew, reached more than their designated audience.[89] Some scholars have thought that the law-code VI Aethelred was not only a version of the 1008 Enham code but drawn up for dissemination at a diocesan synod.[90] The *Northumbrian Priests' Law* states that it was an offence for a priest to be absent from synod or to ignore his bishop's or archdeacon's summons.

Synod was not the only occasion when a bishop could examine or admonish his priests. Another was when, each year, they collected the chrism, namely the holy oils that they used in baptism, anointing the sick and in exorcisms (the purification of elements, such as salt and water, that were used in some services). The bishop blessed these on Maundy Thursday, and charged for them. Some features of the English version of the second pastoral letter that Aelfric wrote for Wulfstan suggest that it was intended for oral delivery on Maundy Thursday. Finally, meetings of the shire court could have been used for ecclesiastical conference. Whatever the meeting, priests might have memorised sermons and instructions that they heard there, in order to preach them to their congregations without needing to own or borrow a written text.[91]

Beyond the English: pastoral care in Scotland and Wales

It seems likely that in Scotland the parishes and centres whose existence has been inferred from the evidence of sculpture were centres and sources of pastoral care for the laity. The Book of Deer is evidence for some such care, at least in one region. Its smallness, portability and content imply a priest travelling around his area, on his own or with a few companions. Its abbreviated Gospels, enhanced by decoration, could have served both for his personal devotion and for use in some teaching and preaching.[92] Its bearer's activities included the visitation of the sick and preparing them for death by giving them Communion, at least from the very late tenth century, when a text for this was added.[93] Since the Church's rules required confession, and acceptance of penance, if applicable, to precede Communion and restricted Communion to baptised persons, we may further deduce that this priest also offered confession and penance, and possibly baptism too. In contrast to practice in England and on the Continent, the Deer priest did not, according to the text, anoint the sick with holy oil. There are several possible explanations, some implying poor standards, others high ones. They are clerical ignorance or neglect; difficulty in obtaining holy oil; difficulty in persuading the laity to pay for it; lay persons' fear of heavy penance and of having to perform it if they survived their illness; priestly performance of anointing from memory; Deer's (hypothetical) desire that people should seek healing from a (hypothetical) relic at Deer itself; and over-conscientious refusal of Communion on the grounds of unworthiness.[94] Such refusal, though not by the dying, is indeed attested, of late-eleventh-century churchmen, even at Easter, in the context of the reform programme inaugurated by Queen – and Saint – Margaret (died 1093). At that time it was, apparently, customary to labour on Sundays, to say Mass only on Sundays, saints' days and days especially approved by the head of the minster in question, and for some people to hear Mass celebrated by some 'barbarian' rite. If this is a reference to the vernacular, as one scholar has suggested, it is our only evidence for any vernacular liturgy.[95]

The evidence for pastoral care in Wales is greater than for Scotland, though sparse. The sources assume that baptism was available though some evidence suggests that British practice was or had been strange in some respect. It may have been that confirmation was by priests rather than by bishops, or even that confirmation was not practised.[96] Churchmen lived in minster communities, though what they were like is not clear. Latin was taught, as evidenced by Welsh glosses to a set of colloquies in a manuscript of the first half or middle of the tenth century, probably Cornish.[97] Churchmen may have travelled to care for the laity, and care could have been provided at the minsters. Ninth-century poetry probably reflects ninth-century conditions despite dealing with earlier heroes, so its references to men doing penance and taking Communion before battle suggests that by the ninth century this was normal. Early- and mid-tenth-century charters attest both penance and synods, in their records of kings making penitential donations of land to churches following judgement in synod. Alms-giving was recommended. Nothing suggests that the laity took Communion regularly or were encouraged to do so.[98]

Three kinds of evidence suggest that localised Welsh cults existed. Names of local saints are preserved in the Llandaff charters, Nennius refers to several holy and wondrous sites that attracted visitors, and many Welsh saints are scarcely known. More than a quarter have only one dedication. Only five have two. Only six have more than two. Such cults were probably dependent on oral tradition, and centred on places and relics (usually non-bodily).[99] They probably generated some pastoral care at their sites. Groups of inscribed and decorated stones may also suggest Christian centres and a possibility of pastoral care there. There is no evidence for parishes until the twelfth century. However, twelfth- and thirteenth-century mother-churches have been shown to be pre-Norman in origin, which might mean that their large parishes, which coincided with secular administrative districts, were also.[100] No portable books survive to compare with the Book of Deer or with English examples. Another dissimilarity between Wales and England is that heathenism and heathen practices never appear in the Welsh sources, such as they are, as a problem or concern.

We can identify aspirations and concerns about the provision of pastoral care to Anglo-Saxon Christians, and something about some of its achievements, including the practice of penance, before the mid-tenth century. Our picture of what was offered by the post-reform English Church is dominated by Aelfric and Archbishop Wulfstan II. The abundant and recurring complaints and anticipation of short-comings can be interpreted as despairing, ineffectual observation of failure or, as preferred here, as testimony to high standards, and meant to be inspirational. Pastoral care for the whole of society was kept under review, great energy was devoted to it and it is likely to have been effective. Alba's Book of Deer is tantalising in implying some pastoral care there. The Welsh evidence does not attest regular care in Wales, yet suggests that there were resources that could have supported it.

Notes

1 Blair, *Church*; Cubitt, *Anglo-Saxon*; Foot, *Monastic*; Yorke, *Nunneries*.
2 Pearce; Yorke, *Conversion*.
3 Cubitt, *Anglo-Saxon*.
4 For penance see Cubitt, 'Bishops'; Meens, 'Frequency'.
5 Paxton.
6 Blair, *Church*, 'Handlist', 'Saint'.
7 Foot, *Monastic*.
8 Pfaff.
9 Foot, *Monastic*; Pestell.
10 Blair, *Church*, 'Saint'.
11 Anlezark; *EHDI*: 806–807; Foot, *Monastic*.
12 Cubitt, 'Bishops'.
13 *EHDI*: 810–813.
14 *EHDI*: 813–817
15 *EHDI*: 820–821.
16 Pfaff, discussing N. Orchard's suggestion.
17 Dumville.
18 *Councils*: 46.
19 *EHDI*: 558–559.
20 Clayton, *Apocryphal*; Gatch; Scragg, 'Corpus'; N.M. Thompson; Toswell; Treharne, 'Form'; Zacher.
21 N.M. Thompson; Zacher.
22 N.M. Thompson.
23 Zacher.
24 *Councils*: 67–68.
25 Wormald, *Making*.
26 Godden; J. Hill.
27 S. Wood.
28 Giandrea; Wilcox, 'Wulfstan's'.
29 Giandrea.
30 J. Hill.
31 Cubitt, 'Virginity'; Stanley.
32 N.M. Thompson; Zacher.
33 Wilcox, *Ælfric's*.
34 Meaney, 'And', 'Old'.
35 Meaney, 'Old'.
36 Clayton, 'Hermits';
37 *Ibid.*
38 *Ibid.*
39 T.E. Powell.
40 Wormald, *Making*.
41 Godden.
42 *Ibid.*
43 Giandrea.
44 Bedingfield, *Dramatic*.
45 Jolly, *Popular*.
46 V. Thompson, 'Pastoral'; Tinti, 'Costs'.
47 A. Williams, 'Thegnly'.

48 Yorke, *Nunneries*.
49 Wilcox, 'Ælfric'.
50 Bedingfield, *Dramatic*.
51 Harte.
52 Jolly, *Popular*; Wilcox, *Ælfric's*, 'Ælfric'.
53 Wilcox, *Ælfric's*.
54 *Ibid.*
55 Godden; J. Hill.
56 Toswell, citing Pamela Robinson; Zacher. See also Giandrea; Tinti, *Sustaining*.
57 Zacher.
58 Tinti, *Sustaining*.
59 T.N. Hall; J. Hill.
60 Upchurch, *Aelfric's*, 'Homiletic'.
61 Jackson.
62 Scragg, 'Corpus'.
63 Conner.
64 Toswell; Treharne, 'Form'; Zacher.
65 Raw, 'Pictures'.
66 Gameson.
67 *Ibid.*
68 Karkov, *Ruler*.
69 Fleming, 'New'.
70 Gameson.
71 Wilcox, *Ælfric's*.
72 Bedingfield, *Dramatic*.
73 Dumville; Gittos, 'Is'.
74 V. Thompson, *Dying*, 'Pastoral'.
75 Gittos, 'Is'.
76 Corrêa, 'Liturgical'.
77 Cubitt, 'Bishops'; Meens, 'Frequency', 'Penitentials'. For penance and penitentials see also Giandrea; Tinti, *Sustaining*.
78 Cubitt, 'Bishops'.
79 Giandrea.
80 Bedingfield, 'Public'; Hamilton.
81 Hamilton.
82 V. Thompson, 'Pastoral'.
83 Gameson.
84 Cubitt, 'Archbishop'; Karkov, *Ruler*.
85 Giandrea.
86 Gwara (ed.), *Anglo-Saxon*.
87 *Ibid.*; and see D. Bullough, 'Educational'.
88 Giandrea.
89 J. Hill.
90 *EHDI*: 405.
91 Giandrea.
92 Henderson, 'Understanding'.
93 Márkus.
94 *Ibid.*
95 Warren and Stevenson.
96 J. Stevenson, in Warren and Stevenson.
97 Gwara, *Education*.
98 W. Davies, *Wales*; Pryce, 'Pastoral'.
99 Pryce, 'Pastoral'; J.R. Davies, 'Saints'.
100 Pryce, *Native*, 'Pastoral'.

12 The Christian's life

Christianity and the Church were ever-present in the life of the individual, throughout society, though how marked their involvement was must have varied over time and space, depending on the extent and quality of the pastoral care that was provided. It probably peaked in late-tenth- and early-eleventh-century England. Most of this chapter relates to that time and place. Everyday life entailed participation in Christian activities, some frequent, some only once, others depending on circumstances. All laity should have attended church weekly, and been baptised and confirmed. Many probably witnessed the baptisms and confirmations of others. Peasants probably saw the dedication of a new church only once, if ever, but aristocrats might have seen it often, in different places. The spectacle of public penance probably involved different penitents each time, but may have been available every year. Congregations were frequently warned about what constituted sin, and how it would affect their fate after death, and at the Last Judgement. Churchmen voiced anxiety about salvation and emphasised both how individuals could help themselves to achieve it, and how they could help others, including the dead, to do so. There was little, if any, sense of distinction between what would today be regarded as different worlds, the natural and the supernatural. The fact that the Old English language does not have different words for them suggests this,[1] and it is clear from the texts. God and the Church were regularly asked for help, about regular and frequent problems and concerns. Some misfortunes and sufferings were attributed to evil spirits, and some to divine punishment for sin.

Routines and special occasions

Ecclesiastics' routines

We know something of what the routine was supposed to be within monastic houses and those of secular canons in England after the reform. What it usually was in practice, however, is not certainly ascertainable. It probably varied. The English reformers themselves varied, despite their original emphasis on uniformity. The monastic routine included educating children. For some pupils, their education was the beginning of life as a religious. It was common for families to offer young children as oblates (dedicatees to a monastic life) among their gifts to monastic houses, as part of their forging of relationships with them. Thirty-five of the forty-one monks who entered Winchester's New Minster between about 1030 and about 1070 did so as oblates.[2] Monastic routine also involved study and meditation, and these were activities that vowesses and pious lay persons with the requisite resources undertook too. Many vernacular poems engage with aspects of Christianity, even if not explicitly, and so offer great scope for thought-provoking interpretation. Many of them were composed by ecclesiastics. They provided educational material in entertaining form, and might have been useful in keeping monks and nuns properly occupied and mentally focused. Homilies more obviously offer the same opportunities. The Vercelli manuscript's collection of sermons and poems together seem to have a theme – penitence, asceticism, confession and repentance.[3] Artworks in church also served this purpose. Ordinary library books seldom had much illustration, but the rich and highly placed could have pondered the illuminations in prestigious manuscripts that were meant for private or ceremonial use.[4] For example, in the ninth-century Book of Cerne the four Evangelist miniatures illustrate the four different facets of Christ's being: Incarnation (Matthew), Passion (Luke), Resurrection (Mark) and Ascension or Majesty (John). They also evoke four rites of inclusion in the Church: catechumenate, baptism, confession, the Eucharist.[5] There seems to have been a trend in Mercia at that time to compile thematic manuals for private devotion, but it was short-lived.[6]

In a monastery most of the time was spent on divine service. This incorporated intercession for both living and dead. Within the liturgical year there were special occasions, for example Easter, and feasts of particular saints, besides the daily and weekly services. Variation between major churches may have been less than some of the evidence implies. Of the surviving calendars from before c. 1100, some are very full and some not, but some compilers may have been trying to compose reference works, and others only to record the observances of their own church.[7] What happened in local churches that had only one priest was probably much more variable. Aelfric's stipulation that Mass priests sing the hours daily implies both that he thought that some did not, and that some actually did. His, and Archbishop Wulfstan II's, concern to limit the number of times a day that a priest said Mass itself implies that in many churches it would have been said at least daily.

The laity's routine

It may be that many lay people did not attain the ideal of church attendance and instruction that Aelfric set out for them: weekly and on all special occasions. Nevertheless, the large number and wide circulation of his sermons suggests that they heard his teaching every year and fairly regularly throughout the year. They would have heard works of other authors too, because Aelfric left out of his provision some feasts that were actually celebrated. Of these, some were observed in western Europe generally but others were particularly Anglo-Saxon: those of the evangelist Luke, the translation of St Benedict, Augustine of Canterbury and the Anglo-Saxons Boniface, Cedd, Dunstan, Eadburh, Edward, Guthlac, Kenelm and Mildthryth.[8] The other authors probably included Wulfstan. Though some of his sermons seem to have been meant especially for bishops, being concerned with their duties, others were not. Many concern aspects of Christian faith, and some, eschatology (the end of the world).[9] It is not entirely clear whether a sermon would normally have been regarded as part of Mass or as a supplement to it.[10] Regular announcements at services probably included notifications of forthcoming feasts and fasts, reminders that everyone should be baptised and confirmed, and, at Easter, the Rogation Days, and, at midsummer, about paying the dues that were owed to the Church. These were spread over the year. Plough-alms were due by fifteen days after Easter, tithe of young animals by Pentecost, Romescot by St Peter's Day, tithe of the fruits of the earth by All Saints, churchscot by Martinmas, lightscot by Easter Eve, Candlemas Eve and All Saints' Eve. The tithes supplied alms for the poor. Priests were to sing psalms when distributing them, and to beg the poor to intercede, that is pray, for the people.

Not every special day involved a sermon for everyone. Aelfric stipulated that there should be none on the three days before Easter Sunday, that is, Maundy Thursday, Good Friday and Holy Saturday. Others, however, disagreed. One of Archbishop Wulfstan II's surviving sermons is for Maundy Thursday. The later biographer of Bishop Wulfstan II of Worcester records that he himself disagreed, and that bishops often preached in that week. Maundy Thursday was actually an obvious and opportune occasion for a bishop to preach, addressing both laity and priests, since it was when bishops reconciled public penitents to the Church and consecrated and distributed to their priests the three holy oils that were used in services.[11]

Most routine proceedings took place inside the church, but some occurred outside, and in processions. The doorway was used at Candlemas as the place of celebration of Symeon's acceptance of the infant Christ into the Temple and served on Palm Sunday as that of the adult Christ's triumphal entry into Jerusalem.[12] Jollification became traditional at Rogationtide, but the official aim of its processions – carrying relics, the Gospels and the Cross – was unity in penance, fasting and prayer for release from suffering, especially to avoid shortage of food.[13]

Not all the days and seasons that were supposed to be observed were explicitly penitential, yet all had an element of purification and fasting about them. This was because Christians were supposed to make themselves spiritually fit, by fasting, to celebrate a Sunday and a festival by taking Communion.[14] Some holidays (a word that derives from holy days) were matters of law. This was not out of any concern that people should have leisure time and relaxation. It was to enable Christians to fulfil their religious obligations, to avoid the divine punishment of king and society that neglecting them would provoke. Alfred's law-code designates the following as holidays for all free men: twelve days at Christmas; the day on which Christ overcame the Devil (15 February); the anniversary of St Gregory (12 March); seven days at Easter and seven after; one day at the feast of saints

Peter and Paul (29 June); a week in harvest time before the feast of St Mary (probably her Nativity, 8 September, but possibly her Assumption, 15 August); and one day at the feast of All Saints (1 November). Slaves were to have the Wednesday of each of the four Ember weeks.[15] Archbishop Wulfstan II's legal texts stipulate that fines be paid for Sunday trading, for working on a feast day and for breaking a legally ordained fast.

As well as attending church and not working on Sundays, the laity's (theoretical) weekly routine included fasting on Fridays. The earliest attestation of this requirement is mid-tenth-century. Fridays between Easter and Pentecost and from Christmas to seven days after Twelfth Night were excepted. Fasting was also necessary on Ash Wednesday, in Lent and the Rogation Days. To observe a fast day probably meant to eat only one meal on that day, but there is some evidence that fasting could be replaced by alms-giving.[16] Children and sick people were exempt. Individuals might also fast, as a penitential act, on days other than those required of everybody. We lack comparable detail for Scotland and Wales. Celebration of Easter and Whitsun is attested in pre-eleventh-century Wales, as is that of some local festivals there in the eleventh century. Surviving Welsh calendars imply that there may have been more such feasts, possibly at an earlier date.[17]

Baptism, confirmation, consecration of churches, marriage, penance and the last rites

The first sacrament anyone received was baptism. This was to take place as soon as possible after birth according to Aelfric, within seven days of it according to Wulfstan's *Canons of Edgar*, but within nine days according to the *Northumbrian Priests' Law*. Baptism involved god-parents, who made promises on their god-children's behalf and were meant to teach them later on. The Church anticipated emergencies, of dying babies needing baptism: priests were always to be ready to administer it and were never to refuse it. There seems not to have been any rule regarding where babies were to be baptised and by which priest and there is some evidence that the laity could and did choose. Many people, from both town and country sought baptism for their children from Wulfstan II of Worcester whilst he was prior of Worcester monastery, that is, before 1062. This was because he did not charge a fee, which implies that other priests did, as is also suggested in Aelfric's pastoral letter for Wulfsige of Sherborne.[18] It is likely that portable fonts were used. Stone fonts became common in local churches only shortly before the Norman Conquest, and the usage of Old English *fant* in the texts suggests that until about the same time this word did not mean font in the modern sense, but rather 'waters of baptism'.[19] Baptism was followed by confirmation. This too created and involved spiritual kin and it was supposed to be performed by the diocesan bishop. There were different rites for children and adults. The latter may have included recent converts, perhaps Scandinavian settlers. Adults were confirmed at Mass, children not.[20] Most confirmations would not have had an especially spectacular context.

Some, however, would have, because, according to the biography of Bishop Wulfstan II of Worcester, preaching and confirmations would occur after a dedication of a new church.

Since the tenth and eleventh centuries saw the foundation of many local churches, this dedication ceremony too was part of episcopal routines. Even for a simple local church it would have been impressive. Its meaning was even more so, and it is likely that post-dedication sermons included explaining it. A Carolingian exposition explains that 'church' means the people who worship in the building, bound by a covenant with God, as well as the building itself. It explicitly connects the rites of baptism and of church dedication, teaching that both the building and its people are baptised and anointed, consecrated and dedicated to the service of God, the people being a New Israel, its leaders a new David and Solomon.[21] Carolingian thinking was one of the things that inspired the English reformers, and similar ideas lie behind a picture in Aethelwold's Benedictional. This implies that the believers are assimilated to the building and the bishop to the altar.[22] The dedication of a great church would have been especially awe-inspiring, because its congregation would have included more of the elite.

Probably most lay people married. In Aelfric's view, marriage was their proper function.[23] The Church's involvement in wedding ceremonies was provided for, and it probably occurred in many cases, especially in the upper levels of society where for centuries laymen had more access than peasants to churches and priests. The tenth-century text that is known as the Egbert Pontifical, which probably reflects later eighth-century practice, contains an Order of Marriage comprising a group of prayers. The same prayers occur in the Durham Collectar, following a Nuptial Mass which itself follows an earlier marriage rite that includes blessing the ring and the marital bedchamber. At parish level, the Red Book of Darley contains blessings for the bedchamber and the bed, to follow Mass.[24] The eleventh-century *Betrothal of a Woman* states that there should be a Mass priest at the marriage to unite the couple with God's blessing. A priest's involvement was not, however, legally necessary for a marriage's validity, as the issue of second and subsequent marriages makes plain. According to Aelfric, no priest was to attend a marriage where either party was taking another spouse, and a widowed layman's second marriage was not to be blessed. But he raises no doubt about such marriages' legality. Curiously, the *Handbook* for confessors does not envisage them having to deal with persons who wished to remarry.[25]

The frequency with which the laity engaged in confession and penance is debatable. Penance was emphasised particularly in Lent, as preparation for Easter. Aelfric taught that everyone should go to church on Ash Wednesday, to be smeared with ashes. Ashes, according to the Carolingian exposition of the dedication of a church, signified the consummation of Christ's Passion, for the atonement of the people. Penance would have entailed visiting the local priest, who, according to Aelfric, should have owned a penitential book. The priest should, according to one of the Vercelli homilies, have asked every penitent about each of the eight capital sins, about their thoughts as well as their deeds, have heard confession for each sin and absolved them of each, individually. It is likely that many people did engage in penance in Lent.[26] It is even more likely that most took part in the special penance that Aethelred II ordered, for 'all the nation', in response to the coming of the Scandinavian Great Army in 1009.[27] This included three days of fasting, going to church and to confession, processing with the relics, paying one penny per hide, which was to be treated like the regular tithe, giving alms and freeing slaves from work so that they could participate in these activities. Alms-giving, fasting, prayer and exclusion from taking Communion were the key elements in the performance of penance, though in some cases pilgrimage was undertaken, or imposed. Early penitential texts include physical punishment.

At least some ecclesiastics regarded confession as a rehearsal, ultimately for the Last Judgement and also for the ritual that immediately preceded death, about which the *Regularis Concordia* and the manuscript Laud Misc. 482 are particularly informative. The former relates to Winchester monks; the latter pertains probably to Worcester and concerns the laity. Other manuscripts that illuminate this subject include the Red Book of Darley and Scotland's Book of Deer. Though differing slightly in detail, the rituals for the monastic and the lay deathbed were much the same. Death was not to be a lonely experience. A priest was to be called to the sick person, to advise the lay person to bequeath their property, to encourage their confession and acceptance of penance, which could be commuted or even arranged to be performed by other people, and then to anoint them and give them Communion.[28] The Deer Book omits anointing but makes clear that the Communion will defend the recipient at the Resurrection and Last Judgement.[29] The Laud manuscript envisages several ecclesiastics participating in the visitation of the sick, perhaps reflecting a greater availability of priests in cathedral towns than in country districts.[30] The emphasis and interpretation of the ritual was much less on its function as an aid to health and recovery than it had been in earlier centuries. Now it was, essentially, preparing the soul for death.[31] In the Laud and Darley rituals the lay person's hands and feet, having been anointed, were to be dressed in linen gloves (without thumbs in the Laud) and socks. Other people would be present, singing the penitential psalms (of which there were seven). When he thought that death was imminent the priest was to read aloud from the Bible, about the death of Christ, and from other holy books, without a break until death came. He was also to ensure that the sick person understood the nature of the Trinity and of the Last Judgement.[32]

Funeral rituals and care of the dead

The dead body would be stripped and washed. Deceased monks would be laid out in clean clothes (shirt, cowl, stockings and shoes, and also a stole in the cases of monk-priests). The lay dead would be clad in a haircloth – a cloth that has penitential significance – which the priest had blessed, with ashes, in the chamber before the death. Lay dead would be laid out with head to the east, eyes covered and mouth closed.[33] Monastic funerals were to be sober and immediate. Monks who died after dark and before dawn were to be buried, if possible, before their brethren had their meal, after the Masses had been celebrated. If there was delay in making the preparations, the deceased's fellow-monks were to take turns to chant psalms continuously by the body. Before its burial the monk's body was to be carried into the church to the sound of psalms being chanted and bells tolling. As for lay funerals, Aelfric warned that priests should not attend a corpse uninvited, should forbid heathen songs and loud laughter, and not eat and drink where a corpse lies, and that prayers are more seemly than feasting and drinking. Aelfric's concerns imply that the laity held a watch over the dead before burial, that there could be competition between priests to be commissioned with it and that bereavement could immediately involve what Aelfric perceived as an improperly jolly party.[34]

This last is particularly interesting. The concern of the early Church Fathers, with whose writings Anglo-Saxon scholars were familiar, had been to discourage the weeping and wailing that had attended Roman pagan funerals, and to promote, instead, joyfulness at the soul's passing to Christ, and psalm- and hymn-singing. One of their images of salvation was in fact the heavenly feast. What Aelfric deprecated looks like a very old-fashioned, if simplistic, adherence to these earlier teachings. In his own time the Church was more pessimistic about salvation, having become so by the ninth century, and was promoting uncertainty, and community prayer to help the dead.[35]

A confraternity movement, in which individuals and monastic houses undertook to pray for each other, had spread through England as well as the Carolingian lands, and a special Office for the Dead had developed. In Winchester, for a Winchester monk the penitential psalms were to be repeated, and the Office of the Dead said in full after burial; then daily with three lessons for a week; in full on the thirtieth day. Each priest was to say a special Mass, each deacon chant the Psalter and each sub-deacon fifty psalms on each of the thirty days. For a deceased monk of another monastery but the same confraternity, the penitential psalms were to be chanted, the Office of the Dead said in full on the first, third, seventh and thirtieth days, but only in the short version on the others. His name was to be added to the list of anniversaries. An 'unknown' monk would be honoured only with prayer and one day's memory. What we know about the multiplication of Masses in monastic houses surely illuminates Aelfric's and Wulfstan's worry that local priests might say Mass too many times a day. They might have been anticipating that local priests would be asked to say Masses on a large scale for their local dead. As we have seen, Mass was regarded as an effective form of intercession, and it seems to have been perceived as making a contribution to a dead sinner's penance.[36]

The role of Mass in salvation gave the Church, and individual priests, a great deal of power and authority, over the living and the dying as well as over the dead. They applied these to the matter of the location of burials.[37] Churchyard burial of lay people was unusual in Britain in 800 but the norm in England in 1066. The change-over happened throughout the tenth century. Royal law addressed churches' entitlement to burial fees, and the earliest surviving rite for dedication of a grave-yard is from the late tenth century. Wales saw the same trend, but there it was perhaps slower and it is certainly less detectable.[38] According to the late-eleventh-century *Life* of Cadog, Llancarfan church had had the right to bury all kings, their companions, nobles, leading men and members of their households, of the kingdom of Gwynllwig, and had provided funeral vigils for laymen who bequeathed goods to the church. Some charter references suggest that Welsh churches had memorial books.[39]

Burial and funerary rites were important to the English laity. This is apparent from the surviving guild statutes, in which they loom large, even overshadowing their other aspects.[40] Guild-members in Cambridge shouldered the tasks of transporting a sick or deceased member to where he wished, or had arranged, to be buried, supplying half the provisions of the funeral feast and money for alms-giving, and paying for Masses and psalms to be said. In Exeter, deceased members would enjoy six Masses or six Psalters from each brother, and there-after, at each of the thrice-yearly meetings, a Mass and the recitation of the Psalter by each brother. Bedwyn's regulations begin with provision for dead members, of Masses or Psalters, and of bread and something to eat with it on the thirtieth day. Death is less prominent in the Abbotsbury statutes, but these too provide for transportation, within sixty miles, by fifteen brothers if the member is merely ill, by thirty if he is dead, and for money to be given for his soul.[41] Thus, just as in earlier centuries, the treatment of the dead could express and maintain social status. But it no longer did so through the material aspects of their disposal, such as the provision of grave-goods.

Burial

There are instances of special burial places for particular groups. Some societies have routinely excluded the deformed, disabled, and those thought to suffer from leprosy, from regular burial sites, but this did not happen in Europe at this date.[42] In central-southern and eastern England, perjurers and other criminals who suffered the death penalty were excluded from regular sites as part of their punishment, and buried in cemeteries that were exclusive to them. Only one execution cemetery has been found in northern England, in Yorkshire. Executed criminals had once, according to Aethelstan's laws, included thieves over the age of twelve who stole goods worth more than 8 pence, but Aethelstan raised the limits to fifteen and 1 shilling. Others were people guilty of treason or witchcraft, thieves who had failed the ordeal, and people who had violated royal or eccle-siastical sanctuary. The sites of the executions, normally by hanging or beheading, and subsequent burials are almost all (some 90 per cent) at boundaries (of hun-dreds, *burhs* or shires). They were in highly visible locations, the vast majority being associated with some sort of earthwork, twelve of the twenty-seven that are known being at mounds, in some cases specially constructed. References in texts, for example in charter boundaries, to stakes on which heads were displayed sug-gest that, though physically marginalised, the dead criminals nevertheless con-tinued to play a part in their community, as an awful warning, and as a noticeable, perhaps constant, feature in the landscape. Yet it is not necessarily the case that executions were very frequent. A rough estimate, taking into account the numbers of burials that have been found and the fact that the cemeteries were used for 500 years, is perhaps one execution per cemetery every ten years.[43]

At regular cemeteries, some parts were preferred to others. At the tenth- and eleventh-century cemetery at Raunds, there were twenty-three planned rows, and less well-ordered burials near the walls of the church.[44] This may imply that proximity to the church was regarded as particularly desirable, as it was in Francia. Children seem to be under-represented in cemeteries, which may mean that their burials involved special treatment, or places, or both, which have yet to be found, or that their mortality rate was not as high as has usually been thought, which has been suggested.[45] The Raunds remains suggest a 20 per cent mortality rate for infants under the age of one. The usual suggestion for children is 30 per cent.[46] Infants at Raunds were buried under the eaves of the church roof. It has been suggested that rainwater dripping from the eaves was thought to have a sanctifying, baptismal effect.[47] Such a belief would have been a natural consequence of how the consecration of a church was accomplished and interpreted, and a logical deduction from it. It is consistent with, and would surely have been encouraged by, what Aelfric says in one of his homilies, about a church of St Michael in Italy. There, apparently, water that dripped from the roof-stone north of the altar was collected and cured sicknesses.

No ecclesiastical ruling about the form of burial survives. Nor can one be deduced from the excavated cemeteries. Practices varied greatly, both between and within cemeteries, and there are no texts to explain the thinking behind any of them.[48] Thus at Winchester there were earth graves, stone coffins, wooden coffins, graves with pillow-stones for the head, burials with charcoal and burials with yellow sand. At York there were stone coffins, wooden coffins, domestic storage chests used as coffins, graves lined with tiles or stones, and burials with charcoal. Charcoal absorbs fluids, which bodily decay generates, and it may have been included for this reason. It may, however, have had a penitential significance. It resembles ash, which certainly did. It may have been thought that charcoal could be spiritually purifying in itself, because it can purify water, and can burn but not be destroyed by fire, which itself was often regarded as an agent of purification. Charcoal was used with coffins, inside or outside, without coffins, with stone head-supports and mixed with other substances. It was particularly common at larger churches, which might imply an element of high status about it since there were more high-status dead there. About one-fifth of the tenth- and eleventh-century excavated burials of the Old and New Minsters at Winchester involved charcoal, as did some 10 per cent of those at St Oswald's, Gloucester, with more north of the church than elsewhere. At Raunds, by contrast, only 4 per cent had pieces of charcoal whereas about half of the graves contained stones.[49] Some burials there involved coffins, and some involved shrouds. All the Raunds dead were interred in the supine position, but the placing of their heads, hands and feet varied. Some seem to have been moved from storage or from a distance rather than having been buried shortly after death. Some Anglo-Saxon bodies enjoyed more than a shroud or minimal clothing. Some pilgrims' staffs have been discovered. Three Winchester graves contained gold thread, and another some cloth of gold and decorated silver garter-tops.[50]

The use of grave-covers and grave-markers was common from the late ninth century onwards. Markers too were very varied, but some large-scale production has been detected, in the east Midlands and at York.[51] As declarations of the status and power of the deceased individual, grave-stones helped to preserve not just that person's memory, but also the power and status of their family. The numerous sculpted monuments from tenth-century northern England that bear hunting and warrior images, and which probably had religious as well as secular meanings, are very likely to have been intended to do this, since this was a time and place of change.[52] Sadly, it seems to have been normal for grave-stones to remain in place for only a few generations. At St Oswald's, Gloucester, grave-stones were removed within 100 to 150 years and broken up to serve as building rubble. At some churches, earlier pieces were set into walls. At York, stones were reused, perhaps replastered and repainted beforehand.[53]

A very few Scandinavian-style and well-furnished burials have been discovered. These too may signify (incomers') statements of control, power and authority, rather than religious dissent, their intended audience being the contemporary and future indigenous inhabitants. There were burials under mounds in the ninth century on the Isle of Man, at Chapel Hill, Balladoole and at Ballateare. What was buried includes, at the former, a boat, under a 40-feet-long and 16-feet-high boat-shaped mound, and, at both, cremated sacrificed animal remains and the body of a woman who might likewise have been a sacrifice.[54]

Evil and misfortune

The Church has always offered explanations for misfortune, methods of coping with it, and means to ward off future ill fortune and to attract good fortune, varying in different periods and places. They are well known for Anglo-Saxon England, very little for Wales and Scotland.

Health and prosperity

One explanation of illness and accident was divine, or saintly, punishment for sin. There is, though, some evidence for a perception of a physiological connection between sin and illness too. One of the Vercelli homilies, for example, states that gluttony (which was sinful) is the cause of many illnesses and of sinful desires.[55] Not everyone, however, expected misfortune to follow misdemeanour. In one of his homilies Aelfric describes, as an event perhaps a generation earlier, in Wessex, the death of someone in a bishop's household. This man had refused to be ashed on Ash Wednesday, and had subsequently been attacked by dogs and accidentally become impaled on his own spear. Another man, apparently, had nearly died while he was eating in the bishop's kitchen when he should have been observing the Lenten fast. A third, likewise in a bishop's household, had drunk in Lent from a cup that his bishop had refused to bless for him, and been subsequently crushed by a bull. The obvious inference, which Aelfric must have meant his audience to draw, is that these men's misfortunes were punishments. Yet the stories clearly demonstrate that there were, or Aelfric imagined there were, people in bishops' households who did not expect Lenten transgressions to have such consequences.

Illness was not necessarily discreditable. It could on the contrary be interpreted as a sign of divine favour, and as something that was spiritually purifying. Asser portrayed King Alfred's youthful suffering from piles as something that Alfred had asked God for, to save him from feeling, and succumbing to, sexual desire. According to Aelfric, God might permit afflictions to test people, or to preserve their true humility, and also to provide an opportunity for the working of God's miracles.

Another explanation of illness was that forces of evil caused it directly.[56] Asser recorded that the illness that Alfred suffered after his wedding feast was attributed by some people to the ill-will of the Devil, and by many others to spells and witchcraft. People believed that witchcraft existed: it appears in law-codes as something that could cause death and was to be punished, and in homilies as sinful. Yet there is almost no evidence for what its practice was thought to involve. Aelfric uses the feminine form of the word for witches, which suggests that he expected witches to be women. For him they were people whom Christians might, though they ought not, consult about their health; who worshipped stones (possibly meaning standing stones), trees and wells; made love-potions; interpreted dreams; sometimes predicted the future accurately; and tried to raise and communicate with the dead, at cross-roads and heathen graves, by which he probably meant barrows or execution cemeteries.[57] Barrows were associated with demons and dragons, as, for example, the *Life* of Guthlac and the poem *Beowulf* attest, and, according to some place-names, with goblins, elves and the Anglo-Saxon pagan god Woden.[58] But neither Aelfric nor any other homilist cites specific cases of (alleged) witchcraft. The only text to do so is a charter. It claims that a widow and her son stuck iron nails into an effigy of someone called Aelfsige, in an attempt to procure his death, and the effigy was found in her cupboard. The widow was seized and drowned. Her son escaped and became an outlaw. No trial is referred to. These events occurred in 948 or, possibly, sometime between 963 and 975. Whether witchcraft was really practised is another matter entirely.[59]

Illness was also attributed to elves. The view that the medical remedies testify to a belief in elf-shot, illness-causing missiles which were thrown by entities that were ever-present but small and hard to see, has been long held but recently challenged. Elves have been restored to human stature. They were regarded, to judge by the poet of *Beowulf*, as belonging to the progeny of Cain, like other human-like monsters, most notably Beowulf's adversaries, Grendel and his mother, all of whom were corporeal. Elves were, according to manuscript glosses, equivalents of the youthful and beautiful female nymphs of classical Antiquity. By the ninth century they were paradigms of dangerous, seductive, female beauty, but they were not normally perceived as demons. Elves' responsibility for illness, and their elf-shot, have also been disputed. The authors of the medical texts did not regard elves as the main cause of illnesses though these texts do refer to elf-associated complaints and elf-magic. In one of the three remedies in Bald's *Leechbook* that refer to elves, for example, the elves (without elf-shot) appear as only a possible, not a certain, cause of the problem.

Exactly which illnesses were thought to be elf-related is not clear. They seem to have been of three sorts: skin problems or wounds; complaints that entailed sudden stabbing pains especially in the torso; and conditions involving mind-altering symptoms, especially associated with fever (which can cause such symptoms). Chicken-pox or measles, rheumatism, arthritis, stitch, and, in the case of cattle, excess methane in the stomach caused by overfeeding on fresh grass, have all been suggested by modern scholars. Fevered conditions may have been perceived as elvish attempts to seduce the victim or to wreak vengeance for previous attempts having been rejected.[60] Finally, illness could be interpreted much more prosaically. Alfred's was thought by some people at the time to be caused by some unfamiliar kind of fever, and was attributed by others to his piles.

Aelfric taught that the holy relics, the house of God and the cross-sign were the only sources of healing that Christians should resort to, apart from 'true' leech-craft, for example the use of medicinal herbs. The relief that the Church offered to sick people was of various kinds. First of all, many healings were claimed for Anglo-Saxon shrines, and advertised in texts and, probably, orally. In late-tenth-century Winchester, St Swithun's tomb was a medical resource. Blind, dumb, paralysed and, most notably, crippled people were cured there. After Swithun's translation to St Peter's, 200 men were healed in ten days, and in twelve months the number was countless. Bishop Aethelwold's requirement that the monks praise God for every healing meant that they sometimes rose to do so four times a night.[61] In Wales, most of the miracles worked by relics were healing miracles, and in the eleventh century most relic-containing shrines were in churches.[62] Second, alms-giving, constantly recommended by the Church, was probably regarded as health improving. This is the implication of one of the psalms, where the psalmist, suffering an evil disease, asks God for mercy, having previously stated that the Lord will preserve, keep alive and deliver in time of trouble he who considers the poor.[63]

Monasteries had long been places of care for the sick: they had their own hospital areas.[64] On Scotland's May Island the church's cemetery contained a group of burials which were mixed in age and sex and showed signs of serious disease, their dates spanning the seventh to the tenth centuries. The deceased may have been on May to seek treatment, prosaically in the monastery's hospital or miraculously at St Ethernan's shrine.[65] One of the conversations in Aelfric Bata's *Colloquies* suggests that monasteries also acted as medical centres. This refers to the gardener of the monastery, the abbot's doctor, as someone who often makes good medicines and ointments and who supplies them to anyone who asks. Local, proto-parish, churches and their priests also had a medical role. Made-up remedies and ingredients that had to have Masses said over them were probably kept under altars.[66] The excessive saying of Mass that concerned Aelfric and Wulfstan might have been only partly due to parishioners wanting Masses for the dead. It could also have arisen from running out of medical supplies. It has been suggested that there were, in addition, some Church-approved medical practitioners who were not ecclesiastics. Some illustrations depict physicians without the ecclesiastical tonsure, and the relative lack in Bald's *Leechbook* of female problems (for example relating to pregnancy) may have been because, and an indication that, there were women who treated them.

Both laity and ecclesiastics had extensive recourse, in health care and in striving for prosperity, to things that had somehow been sanctified, to Christian symbols and to prayers, quite apart from using things that had had Masses said over them. Some remedies prescribe water that had been hallowed for use in baptism. One example is an ointment for headaches needing font-holy wax, which has been taken to mean wax that had been dipped in, or sprinkled with, baptismal water. Although Aelfric did not mention it, the practice of priests distributing water that had been blessed but not yet had chrism added to it had probably been allowed on the Continent, and may have been followed in England.[67] A recurrent instruction in remedies is to make the sign of the cross, or invoke it verbally. The cross was often recommended as a protective device, to ward off the Devil. One of the Blickling homilies recommends that the sign of the cross be made seven times a day. Doing so would have mimicked the liturgical hours and symbolised Creation. Aelfric taught that it should be made with three fingers, symbolising the Trinity, and made on every occasion and in every trouble.[68] Another common requirement in medical recipes is to say specified prayers, for a specified number of times, whilst making the remedy and as part of treatment. Some remedies involve exorcism of evil or alien forces, depending on words and prayer as much as, or more than, medicines.

Those who compiled and used the medical collections were not concerned merely with human ailments. They addressed veterinary, horticultural and agricultural matters too, and misfortunes such as cattle straying or being stolen.[69] The eleventh-century *aecerbot* ritual, for example, was to make land that had become unfruitful, fruitful, and to protect it from foes and from witchcraft. It too is permeated by Christianity. It includes taking a sod from each corner of the estate, blessing them, making four wooden crosses, writing the names of the four Evangelists on the four ends of each, burying them where the sods had come from and replacing the sods. It also includes prayers. Its author seems to have assumed that the practitioner would be a priest, since he had to know several prayers by heart and to be able to sing them in good Latin.[70]

Such remedies may have been effective. Not only did they express and invoke the community's commitment to whatever was at stake, but some elements were, in modern terms, scientifically sensible. The *aecerbot* ritual, including procession from fields to church and back, and lasting all day, was a communal activity that must have focused everybody's attention on the fields and their needs. In addition, it required unknown seed, taken from beggars who were to receive (twice the amount of) old seed in recompense. The new would have been free of whatever problems had afflicted the old.[71] As for the clinical effectiveness of officially sanctioned medicine, opinions have varied. Once regarded with great disfavour, it has been rehabilitated, and the rehabilitation recently challenged.[72]

There remain nevertheless at least two reasons to think that it was not useless. One is the placebo effect. The other is the beneficial effect of a sufferer's positive outlook, promoted by a specialist's care, authoritative manner and pronouncements.[73] This last, which may also have been an important element in miraculous healings, sometimes enables patients to recover, and usually helps them better to adjust to limitations caused by disease and injury, and more confidently to resume normal activity after treatment and convalescence. In this respect, the remedy for pains in the torso, which reads like a magic spell and which attributes the pains to elves, is particularly interesting. Whatever its cause, pain is generally worsened by stress and anxiety, and ameliorated by relieving them, even if only minimally. Chronic anxiety often presents as suspect sensation in the digestive tract. It is not hard to imagine many Anglo-Saxons being anxious, perhaps rationally so.

Interpretations and responses

The Church taught that the various misfortunes of humankind were consequences of the Fall, that the Devil was the ultimate source of evil, that he had the power to do harm and that his purpose in doing so was to undermine people's faith and to estrange them from God. Thus Archbishop Wulfstan II thought that the Devil not only sent afflictions but also prompted people to respond to them by vowing offerings to a spring or stone or 'forbidden' things. The correct Christian response was to rely on faith and God's power, and to refuse to permit any evil to be done to one's soul: whatever happened to one's body, one's soul could be protected.

Misfortune did not necessarily suggest divine disfavour. There was nevertheless an expectation that divine disfavour and approval would indeed manifest themselves through ill or good fortune. Behind the law-code IV Edgar, for example, was clearly a perception that recent pestilence was punishment. King and archbishop command that nobody merit death by any withholding of God's dues. Instead, everyone is to pay their tithes. In his 966 charter for New Minster, Winchester, Edgar justified the expulsion of the canons from his kingdom's monasteries on the grounds that they 'provoked God's vengeance', doing things which God did not wish and not things which He did wish.[74] Later, Aelfric used Old Testament figures to show that idolatry led to shame and failure, pious living to worldly success.[75] So did authors of vernacular poems about biblical events and figures. Victories in battle were interpreted as signs of piety, correct worship and God's blessing, and defeats as punishments for abandoning His law.

Such teaching is sometimes uncomfortable, and can give rise to perplexity, to difficult cases of interpretation, and to new interpretations. One such was that of the early-ninth-century Welsh Nennius. Nennius provided a different interpretation of the fifth-century invasions and conquests which he recounted to that of Bede, whose view had been that they were divine punishment for the sinfulness of the Britons, blaming their leader Vortigern instead and offering hope of future

British success against the Anglo-Saxons.[76] Other reinterpretations may lie in the cults of murdered kings and other royal persons in Anglo-Saxon England. It has been suggested that they were not essentially or entirely political, originating in royal sponsorship, but rather a popular reaction to the unexpectedness and injustice of the events in question and a rebuttal of their implications of divine disfavour.[77] The best example is that of King Edmund of East Anglia.[78] The late-ninth-century evidence concerning his death in 869 is that he died in battle against Vikings. Abbo's late-tenth-century (sometime between 985 and 987) account, in which he used oral tradition that included stories told by Edmund's arms-bearer to Archbishop Dunstan and then by Dunstan to Abbo, shows that Edmund had subsequently come to be seen very differently. In this version Edmund had refused to fight, but had offered to submit if the Viking leader would convert to Christianity, which he would not. This meant that Edmund had effectively chosen to die, and had not truly been defeated. Since this is what the Church teaches about Christ, Edmund's choice had been Christ-like. This interpretation would certainly have offered political advantages to East Anglians if West Saxon kings had ever tried to use Edmund's defeat to claim divine approval of their conquest of the East Anglian Danelaw. But it may have originated in spontaneous lay devotion. In this and some other cults certain features indicative of such an origin recur in the stories: severed heads, dismembered corpses, holy trees and wells, a strong topographical element, and vengeance miracles. Royal cults of this kind are detectable before as well as after the coming of the Vikings. An earlier East Anglian king, Aethelbert, who fell victim to Offa of Mercia in 794, was seen as a saint in the ninth century, according to the list of saints' resting places, though the earliest surviving account is that by Byrhtferth of Ramsey, written after 997.[79]

Some people in the late tenth and early eleventh centuries thought that England's political and social misfortunes were caused by sin, though not by especially personal ones, such as sexual sins. They feared that failure to reform carried the risk of losing dominion over England and of being expelled from it, that God might use the Vikings to punish the English just as He had once used the English to punish the Britons.[80] This anxiety permeates Archbishop Wulfstan II's writings, and explains his attempts to provide blueprints for a People of God. It is especially marked in his 1014 *Sermon of the Wolf*. There he explicitly recalls the Britons and their fate, accuses the English of worse deeds than were known of the Britons and urges repentance and reform. He picks out failure to keep God's laws, meaning for example rules about marriage and respecting widows and sanctuary, failure to pay God's dues, meaning spoliation of ecclesiastical property as well as failure to pay Church dues, and failures of loyalty that marked recent political events.[81] To these sins Wulfstan attributed various unpleasant experiences, including Viking violence and oppression. Earlier, Aelfric had stated that the heathens (Scandinavians) were a punishment for monasteries having been cast down and God's worship having been held in scorn. This complaint dovetails with evidence in charters that Aethelred II and his advisers worried that the lay confiscation or repossession of monastic property that

Aethelred had allowed early in his reign had displeased God and thus produced the Viking raids.[82] Such fears were entirely logical, given the sanctions contained in some earlier charters. Edgar's 966 Winchester New Minster charter had in fact threatened exactly what had happened and was happening. Its curse on anyone who diminished the monastery's property included misery and misfortune, the hatred of the Virgin and the saints, and ravaging enemies to plunder all their property.

There is some evidence, especially in the poetry, that history was conceived as cyclical, with a repeating pattern: kingdoms would rise and fall; peoples would deserve and receive God's favour, then become proud, then sinful, then be punished and replaced by others.[83] Large-scale and continuing misfortunes also prompted a different view, namely that the end of the world was near. For the Bible predicts that the end will be preceded by signs, which include various misfortunes and sufferings that are very similar to things that actually happened between 800 and 1066. The unorthodox teaching of Pehtred, which circulated in Northumbria in the 830s, seems to have expressed and appealed to apocalyptic fears inspired by the Vikings. Two homilies that draw ultimately on Pehtred's (lost) book developed the motif of Noah as an apocalyptic preacher. They testify to a long and continuing tradition of these ideas, for they draw on a lost homily that was written after 962, contain elements that go back to the 920s at least and survive in eleventh-century manuscripts.[84]

The imminence of the year AD 1000 made no significant contribution to the stimulation of English apocalyptic expectations. One of the Blickling homilies announces that the end is very near. Another stresses that its time is secret, known only to the Lord. Its author regarded the several thousands of years into which God had supposedly divided the ages of the world, the one inaugurated by the life of Christ being the final one, as only approximations. In his view they had varied in length, and whether the current thousand would turn out to be shorter or longer only the Lord knew. Aelfric anticipated that there would be many more perils before the end and he was very cautious about its timing, since, as he said, battle comes after battle and famine after famine but still the end does not. Nevertheless, he also thought that it was close, and that people needed scholarly teaching that would strengthen them against a temptation that was to beset them. For the Antichrist, an entity that was both man and devil, was to come, and reign for three and a half years. He would try to persuade people to accept him as God, by proclaiming himself to be God, by working signs and wonders, including miracles of healing, though only where he himself had caused the affliction, and by terror and persecution. Those who resisted him would be martyred and go to Heaven, those who were deceived or yielded would be damned.[85] In 1014 Wulfstan implied, in his *Sermon of the Wolf*, that the end would be very soon. It is possible that he equated Danish conquest, which he feared might happen, with the rule of Antichrist. His successive versions of the sermon show that he subsequently reverted to a cyclical view of history, though even in Cnut's reign he warned that everyone should be prepared for the end.[86]

Sin and salvation

Sin

Anglo-Saxons did not all define sin and its causes in the same way, or have the same ideas about how to secure salvation or about life after death. There were changes over time, and differences of opinion between contemporaries. Instances we have seen are the West Saxon kings' turning sin into crime against king and state, and vice versa, and debate about the sinfulness of clerical marriage and of ecclesiastical involvement in war.

There was generally agreement that waging war was not sinful in itself. Nevertheless, shades of opinion about war are identifiable. Aelfric followed the Church Fathers in distinguishing between unjust and just war. He defined as just war that which was waged 'against the violent seamen or against other peoples that wish to destroy a land'.[87] He tried in his teaching to encourage such war, as some of the omissions and inclusions of his coverage of saints suggest. He omitted Guthlac from his *Lives of Saints* despite Guthlac's popularity, perhaps because, as a warrior who withdrew from the world, he did not seem to Aelfric an appropriate model to offer to his lay audience. His decision to include the forty soldiers of Sebasteia, in Armenia, must have been a considered one, for their feast seems not to have been observed in Winchester, where Aelfric had been trained, though it was elsewhere in England. These martyrs had been successful soldiers. They had refused to give up Christianity when they were ordered to, and been tortured. Only one of them had betrayed the faith, and their number had been made back up to forty by a guardsman who, impressed by them, changed sides. They must have seemed to be appropriate models, because their story showed not only that war was acceptable to God, but also that warriors could become saints. Aelfric was concerned not only about ecclesiastics' wrongly thinking that it was right for ecclesiastics to fight, but about laymen wrongly thinking that it was wrong to do so themselves.[88]

Different views about the righteousness of war are also discernible in the vernacular poetry, though the difficulty of dating the poems precisely means that such differences are less easy to explain by reference to the Viking threat. *Elene* seems to sanctify defensive war, the not-yet-Christian emperor Constantine being represented as acting defensively against non-Christian enemies. *Juliana*, by contrast, seems to recommend spiritual rather than physical struggle, judging by its heroine's activity and by the fact that it is less violent than the Latin original that lies behind it. Different again is *Andreas*, whose hero is a model not only of willing martyrdom but also of a holy warrior. He is presented as willingly putting himself at risk, to rescue the apostle Mathew from cannibals, and as engaging in offensive as well as defensive acts.[89]

Sin is treated in a variety of texts. Some refer to it in rather general terms, others much more precisely, and the same authors offered their audience variations on the same theme. Archbishop Wulfstan II's works for example provide several lists of sins.[90] They include: disloyalty and treachery; sale of family members; buying and selling women for sexual purposes; forcing widows to marry; selling the poor to foreigners; enslaving children for petty theft; violating sanctuary; the worship of springs, stones, trees, idols, heathen gods, sun, moon, fire, flood; sacrifice and divination; witchcraft. Some sins were omissions, or deeds, that deprived God of His due.[91] These included failure to fast in the six weeks of Lent. This was because the exemption of Sundays made the fast thirty-six days, that is, one-tenth of a year (conceived as 360 days), and thus an offering to God of a tithe of one's body. Sexual intercourse in Lent was a worse offence than breaking the Lenten fast. Failure to observe Sundays, which caused Pehtred great concern in the ninth century and was castigated in later legal texts, could also be considered as refusing God His dues.

Some sins were deemed trivial, others major. Sins were sometimes defined as actions, like murder, and sometimes as attitudes that might lead to sinful actions, like covetousness, which might lead to stealing and false witness. Aelfric regarded greed as the root of all evil, and defined 'light offences' as idle speech, too much food and drink, sexual intercourse more often than was necessary for procreation, unnecessary or spiteful chiding, flattery, reviling the imploring poor and immoderate gaming. His 'deadly sins' in the same homily are murder, church-breach, sex with someone else's wife, false witness, stealing, rapine, covetousness, vainglory, pride, envy, constant drunkenness, idolatry, sorcery and witchcraft. Eight is often the number of major sins. In the Vercelli homilies the eight capital sins are greed for food, adultery, slackness and sadness, avarice, vainglory, envy, anger, and pride – pride being deemed the worst. One Blickling homily regards envy and slander as kinds of murder, and includes among the inhabitants of Hell those who deprive men wrongfully of their property, the proud, magicians who practise enchantments and deceits and wean men from contemplation of God, evil reeves who give wrong judgements and evil judges. Sexual activity was permissible only within marriage, and to be eschewed in Lent, on feast and fast days, during menstruation and pregnancy and for a period after childbirth. The penitential texts suggest that homosexual activity, both male and female, occurred and was censured.[92] Behaviour that confused the ordering of society could also be thought sinful. Secular clergy were not to wear monks' or laymen's clothes, for which offence they were to be excommunicated, as were men wearing women's clothes and women wearing men's. One of the Vercelli homilies states that suicides are damned when they die, as are heathen men and Jews.

The repeated stress, for example in homilies and in the deathbed ministry of priests, on the necessity of all the people having right belief, especially about the Trinity and the nature of Christ (both divine and human), suggests that something else that counted as a sin was wrong belief.[93] The writers do not, however, suggest that they thought, rightly or wrongly, that there was any active heretical movement holding and spreading incorrect views about basic points of doctrine: Aelfric, for example, presents the fourth-century Arius as a dangerous and heretical figure in history, not as a current threat. Their anxiety seems to have been about the possibility of the people's misunderstanding complex ideas, and as such is suggestive of active teaching and thinking. Wulfstan did not include heresy in his catalogues of offences, but he did include lack of belief. In one of his sermons he presents belief in the true resurrection of the flesh as essential for salvation. Finally, some sins were peculiar to priests and bishops. Neglect of their duty of instructing the people, especially about confession and penance, would cause their eternal condemnation.

Sins were the opposite of virtues, and virtues too were identified and defined for the faithful. Right belief, namely knowledge, acceptance and some under-standing of the Creed, was one. The Virgin Mary was praised for her obedience and meekness. Aelfric required penitents to forgive those who had angered them. He thought that the chief sins could be overcome by moderation, chastity, gen-erosity, patience, 'ghostly' joy, steadfastness, inward love and humility. Aelfric Bata defined Christian works both negatively and positively: fleeing drunkenness; not being proud or envious; not stealing, lying, perjuring, bearing false witness or committing adultery; chastity; frequent visits to church to pray; honouring elders; giving to the poor; hospitality to strangers; promoting harmony; teaching one's son and neighbours, by admonition and good example, to live chastely and soberly; remembering and obeying the Creed, Lord's Prayer and other prayers; teaching one's own and others' sons to keep themselves faithful.

Routes to Heaven

Baptism cleansed a person from sin and was a requirement for salvation, but unless it was a deathbed baptism it was not enough. Baptised people sinned and their sins had to be dealt with. One method was donation to the Church. This was often in exchange for intercession, but the English may have shared the view attested by the charters of the influential monastery of Cluny in Burgundy, that donation had a redemptive effect in itself.[94] The Britons in Wales probably agreed. Inscriptions there recording that so-and-so raised a cross for the soul of another imply that the very act would benefit the deceased. It is possible too that the monument itself was perceived as engaging in intercession.[95] It was this redemptive effect of donation that made the offence of spoliation of church property especially dangerous for its perpetrators. Taking ecclesiastical property entailed taking responsibility for the sins of the original donor(s), as many English charters threaten. Grants had been made, as it were, as compensation to God for these sins, or to sustain the religious who interceded for the dead. To deprive God of His compensation and a church of its financial resource was simulta-neously to resurrect the debt of the donor(s), and to deprive them of intercession.

The belief that donation and intercession were efficacious is manifest in the texts, especially wills and charters. Perhaps the most explicit statement about the importance of intercession is Edgar's, in his 966 New Minster charter, justifying his expulsion of canons: they had been of no benefit to him with their intercessory prayers and he had replaced them with monks who were pleasing to the Lord. Records routinely state that donations, including manumissions of slaves, have been made for the salvation of the soul. Donors request prayers for the souls and for those of their relatives, and occasionally the details of what donor and beneficiary had agreed are specified.[96] Examples abound. In the late-tenth-century will of Aethelgifu, freedom for a slave is conditional on the singing of a stated number of Psalters. The early-eleventh-century manumission at Liskeard in Cornwall of Aelfgyth, by Aethelflaed, wife of Ealdorman Aethelweard, was for her own and her husband's souls. In Wales, monuments at the monastery of Llantwit Major were erected for the benefit of their patrons and others, these being kings and their families, other lay patrons and churchmen. The inscription at Odda's chapel at Deerhurst, which was dedicated in 1056, states that Odda founded the chapel for the soul of his brother Aelfric.

Exactly how the dead were prayed for varied, according to place, period and resources. The greatest in society and at least some others profited from daily prayer. King Edward the Elder, according to his charters, built Winchester's New Minster for the sake of his and his father, King Alfred's, souls and required daily prayers of intercession for both of them and for their ancestors. Edward's sister, Aethelflaed of Mercia, and her husband gave rights in Worcester to the bishopric of Worcester and in return, both before and after their deaths, the canons were to sing a specified psalm at three daily offices and thirty psalms and a Mass every Saturday. According to Winchester New Minster's *Liber Vitae*, the names in the list of those to be commemorated were recited daily in one of the Masses. Aethelgifu's will stipulates three Masses each week for herself and her husband. Less frequent prayer was also requested and anticipated. The inscription in a manuscript that King Aethelstan gave to Bath Abbey, possibly contemporary, requests whoever reads it to pray for him and his friends. In the ninth century, the inscription on the Cornish Redgate, or Doniert, stone requested prayer for Doniert's soul, and that on the Welsh Elise Pillar did the same for Elise's. A complete catalogue of such requests and requirements would be overwhelming. The efficacy of Masses, and prayers for the dead, was, according to one of the Blickling homilies, very annoying for the devils. This was because they had many souls in their power that would ultimately escape because of intercession.

Living canons, priests, monks and nuns were not the only intercessors available. Beyond them were the dead saints, and above these and the angels was the Virgin Mary.[97] Some people thought that Mary would have an effective intercessory role even at Judgement Day, saving some sinners after Christ had condemned them. In some anonymous texts and in an ivory, she is pictured to the right of Christ at Judgement Day, whilst St Peter is to His left. Both of them, as also the archangel Michael, intercede with Him for sinners. One Vercelli homily represents Mary, Michael and Peter successively saving one-third of the crowd of sinners.[98] The number, though not the proportion, of individuals saved is smaller in each round. Only one-third (nearly) of the original damned crowd remain damned. And at a mundane level, kin, friends and especially the poor were thought to be effective intercessors. Alms-giving is continually recommended, both in Welsh sources and in Anglo-Saxon ones, where it is repeatedly stressed as efficacious for salvation. In the Vercelli homilies three kinds of alms-giving are identified: bodily (the giving of gifts); spiritual (forgiving people who have sinned against oneself); and the reproof of sinners and bringing the erring to right. In the Blickling homilies, failure to give alms is something that will lead to Hell. Alms-giving, it is implied, is redemptive in itself. Sometimes, however, it is explicitly stated that the beneficiaries have a duty to pray for their benefactors. Aelfric taught that rich and poor needed each other – the rich to give alms, the destitute to pray for their benefactors – and that the poor are the way to God's kingdom, giving the rich eternal life. The poor themselves were not exempt from alms-giving: the needy were to give alms according to their capacity.

A virtuous life, patronage, alms-giving and intercession could each lead to Heaven. A fifth route was through pilgrimage. There are very few specific references to people below the highest levels of society going on pilgrimage to foreign sites. Yet such pilgrimage may be under-reported. The will of the thegn Ketel, made some time between 1052 and 1066, refers to a forthcoming visit to Rome. Another will, made between November 1066 and about 1068, by Ulf and his wife Madselin, was apparently made 'when they went to Jerusalem'. The Exeter guild statutes require members to contribute 5 pence each if one of their number undertakes a pilgrimage south, which can only mean overseas.[99] Such an eventuality seemed, in Exeter, as plausible and normal as the deaths and burning down of houses that the statutes also provided for.

Like donations and alms-giving, pilgrimage could be undertaken as a penitential act. Penance was not merely one among several mechanisms for attaining salvation. It was the most efficacious, and an essential requirement. This is clear from the Church's stress on priests' deathbed duties and the reiteration that no person near to death who wished to confess, including healthy but condemned criminals, should ever be refused. Furthermore, in sermon after sermon, by author after author, the audience is urged to repent, and is warned that intercession after their deaths will not release them from eternal torments if they have not repented beforehand, by confession and making satisfaction to a man of God. But it is reassured that there was no sin so great that confession and true repentance (which included atonement and cessation of the sin) would be in vain.

Salvation could, therefore, be represented as possible for everybody. Aelfric was optimistic about it. Another cause for optimism was teaching about the causes of sin. Sin was thought to be the result of demonic temptation, and the Devil the source of all misdeeds. But, as was most clearly and often proclaimed by Aelfric, sin was also a matter of free will, and although Christians needed God's help to do good, and God had foreknowledge of what would occur, there was no predestination. Christians were advised to pray, to strengthen their willpower and for God's help.

Christians had invisible enemies, devils who set traps for them. They also had powerful invisible allies, the angels. Aelfric featured angels in nearly three-quarters of his sermons and enunciated the view, derived from St Paul, that every Christian has a guardian angel, to support them in virtue and to shield them against demonic machinations and temptations. The Blickling homilies are a little more circumspect, implying that only particularly holy people have them, but they are equally clear that the role of the angels is to help against hell-fiends, acting as a shield. Angels were also thought to attend the liturgy, and in the liturgy men were thought to be joining in the angels' perpetual worship of God. Some Mass prayers were thought to be of angelic origin.[100] Archbishop Wulfstan II states, in Cnut's laws, that angels hover around and protect baptisms and the consecration of the host in Mass, helping the priests.

After death

There are apparent inconsistencies in what was taught and believed about what would happen after death. Some of these may arise from literary and rhetorical devices, not meant literally. Thus one vernacular poem announces that the soul will visit the body in the grave every week for 300 years unless the end of the world happens before this time is up, to rebuke it for its sins, for which the soul will be suffering. The poet implies that the body is sentient, though unable to speak. There is other evidence too for an expectation of life in the grave. This includes Aelfric's ideas about the activities of witches. Some people thought that *mod* (the mind or emotion) was part of the body, and some burials suggest a concern, perhaps for symbolic, but possibly for literal, comfort in the grave, for example in provision of a pillow-stone for the head. Yet there was also conviction that the body would rot, be food for worms, and become dust, spelt out in the poetry and sermons.[101]

Though it is clear that people wanted intercession, exactly what intercession was thought to be for is less so.[102] One purpose was to complete penances that sinners had accepted but not finished. Ecclesiastical intercession may sometimes have been regarded as an act of formal absolution of the dead penitent. Sometimes intercession may have been meant to protect the soul on its journey from the body to its next domicile. Accounts of deaths of martyrs of the early Church involve souls being borne to Heaven by angels, with demons trying to prevent their passage, and a prayer in the Book of Cerne hopes for a safe journey, to a pleasant place, to rest there until the Resurrection.[103] The otherworld had been scrutinised by Christian writers long before the conversion of the Anglo-Saxons, and they continued the process. A vision recounted, and thus endorsed, by Bede, teaches that it is four-fold in structure, but will be only two-fold after the Last Judgement. In the vision there is Hell, Heaven and two waiting places for souls who will eventually reside in Heaven. Condemned souls are suffering in Hell. Souls who had repented and confessed but only at the point of death are awaiting Judgement Day in a very unpleasant place of painful punishment. Others, who had died practising good works, are waiting in a pleasant, flowery place. Those who were perfect at death are in Heaven itself. Prayers, alms, fastings and especially Masses are stated to help free many of the souls from the punishment place before Judgement Day. So intercession must have been thought to help a soul to progress from the unpleasant waiting place to the pleasant one.[104] A cynical view would be that this two-fold purgatory had been shaped by the Church to explain and justify the demands that it made on the living, rather than that the Church made those demands in response to belief and anxiety about the afterlife.

The teaching of the vision seems to be that the flowery place is an interim paradise, and that passage from it to Heaven, eventually, will be automatic. This, however, was not the only view. There are other ideas elsewhere in Bede's works. Late-eighth- and early-ninth-century private prayers and some anonymous homilies accept the interim paradise, but the funeral liturgy that is likely to have been used then seems not to. Some of the Cerne prayers give it the function of a courtroom. It seems that by the eleventh century, official teaching was that intercession was necessary both for admission to the pleasant waiting area and for transfer thence to Heaven.[105]

The end of the world and the Last Judgement were expected to follow the reign of Antichrist and be preceded by a series of signs. According to one anonymous text, six days before Doomsday all the limbs of dead people, however scattered they are, will reassemble themselves, and each body will rise as far as the top margin of the grave, and four days later all living people will die.[106] After the cleansing of the earth by fire and flood will come the bodily resurrection. In this, one of the Blickling homilies says, the body will be as transparent as glass. According to Aelfric, it will be clad in spiritual garments, and according to some others, Aelfric implies, its grave-shroud. The Last Judgement will follow. This, according to another Blickling homily, was expected to be around Good Friday, the day of Christ's Crucifixion, though in another, at the season of Easter Day.

There is only one surviving narrative representation of the Last Judgement in Anglo-Saxon art. The drawings in the *Liber Vitae* of the New Minster in Winchester show first a procession into Heaven, with a group led by an abbot and by a lay figure who looks like King Cnut. This group has been presumed to represent the people whose names were, and would be, inscribed in the book. On the next page is a scene representing the trial of souls. St Peter has the key to Heaven, an angel and a demon each have a book, presumably recording good and bad deeds respectively, a figure is held by Peter and a demon and two figures are carried away by a winged demon. Above this scene is Peter with his key at Heaven's gate; below it an angel locks the door of Hell with two keys. By contrast, in a Vercelli homily it is Peter who locks Hell.[107]

Hell is represented in poetry and sermons as an abyss, a dwelling place of fiends, dark, fiery, a prison and place of everlasting torments, of extreme heat and cold, wild beasts, gnawing serpents and devils' taunting, terror, hunger and nakedness, misery and anxiety, sickness and weeping, where figures writhe.[108] It is a place of bodily suffering. In a Christ Church, Canterbury, manuscript, one artist gives the demons talons and claws, breasts and genitalia; another suggests that Hell was underground the present earth, as indeed Pope Gregory I had thought.[109] Ideas in Scotland may have been similar, for some of the sculpture there, for example at Meigle, depicts torments of the damned and what may be a purgatory.[110]

Heaven, traditionally referred to as a heavenly city – heavenly Jerusalem – seems to have been felt to be unknowable and indescribable: Aelfric commented that no man's heart can conceive the things that God prepares for those that love Him. In Anglo-Saxon texts, visions of Hell are more numerous and more detailed than those of Heaven, which tends to be described in terms of abstractions and in opposition to Hell, for example, joy, rest, freedom from pain and from care, lightness and brightness. It was also conceptualised in terms of the 'ideal indoors': a lord's splendid hall, and in a *burh*, securely fortified but containing also the green open space, or garden, with sweet-scented flowers, which are associated with the interim paradise.[111] In the Winchester drawing it resembles a castle, with towers and a courtyard.[112]

English evidence allows us partially to reconstruct the regular and less routine experiences of Christians in later Anglo-Saxon England, professional and lay, individuals and communities, high and low, personal and public, their timetables through the year, their rites of passage and how the Church offered practical and effective help in matters of health. We do not know what everybody thought about the questions that perplex humanity: Why are we here? What is it all for? Why do we suffer? How can we bear it? The meaning of life, the universe, everything? Is there anything more? But we know what they were taught to think, and what they were offered: Heaven, or the interim paradise, which some texts suggest was the Garden of Eden. This was the homeland, from which, because of the Fall, we are exiles in this world.

Notes

1 V. Thompson, *Dying*.
2 Cubitt, 'Virginity'.
3 Toswell.
4 Gameson; Raw, 'Pictures'.
5 Brown, *Book*.
6 *Ibid.*
7 Rushforth.
8 Lapidge, 'Ælfric's'.
9 T.N. Hall; J. Hill.
10 Gatch; N.M. Thompson.
11 Teresi; Tinti, *Sustaining*.
12 Gittos, 'Architecture'.
13 S.J. Harris, 'Liturgical'; Harte.
14 Lee; Upchurch, *Ælfric's*.
15 *EHDI*: 380.
16 Lee.
17 W. Davies, *Wales*.
18 Tinti, *Sustaining*.
19 Blair, *Church*; C.A. Jones, 'Old'.
20 Giandrea; Tinti, *Sustaining*.
21 Repsher.
22 Karkov, *Ruler*.
23 Jackson.
24 K.W. Stevenson.
25 Fletcher; McCarthy.
26 Bedingfield, 'Public'; Cubitt, 'Bishops'; Giandrea; Means, 'Frequency', 'Penitentials'; Tinti, *Sustaining*.
27 *EHDI*: 410.
28 V. Thompson, *Dying*.

29 Márkus.
30 V. Thompson, *Dying*.
31 Márkus.
32 V. Thompson, *Dying*; Tinti, *Sustaining*.
33 Tinti, *Sustaining*.
34 Lee. For funerals see also Fleming, 'Rural'; Lee; Thompson, *Dying*; Tinti, *Sustaining*; H. Williams.
35 Paxton; McLaughlin.
36 McLaughlin; Cubitt, 'Virginity'; Muschcol.
37 Effros.
38 H. James; Longley.
39 W. Davies, *Wales*.
40 A. Williams, 'Thegnly'.
41 V. Thompson, *Dying*; *EHDI*: 557–560.
42 For England see S. Crawford, 'Differentiation'; Hadley, 'Burying'.
43 A. Reynolds, *Anglo-Saxon*.
44 Blair, *Church*; Boddington.
45 S. Crawford, *Childhood*, 'Children'; Steckel.
46 F. Powell.
47 Blair, *Church*.
48 V. Thompson, *Dying*. For burial practices see also Hadley, 'Negotiating', 'Burial'; Hadley and Buckberry; Lucy and Reynolds; Tinti, *Sustaining*.
49 V. Thompson, *Dying*; Holloway.
50 V. Thompson, *Dying*.
51 *Ibid.*
52 Hadley, 'Negotiating'.
53 Heighway; V. Thompson, *Dying*.
54 H. Williams.
55 Scheil.
56 For illness, magic, medicine, see Cameron; B. Griffiths; A. Hall; Pollington.
57 J. Crawford.
58 Semple, 'Fear'.
59 J. Crawford; Pollington.
60 A. Hall.
61 Webb, *Pilgrimage*.
62 W. Davies, *Wales*.
63 Pratt, 'Illnesses'.
64 Foot, *Monastic*.
65 Yeoman.
66 Jolly, *Popular*.
67 C.A. Jones, 'Old'.
68 D.F. Johnson; Jolly, 'Cross-Referencing', 'Tapping'.
69 Jolly, 'Tapping'.
70 Niles, 'Æcerbot'.
71 *Ibid.*
72 Cameron; Pettit; Pollington.
73 Pollington.
74 Trans. in Rumble, *Property*.
75 Klein.
76 Higham, *King*.
77 Cubitt, 'Sites'; Damon.
78 Damon.
79 Cubitt, 'Sites'.
80 Howe, *Migration*.

81 Cowen.
82 Cubitt, 'Archbishop'.
83 Anlezark; Lionarons; Scheil.
84 Anlezark.
85 Cowen; Lionarons.
86 Lionarons.
87 Bachrach; Damon; Whatley.
88 Damon; Whatley.
89 Damon.
90 Meaney, 'And', 'Old'.
91 Baxter, 'Archbishop'.
92 Payer.
93 Raw, *Trinity*.
94 Rosenwein, *Neighbor*.
95 Higgitt, 'Words'.
96 Foot, *Monastic*, *Veiled* I; Giandrea; Yorke, *Nunneries*.
97 Mayr-Harting, 'Idea'.
98 Clayton, *Cult*.
99 Wareham, *Lords*.
100 Mayr-Harting, *Perceptions*; Peterson; Rios.
101 V. Thompson, *Dying*.
102 Kabir.
103 *Ibid*.
104 *Ibid*. For afterlife and otherworld, see also Gurevich; Semple, 'Fear', 'Illustrations'; V. Thompson, *Dying*.
105 Kabir.
106 B. Griffiths.
107 Karkov, *Ruler*.
108 Kabir.
109 Semple, 'Illustrations'.
110 G. Henderson and I. Henderson.
111 Kabir.
112 Karkov, *Ruler*.

Conclusion

1066

There was much that was unpleasant about politics and society and difficult about life in Britain between 800 and 1066, as studies of the material remains have made plain.[1] Responsibility for some of its unprepossessing features lay with its Christian inhabitants and in the wider context of the history of Christianity and the Church some episodes offer readers a tale of sexism, villainy, mis-information and persecution. Nevertheless, in this case their contributions to the human experience were overwhelmingly positive, though not faultless. This conclusion follows from scrutiny of the provenance, context, purpose and layers of meaning of the evidence, not merely its overt content.

Nowadays stimulating national identity can seem dangerous and unfortunate. The Church seems not to have done this in Wales and Scotland but certainly did in England, where it also contributed to the formation of a state, and strong government and sophisticated administration that was unmatched in western Europe at the time. Justice, order, security, wealth, health, psychological support, respect for women and their contributions to the good of society and what it valued, the decline of slavery, enhancement of the landscape and built environ-ment, engagement with the entirety of the population, an inclusive society, pro-fessional self-appraisal, a sense of belonging to a world wider than the European, that of Christendom, can be set to its account. What the Church achieved in Wales and Scotland is frustratingly far less within our reach, but similarities included sophistication of thought and learning, broad horizons, individuality and idiosyncrasy. Evocative, and in Pictland often mysterious, sculpture connected generations over centuries.

In 1065 the English Church was on the eve of two of the most dramatic and far-reaching upheavals in British and in European history, though it is often difficult to distinguish the consequences of one from the other. The conquest of England by William of Normandy in 1066 installed a new military aristocracy and royal government of brutal power. In Rome control of the Papacy was seized by reformers who aimed at nothing less than a transformation of the Church in Latin Christendom, embodied in the demand for a celibate priesthood free of obligation to secular lords. Both were revolutionary, involved sudden and violent upheaval, and were justified by their proponents by sweeping repudiation of the old order as illegitimate, corrupt and condemned by its defiance of the will of

God.[2] In England they were consciously and deliberately allied. William launched his invasion under a banner of St. Peter – sent by Pope Alexander II, who boosted his own authority in doing so – to legitimise his claim to the English throne. Just as English lords were replaced in their lands by his Norman followers, English bishops and abbots were denounced as corrupt and immoral, and their sees and monasteries, in the name of reform, were filled by William's men, drawn from the courts, as well as the monasteries, of Normandy and its neighbours. Among the transformations wrought by the new order one of the fastest, and certainly the most visible, was that of the sacred landscape. Cathedrals, abbeys and parish churches in the latest and grandest architectural style, larger by far than those they replaced, towered over settlements and dominated skylines, as many of them still do today.

Disregard for, even obliteration of the history and achievements of the English Church was as necessary to this work as the destruction of its leaders and buildings. Its defamation prevailed until the mid-twentieth century, and lingered beyond. It was perceived through a thick and distorting lens of victors' hindsight, all the more effective because it was crafted by one of the most talented generations of historians that England has ever seen, including Ordericus Vitalis and William of Malmesbury, Henry of Huntingdon and John of Worcester, whose account this book has chosen to set aside. Yet the victory was not quite so complete as it looks, in two ways at least that are particularly revealing. Despite identifying with the achievements of the conquerors in Church and State, many of the post-Conquest historians were of English or part-English descent, knew that they drew on a tradition of monastic learning that went back far beyond the conquest, and did much to preserve its memory. In the same years communities throughout the land venerated hermits and holy men and women, many again of English blood. These individuals resolved communities' quarrels and nourished their memories, and often acted as intermediaries with the conquerors, translating for village priests who could not speak the language of their bishops, and, through the influence that they secured over many leaders of the new order, softening the brutalities of conquest. They represented the lasting influence of the Anglo-Saxon Church among its people, the last instances of its leadership and its service to them.

Notes

1 Fleming, *Britain*.
2 Moore, *First*.

Bibliography

Primary sources

Aelfric, *Catholic Homilies*, translated in B. Thorpe (ed. and trans.), *The Homilies of the Anglo-Saxon Church*, 2 vols. (1844–186).

——, *Lives of the Saints*, translated in W.W. Skeat (ed. and trans.), *Aelfric's Lives of Saints*, 4 vols. (1881–1900, reprinted 1966 as 2 vols.).

——, *Lives of the Virgin Spouses*, translated in R.K. Upchurch, *Ælfric's Lives of the Virgin Spouses* (2007).

——, *Prefaces*, translated in J. Wilcox, *Ælfric's Prefaces* (1994).

Aelfric Bata, *Colloquies*, translated in S. Gwara (ed.).

Alfred, translations of some of his work in *EHDI*; Keynes and Lapidge, *Alfred*.

Anglo-Saxon Chronicle, translated in *EHDI*.

Apocryphal Gospels of Mary, texts and translations in Clayton, *Apocryphal*.

Armes Prydein (The Prophecy of Britain), translated in R. Bromwich, *Armes Prydein: The Prophecy of Britain* (1972), J.P. Clancy, and Isaac.

Asser, *Life of King Alfred*, translated in Keynes and Lapidge, *Alfred*.

Bald, *Leechbook*, Book III, text and translation in Pollington, 378–407.

The Blickling Homilies, translated in R. Morris (ed. and trans.), *The Blickling Homilies of the Tenth Century* (1880, reprinted 1967).

Calendars, see Rushforth.

Charms, translated in B. Griffiths, 171–204.

Charters, texts and translations at www.aschart.kcl.ac.uk; translations of some in *EHDI*; text and translation of King Edgar's Winchester New Minster refoundation charter in Rumble, *Property*, 74–97.

Chronicle of the Kings of Alba, translated in Hudson, 'Scottish', 152–161.

Church Councils, see *Councils and Synods*.

Corpus of Anglo-Saxon Stone Sculpture, Volumes I (Part 1 and Part 2, 2 vols.), II–IX, various authors (1984–2010).

A Corpus of Early Medieval Inscribed Stones and Stone Sculpture in Wales, Volume I, M. Redknap and J.M. Lewis, *Breconshire, Glamorgan, Monmouthshire, Radnorshire, and Geographically Contiguous Areas of Herefordshire and Shropshire* (2007). Volume II, N. Edwards, *South-West Wales* (2007).

Councils and Synods, texts and translations in D. Whitelock, M. Brett, and C.N.L. Brooke (eds.), *Councils and Synods with Other Documents Relating to the English Church* (2 vols.), Volume I 871–1204, Part I 871–1066 (1981).

Domesday Book, Domesday Book: A Complete Translation (2002).

The Early Christian Monuments of Scotland, John Romilly Allen's and Joseph Anderson's *The Early Christian Monuments of Scotland: A Classified, Illustrated, Descriptive List of the Monuments, with an Analysis of their Symbolism and Ornamentation* (1903): reissued with introduction by I. Henderson (2 vols.) (1993).

The Early Christian Monuments of Wales, see Nash-Williams.

EHDI, D. Whitelock (ed.), *English Historical Documents* c. *500–1042* (1968).

Historia de Sancto Cuthberto, text and translation in Johnson South.

Hywel Dda, *Laws*, translated in M. Richards, *The Laws of Hywel Dda (The Book of Blegywryd)* (1954). And in D. Jenkins, *The Law of Hywel Dda: Law Texts from Medieval Wales. Translated and Edited* (1990).

Inscriptions, see *Corpus*; *Early Christian*; Nash-Williams; Okasha.

Lacnunga (Remedies), text and translation in Pollington, 184–247, and in Pettit, Volume I, 4–131.

Laws (English), see *EHDI* for translations.

Liber Eliensis, translated in Fairweather.

The Life of King Edward who rests at Westminster, translated in F. Barlow (ed. and trans.), *The Life of King Edward who Rests at Westminster, Attributed to a Monk of Saint Bertin* (2nd edn. 1992).

Litanies, see Lapidge (ed.), *Anglo-Saxon*.

Liturgy, see Corrêa (ed.), *Durham*; Warren and Stevenson.

Nennius, *History of the British*, text and translation in J. Morris (ed. and trans.), *Nennius: British History and the Welsh Annals* (1980).

Old English Martyrology, translated in G. Herzfeld (ed. and trans.), *An Old English Martyrology* (1900).

Old English Orosius, translated by B. Thorpe in R. Pauli, *The Life of Alfred the Great* (1853), 238–528.

Penitentials, translated in Gamer and McNeill.

Poetry (Old English), translated in S.A.J. Bradley (ed. and trans.), *Anglo-Saxon Poetry: An Anthology of Old English Poems in Prose Translation with Introduction and Headnotes* (1982).

Poetry (Scottish), translated in T.O. Clancy, *Triumph*.

Poetry (Welsh), translated in J.P. Clancy.

Prophecy of Berchán, translated in Hudson, *Prophecy*.

Regularis Concordia … , text and translation in T. Symons (ed. and trans.), *Regularis concordia Anglicae nationis monachorum sanctimonialiumque: the Monastic Agreement of the Monks and Nuns of the English Nation* (1953).

Rhygyfarch, *Life of Saint David*, text and English translation in R. Sharpe and J.R. Davies, 'Rhygyfarch's *Life* of St David' in Evans and Wooding (eds.), 107–155.

Rite of Church Dedication (Carolingian), translated in Repsher.

Sculpture, see entries for *Corpus*; *Early Christian*; Fisher.

Symeon of Durham, *Libellus de Exordio atque Procursu istius, hoc est Dunhelmensis Ecclesiae*, translated in D. Rollason (ed. and trans.), *Symeon of Durham: Libellus de Exordio atque Procursu istius, hoc est Dunhelmensis Ecclesiae. Tract on the Origins and Progress of this, the Church of Durham* (2000).

The Vercelli Book Homilies, translated in L.E. Nicholson (ed.), *The Vercelli Book Homilies: Translations from the Anglo-Saxon* (1991).

Welsh Annals, text and translation in J. Morris (ed. and trans.), *Nennius: British History and the Welsh Annals* (1980).

Wills, D. Whitelock, *Anglo-Saxon Wills. Edited with Translation and Notes* (1930).

Wulfstan of Winchester, *The Life of St. Æthelwold*, translated in Lapidge and Winterbottom.

Wulfstan of Worcester and York, *Canon Law Collection*, text and translation in J.E. Cross and A. Hamer (eds.), *Wulfstan's Canon Law Collection* (1999).

——, Laws, see *Councils and Synods*; *EHDI*.

——, *Sermon of the Wolf to the English*, translated in *EHDI*, 855–859.

Secondary sources

Abels, R., *Alfred the Great. War, Kingship and Culture in Anglo-Saxon England* (1998).

Abrams, L., *Anglo-Saxon Glastonbury: Church and Endowment* (1996).

——, 'The Conversion of the Danelaw', in Graham-Campbell, Hall, Jesch and Parsons (eds.), 31–44.

——, 'Edward the Elder's Danelaw', in Higham and Hill (eds.), 128–143.

——, 'Conversion and the Church in the Hebrides in the Viking Age: "A Very Difficult Thing"', in B.B. Smith, S. Taylor and G. Williams (eds.), *West Over Sea: Studies in Scandinavian Sea-Borne Expansion and Settlement Before 1300* (2007), 169–193.

——, 'King Edgar and the Men of the Danelaw', in Scragg (ed.), 171–191.

Abrams, L. and Parsons, D.N., 'Place-names and the History of Scandinavian Settlement in England', in Hines, Lane and Redknap (eds.), 379–431.

Airlie, S., 'The View from Maastricht', in B.E. Crawford (ed.), 33–46.

Aitchison, N., *Forteviot: A Pictish and Scottish Royal Centre* (2006).

Alcock, E. 'Burials and Cemeteries in Scotland', in Edwards and Lane (eds.), 125–129.

Anderson, B., *Imagined Communities: Reflections on the Origin and Spread of Nationalism* (1983).

Anderton, M. (ed.), *Anglo-Saxon Trading Centres: Beyond the Emporia* (1999).

Anlezark, D., *Water and Fire: The Myth of the Flood in Anglo-Saxon England* (2006).

Arnold, C.J. and Davies, J.L., *Roman and Early Medieval Wales* (2000).

Astill, G., 'Community, Identity and the Later Anglo-Saxon Town: The Case of Southern England', in Davies, Halsall and Reynolds (eds.), 233–254.

Audouy, M. and Chapman, A. (ed.), *Raunds: The Origin and Growth of a Midland Village AD 450–1500* (2009).

Bachrach, D.S., *Religion and the Conduct of War c.300–1215* (2003).

Bailey, M., 'Ælfwynn, Second Lady of the Mercians', in Higham and Hill (eds.), 112–127.

Baker, N. and Holt, R., 'The Origins of Urban Parish Boundaries', in T.R. Slater and G. Rosser (eds.), *The Church in the Medieval Town* (1998), 209–235.

Balchin, W.G.V., *The Cornish Landscape* (1983).

Barrett, J.H., 'Culture Contact in Viking Age Scotland', in J.H. Barrett (ed.), *Contact, Continuity, and Collapse: The Norse Colonization of North Atlantic* (2003), 73–111.

Barrow, J., 'The Community of Worcester, 961–c.1100', in Brooks and Cubitt (eds.), 84–99.

——, 'Churches, Education and Literacy in Towns, 600–1300', in D.M. Palliser (ed.), *The Cambridge Urban History of Britain I: 600–1540* (2000), 127–152.

——, 'Survival and Mutation: Ecclesiastical Institutions in the Danelaw in the Ninth and Tenth Centuries', in Hadley and Richards (eds.), 155–176.

——, 'Wulfstan and Worcester: Bishop and Clergy in the Early Eleventh Century', in Townend (ed.), 141–159.

——, 'The Clergy in English Dioceses c. 900–c. 1066', in Tinti (ed.), 17–26.

——, 'The Chronology of Forgery Production at Worcester from *c.* 1000 to the Early Twelfth Century', in Barrow and Brooks (eds.), 105–122.

——, 'The Chronology of the Benedictine "Reform"', in Scragg (ed.), 211-23.

Barrow, J. and Brooks, N.P. (eds.), *St Wulfstan and his World* (2005).

Barrow, J. and Wareham, A. (eds.), *Myth, Rulership, Church and Charters: Essays in Honour of Nicholas Brooks* (2008).

Bassett, S., 'The Administrative Landscape of the Diocese of Worcester in the Tenth Century', in Brooks and Cubitt (eds.), 147–173.

——, *The Origins of the Parishes of the Deerhurst Area* (1998).

——, 'Boundaries of Knowledge: Mapping the Land Units of Late Anglo-Saxon and Norman England', in Davies, Halsall and Reynolds (eds.), 115–142.

Baxter, S., 'Archbishop Wulfstan and the Administration of God's Property', in Townend (ed.), 161–205.

——, *The Earls of Mercia: Lordship and Power in Late Anglo-Saxon England* (2007).

Baxter, S., Karkov, C., Nelson, J.L. and Pelteret, D. (eds.), *Early Medieval Studies in Memory of Patrick Wormald* (2009).

Beckett, K.S., *Anglo-Saxon Perceptions of the Islamic World* (2003).

Bedingfield, M. Bradford, *The Dramatic Liturgy of Anglo-Saxon England* (2002).

——, 'Public Penance in Anglo-Saxon England', *Anglo-Saxon England* 31 (2002), 223–255.

Biddle, M. and Kjølbye-Biddle, B., 'Repton and the "Great Heathen Army" 873–4', in Graham-Campbell, Hall, Jesch and Parsons (eds.), 45–96.

Biggs, F.M., 'Edgar's Path to the Throne', in Scragg (ed.), 124–139.

Blackburn, M., 'Expansion and Control: Aspects of Anglo-Scandinavian Minting South of the Humber', in Graham-Campbell, Hall, Jesch and Parsons (eds.), 125–142.

——, 'Alfred's Coinage Reforms in Context', in Reuter (ed.), 199–217.

Blair, J., 'A Saint for Every Minster? Local Cults in Anglo-Saxon England', in Thacker and Sharpe (eds.), 455–494.

——, 'A Handlist of Anglo-Saxon Saints', in Thacker and Sharpe (eds.), 495–565.

——, *The Church in Anglo-Saxon Society* (2005).

Blair, J. and Sharpe, R. (eds.), *Pastoral Care Before the Parish* (1992).

Blanton, V. and Scheck, H. (eds.), *Intertexts: Studies in Anglo-Saxon Culture Presented to Paul E. Szarmach* (2008).

Blinkhorn, P., 'Of Cabbages and Kings: Production, Trade and Consumption in Middle-Saxon England', in Anderton (ed.), 4–23.

Boardman, S., Davies, J.R. and Williamson, G., *Saints' Cults in the Celtic World* (2009).

Boddington, A., *Raunds Furnells. The Anglo-Saxon Church and Churchyard* (1996).

Boenig, R. and Davis, K. (eds.), *Manuscript, Narrative, Lexicon: Essays on Literacy and Cultural Transmission in Honor of Whitney F. Bolton* (2000).

Bonner, G., Rollason, D. and Stancliffe, C. (eds.), *St Cuthbert, His Cult and His Community to AD 1200* (1989).

Breeze, A., 'Cornwall and the Authorship of the Old English Orosius', *Notes and Queries* n.s., 38 (June 1991), 152–154.

——, 'Cornish *Donua* "Danube" and the Old English Orosius', *Notes and Queries* n.s., 39 (December 1992), 431–433.

——, 'Edgar at Chester in 973: A Breton Link?', *Northern History* 44 (1) (2007), 153–157.

Brooks, N., 'Canterbury, Rome and the Construction of English Identity', in J.M.H. Smith (ed.), *Early Medieval Rome and the Christian West: Essays in Honour of Donald A. Bullough* (2000), 221–247.

Brooks, N. and Cubitt, C. (eds.), *St Oswald of Worcester: Life and Influence* (1996).

Broun, D., 'The Origin of Scottish Identity in its European Context', in B.E. Crawford (ed.), 21–31.

——, 'The Birth of Scottish History', *Scottish Historical Review* 76 (1997), 4–22.

——, 'Pictish Kings 761–839: Integration with Dál Riata or Separate Development?', in Foster (ed.), 71–83.

——, '*Alba* as "Britain" after 900 and the Pictish Antecedents of the Kingdom of the Scots', in his *Scottish Independence and the Idea of Britain* (2007), 71–97.

——, 'The Property Records in the Book of Deer as a Source for Early Scottish Society', in Forsyth (ed.), 313–360.

Brown, M.P., *The Book of Cerne: Prayer, Patronage and Power in Ninth-Century England* (1996).

——, 'Building Babel: the Architecture of the Early Written Western Vernaculars', in A.J. Duggan, J. Greatrex and B. Bolton (eds.), *Omnia disce: Medieval Studies in Memory of Leonard Boyle, O.P.* (2005), 109–128.

Brubaker, L. and Smith, J.M.H. (eds.), *Gender in the Early Medieval World. East and West, 300–900* (2004).

Bruce-Mitford, R. and others, *Mawgan Porth: A Settlement of the Late Saxon Period on the North Cornish Coast* (1997).

Buchelt, L.C., 'All About Eve: Memory and Re-Collection in Junius 11's Epic Poems *Genesis* and *Christ and Satan*', in S.S. Poor and J.K. Schulman (eds.), *Women and Medieval Epic: Gender, Genre, and the Limits of Epic Masculinity* (2007), 137–158.

Buckberry, J. and Cherryson, A. (eds.), *Burial in Later Anglo-Saxon England c. 650–1100* AD (2010).

Bullough, D.A., 'The Educational Tradition in England from Alfred to Ælfric: Teaching *utriusque linguae*', *Settimane di Studi del Centro Italiano di Studi sull' Alto Medioevo* 19 (1972), 453–494.

——, 'Hagiography as Patriotism: Alcuin's "York Poem" and the Early Northumbrian "vitae sanctorum"', in E. Patlagean and P. Riché (eds.), *Hagiographie, cultures, et sociétés. IVe–XIIe siècles* (1981), 339–359.

——, 'Alcuin and the Kingdom of Heaven: Liturgy, Theology, and the Carolingian Age', in U.-R. Blumenthal (ed.), *Carolingian Essays* (1983), 1–69.

——, 'Burial, Community and Belief in the Early Medieval West', in P. Wormald et al. (eds.), *Ideal and Reality in Frankish and Anglo-Saxon Society* (1983), 177–201.

——, 'St Oswald: Monk, Bishop and Archbishop', in Brooks and Cubitt (eds.), 1–22.

Bullough, V. and Campbell, C., 'Female Longevity and Diet in the Middle Ages', *Speculum* 55 (1980), 317–335.

Burghart, A., Review of Pratt, *The Political …* , *The Times Literary Supplement* no. 5450 (14 September 2007).

Burghart, A. and Wareham, A., 'Was there an Agricultural Revolution in Anglo-Saxon England?', in Barrow and Wareham (eds.), 89–99.

Cameron, M.L., *Anglo-Saxon Medicine* (1993).

Campbell, J., 'The Church in Anglo-Saxon Towns', in D. Baker (ed.), *Studies in Church History* 16 (1979), 119–135.

——, *Bede's* Reges *and* Principes (Jarrow Lecture 1979).

——, 'Asser's *Life of Alfred*', in C.J. Holdsworth and T.P. Wiseman (eds.), *The Inheritance of Historiography 350–900* (1986), 115–135.

——, 'The United Kingdom of England: The Anglo-Saxon Achievement', in A. Grant and K.J. Stringer (eds.), *Uniting the Kingdom? The Making of British History* (1995), 31–47.

——, 'What is Not Known about the Reign of Edward the Elder', in Higham and Hill (eds.), 12–24.

——, 'Domesday Herrings', in C. Harper-Bill, C. Rawcliffe and R.G. Wilson (eds.), *East Anglia's History: Studies in Honour of Norman Scarfe* (2002), 5–17.

——, 'Aspects of Nobility and Mobility in Anglo-Saxon society', in P. Coss and C. Tyerman (eds.), *Soldiers, Nobles and Gentlemen: Essays in Honour of Maurice Keen* (2009), 17–31.

——, 'Archipelagic Thoughts: Comparing Early Medieval Polities in Britain and Ireland', in Baxter, Karkov, Nelson and Pelteret (eds.), 47–63.

——, 'Questioning Bede', in M. Henig and N. Ramsay (eds.), *Intersections: The Archaeology and History of Christianity in England, 400–1200* (2010), 119–127.

Cannadine, D. and Price, S. (eds.), *Rituals of Royalty. Power and Ceremonial in Traditional Societies* (1987).

Carver, M., *Portmahomack: Monastery of the Picts* (2008).

Ciggaar, K.N., *Western Travellers to Constantinople: The West and Byzantium, 962–1204: Cultural and Political Relations* (1996).

Charles-Edwards, T.M. (ed.), *After Rome* (2003).

Charles-Edwards, T.M. 'The Making of Nations in Britain and Ireland in the Early Middle Ages', in Evans (ed.), 11–37.

——, 'Picts and Scots', *Innes Review* 59 (2) (2008), 168–188.

——, *Wales and the Britons 350–1064* (2013).

Clancy, J.P., *Medieval Welsh Poems* (2003).

Clancy, T.O. (ed.), *The Triumph Tree. Scotland's Earliest Poetry AD 550–1350* (1998).

Clancy, T.O., 'Scottish Saints and National Identities in the Early Middle Ages', in Thacker and Sharpe (eds.), 397–421.

——, 'Deer and the Early Church in North-Eastern Scotland', in Forsyth (ed.), 363–397.

Clayton, M. (ed. and trans.), *The Apocryphal Gospels of Mary in Anglo-Saxon England* (1998).

Clayton, M., *The Cult of the Virgin Mary in Anglo-Saxon England* (1990).

——, 'Hermits and the Contemplative Life in Anglo-Saxon England', in Szarmach (ed.), 147–175.

Coatsworth, E., 'The Embroideries from the Tomb of St Cuthbert', in Higham and Hill (eds.), 292–306.

Conner, P.W., 'Parish Guilds and the Production of Old English Literature in the Public Sphere', in Blanton and Scheck (eds.), 255–271.

Cooper, J. (ed.), *The Battle of Maldon: Fiction and Fact* (1993).

Corrêa, A. (ed.), *The Durham Collectar* (1992).

Corrêa, A., 'Daily Office Books', in R.W. Pfaff (ed.), *The Liturgical Books of Anglo-Saxon England* (1995), 45–60.

——, 'The Liturgical Manuscripts of Oswald's Houses', in Brooks and Cubitt (eds.), 285–324.

Cowen, Alice, '*Byrstas* and *bysmeras*: The Wounds of Sin in the *Sermo Lupi ad Anglos*', in Townend (ed.), 397–411.

Coz, Y., 'The Image of Roman History in Anglo-Saxon England', in Rollason, Leyser and Williams (eds.), 545–558.

Cramer, P., *Baptism and Change in the Early Middle Ages, c. 200–c. 1150* (1993).

Crawford, B.E. (ed.), *Scotland in Dark Age Britain* (1996).

Crawford, B.E., *Scandinavian Scotland* (1987).

Crawford, J., 'Evidences for Witchcraft in Anglo-Saxon England', *Medium Aevum* 32 (1963), 99–116.

Crawford, S., 'Children, Death and the Afterlife in Anglo-Saxon England', *Anglo-Saxon Studies in Archaeology and History* 6 (1993), 83–91.

——, *Childhood in Anglo-Saxon England* (1999).

——, 'Differentiation in the Later Anglo-Saxon Burial Ritual on the Basis of Mental or Physical Impairment', in Buckberry and Cherryson (eds.), 93–102.

Crick, J., 'Women, Posthumous Benefaction and Family Strategy in Pre-Conquest England', *The Journal of British Studies* 38 (4) (1999), 399–422.

——, 'Edgar, Albion and Insular Dominion', in Scragg (ed.), 158–170.

——, 'Insular History? Forgery and the English Past in the Tenth Century', in Rollason, Leyser and Williams (eds.), 515–544.

Cross, J.E. and Hamer, A., (eds.), *Wulfstan's Canon Law Collection* (1998).

Cubitt, C., *Anglo-Saxon Church Councils c.650–c.850* (1995).

——, 'Sites and Sanctity: Revisiting the Cult of Murdered and Martyred Anglo-Saxon Royal Saints', *Early Medieval Europe* 9 (2000), 53–83.

——, 'Virginity and Misogyny in Tenth- and Eleventh-Century England', *Gender and History* 12 (2000), 1–32.

——, 'Universal and Local Saints in Anglo-Saxon England', in Thacker and Sharpe (eds.), 423–454.

——, 'Bishops, Priests and Penance in Late Saxon England', *Early Medieval Europe* 14 (2006), 41 63.

——, 'Archbishop Dunstan: A Prophet in Politics?', in Barrow and Wareham (eds.), 145–166.

Damico, H., '*Beowulf*'s Foreign Queen and the Politics of Eleventh-Century England', in Blanton and Scheck (eds.), 209–240.

Damon, J.E., *Soldier Saints and Holy Warriors: Warfare and Sanctity in the Literature of Early England* (2003).

Darby, H.C., *Domesday England* (1977).

Davidson, A., 'The Early Medieval Church in North-West Wales', in Edwards (ed.), *Archaeology*, 41–60.

Davies, J.R., 'The Book of Llandaf: a Twelfth-Century Perspective', *Anglo-Norman Studies* 21 (1999), 31–46.

——, 'The Saints of South Wales and the Welsh Church', in Thacker and Sharpe (eds.), 361–395.

——, 'Bishop Kentigern among the Britons', in Boardman, Davies and Williamson (eds.), 66–90.

Davies, W., *An Early Welsh Microcosm: Studies in the Llandaff Charters* (London: Royal Historical Society, 1978).

——, *The Llandaff Charters* (1979).

——, *Wales in the Early Middle Ages* (1982).

——, *Patterns of Power in Early Wales* (1990).

——, 'The Myth of the Celtic Church', in Edwards and Lane (eds.), 12–21.

——, 'Adding Insult to Injury: Power, Property and Immunities in Early Medieval Wales', in Davies and Fouracre (eds.), *Property* … , 137–164.

Davies, W. and Fouracre, P.J. (eds.), *The Settlement of Disputes in Early Medieval Europe* (1986).

——, *Property and Power in the Early Middle Ages* (1995).

Davies, W., Halsall, G. and Reynolds, A. (eds.), *People and Space in the Middle Ages, 300–1300* (2006).

Davis, Kathleen, 'National Writing in the Ninth Century: A Reminder for Postcolonial Thinking about the Nation', *Journal of Medieval and Early Modern Studies* 28 (1998), 611–637.

——, 'The Performance of Translation Theory in King Alfred's National Literacy Program', in Boenig and Davis (eds.), 149–170.

Davison, M.R., 'The (Non)Submission of the Northern Kings in 920', in Higham and Hill (eds.), 200–211.

Dekker, K., 'Pentecost and Linguistic Self-Consciousness in Anglo-Saxon England: Bede and Ælfric', *Journal of English and Germanic Philology* 104 (2005), 345–372.

Deshman, R., *The Benedictional of Æthelwold* (1995).

Driscoll, S.T., 'Formalising the Mechanisms of State Power: Early Scottish Lordship from the Ninth to the Thirteenth Centuries', in S.M. Foster, A. MacInnes and R. MacInnes (eds.), *Scottish Power Centres from the Early Middle Ages to the Twentieth Century* (1998), 33–58.

——, *Alba: The Gaelic Kingdom of Scotland, AD 800–1124* (2002).

——, *Govan: From Cradle to Grave* (2004).

——, 'Pictish Archaeology: Persistent Problems and Structural Solutions', in Driscoll, Geddes and Hall (eds.), 245–279.

Driscoll, S.T., Geddes, J. and Hall, M.A., (eds.), *Pictish Progress: New Studies on Northern Britain in the Early Middle Ages* (2011).

Dumville, D.N., *Liturgy and the Ecclesiastical History of Late Anglo-Saxon England: Four Studies* (1992).

Duncan, A.A.M., *The Kingship of the Scots, 842–1292: Succession and Independence* (2002).

Dyas, D., *Pilgrimage in Medieval English Literature, 700–1500* (2001).

Dyer, C., 'Towns and Cottages in Eleventh-Century England', in H. Mayr-Harting and R.I. Moore (eds.), *Studies in Medieval History Presented to R.H.C. Davis* (1985), 91–106.

——, 'St Oswald and 10,000 West Midland peasants', in Brooks and Cubitt (eds.), 174–193.

——, *Making a Living in the Middle Ages: The People of Britain, 850–1520* (2002).

——, 'Bishop Wulfstan and his Estates', in Barrow and Brooks (eds.), 137–149.

Edwards, N., 'Identifying the Archaeology of the Early Church in Wales and Cornwall', in J. Blair and C. Pyrah (eds.), *Church Archaeology Research Directions for the Future* (1996), 49–62.

——, 'Landscape and Settlement in Medieval Wales: An Introduction', in Edwards (ed.), *Landscape*, 1–11.

——, 'The Irish Connection', in Foster (ed.), 227–239.

——, 'Early-Medieval Inscribed Stones and Stone Sculpture in Wales: Context and Function', *Medieval Archaeology* 45 (2001), 15–39.

——, 'Monuments in a Landscape: The Early Medieval Sculpture of St David's', in Hamerow and MacGregor (eds.), 53–77.

——, 'Celtic Saints and Early Medieval Archaeology', in Thacker and Sharpe (eds.), 225–265.

——, 'Rethinking the Pillar of Eliseg', *Antiquaries Journal* 89 (2009), 143–177.

——, 'Viking-Age Sculpture in North-West Wales: Wealth, Power, Patronage and the Christian Landscape', in F. Edmonds and P. Russell (eds.), *Tome: Studies in Medieval Celtic History and Law in Honour of Thomas Charles-Edwards* (2011), 73–87.

Edwards, N. (ed.), *Landscape and Settlement in Medieval Wales* (1997).

——, *The Archaeology of the Early Medieval Celtic Churches: Proceedings of a Conference on the Archaeology of the Early Medieval Celtic Churches, September 2004* (2009).

Edwards, N. and Lane, A. (eds.), *The Early Church in Wales and the West* (1992).

Effros, B., 'Beyond Cemetery Walls: Early Medieval Funerary Topography and Christian Salvation', *Early Medieval Europe* 6 (1997), 1–23.

Evans, J.W. and Wooding, J.M. (eds.), *St David of Wales: Cult, Church and Nation* (2007).

Evans, R. (ed.), *Lordship and Learning. Studies in Memory of Trevor Aston* (2004).

Fairweather, J., *Liber Eliensis. A History of the Isle of Ely from the Seventh Century to the Twelfth* (2005).

Faith, R., *The English Peasantry and the Growth of Lordship* (1997).

——, 'Cola's *tūn*: Rural Social Structure in Late Anglo-Saxon Devon', in Evans (ed.), 63–78.

Faull, M.L., 'The Semantic Development of Old English *Wealh*', *Leeds Studies in English* n.s., 8 (1975), 20–44.

Fell, C.E., *Women in Anglo-Saxon England* (1984).

Fisher, I., *Early Medieval Sculpture in the West Highlands and Islands* (2001).

Fleming, R., 'Monastic Lands and England's Defence in the Viking Age', *English Historical Review* 100 (1985), 247–265.

——, 'Rural Elites and Urban Communities in Late-Saxon England', *Past and Present* 141 (1993), 3–37.

——, 'The New Wealth, the New Rich and the New Political Style in Late Anglo-Saxon England', *Anglo-Norman Studies* 23 (2001), 1–22.

——, *Britain After Rome: The Fall and Rise 400 to 1070* (2011: first published 2010).

Fletcher, R., *Bloodfeud: Murder and Revenge in Anglo-Saxon England* (2003).

Foot, S., 'The Making of *Angelcynn*: English Identity before the Norman Conquest', *Transactions of the Royal Historical Society* 6th series, 6 (1996), 25–49.

——, 'Remembering, Forgetting and Inventing: Attitudes to the Past in England at the End of the First Viking Age', *Transactions of the Royal Historical Society* 6th series, 9 (1999), 185–200.

——, *Veiled Women Volume I: The Disappearance of Nuns from Anglo-Saxon England* (2000).

——, *Veiled Women Volume II: Female Religious Communities in England, 871–1066* (2000).

——, 'The Historiography of the Anglo-Saxon "Nation-state"', in Scales and Zimmer (eds.), 125–142.

——, *Monastic Life in Anglo-Saxon England, c. 600–900* (2006).

——, 'When English Becomes British: Rethinking Contexts for *Brunanburh*', in Barrow and Wareham (eds.), 127–144.

——, 'Dynastic Strategies: The West Saxon Royal Family in Europe', in Rollason, Leyser and Williams (eds.), 237–53.

——, *Æthelstan: The First King of England* (2011).

Forde, S., Johnson, L. and Murray, A.V. (eds.), *Concepts of National Identity in the Middle Ages* (1995).

Forsyth, K. (ed.), *Studies on the Book of Deer* (2008).

Forsyth, K., 'Literacy in Pictland', in Pryce (ed.), 39–61.

——, 'The Stones of Deer', in Forsyth (ed.), 398–438.

Forsyth, K., Broun, D. and Clancy, T., 'The Property Records: Text and Translation', in Forsyth (ed.), 131–144.

Foster, S.M. (ed.), *The St Andrews Sarcophagus. A Pictish Masterpiece and its International Connections* (1998).

Foster, S.M., *Picts, Gaels and Scots* (2004).

Fraser, J.E., *From Caledonia to Pictland: Scotland to 795* (2009).

——, 'Rochester, Hexham and Cennrígmonaid: The Movements of St Andrew in Britain, 604–747', in Boardman, Davies and Williamson (eds.), 1–17.

——, 'From Ancient Scythia to *The Problem of the Picts*: Thoughts on the Quest for Pictish Origins', in Driscoll, Geddes and Hall (eds.), 15–43.

Gamer, H.M. and McNeill, J.T. (trans.), *Medieval Handbooks of Penance* (1979).

Gameson, R., *The Role of Art in the Late Anglo-Saxon Church* (1995).

Gameson, R. and Leyser, H. (eds.), *Belief and Culture in the Middle Ages: Studies Presented to Henry Mayr-Harting* (2001).

Gatch, M.McC., *Preaching and Theology in Anglo-Saxon England: Ælfric and Wulfstan* (1977).

Geary, P.J., 'The Saint and the Shrine. The Pilgrim's Goal in the Middle Ages', in Kriss-Rettenbeck and Möhler (eds.), 265–273.

——, *Living with the Dead in the Middle Ages* (1994).

Gellner, E., *Nations and Nationalism* (1983).

Gem, R., 'How Much can Anglo-Saxon Buildings Tell us about Liturgy?', in Gittos and Bedingfield (eds.), 271–289.

Genicot, L., *Rural Communities in the Medieval West* (1990).

Gerchow, J., 'The Origins of the *Liber Vitae*', in Rollason, Piper, Harvey and Rollason (eds.), 45–61.

Giandrea, M.F., *Episcopal Culture in Late Anglo-Saxon England* (2007).

Gittos, H., 'Creating the Sacred: Anglo-Saxon Rites for Consecrating Cemeteries', in Lucy and Reynolds (eds.), 195–208.

——, 'Architecture and Liturgy in England c. 1000: Problems and Possibilities', in N. Hiscock (ed.), *The White Mantle of Churches: Architecture, Liturgy and Art around the Millennium* (2003), 91–106.

——, 'Is There any Evidence for the Liturgy of Parish Churches in Late Anglo-Saxon England? The Red Book of Darley and the Status of Old English', in Tinti (ed.), 63–82.

Gittos, H. and Bedingfield, M.B. (eds.), *The Liturgy of the Late Anglo-Saxon Church* (2005).

Gneuss, H., 'The Origin of Standard Old English and Æthelwold's School at Winchester', *Anglo-Saxon England* 1 (1972), 63–83.

——, 'King Alfred and the History of Anglo-Saxon Libraries', in P.R. Brown et al. (eds.), *Modes of Interpretation in Old English Literature* (1986), 29–49.

Godden, M., 'The Relations of Wulfstan and Ælfric: A Reassessment' in Townend (ed.), 353–374.

Godden, M. and Irvine, S. (eds.), *The Old English Boethius: An Edition of the Old English Versions of Boethius's* De Consolatione Philosophiae *With a chapter on the Metres by Mark Griffith and contributions by Rohini Jayatilaka* (2009).

Graham-Campbell, J., 'The Northern Hoards from Cuerdale to Bossall/Flaxton', in Higham and Hill (eds.), 212–229.

Graham-Campbell, J. and Batey, C.E., *Vikings in Scotland: An Archaeological Survey* (1998).

Graham-Campbell, J., Hall, R., Jesch, J. and Parsons, D.N. (eds.), *Vikings and the Danelaw: Select Papers from the Proceedings of the Thirteenth Viking Congress* (2001).

Grant, A., 'The Construction of the Early Scottish State', in Maddicott and Palliser (eds.), 47–71.

Gretsch, M., *The Intellectual Foundations of the English Benedictine Reform* (1999).

——, 'The Junius Psalter Gloss: Tradition and Innovation', in Higham and Hill (eds.), 280–291.

——, *Ælfric and the Cult of Saints in Late Anglo-Saxon England* (2005).

Griffiths, B., *Aspects of Anglo-Saxon Magic* (1996).

Griffiths, D., 'The North-West Frontier', in Higham and Hill (eds.), 167–187.

Gurevich, A., *Medieval Popular Culture: Problems of Belief and Perception*, trans. J.M. Bak and P.A. Hollingsworth (1988).

Gwara, S. (ed.), *Anglo-Saxon Conversations: The Colloquies of Ælfric Bata*, trans. with an introduction by D.W. Porter (1997).

Gwara, S., *Education in Wales and Cornwall in the Ninth and Tenth Centuries: Understanding* De raris fabulis (2004).

Hadley, D.M., 'Conquest, Colonization and the Church: Ecclesiastical Organization in the Danelaw', *Historical Research* 69 (1996), 109–128.

——, 'Burial Practice in the Northern Danelaw, c.650–1100', *Northern History* 36 (2) (2000), 199–216.

——, '"Cockle Amongst the Wheat": The Scandinavian Settlement of England', in W.O. Fraser and A. Tyrrell (eds.), *Social Identity in Early Medieval Britain* (2000), 111–135.

——, *The Northern Danelaw: Its Social Structure, c.800–1100* (2000).

——, 'Viking and Native: Re-thinking Identity in the Danelaw', *Early Medieval Europe* 11 (2002), 45–70.

——, 'Negotiating Gender, Family and Status in Anglo-Saxon Burial Practices, *c.* 600–950', in Brubaker and Smith (eds.), 301–23.

——, *The Vikings in England: Settlement, Society and Culture* (2006).

——, 'Burying the Socially and Physically Distinctive in Anglo-Saxon England', in Buckberry and Cherryson (eds.), 103–115.

Hadley, D.M. and Buckberry, J., 'Caring for the Dead in late Anglo-Saxon England', in Tinti (ed.), 121–147.

Hadley, D.M. and Richards, J.D. (eds.), *Cultures in Contact: Scandinavian Settlement in England in the Ninth and Tenth Centuries* (2000).

Hall, A., *Elves in Anglo-Saxon England: Matters of Belief, Health, Gender and Identity* (2007).

Hall, R., 'A Kingdom too Far: York in the Early Tenth Century', in Higham and Hill (eds.), 188–199.

Hall, T.N., 'Wulfstan's Latin Sermons', in Townend (ed.), 93–139.

Halsall, G., *Violence and Society in the early Medieval West* (1998).

——, *Warfare and Society in the Barbarian West, 450–900* (2003).

Hamerow, H. and MacGregor, A. (eds.), *Image and Power in the Archaeology of Early Medieval Britain: Essays in Honour of Rosemary Cramp* (2001).

Hamerow, H., Hinton, D.A. and Crawford, S. (eds.), *Oxford Handbook of Anglo-Saxon Archaeology* (2011).

Hamilton, S., 'Remedies for "Great Transgressions": Penance and Excommunication in Late Anglo-Saxon England', in Tinti (ed.), 83–105.

Handley, M., 'The Early Medieval Inscriptions of Western Britain: Function and Sociology', in Hill and Swan (eds.), 339–361.

Hardt, M., 'Royal Treasures and Representation in the Early Middle Ages', in W. Pohl and H. Reimitz (eds.), *Strategies of Distinction: the Construction of Ethnic Communities, 300–800* (1998), 255–280.

Harris, J., 'Wars and Rumours of Wars: England and the Byzantine World in the Eighth and Ninth Centuries', *Mediterranean Historical Review* 14 (2) (1999), 29–46.

Harris, S.J., *Race and Ethnicity in Anglo-Saxon Literature* (2003).

——, 'The Liturgical Context of Ælfric's Homilies for Rogation', in Kleist (ed.), 143–169.

Harte, J., 'Rethinking Rogationtide', *Third Stone* 42 (Spring 2002), 29–35.

Hastings, A., *The Construction of Nationhood: Ethnicity, Religion and Nationalism* (1997).

Heighway, C., 'Gloucester and the New Minster of St. Oswald', in Higham and Hill (eds.), 102–111.

Helmholz, R.H., *The Oxford History of the Laws of England, Volume I: The Canon Law and Ecclesiastical Jurisdiction from 597 to the 1640s* (2004).

Henderson, G. and Henderson, I., *The Art of the Picts: Sculpture and Metalwork in Early Medieval Scotland* (2004).

Henderson, I., 'The "David Cycle" in Pictish Art', in Higgitt (ed.), 87–123.

——, '*Primus inter Pares*: the St Andrews Sarcophagus and Pictish Sculpture', in Foster (ed.), 97–167.

——, 'Understanding the Figurative Style and Decorative Programme of the Book of Deer', in Forsyth (ed.), 32–66.

Higgitt, J. (ed.), *Early Medieval Sculpture in Britain and Ireland* (1986).

Higgitt, J., 'Words and Crosses: The Inscribed Stone Cross in Early Medieval Britain and Ireland', in Higgitt (ed.), 125–152.

——, 'Form and Focus in the Deerhurst Dedication Inscription', in Higgitt, Forsyth and Parsons (eds.), 89–93.

Higgitt, J., Forsyth, K. and Parsons, D.N. (eds.), *Roman, Runes and Ogham: Medieval Inscriptions in the Insular World and on the Continent* (2001).

Higham, N.J., *The Death of Anglo-Saxon England* (1997).

——, *King Arthur: Myth-Making and History* (2002).

Higham, N.J. and Hill, D.H. (eds.), *Edward the Elder 899–924* (2001).

Hill, D., *An Atlas of Anglo-Saxon England* (1981).

——, 'The Shiring of Mercia – Again', in Higham and Hill (eds.), 144–159.

Hill, J., 'Archbishop Wulfstan: Reformer?', in Townend (ed.), 309–324.

Hill, J. and Swan, M. (eds.), *The Community, the Family and the Saint: Patterns of Power in Early Medieval Europe* (1998).

Hines, J., Lane, A. and Redknap, M. (eds.), *Land, Sea and Home* (2004).

Hollis, S., '"The Protection of God and the King": Wulfstan's Legislation on Widows', in Townend (ed.), 443–460.

Holloway, J., 'Material Symbolism and Death: Charcoal Burial in Later Anglo-Saxon England', in Buckberry and Cherryson (eds.), 83–92.

Holman, K., 'Defining the Danelaw', in Graham-Campbell, Hall, Jesch and Parsons (eds.), 1–11.

Holt, R., 'The City of Worcester in the Time of Wulfstan', in Barrow and Brooks (eds.), 123–135.

Hood, A.B.E., 'Lighten Our Darkness – Biblical Style in Early Medieval Britain and Ireland', *Early Medieval Europe* 8 (1999), 283–296.

Howe, N., *Migration and Mythmaking in Anglo-Saxon England* (1989).

——, 'Rome: Capital of Anglo-Saxon England', *Journal of Medieval and Early Modern Studies* 34 (2004), 147–172.

——, *Writing the Map of Anglo-Saxon England: Essays in Cultural Geography* (2008).

Hudson, B.T., *Prophecy of Berchán, Irish and Scottish High-Kings of the Early Middle Ages* (1996).

——, 'The Scottish Chronicle', *Scottish Historical Review* 77 (1998), 129–161.

Hughes, K., 'Where are the Writings of Early Scotland', in D. Dumville (ed.), *Celtic Britain in the Early Middle Ages: Studies in Scottish and Welsh Sources by the Late Kathleen Hughes* (1980), 1–21.

Hurley, C., 'Landscapes of Gwent and the Marches as seen through the Charters of the Seventh to Eleventh Centuries', in Edwards (ed.), *Landscape*, 31–40.

Insley, C., 'Assemblies and Charters in Late Anglo-Saxon England', in P.S. Barnwell and M. Mostert (eds.), *Political Assemblies in the Earlier Middle Ages* (2003), 47–59.

——, 'Athelstan, Charters and the English in Cornwall', in M.T. Flanagan and J.A. Green (eds.), *Charters and Charter Scholarship in Britain and Ireland* (2005), 15–31.

Irvine, M., *The Making of Textual Culture: 'Grammatica' and Literary Theory, 350–1100* (1994).

Irvine, S., 'The *Anglo-Saxon Chronicle* and the Idea of Rome in Alfredian Literature', in Reuter (ed.), 63–77.

Isaac, G.R., '*Armes Prydain Fawr* and St David', in Evans and Wooding (eds.), 161–181.

Jackson, P., 'Ælfric and the Purpose of Christian Marriage: A Reconsideration of the *Life of Æthelthryth*, Lines 120-30', *Anglo-Saxon England* 29 (2000), 235–260.

James, E., 'The Continental Context', in Foster (ed.), 240–249.

James, H., 'Early Medieval Cemeteries in Wales', in Edwards and Lane (eds.), 90–104.

James, T.A., 'Air Photography of Ecclesiastical Sites in South Wales', in Edwards and Lane (eds.), 62–76.

Jankulak, K., *The Medieval Cult of St Petroc* (2000).

Jayakumar, S., 'Eadwig and Edgar: Politics, Propaganda, and Faction', in Scragg (ed.), 83–103.

Jennings, A. and Kruse, A., 'One Coast-Three Peoples: Names and Ethnicity in the Scottish West during the Early Viking Period', in Woolf (ed.), 75–102.

John, E., 'The King and the Monks in the Tenth-Century Reformation', *Bulletin of the John Rylands Library* 42 (1959–60), 61–87.

——, 'The Church of Worcester and St Oswald', in Gameson and Leyser (eds.), 142–157.

——, 'The Annals of St Neots and the Defeat of the Vikings', in R. Evans (ed.), *Lordship and Learning. Studies in Memory of Trevor Aston* (2004), 51–62.

Johnson, D.F., 'The *Crux Usualis* as Apotropaic Weapon in Anglo-Saxon England', in Karkov, Keefer and Jolly (eds.), 80–95.

Johnson South, T., *Historia de Sancto Cuthberto: A History of Saint Cuthbert and a Record of his Patrimony* (2002).

Jolly, K.L., *Popular Religion in Late Saxon England: Elf Charms in Context* (1996).

——, 'Elves in the Psalms? The Experience of Evil from a Cosmic Perspective', in A. Fereiro (ed.), *The Devil, Heresy and Witchcraft in the Middle Ages: Essays in Honor of Jeffrey B. Russell* (1998), 19–44.

——, 'Cross-Referencing Anglo-Saxon Liturgy and Remedies: The Sign of the Cross as Ritual Protection', in Gittos and Bedingfield (eds.), 213–243.

——, 'Tapping the Power of the Cross: Who and for Whom?', in Karkov, Keefer and Jolly (eds.), 58–79.

Jones, C.A. (ed. and trans.), *Ælfric's Letter to the Monks of Eynsham* (1998).

Jones, C.A., 'Old English *Fant* and its Compounds in the Anglo-Saxon Vocabulary of Baptism', *Mediaeval Studies* 63 (2001), 143–192.

——, 'Wulfstan's Liturgical Interests', in Townend (ed.), 325–352.

——, 'The Chrism Mass in Later Anglo-Saxon England', in Gittos and Bedingfield (eds.), 105–142.

Jones, O.W., '*Hereditas Pouoisi*: The Pillar of Eliseg and the History of Early Powys', *Welsh History Review* 24 (4) (2009), 41–80.

Kabir, A.J., *Paradise, Death and Doomsday in Anglo-Saxon Literature* (2001).

Karkov, C.E., *The Ruler Portraits of Anglo-Saxon England* (2004).

——, 'The Frontispiece to the New Minster Charter and the King's Two Bodies', in Scragg (ed.), 224–241.

Karkov, C.E., Keefer, S.L. and Jolly, K.L. (eds.), *The Place of the Cross in Anglo-Saxon England* (2006).

Keefer, S.L., '*Ut in omnibus honorificetur Deus*: The *Corsnæd* Ordeal in Anglo-Saxon England', in Hill and Swan (eds.), 237–264.

——, '*Ðonne se cirlisca man ordales weddigeð*: The Anglo-Saxon Lay Ordeal', in Baxter, Karkov, Nelson and Pelteret (eds.), 353–367.

Kelly, S., 'Anglo-Saxon Lay Society and the Written Word', in McKitterick (ed.), 36–62.

Kempshall, M., 'No Bishop, No King: The Ministerial Ideology of Kingship and Asser's *Res Gestae Ælfredi*', in Gameson and Leyser (eds.), 106–127.

Keynes, S., 'Royal Government and the Written Word in Late Anglo-Saxon England', in McKitterick (ed.), 226–257.

——, *The Councils of Clofesho* (1994).

——, 'Edward, King of the Anglo-Saxons', in Higham and Hill (eds.), 40–66.

——, 'The *Liber Vitae* of the New Minster, Winchester', in Rollason, Piper, Harvey and Rollason (eds.), 149–163.

——, 'Edgar, *rex admirabilis*', in Scragg (ed.), 3–59.

——, 'A Conspectus of the Charters of King Edgar, 957-975', in Scragg (ed.), 60–80.

Keynes, S. and Lapidge, M. (eds. and trans.), *Alfred the Great: Asser's* Life of King Alfred *and Other Contemporary Sources* (1983).

King, V., 'St Oswald's Tenants', in Brooks and Cubitt (eds.), 100–116.

Kissock, J., '"God Made Nature and Men Made Towns": Post-Conquest and Pre-Conquest Villages in Pembrokeshire', in Edwards (ed.), *Landscape*, 123–137.

Klein, S.S., *Ruling Women. Queenship and Gender in Anglo-Saxon Literature* (2006).

Kleist, A.J. (ed.), *The Old English Homily. Precedent, Practice and Appropriation* (2007).

Klinck, A.L., 'Anglo-Saxon Women and the Law', *Journal of Medieval History* 8 (1982), 107–121.

Kriss-Rettenbeck, L. and Möhler, G. (eds.), *Wallfahrt kennt keine Grenzen* (1984).

Lapidge, M. (ed.), *Anglo-Saxon Litanies of the Saints* (1991).

Lapidge, M., 'Æthelwold as Scholar and Teacher', in Yorke (ed.), 89–117.

——, 'Ælfric's *Sanctorale*', in Szarmach (ed.), 115–129.

——, 'Byzantium, Rome and England in the Early Middle Ages', in *Settimane di Studi del Centro Italiano di Studi sull' Alto Medioevo* 49 (2002), 363–400.

Lapidge, M. and Winterbottom, M. (ed. and trans.), *Wulfstan of Winchester, Life of St Æthelwold* (1991).

Lee, C., *Feasting the Dead: Food and Drink in Anglo-Saxon Burial Rituals* (2007).

Lees, C.A. and Overing, G.R., *Double Agents: Women and Clerical Culture in Anglo-Saxon England* (2009).

Lerer, S., *Literacy and Power in Anglo-Saxon Literature* (1991).

Lewis, C.P., 'Edgar, Chester, and the Kingdom of the Mercians, 957-9', in Scragg (ed.), 104–123.

Lionarons, J.T., 'Napier Homily L: Wulfstan's Eschatology at the Close of his Career', in Townend (ed.), 413–428.

Longley, D., 'Early Medieval Burial in Wales', in Edwards (ed.), *Archaeology*, 105–132.

Loveluck, C.P., 'Wealth, Waste and Conspicuous Consumption: Flixborough and its Importance for Middle and Late Saxon Rural Settlement Studies', in Hamerow and MacGregor (eds.), 78–130.

——, *Rural Settlement, Lifestyles and Social Change in the Later First Millennium* AD: *Anglo-Saxon Flixborough in its Wider Context* (2007).

Loyn, H.R., *The English Church, 940–1154* (2000).

Lucy, S. and Reynolds, A. (eds.), *Burial in Early Medieval England and Wales* (2002).

Ludlow, N., 'Identifying Early Medieval Ecclesiastical Sites in South-West Wales', in Edwards (ed.), *Archaeology*, 61–84.

Lynch, J.H., *Christianizing Kinship. Ritual Sponsorship in Anglo-Saxon England* (1998).

Lyon, S., 'The Coinage of Edward the Elder', in Higham and Hill (eds.), 67–78.

McCarthy, C. (ed.), *Love, Sex and Marriage in the Middle Ages: A Sourcebook* (2004).

McCarthy, C., *Marriage in Medieval England: Law, Literature and Practice* (2004).

McInerney, M.B., *Eloquent Virgins from Thecla to Joan of Arc* (2003).

McKitterick, R. (ed.), *The Uses of Literacy in Early Medieval Europe* (1990).

McLaughlin, M., *Consorting with Saints. Prayer for the Dead in Early Medieval France* (1994).

Mac Lean, D., 'The Northumbrian Perspective', in Foster (ed.), 179–201.

McNeill, P.G.B. and MacQueen, H.L. (eds.), *Atlas of Scottish History to 1707* (1996).

Macquarrie, A., 'Early Christian Religious Houses in Scotland: Foundation and Function', in Blair and Sharpe (eds.), 110–133.

——, *The Saints of Scotland. Essays in Scottish Church History* AD *450–1093* (1997).

Maddicott, J.R. and Palliser, D.M. (eds.), *The Medieval State: Essays Presented to James Campbell* (2000).

Márkus, G., 'The Sick and the Dying in the Book of Deer. Appendix: Four Rites Compared', in Forsyth (ed.), 67–97.

Marvin, W.P., *Hunting Law and Ritual in Medieval English Literature* (2006).

Mason, E., 'St Oswald and St Wulfstan', in Brooks and Cubitt (eds.), 269–284.

Mayr-Harting, H., *Two Conversions to Christianity: The Bulgarians and the Anglo-Saxons* (1994).

——, *Perceptions of Angels in History* (1998).

——, 'The Idea of the Assumption of Mary in the West, 800–1200', in R.N. Swanson (ed.), *The Church and Mary* (2004), 86–111.

Meaney, A.L., '"And we forbeodoð eornstlice ælcne hæðenscipe": Wulfstan and Late Anglo-Saxon and Norse "Heathenism"', in Townend (ed.), 461–500.

——, 'Old English Legal and Penitential Penalties for "Heathenism"', in S. Keynes and A.P. Smyth (eds.), *Anglo-Saxons: Studies Presented to Cyril Roy Hart* (2006), 127–158.

Meens, R., 'Magic and the Early Medieval World View', in Hill and Swan (eds.), 285–295.

——, 'The Frequency and Nature of Early Medieval Penance', in P. Biller and A.J. Minnis (eds.), *Handling Sin: Confession in the Middle Ages* (1998), 35–61.

——, 'Penitentials and the Practice of Penance in the Tenth and Eleventh Centuries', *Early Medieval Europe* 14 (1) (2006), 7–21.

Metcalf, D.M., 'How Large was the Anglo-Saxon Currency?', *Economic History Review* 18 (1965), 475–482.

——, 'Monetary Expansion and Recession: Interpreting the Distribution Patterns of Seventh and Eighth Century Coins', in J. Casey and R. Reece (eds.), *Coins and the Archaeologist* (2nd edn. 1988), 230–253.

Miller, E., *The Abbey and Bishopric of Ely* (1951).

Miller, M., *The Saints of Gwynedd* (1979).

Minnis, A. and Roberts, J. (eds.), *Text, Image, Interpretation. Studies in Anglo-Saxon Literature and its Insular Context in Honour of Éamonn Ó Carragáin* (2007).

Moore, R.I., *The First European Revolution* (2001).

——, *The War on Heresy* (2012).

——, 'R. I. Moore: Homepage' available online at www.rimoore.net.

Morris, C.J., *Marriage and Murder in Eleventh-century Northumbria: A Study of 'De Obsessione Dunelmi'* (1992).

Muschol, G., 'Men, Women and Liturgical Practice in the Early Medieval West', in Brubaker and Smith (eds.), 198–216.

Nash-Williams, V.E., *The Early Christian Monuments of Wales* (1950).

Nelson, J.L., 'Reconstructing a Royal Family: Reflections on Alfred, From Asser, Chapter 2', in Wood and Lund (eds.), 47–66.

——, 'Gendering Courts in the Early Medieval West', in Brubaker and Smith (eds.), 185–197.

——, 'The First Use of the Second Anglo-Saxon *Ordo*', in Barrow and Wareham (eds.), 117–126.

Neuman de Vegvar, C., 'Converting the Anglo-Saxon Landscape: Crosses and their Audiences', in Minnis and Roberts (eds.), 407–430.

Niles, J.D. (ed.), *Old English Literature in Context: Ten Essays* (1980).

Niles, J.D., 'The *Æcerbot* Ritual in Context', in Niles (ed.), 44–56.

——, 'Trial by Ordeal in Anglo-Saxon England: What's the Problem with Barley?', in Baxter, Karkov, Nelson and Pelteret (eds.), 369–382.

Noble, T.F.X., 'The Interests of Historians in the Tenth Century', in Rollason, Leyser and Williams (eds.), 495–513.

Norton, C., 'York Minster in the Time of Wulfstan', in Townend (ed.), 207–234.

Okasha, E., *Hand-List of Anglo-Saxon Non-Runic Inscriptions* (1971).

——, 'A Supplement to *Hand-List of Anglo-Saxon Non-Runic Inscriptions*', *Anglo-Saxon England* 11 (1983), 83–118.

——, 'A Second Supplement to *Hand-List of Anglo-Saxon Non-Runic Inscriptions*', *Anglo-Saxon England* 21 (1992), 37–85.

——, *Corpus of Early Christian Inscribed Stones of South-west Britain* (1993).

——, 'Anglo-Saxon Women: The Evidence from Inscriptions', in Higgitt, Forsyth and Parsons (eds.), 79–88.

O'Loughlin, T., 'The Biblical Text of the Book of Deer: Evidence for the Remains of a Division System from its Manuscript Ancestry. Appendix: A Concordance of the Display Initials of the Book of Deer with the Ammonian Sections/Eusebian Canons', in Forsyth (ed.), 3–31.

Olson, L. and Padel, O.J., 'A Tenth-Century List of Cornish Parochial Saints', *Cambridge Medieval Celtic Studies* 12 (1986), 33–71.

Ó'Maolalaigh, R., 'The Property Records: Diplomatic Edition including Accents', in Forsyth (ed.), 119–130.

Opland, J., 'From Horseback to Monastic Cell: The Impact on English Literature of the Introduction of Writing', in Niles (ed.), 30–43.

Orchard, A., 'Wulfstan as Reader, Writer, and Rewriter', in Kleist (ed.), 311–341.

Ortenberg, V., '"The King from Overseas": Why Did Æthelstan Matter in Tenth-Century Continental Affairs?', in Rollason, Leyser and Williams (eds.), 211–236.

Padel, O.J., 'Local Saints and Place-Names in Cornwall', in Thacker and Sharpe (eds.), 303–360.

——, 'Place-Names and the Saxon Conquest of Devon and Cornwall', in N.J. Higham (ed.), *Britons in Anglo-Saxon England* (2007), 214–230.

——, *Slavery in Saxon Cornwall: The Bodmin Manumissions* (2009).

Pagan, H., 'The Pre-Reform Coinage of Edgar' in Scragg (ed.), 192–205.

Parsons, D., 'Odda's Chapel, Deerhurst: Place of Worship or Royal Hall?', *Medieval Archaeology* 44 (2000), 225–228.

Paxton, F.S., *Christianizing Death: The Creation of a Ritual Process in Early Medieval Europe* (1990).

Payer, P.J., *Sex and the Penitentials* (1984).

Pearce, S., *South-western Britain in the Early Middle Ages* (2004).

Pelteret, D.A.E., *Slavery in Early Mediaeval England from the Reign of Alfred until the Twelfth Century* (1995).

Pestell, T., *Landscapes of Monastic Foundation: The Establishment of Religious Houses in East Anglia c. 650–1200* (2004).

Peterson, E., *The Angels and the Liturgy: The Status and Significance of the Holy Angels in Worship*, trans. R. Walls (1964).

Pettit, E., *Anglo-Saxon Remedies, Charms and Prayers from British Library MS Harley 585: The Lacnunga* (2 vols.), Volume I: *Introduction, Text, Translation, and Appendices* (2001).

Petts, D., 'Cemeteries and Boundaries in Western Britain', in Lucy and Reynolds (eds.), 24–46.

Pfaff, R.W., *The Liturgy in Medieval England: A History* (2009).

Plunkett, S.J., 'The Mercian Perspective', in Foster (ed.), 202–226.

Pollington, S., *Leechcraft: Early English Charms, Plant Lore and Healing* (2000).

Powell, F., 'The Human Remains', in Boddington (ed.), 113–124.

Powell, T.E., 'The "Three Orders" of Society in Anglo-Saxon England', *Anglo-Saxon England* 23 (1994), 103–132.

Pratt, D., 'The Illnesses of King Alfred the Great', *Anglo-Saxon England* 30 (2001), 39–90.

——, *The Political Thought of King Alfred the Great* (2007).

———, 'Written Law and the Communication of Authority in Tenth-Century England', in Rollason, Leyser and Williams (eds.), 331–350.

Preston-Jones, A., 'Decoding Cornish Churchyards', in Edwards and Lane (eds.), 104–124.

Pryce, H. (ed.), *Literacy in Medieval Celtic Societies* (1998).

Pryce, H., 'Ecclesiastical Wealth in Early Medieval Wales', in Edwards and Lane (eds.), 22–32.

———, 'Pastoral Care in Early Medieval Wales', in Blair and Sharpe (eds.), 41–62.

———, *Native Law and the Church in Medieval Wales* (1993).

Rauer, C., *Beowulf and the Dragon: Parallels and Analogues* (2000).

Raw, B.C., *Trinity and Incarnation in Anglo-Saxon Art and Thought* (1997).

———, 'Pictures: The Books of the Unlearned?', in P. Cavill (ed.), *The Christian Tradition in Anglo-Saxon England. Approaches to Current Scholarship and Teaching* (2004), 103–119.

Redgate, A.E., 'Vernacular Liturgy in England and Armenia from the Fifth to the Eleventh Centuries', *Armenian Folia Anglistika: International Journal of English Studies* 2 (4) (2007), 144–161.

Redknap, M., *Vikings in Wales: An Archaeological Quest* (2000).

———, 'Viking-Age Settlement in Wales and the Evidence from Llanbedrgoch', in Hines, Lane and Redknap (eds.), 139–175.

———, 'Early Medieval Metalwork and Christianity: A Welsh Perspective', in Edwards (ed.), *Archaeology*, 351–373.

Repsher, B., *The Rite of Church Dedication in the Early Medieval Era* (1998).

Resnick, I.M., 'Lingua Dei, Lingua Hominis: Sacred Language and Medieval Texts', *Viator* 21 (1990), 51–74.

Reuter, T. (ed.), *Alfred the Great: Papers from the Eleventh-Centenary Conferences* (2003).

Reynolds, A., 'Burials, Boundaries and Charters in Anglo-Saxon England: A Reassessment', in Lucy and Reynolds (eds.), 171–194.

———, *Anglo-Saxon Deviant Burial Customs* (2009).

Reynolds, S., 'Medieval *Origines Gentium* and the Community of the Realm', *History* 68 (1983), 375–390.

———, *Kingdoms and Communities in Western Europe 900–1300* (1984).

Richards, J.D., *Viking Age England* (2nd edn. 2000).

———, 'Boundaries and Cult Centres: Viking Burial in Derbyshire', in Graham-Campbell, Hall, Jesch and Parsons (eds.), 97–104.

———, 'Finding the Vikings: The Search for Anglo-Scandinavian Rural Settlement in the Northern Danelaw', in Graham-Campbell, Hall, Jesch and Parsons (eds.), 269–277.

———, 'The Case of the Missing Vikings: Scandinavian Burial in the Danelaw', in Lucy and Reynolds (eds.), 156–170.

Riggs, C.H., *Criminal Asylum in Anglo-Saxon Law* (1963).

Rios, R., 'Angels in the Liturgy', *Clergy Review* n.s., 19 (1940), 295–305.

Rodwell, W., Hawkes, J., Howe, E. and Cramp, R., 'The Lichfield Angel: A Spectacular Anglo-Saxon Painted Sculpture', *Antiquaries Journal* 88 (2008), 48–108.

Rollason, D.W., *Two Anglo-Saxon Rituals: The Dedication of a Church and the Judicial Ordeal* (1988).

———, 'St Cuthbert and Wessex: The Evidence of Cambridge, Corpus Christi College MS 183', in Bonner, Rollason and Stancliffe (eds.), 413–424.

———, *Northumbria, 500–1100: Creation and Destruction of a Kingdom* (2003).

Rollason, D., Leyser, C. and Williams, H. (eds.), *England and the Continent in the Tenth Century: Studies in Honour of Wilhelm Levison (1876–1947)* (2010).

Rollason, D., Piper, A.J., Harvey, M. and Rollason, L. (eds.), *The Durham* Liber Vitae *and its Context* (2004).

Rosenwein, B.H., *To Be the Neighbor of Saint Peter: The Social Meaning of Cluny's Property, 909–1049* (1989).

——, *Negotiating Space: Power, Restraint and Privileges of Immunity in Early Medieval Europe* (1999).

Ross, M.C., 'Concubinage in Anglo-Saxon England', *Past and Present* 108 (1985), 3–34.

Rumble, A.R., 'Edward the Elder and the Churches of Winchester and Wessex', in Higham and Hill (eds.), 230–247.

——, *Property and Piety in Early Medieval Winchester* (2002).

——, 'The Laity and the Monastic Reform in the Reign of King Edgar', in Scragg (ed.), 242–251.

Rushforth, R., *Saints in English Kalendars before A.D. 1100* (2008).

Salvador-Bello, M., 'The Edgar Panegyrics in the *Anglo-Saxon Chronicle*', in Scragg (ed.), 252–272.

Scales, L. and Zimmer, O. (eds.), *Power and the Nation in European History* (2005).

Scharer, A., 'The Writing of History at King Alfred's Court', *Early Medieval Europe* 5 (2) (1996), 177–206.

Scheil, A.P., *The Footsteps of Israel: Understanding Jews in Anglo-Saxon England* (2004).

Schwab, U., '*The Battle of Maldon*: A Memorial Poem', in Cooper (ed.), 63–85.

Scragg, D. (ed.), *Edgar, King of the English 959–975: New Interpretations* (2008).

Scragg, D.G., '*The Battle of Maldon*: Fact or Fiction?', in Cooper (ed.), 19–31.

——, 'The Corpus of Anonymous Lives and Their Manuscript context', in Szarmach (ed.), 209–234.

Searle, E., *Predatory Kinship and the Creation of Norman Power 840–1066* (1988).

Semple, S., 'A Fear of the Past: The Place of the Prehistoric Burial Mound in the Ideology of Middle and Later Anglo-Saxon England', *World Archaeology* 30 (1998), 109–126.

——, 'Illustrations of Damnation in Late Anglo-Saxon Manuscripts', *Anglo-Saxon England* 32 (2004), 231–245.

Senecal, C., 'Keeping up with the Godwinesons: In Pursuit of Aristocratic Status in Late Anglo-Saxon England', *Anglo-Norman Studies* 23 (2000) (2001), 251–266.

Sharp, S., 'The West Saxon Tradition of Dynastic Marriage: With Special Reference to the Family of Edward the Elder', in Higham and Hill (eds.), 79–88.

Sharples, N. and Smith, R., 'Norse Settlement in the Western Isles', in Woolf (ed.), 103–130.

Shepard, J., 'The Ruler as Instructor, Pastor and Wise: Leo VI of Byzantium and Symeon of Bulgaria', in Reuter (ed.), 339–358.

Silvester, R., 'New Radnor: The Topography of a Medieval Planned Town in Mid-Wales', in Edwards (ed.), *Landscape*, 157–164.

Silvester, R.J., and Evans, J.W., 'Identifying the Mother Churches of North-East Wales', in Edwards (ed.), *Archaeology*, 21–40.

Simpson, L., 'The King Alfred/St Cuthbert Episode in the *Historia de sancto Cuthberto*: Its Significance for Mid-tenth-century English History', in Bonner, Rollason and Stancliffe (eds.), 397–411.

Sims-Williams, P., 'The Uses of Writing in Early Medieval Wales', in Pryce (ed.), 15–38.

——, 'The Five Languages of Wales in the Pre-Norman Inscriptions', *Cambrian Medieval Celtic Studies* 44 (2002), 1–36.

Smith, A.D., *Chosen Peoples* (2003).

Smyth, A.P., *Warlords and Holy Men: Scotland AD 80–1000* (1984).

——, *King Alfred the Great* (1995).

Stacey, R.C., *The Road to Judgement: From Custom to Court in Medieval Ireland and Wales* (1994).

Stafford, P., *Queens, Concubines and Dowagers* (1983).

——, *Unification and Conquest. A Political and Social History of England in the Tenth and Eleventh Centuries* (1989).

——, *Queen Emma and Queen Edith* (1997, and 2001).

——, '"The Annals of Æthelflaed": Annals, History and Politics in Early Tenth-Century England', in Barrow and Wareham (eds.), 101–116.

Stanley, E., 'Wulfstan and Ælfric: "the true Difference between the Law and the Gospel"', in Townend (ed.), 429–441.

Stanton, R., *The Culture of Translation in Anglo-Saxon England* (2002).

Steckel, R.H., 'New Light on the "Dark Ages": The Remarkably Tall Stature of Northern European Men during the Medieval Era', *Social Science History* 28 (2) (2004), 211–228.

Stenton, F., *Anglo-Saxon England* (1943, 3rd edn. 1971).

Stevenson, K.W., *Nuptial Blessing: A Study of Christian Marriage Rites* (1982).

Stocker, D., 'Monuments and Merchants: Irregularities in the Distribution of Stone Sculpture in Lincolnshire and Yorkshire in the Tenth Century', in Hadley and Richards (eds.), 179–212.

Stocker, D. and Everson, P., 'Five Towns Funerals: Decoding Diversity in Danelaw Stone Sculpture', in Graham-Campbell, Hall, Jesch and Parsons (eds.), 223–243.

Symons, T. and Spath, S. (eds.), '*Regularis Concordia*', in K. Hallinger (ed.), *Consuetudinum Saeculi X/XI/XII Monumenta non-Cluniacensia* (*Corpus Consuetudinum Monasticarum*, vii. 3) (1984), 61–147.

Szarmach, P.E. (ed.), *Holy Men and Holy Women: Old English Prose Saints' Lives and Their Contexts* (1996).

Szarmach, P.E., 'Alfred, Alcuin and the Soul', in Boenig and Davis (eds.), 127–148.

Taylor, S. (ed.), *Kings, Clerics and Chronicles in Scotland, 500–1297: Essays in Honour of Marjorie Ogilvie Anderson on the Occasion of her Ninetieth Birthday* (2000).

Taylor, S., 'The Toponymic Landscape of the Gaelic Notes in the Book of Deer. Appendix: Early Forms of Place-names Discussed in the Text', in Forsyth (ed.), 275–308.

Teresi, L., 'Ælfric's or Not? The Making of a *Temporale* Collection in Late Anglo-Saxon England', in Kleist (ed.), 285–310.

Thacker, A., 'Æthelwold and Abingdon', in Yorke (ed.), 43–64.

——, 'Monks, Preaching and Pastoral Care in Early Anglo-Saxon England', in Blair and Sharpe (eds.), 137–170.

——, 'Saint-making and Relic Collecting by Oswald and his Communities', in Brooks and Cubitt (eds.), 244–268.

——, '*Peculiaris Patronus Noster*: The Saint as Patron of the State in the Early Middle Ages', in Maddicott and Palliser (eds.), 1–24.

——, 'Dynastic Monasteries and Family Cults: Edward the Elder's Sainted Kindred', in Higham and Hill (eds.), 248–263.

Thacker, A. and Sharpe, R. (eds.), *Local Saints and Local Churches in the Early Medieval West* (2002).

Thomas, C., *Christian Celts: Messages and Images* (1998).

——, 'Form and Function', in Foster (ed.), 84–96.

Thompson, N.M., 'The Carolingian *De festivitatibus* and the Blickling Book', in Kleist (ed.), 97–119.

Thompson, S.D., *Anglo-Saxon Royal Diplomas: A Palaeography* (2006).

Thompson, V., *Dying and Death in Later Anglo-Saxon England* (2004).

——, 'The Pastoral Contract in Late Anglo-Saxon England: Priest and Parishioner in Oxford, Bodleian Library, MS Laud Miscellaneous 482', in Tinti (ed.), 106–120.

Tinti, F. (ed.), *Pastoral Care in Late Anglo-Saxon England* (2005).

Tinti, F., 'The "Costs" of Pastoral Care: Church Dues in Late Anglo-Saxon England', in Tinti (ed.), 27–51.

——, 'England and the Papacy in the Tenth Century', in Rollason, Leyser and Williams (eds.), 163–184.

——, *Sustaining Belief. The Church of Worcester from c. 870 to c. 1100* (2010).

Toswell, M.J., 'The Codicology of Anglo-Saxon Homiletic Manuscripts, Especially the Blickling Homilies', in Kleist (ed.), 209–226.

Townend, M. (ed.), *Wulfstan, Archbishop of York: The Proceedings of the Second Alcuin Conference* (2004).

Townend, M., *Language and History in Viking Age England: Linguistic Relations between Speakers of Old Norse and Old English* (2002).

Treharne, E., 'The Form and Function of the Vercelli Book', in Minnis and Roberts (eds.), 253–266.

——, *Living Through Conquest: The Politics of Early English, 1020–1220* (2012).

Turner, S., *Making a Christian Landscape: The Countryside in Early Medieval Cornwall, Devon and Wessex* (2006).

Turner, V. and Turner, E., *Image and Pilgrimage in Christian Culture: Anthropological Perspectives* (1978).

Upchurch, R.K. (ed. and trans.), *Ælfric's Lives of the Virgin Spouses. With Modern English Parallel-Text translations: Julian and Basilissa, Cecilia and Valerian, and Chrysanthus and Daria* (2007).

Upchurch, R.K., 'Homiletic Contexts for Ælfric's Hagiography: The Legend of Saints Cecilia and Valerian', in Kleist (ed.), 265–284.

Valtonen, I., *The North in the Old English Orosius. A Geographical Narrative in Context* (2008).

Wallace-Hadrill, J.M., 'The Bloodfeud of the Franks', *Bulletin of the John Rylands Library* 41 (1958–1959), 459–487.

Ward, S., 'Edward the Elder and the Re-establishment of Chester', in Higham and Hill (eds.), 160–166.

Wareham, A., 'St Oswald's family and Kin', in Brooks and Cubitt (eds.), 46–63.

——, *Lords and Communities in Early Medieval East Anglia* (2005).

Warren, F.E. and Stevenson, J., *The Liturgy and Ritual of the Celtic Church*, Studies in Celtic History 9 (2nd edn. J. Stevenson) (1987: first published 1881).

Webb, D., *Pilgrims and Pilgrimage in the Medieval West* (1999).

——, *Pilgrimage in Medieval England* (2000).

Webster, L., '*Ædificia nova*: Treasures of Alfred's Reign', in Reuter (ed.), 79–103.

Whatley, E.G., 'Hagiography and Violence: Military Men in Ælfric's *Lives of Saints*', in Wright, Biggs and Hall (eds.), 217–238.

Wilcox, J. (ed.), *Ælfric's Prefaces* (1994).

Wilcox, J., 'Wulfstan's *Sermo Lupi ad Anglos* as Political Performance: 16 February 1014 and Beyond', in Townend (ed.), 375–396.

——, 'Ælfric in Dorset and the Landscape of Pastoral Care', in Tinti (ed.), 52–62.

Williams, A., 'Thegnly Piety and Ecclesiastical Patronage in the Late Old English Kingdom', *Anglo-Norman Studies* 24 (2002), 1–24.

——, *Æthelred the Unready: The Ill-Counselled King* (2003).

Williams, H., *Death and Memory in Early Medieval Britain* (2006).

Williamson, R., 'Medieval English Pilgrims and Pilgrimages', in Kriss-Rettenbeck and Möhler (eds.), 114–126.

Withers, B.C., *The Illustrated Old English Hexateuch, Cotton Claudius B. iv: The Frontier of Seeing and Reading in Anglo-Saxon England* (2007).

Wood, I.N. and Lund, N., *People and Places in Northern Europe, 500–1600: Essays in Honour of Peter Hayes Sawyer* (1991).

Wood, M., 'The Making of King Æthelstan's Empire: An English Charlemagne?', in Wormald et al. (eds.), 250–272.

Wood, S., *The Proprietary Church in the Medieval West* (2006).

Woolf, A. (ed.), *Scandinavian Scotland – Twenty Years After: The Proceedings of a Day Conference held on 19 February 2007* (2009).

Woolf, A., 'View from the West: An Irish Perspective on West Saxon Dynastic Practice', in Higham and Hill (eds.), 89–101.

——, *From Pictland to Alba, 789–1070* (2007).

Wormald, [C.]P., '*Lex Scripta* and *Verbum Regis*: Legislation and Germanic Kingship from Euric to Cnut' in P.H. Sawyer and I.N. Wood (eds.), *Early Medieval Kingship* (1977), 105–138.

——, 'Charters, Law and the Settlement of Disputes in Anglo-Saxon England', in Davies and Fouracre (eds.), *Settlement …* , 149–168.

——, 'A Handlist of Anglo-Saxon Lawsuits', *Anglo-Saxon England* 17 (1988), 247–281.

——, 'Æthelwold and his Continental Counterparts: Contact, Comparison, Contrast', in Yorke (ed,), 13–42.

——, 'In Search of King Offa's "Law-code"', in Wood and Lund (eds.), 201–124.

——, '*Engla Lond*: The Making of an Allegiance', *Journal of Historical Sociology* 7 (1994), 1–24.

——, 'Lordship and Justice in the Early English Kingdom: Oswaldslow Revisited', in Davies and Fouracre (eds.), *Property …* , 114–136.

——, 'The Emergence of the *Regnum Scottorum*: A Carolingian Hegemony?', in B.E. Crawford (ed.), 131–153.

——, 'Oswaldslow: an Immunity?', in Brooks and Cubitt (eds.), 117–128.

——, 'Archbishop Wulfstan and the Holiness of Society', in his *Legal Culture in the Early Medieval West* (1999), 225–251.

——, *The Making of English Law: King Alfred to the Twelfth Century Volume I. Legislation and its Limits* (1999).

——, 'The Strange Affair of the Selsey Bishopric, 953–963', in Gameson and Leyser (eds.), 128–141.

——, '*On tha wæpnedhealfe*: Kingship and Royal Property from Æthelwulf to Edward the Elder', in Higham and Hill (eds.), 264–279.

——, 'Archbishop Wulfstan: Eleventh-Century State-Builder', in Townend (ed.), 9–27.

——, 'Did Harold Really Get It in the Eye?', *London Review of Books* 26 (11) (3 June 2004), 30–32.

——, 'Germanic Power Structures: The Early English Experience', in Scales and Zimmer (eds.), 105–124.

Wormald, [C.]P. et al. (eds.), *Ideal and Reality in Frankish and Anglo-Saxon Society* (1983).

Wright, C.D., 'A New Latin Source for Two Old English Homilies (Fadda I and Blickling I): Pseudo-Augustine, Sermo App. 125 and the Ideology of Chastity in the Anglo-Saxon Benedictine Reform', in Wright, Biggs and Hall (eds.), 239–265.

Wright, C.D., Biggs, F.M. and Hall, T.N. (eds.), *Source of Wisdom: Old English and Early Medieval Latin Studies in Honor of Thomas D. Hill* (2007).

Yeoman, P., 'Investigations on the May Island, and Other Early Medieval Churches and Monasteries in Scotland', in Edwards (ed.), *Archaeology*, 227–244.

Yorke, B.A.E., (ed.), *Bishop Æthelwold: His Career and Influence* (1988).

Yorke, B.A.E., 'Æthelwold and the Politics of the Tenth Century', in Yorke (ed.), 65–88.

——, 'Edward as Ætheling', in Higham and Hill (eds.), 25–39.

——, *Nunneries and the Anglo-Saxon Royal Houses* (2003).

——, *The Conversion of Britain: Religion, Politics and Society in Britain, 600–800* (2006).

——, 'The Women in Edgar's Life', in Scragg (ed.), 143–157.

Zacher, S.P., 'Re-Reading the Style and Rhetoric of the Vercelli Homilies', in Kleist (ed.), 173–207.

Zadora-Rio, E., 'The Role of Cemeteries in the Formation of Medieval Settlement Patterns in Western France', in C.L. Redman (ed.), *Medieval Archaeology* (1989), 177–186.

——, 'The Making of Churchyards and Parish Territories in the Early-Medieval Landscape of France and England in the 7th–12th Centuries: A Reconsideration', *Medieval Archaeology* 47 (2003), 1–19.

Zeitler, B., 'Cross-Cultural Interpretations of Imagery in the Middle Ages' *Art Bulletin* 56 (4) (1994), 680–694.

Index